THE
STATUS OF WOMEN IN INDIA

Owing to the antiquity and rarity of this book, certain pages are regrettably absent, and readability is compromised due to the blurring of the original text. If you possess any insights regarding the availability of these missing sections, kindly inform us. Your assistance is crucial in ensuring the completion of this significant work for the benefit of future generations.

THE STATUS OF WOMEN IN INDIA:

OR

A HAND-BOOK FOR HINDU SOCIAL REFORMERS

DAYARAM GIDUMAL

GYAN

Published by

Gyan Publishing House
5, Ansari Road
Daryaganj, New Delhi-110002
Phone: 011-47034999, 9811692060
E-mail: books@gyanbooks.com

Distribution Network
gyanbooks.com
India, USA, Canada, UK, Australia

ISBN: 978-93-6920-067-2 (PB)

First Published, 1889

2nd Impression 2025

Printed at: Gyan Press, Delhi.

THE STATUS OF WOMEN IN INDIA
Author: DAYARAM GIDUMAL

THE

STATUS OF WOMAN IN INDIA:

OR

A HAND-BOOK FOR HINDU SOCIAL REFORMERS.

BY

DAYARAM GIDUMAL, B.A., LL.B., C.S.,

FELLOW OF THE BOMBAY UNIVERSITY.

"Man is his own star; and the soul that can
Render an honest and a perfect man,
Commands all light, all influence, all fate;
Nothing to him falls early or too late.
Our acts our angels are, or good or ill,
Our fatal shadows that walk by us still."

Bombay:

PRINTED AT THE "FORT PRINTING PRESS."

1889.

[" All history resolves itself very easily into the biography of a few stout and earnest persons."]

DEDICATED

TO

ALL EARNEST WORKERS

IN THE CAUSE

OF

HINDU SOCIAL REFORM.

TABLE OF CONTENTS.

CHAPTER VIII.

CHAPTER IX.

APPENDIX I.

APPENDIX II.

APPENDIX III.

APPENDIX IV.

APPENDIX V.

APPENDIX VI.

APPENDIX VII.

A SYMPOSIUM OF HINDU DOMESTIC REFORMERS AND ANTI-REFORMERS.

SIR T. MADAVA RAO.—We cannot dine together or drink together, my dear friends, but we can have a talk together at least. Let us then "expatiate free" over this vexed question of Hindu Domestic Reform, and try to come to some practical conclusions. More than a year ago, I said: "The great danger is lest the present generation should pass away in total inaction." I am afraid, my dear brethren, we have been all inactive. We have certainly talked away and written away to our hearts' content, but, I am sorry to say, we have set no examples.

MR. A. SANKARIAH.—But, my dear sir, what examples are we to set? Your Social Reformers agitate for freedom to widows and girls to marry at any age, but this freedom is not denied now, and was not denied at any time; and, I say the agitators are not just and even honest, in interfering with those who do not religiously or socially approve of that freedom.

RAO SAHIB VISHWANATH N. MANDLIK.—And I say there is certainly no *enforced* widowhood in India at present, nor is there any such a general early marriage system prevalent as can be remedied by Government. I do not understand what reform is needed.

MR. T. PATTABHIRAM.—Let me introduce myself, gentlemen. I hail from the Southern Presidency, and in my humble opinion, Mr. Mandlik and Mr. Sankaria are certainly right as to the freedom of widows to re-marry—for to a Hindu widow, who makes up her mind to resume her married state, at the risk of losing her caste, her religion, and the affection and society of her relations. there now exists, most assuredly, no obstruction at all to marrying a caste Hindu if she succeeds in finding one who is willing (like the famous Barkis)—or to marrying a Christian or a Mahomedan if she does not so succeed.

MESSRS. BHASKARRAO BALKRISHNAJI PITALE AND NANA MOROBA.—We cannot go so far as Mr. Mandlik—but so far as we know, we say, it is only in the higher castes of the Hindu community, that the system of early marriages and widow celibacy prevails. We think, with Mr. Telang, that the majority of widows will not listen to, but actually shun the company of, nay detest, those sympathising philanthropists who volunteer advice to young widows to re-marry—for the sin of re-marriage is deeply engraven at present on their minds.

MR. AMBALAL S. DESAI.—I too can testify that there are mothers and fathers who rather than their widowed daughters should re-marry would commit suicide.

A HINDU ANTIQUARY—And formerly it was a moot question whether a re-married widow would in heaven join her first husband or her second; and such widows were so dearly loved that a special offering used to be made for the purpose of securing their society in the next world. The Atharva Veda says:—"When a woman has had one husband before, and gets another, if they present the *aja panchaudana* offering, they shall not be separated. A second husband dwells in the same world with his re-wedded wife, if he offers the *aja panchaudana*."* But now of course the sin of re-marriage is deeply graven on our minds —for it appears the Vedas sanctioned a sinful practice.

A HINDU SOCIAL REFORM MISSIONARY.—You forget, my dear sir, that life in the good old days was extremely enjoyable and the Vedic poets could sing to their Father: "Do thou conduct us to heaven—let us be with our wives and children."

* Muir's Sanscrit Texts, Vol. V. p. 306. (3rd Edition.)

Those days are gone, and life has gradually, through our unrighteousness, become such a burden that our highest ideal of bliss is utter extinction.

A HINDU LAWYER.—You are both treading on dangerous ground. I think we might let alone the *aja panchaudana*—and let alone the widows too for the present—and discuss first of all whether infant marriages in the strict and literal sense of the term prevail among us. 'Infant' originally meant, of course, a child not able to speak. But following a physiological theory, the Emperor Theodosius fixed seven years as the period of infancy—and our Penal Code follows his Constitution. The Roman lawyers called a child under seven, an infant, and considered a child under fourteen as *puberta proximus* and as possessing *intelluctus* but not *judicium,* while an adult was supposed to have both *intelluctus* and *judicium*—that is understanding as well as discretion.

RAO SAHIB S. H. CHIPLONKAR.—Adopting these useful distinctions, I say, that except in Gujarat and the adjoining Native States, infant marriages are almost unknown; and even there, they are confined to Kadwa Kanbis only.

PANDIT GATULAL.—I don't know what the Roman or the English law is—but in the Brahma Purana and in the Gautama Mahatamya, it is laid down that, "a father should try his best to perform the marriage of his daughter from the fourth year of her age upwards, till before the completion of the tenth year." In several other text-books, however, there is a prohibition against the marriage of a girl before the sixth year. My opinion, therefore, is that it is not lawful to marry a girl before that year—but that she should be married after the 8th and before the completion of the 12th year. I regret, however, to find that the institution of child marriage—that is marriage in which the bridegroom and the bride are children, and have not attained the marriageable age—is now prevalent in spite of its being opposed to the Shastras and to reason.

Sir T. Madava Rao.—The Panditji, Mr. Chiplonkar, is, as you know, one of the best exponents of conservative Hindu views and, I think, his testimony is not a little strong.

Mr. Ramanujchari.—His testimony is as to Bombay. But I can say, sir, that the evil custom of marrying young girls, whose ages range from six months up to twelve years, obtains among all classes of the people, especially among the Brahmins, in Southern India.

Mr. Navalram Lakshmiram.*—In Gujarat the common saying, "my children were betrothed while yet in their cradle" is the proud expression of the completely satisfied aspirations of a Gujarati parent. Among Kadwa Kanbis, betrothals are sometimes made before the children are born.

Babu Hari Mohan Chandra.—As to Bengal, I see Mr. Bourdillon says, in the last Census Report: "It may be assumed that no marriages take place during the first quinquennial period. Among that people (*i. e.* the Hindus) more than 10 boys in every 100, *between* 5 *and* 10 *years old,* are bridegrooms, while of the girls 28 in 100, *or more than* 1 *in* 4, *are wives or widows at an age, when if they were in Europe, they would be in the nursery or the infant school.*

Sir T. Madava Rao.—I take it that no authoritative Shastra recommends a marriage before the age of ten—while these figures show that such marriages do take place. Perhaps it will tend to clearness, if we style marriages of infants under seven, 'infant marriages,' and marriages of children under ten, as 'child marriages.'

Mr. Gurshidappa Virbasappa.—This is, I think, a good distinction. But my experience is that child marriages are becoming scarce,

Mr. S. Subramania Aiyar.—I think there is a strong re-action in the minds of the educated classes, and the percentage of such marriages is on the decrease.

---

* This good man is no more. The readers may suppose his spirit to speak

MR. VENAYEK VASUDEV.—This is my information also

MR. BHAU MANSARAM.—Yes, the custom is gradually but surely dying out of itself.

MR. MAHDEV VASUDEV BARVE.—The tendency of the general public is certainly much opposed to it.

MR. VENKAT RANGO KATTI.—I and my brother, gentlemen, were married at twelve to girls who were not yet seven. Forty years ago marriages were of this type. But the age of the bride is now generally from 8 to 10, and of the bridegroom from 13 to 15. I have selected a girl of twelve—the daughter of a Shastri too—for my son who will shortly complete his sixteenth year. I am told, however, that child marriages are much in vogue in Gujarat.

DR. SAKHARAM ARJUN*.—I too am aware that Gujarat and parts of the Mofussil—far too much removed from the beneficial influences of Western culture—occasionally indulge in the suicidal and demoralising luxury of child marriages. But this very fact ráther proves the exception than the rule.

RAO SAHIB S. H. CHIPLONKAR—During the last 20 years, a great deal has been effected in the direction of discountenancing such marriages, so much so that, as justly observed by the learned writer of the Baroda Census Report, the average marriage age for girls among the Hindus is now between 10 and 11, whereas only 20 years ago, it was quite different. During the next 10 or 20 years, we shall see a still greater change in the same direction, if the Hindu mind, which is very conservative, and impatient, nay suspicious of all external influences, does not undergo any revulsion of feeling in consequence of any outside pressure, however benevolent in itself.

MR. PANDURANG BALIBHADRA.—In the Prabhu caste to which I belong, child marriages are very rare indeed.

---

* This gentleman—the step-father of Rukhmabai—is also no more.

Within the last decade, I have not seen or heard of any. So far as my experience goes, I think the practice has become almost obsolete.

MR. C. RAMCHANDRA AIYAR.—Well, I can't say whether child marriages are a mania at Poona or Belgaum or among the Prabhus—but my 23 years' experience of several districts in the Madras Presidency is, that in spite of liberal education and a painful consciousness on the part of educated men of the evils arising from them, child marriages are very numerous, and I should say they have become the mania of the people at large. Even graduates of the University, and educated men generally, have been disposing of their infant girls of two or three years by marriage, simply from an apprehension that they could scarcely get rich boys or sons of rich men at a future time. To substantiate my assertion, I would respectfully ask, if there is to-day any graduate or educated man who, as father of infant girls, has not got them married when they were infants, or if there is any graduate or educated man who has had the moral courage to keep his daughter unmarried until she has attained her puberty. No one will come forward to say he has done either.

A HINDU LAWYER—This reminds me of what Mr. A. Mackenzie says regarding some of my countrymen: "Many of my native friends who were sound enough in theory on the subject, failed when the question came to personal and practical issues. They could be pilots of others but sank themselves to be castaways." We are all beautiful "burning and shining lights" to others—but like the lamp in the vernacular proverb can't be such lights to ourselves.

A HINDU SOCIAL REFORM MISSIONARY.—And why is it that we can't be? It is because we do not know what true sacrifice means. As Parásara says to Maitreya in the Vishnu Purana, "daily sacrifice" (he uses this in the sense of rites for exoteric readers) "daily sacrifice makes a man sinless", and it is because we have disregarded sacrifice, and "cut off the path of activity" that we have "become malignant, vicious and perverse."* This is the true meaning of the Kaliyuga—and it is a mournful meaning.

MR. LALSHANKAR UMIASHANKAR.—I know little of the mystery of Yugas—but I know that we had an association, at Ahmedabad, of more than 200 members, all pledged not to celebrate the marriage of their sons before a certain age; but only a few kept the pledge, while several broke it and said that their caste members in the association being few, they were unable to keep it.

H. H. THE THAKORE SAHIB OF MORVI.—I am bound to say, in our part of the country, the evil is as growing as anywhere else. I think there are not, and cannot be, in these days of civilization, two opinions as to the enormity of the evil, and that it ought to be put a stop to.

A HINDU SOCIAL REFORM MISSIONARY.—Then why does not your Highness put a stop to it in your own territory?

MR. NAVALRAM LAKSHMIRAM.—That is a consummation devoutly to be wished. His Highness's example will produce a wholesome effect in Gujarat, where generally all classes give away their daughters in marriage before they have completed their seventh year. In Kattyawar the marriageable age is a little higher, and the Rajputs also form a noteworthy exception in many respects.

BABU K. C BHATTACHARJI.—I am Head Master of the Zilla School, Noakhally, and I can say that, generally, the seeking of a bridegroom begins with the girl's stepping into the 7th or 8th year of her age. The feelings of the educated guardians in all communities are against the custom; but no one is, in his own case, prepared yet to put up with the social ignominy attaching to the departure from a deep-rooted and time-honoured custom enjoined by the Shastras.

---

* Muir's Sanscrit Texts, Vol. I p. 63 (2nd Edition.)

DIWAN BAHADUR MANIBHAI JASBHAI.—Generally Hindu parents do not keep their daughters unmarried beyond the age of twelve years; for education has as yet made very little progress.

RAO SAHIB V. N. MANDLIK.—I say it, with all submission, that there is no royal road to these things any more than to others. People must try to be, to live what they preach. It is a slow painful process—but what is higher education, I should like to know, if it will not prepare men for lives of self-sacrifice and noble self-abnegation?

SIRDAR JAYASING RAO, REGENT OF KOLAHPUR.—And I say it with all submission, that the educated classes, though fully feeling the evil, have not the moral courage to take action in the matter.

THE HON'BLE MR. DAYARAM JETHMUL.*—The truth is education cannot help you much. In the first place, it will take a long time before education can effect a regular upheaval in society. In the second place, if there are some highly educated men who are thoroughly convinced of the evils arising from early marriage, they are powerless to prevent such marriage taking place in their families, either because they have elders who manage their affairs, or for fear that, owing to the prevalence of the custom of early marriages among persons of position, suitable matches will not be procurable if the children are allowed to grow up; or because of the necessity they may be under, owing to limited pecuniary means, of getting presents on accouut of their sons to transfer them to their growing daughters. Supposing none of these obstacles exists, an educated man may set an example by postponing the marriage of his son or daughter, but the example is at the best of a negative character and will hardly act on others. Every one wants the *custom to be created*—for every one wants the whole of his community to follow a certain line of conduct. Voluntary effort can, therefore, achieve but little.

---

* Now unfortunately no more.

A HINDU SOCIAL REFORM MISSIONARY.—It is instructive to notice that, while educated men are doing next to nothing to check the evil, it is ramifying in several directions. Have any of you, gentlemen, read a small manual called "Coorg Civil Law" published in 1871? The Chief Commissioner of Coorg refers to it, and says that within the last 40 years, child marriages, which were unknown before, have come into vogue, and that the Coorgs have not been "superior to the temptation of following the example set by the Brahmins, Rajputs and other caste races, who have come to settle among them in increasing numbers." These caste races ought therefore to realise their heavy responsibility, and effect some reform.

MR. BAJABA RAMCHANDRA PRADHAN.—There is no doubt that any reform adopted by the higher castes will be taken up by the lower and less educated classes of the people.

MR. SHANTARAM NARAYAN.—Most certainly. The lower classes of course regulate their social procedure by the example of the higher classes. I can mention non-Brahmin communities among whom widow-marriage was allowed and practised formerly, but who within living memory declared themselves against the custon.

KUMAR P. BHUSHANA DEVA, RAJA OF NALDANGA.—In Bengal, society is led by rich men of the upper classes, the mass of the people following in their wake. The priests and the pandits watch which way the wind blows, and shape their opinions accordingly.

RAO SAHIB S. H. CHIPLONKAR.—I too do not deny that the larger and more predominant caste almost invariably sets the fashion, and thus the contagion spreads. But I maintain that this system of marriage is least prevalent amongst the Brahmins as compared with the non-Brahminical sections of the Hindu community, and that therefore the Brahmins are no way responsible for it.

Mr. N. C. Biswas.—It is only low-caste Hindus that countenance it in Bengal, and I am happy to say this abominable custom does not now-a-days suit the taste of the upper ten of the Hindu community.

R. S. Vishram Ramji Ghollay.—I cannot understand this at all. Among our Brahmins some girls above the age of twelve are found unmarried, but as a rule the Brahmins are bound, so to say, to get their girls married before this age. The girls of high-caste Mahrattas—called Mahrattas proper—however do remain unmarried in very many instances till twenty or more years.

Pandit Gattulal.—A caste can't be a high caste, Rao Sahib, if it defers the marriage of its girls to such an age The Shastras say: "A girl is called Gauri in the 8th year of her age, a Rohini in the 9th year, a Kanya in the 10th year, and after that a Rajasvala, that is, one having the menses. The menses are found in women in their 11th or 12th year. If the flower does not disclose itself, still it exists within. One goes to the Nak world by giving a Gauri in marriage, to the Vaikunth by giving a Rohini, to the Brahma world by giving a Kanya, and to the Raurav hell, by giving a Rajasvala." All these high-caste people that you speak of, Rao Sahib, will go to this place.

A Hindu Democritus.—Yes, most certainly, unless they give gold to Brahmins. When the doughty Parasurama, 'after having thrice seven times cleared the world of Kshatrias and conquered the whole earth' went to Vasishtha, Agastya, and Kasyapa, and inquired what the best penance was for deeds of violence, their reply was: 'gifts of cows, land and especially gold to Brahmins.' Why 'especially gold?'—asked Parasurama and they said: 'The purifying power of gold, oh Parasurama, is very great. Those who bestow it, bestow the gods.' 'How so' asked again the puzzled son of Jamadagni. 'Know oh Brahmin hero', was the rejoinder, 'know that Agni (Fire) comprehends all the gods, and gold is of the essence of Agni.'* So Parasurama gave gold and was cleansed of all sin. The Panditji ought therefore to make this important qualification, for Brahmins, as he knows, hold, as it were, the keys of all transmigrations. As Bhisma is made to say in the Mahabharata: "The prowess of Brahmins can destroy even the gods......They can turn what is not divine into what is divine and the converse; and can, in anger, create other worlds with their guardians. They are the gods of the gods and the cause of the cause. An ignorant Brahmin is a god, whilst a learned Brahmin is yet more a god, like the full ocean.† I bow with 'bated breath' to the Brahmins—for by their favour the Himalaya stands and the Ganga flows,‡ and I suppose even the British rule also.

A HINDU HERACLITUS.—No profane banter, please. I say woe unto those who have corrupted our Shastras in this fashion.

RAM SHASTRI.—There is no corruption at all. I can quote at least fourteen authorities to prove that the girl who sees the menses in her father's house, before marriage, is impure, and her father is guilty of bhorunmahatya—that is fœticide. Such a girl is rightly considered to be a Vrishali or Shudra female.

RAO SAHIB VISHRAM R. GHOLLAY.—Do you mean to say all pure Maharatta girls married late are Shudras? Pray, Shastriji, remember this is insulting language. I cannot stand it.

MR. VENKUT RANGO KATTI.—But, Rao Sahib, Ram Shastri tells the truth. The reason assigned for not marrying a girl under six is that Soma, Gandharva and Agni claim her each for two years from her birth. To get her married between six and eight is the very best, between nine and ten, a middling,

---

* Mahabharata Anusasanaparva 3960—4183 Muir's Sanskrit Texts Vol. 1 (2nd Edition) p. 461.

† Ibid 7164-7181 Muir I-473.

‡ Ibid 2160 Muir I-130.

and between eleven and twelve an undesirable course, according to the Shastras.

MR. CHENTSAL RAO.—According to custom also, which is regarded, I think, erroneously, as the law, every girl has to be married before she attains her puberty, and if she is not so married, she loses her caste. Girls in this country usually attain puberty at twelve or thirteen, and sometimes even so early as eleven, so that the latest period up to which a girl can be safely kept unmarried is ten.

MR. NANDSHANKAR.—There is no excommunication for prolonged virginity, that I know of. But a girl of thirteen or fourteen is certainly regarded by her parents as a "bundle of snakes."

BABU PEARY MOHAN SIRKAR.—Generally, puberty is attained after the twelfth and before the fourteenth year. But as there is no knowing when this event will happen, Hindu parents marry their girls at or before the age of twelve.

HON'BLE MR. NANABHAI HARIDAS.—The performance of the marriage sacrament in the case of a girl, according to all the authorities on the subject, cannot be delayed beyond the period of puberty which is generally attained in India at the age of twelve. According to some authorities, its performance a year or two before is meritorious.

MR. GAURISHANKER.—How do you explain the text in the Dharma Sindhu that eleven is a bad age, and twelve is one requiring the observance of a penance to wipe away the sin?

A HINDU LAWYER—And how do you explain the following passage in Steele's "Law and Custom of Hindu Castes within the Dekhan Provinces?"—"A Brahmin is enjoined to remain with his Guru as a student until twenty years of age, or at east sixteen, and on leaving him, to marry. Beyond that period there is no limit at which he may not be married (Koustoobh.) A female should be married at eight years of age, but not under six (Niranaysindhu and Mitakshara.) Nor can the marriage be delayed to her twelfth year, except by reason of distress. (Koustoobh and Mitakshara.) Should the signs of puberty appear before the marriage of a Brahmini, she may be married after certain prescribed ceremonies (Niranaysindhu); or married privately as one who has lost caste; or even abandoned altogether (Skand Purana.)" If you follow these shastras, then ten is the proper age, if not eight.

PROFESSOR R. G. BHANDARKAR.—There is no insuperable religious objection to marrying a girl after ten or twelve, for the penance enjoined is not heavy.

RAO SAHIB V. N. MANDLIK.—In the old Hindu institutes the marriageable age for females is twelve; but that for males has been contracted by the gradual curtailment of student-life, and a change in the social usages of the people.

A HINDU SOCIAL REFORM MISSIONARY.—I should like to know how this age of twelve has been contracted to ten. Are we to follow the old institutes—or are we to follow the new usage? It won't do to say that Manu enjoins a low age for girls and they must therefore be married at that age, but that boys may be married at an age not allowed by Manu. If you say the usage should be followed—even if it be opposed to Manu—then it follows that Manu's code has been departed from and may be departed from with impunity, but that any attempt to revert to it should be tabooed as a violation of the Shastras and visited with excommunication. A fine pass have we come to!

MR. K. T. TELANG.—The conclusion that I have come to is that neither caste nor Shastra, as popularly understood, exacts anything more than that girls should not remain unmarried after attaining puberty.

MR. M. G. RANADE.—Yes, for the declarations made at the marriage celebration by the bride and the bride-groom, the significance of certain of the rites themselves, especially the fourth day ceremony, all tend to show that these rites and declarations were not meant for children in their teens.

BABU HORI M. CHANDRA.—Manu says in chap. IX: "Three years let a damsel wait, though she be marriageable, but after that term let her choose for herself a bridegroom of equal rank." He also says: "A damsel, though marriageable, may stay at home till her death, if a suitable bridegroom cannot be found."

A HINDU ANTIQUARY.—And one of the oldest precedents is that of the royal maiden Sulabha who could find no suitable husband and devoted herself to pious deeds.*

MR. TRIMULRAO VENKATESH.—I tell you what, gentlemen. Suppose the dates and numbers of all Regulations and Acts passed up to date by the Government of India and the Local Governments, together with those sections which repeal former enactments or define the territorial extent over which an Act is to operate, were effaced altogether, and the bare enactments placed in the hands of the public—what a beautiful Babel of Law would we all have, and how mighty glad the lawyers would be to have confusion worse confounded? Well this is the real state of what we call our Hindu Law—so let us no more pelt texts at one another.

A HINDU SOCIAL REFORM MISSIONARY.—Then let us at least see if 10 or 12 or a higher age is a proper age for girls.

RAO SAHIB S. H. CHIPLONKAR.—Why, even in England a Law book tells us that "if a boy under 14 or a girl under 12 years of age marries, their marriage is only inchoate and imperfect, but not necessarily void."

---

* Santiparvan 7882-7983 Muir-1430

Rao Saheb V. N. Mandlik.—And in such an advanced country as the United States of America, the age of consent is the same, viz., 12 for females and 14 for males. In New York an attempt was made to raise these periods to 14 and 17 respectively, but they were so disrelished by the people that a law was passed in 1830, restoring the old periods of 12 and 14 as before.

A Hindu Lawyer.—I don't know anything about the laws of New York, but I know that our own Legislature has considered these limits too low. Act XV. of 1872, for example, lays down, as regards Native Christians, that "the age of the man intending to be married shall exceed 16 years, and the age of the woman intending to be married shall exceed 13 years". (S. 60.) Act XXI. of 1866 which also related to such converts, prohibited them from suing for the conjugal society of their unconverted wives, unless these latter had completed the age of thirteen years. (S. 4 and the Definitions.) In Act XV. of 1865, the Legislature enacted for the Parsis that, "no suit shall be brought in any court to enforce any marriage between Parsis, or any contract connected with or arising out of any such marriage, if at the date of the institution of the suit, the husband shall not have completed the age of sixteen years, or the wife shall not have completed the age of fourteen years". (S. 37.) And lastly, in Act III. of 1872 it laid down for Brahmos that, at the time of the marriage, the age of the husband and wife must be 18 and 14 respectively. (S. 2) It is remarkable that the Rajput Sirdars, at their recent meeting in Ajmere, adopted these latter limits, and in my humble opinion a marriage contracted by parties under this age is a premature marriage which often ruins both body and mind. The low age of consent in England has also been recently raised, and it should not be forgotten that in England, if not the United States, the people are always in advance of their laws. One small fact will make this clear. In England the proportion of married women between 15 and 20 years of age is only 3·1 per cent, while in the North-West Provinces alone it is 87·8 per cent.

MR. T. PATTABHIRAM.—I don't understand how early marriage ruins body and mind. I always thought the Brahmins had introduced this custom of child marriage after the Vedic period, to keep their blood and stock pure and untainted, and I always believed that, though weak in physique, their superior intellect was due to this cause.

A HINDU SOCIAL REFORM MISSIONARY.—This is a most novel theory. I don't know whether by purity you mean poverty of blood, for this last is most certainly the result of this pernicious usage, according to the medical opinions collected by the late lamented Keshub Chunder Sen. Even Parasara—the supposed author of the principal text quoted a little while ago by our right reverend Pandit Gattulal—says: "A son is the very same as he by whom he was begotten."* Probably Messrs. Chiplonkar and Pradhan are right in holding that the custom is of recent growth among the Deccan Brahmins, and hence they retain their old intellectual superiority—for sufficient time has not yet elapsed to develop by heredity the effects of the new custom to such an extent as to bring them home to every observer. I don't know if any other class of Brahmins given to premature marriages possess any intellectual superiority.

MR. GAURISHANKAR UDEYSHANKAR.—Whatever may be the Hindu law on the subject, and whatever may be the effects of the custom, let us first discuss whether the custom prevails among us. I cannot say how the case stands in the Deccan, but in Gujarat child marriages are confined to a few among the upper classes, such as Brahmins, Kshatryas and Wanias.

MR. R. B. TALVALKAR.—I should say such marriages are very rife in some sections of the Gujarati Brahmins. If these Brahmins are excepted, the number of girls married under fifteen in the Bombay Presidency will be not more than 30 per cent.

---

* Santiparvan 10861, Mahabharata, Muir I-131.

Mr. S. H. Chiplonkar.—It is only 26 per cent. even if the Brahmins are included. The proportion of Hindu married girls under fifteen to their total number, is 27 per cent. in Gujarat, 26 per cent. in the Deccan, 21 per cent. in the Konkan, 33 per cent. in the Western Carnatic, 28 per cent. in the city of Bombay, and 6 per cent. in Sind. The total number of Hindu girls under ten, at the last census was, in Gujarat, 287,840, and out of these 250,113 were single, 36,582 married, and 1,145 widowed. In the Deccan, out of 659,379 girls under ten, 594,849 were found single, 63,077 married, and 1,453 widowed.

Mr. Ramanujchari.—My hair stand on end when I hear of virgin widows under ten. In Southern India the evil is much more rampant. There girls are married from 6 months up to 12 years, especially among the Brahmins.

Mr. C. Subbaraya Aiyar.—The figures given in the Madras Census report suggest that between 6 and 7 is the average age for females among Brahmins. To quote the words of the report :—"Some are married before seven, and nearly all are married before ten."

Mr. T. Pattabhiram.—The Brahmins are only 4·94 per cent. of the whole Indian population. The Brahmin female population for the whole of India is 6,606,000, and of this number, 31 per cent. are widows, $21\frac{2}{3}$ per cent. unmarried and the rest married. These are not discreditable figures.

Mr. S. H. Chiplonkar.—So also the figures for all Hindus generally do not show any very high averages. In the Panjaub the percentages of Hindu married and widowed girls and boys under ten, respectively, are $3\frac{1}{2}$ and $1\frac{1}{9}$; in the Madras Presidency $4\frac{1}{2}$ and $\frac{4}{5}$; in the North-West Provinces $5\frac{1}{2}$ and $2\frac{2}{5}$; in the Central Provinces 8 and $2\frac{1}{2}$; in the Bombay Presidency $10\frac{1}{2}$ and $2\frac{1}{2}$; in the Bengal Presidency 14 and $5\frac{1}{2}$; in the Berars $21\frac{3}{4}$ and 4.

A Hindu Social Reform Missionary.—I say these figures do not show the real extent of the evil, for they only show how many girls and boys under ten were *found* married or widowed at the Census of 1881, and not how many were really married or widowed under ten. A girl, for example, married at the age of six in 1875 and being nearly 12 years old in 1881, would not appear in the statistics relating to married girls under ten. If you suppose that the girls found married under ten were the only girls so married, then it would follow that the Hindu women shown as married in the 7th decade in the Census report, were married in that decade. But none believes that 6,84,000 Hindu women are married when past the age of sixty, or that 17,53,000 are married between 50 and 60, or that 43,42,000 are married between 40 and 50, or that 87,97,000 are married between 30 and 40, or that 66,51,000 are married between 20 and 25, or even that 53,23,000 are married between 15 and 20. No candid Hindu can deny what Mr. Telang says that the custom of premature marriage is "all but universal." Taking, however, the Census figures as to girls under ten and fourteen into consideration, is it not a mournful fact that no less than 19,32,000 Hindu girls under ten were found married, and no less than 63,000 widowed, at the Census? Twenty lakhs of married and widowed girls under ten is a sight not seen anywhere out of India. Then, besides these twenty lakhs, we have no less than 43,95,000 Hindu married, and 1,74,000 widowed, girls from ten to fourteen years of age. This gives us, then, 45 lakhs and three quarters more. We have thus 65 lakhs of married and widowed girls under fourteen. The aggregate number of Hindu single, married, and widowed males in 1881 was roundly 8,44,00,000, and of Hindu females 8,16,00,000. Of these former 3,97,00,000 were married and of the latter 2,50,00,000; but mark, gentlemen, that while there were only 44,05,000 widowers, there were no less than 1,61,00,000 widows, in other words the widows were to widowers as 3 to 1. So also, if you examine the figures in detail, you find that the widows keep up this proportion in the first three decades, while in the latter three their proportion is nearly as 4 to 1. Contrast, again, the proportion of widowed males to married males with the proportion of widowed females to married females. The former is as 1 to 9; the latter is as 1 to 2½! What is the significance of this last fact? It is that out of every 4 married women one at least is a widow. And who does not know how this takes place?

Sir T. Madava Row.—Babu H. M. Chandra has shown to us that in Bengal more than one in four girls are wives or widows between 5 and 10 years of age. The Madras Census Report contains a passage about Brahmins, which is especially instructive, as there is little doubt that if a better custom were adopted by them it would, in all probability, be imitated. This is the passage: "There are proportionately 50 per cent. more widows among Brahmins than among other castes, and this surplus may be wholly attributed to the greater extent to which infant marriages occur among Brahmins than is the case with other castes. Certainly one-third, probably a larger portion of the number of Brahmin widows, are widows owing to this custom; that is to say, if Brahmins countenanced infant marriage only to the extent that other castes do, there would be nearly 60,000 fewer unhappy women in their caste. The total figures show that there are 80,000 widows under twenty, and the foregoing remarks suggest that the Brahmin custom is responsible for three-fourths of this."

Dr. Rajendralala Mitra.—But, Sir, the less the number of widows, the greater the number of maids who can never have husbands. You know well enough that in England maids number not by thousands—but by hundreds of thousands, and you will not have the hardihood to tell me that all of them or the bulk of them are chaste.

Mr. Kalianrai H. Desai.—I say 'ditto' to the learned doctor.

Mr. T. Pattabhiram.—The unmarried and widowed females among the Brahmins come up to 52$\frac{2}{3}$ per cent., while in Europe they come up to 67 per cent. of the total female population there, or 14$\frac{1}{3}$ per cent. more.

Mr. M. T. Pillai.—I must ask you, gentlemen, to consider the difference between the conditions of women leading lives of celibacy of their own accord, enjoying all the innocent comforts and pleasures of life, and those of the Hindu widows who are looked down upon as inauspicious, sinful creatures, destined to live miserably without the comforts and pleasures of life.

It is true, as Sir Alfred Lyall says, that "the general social effect and result must be detrimental wherever a large body of unmarried women exists, whether these be widows or spinsters." But "the position of a single woman is", he continues, "no doubt more tolerable in England from the greater freedom and security and the much higher social consideration and sympathy that women of every status enjoy there", while Mr. White's inquiries (at the time of the Census) went to show that, at 30 years of age, a Hindu woman is generally an old woman; and Sir Alfred states that "this most likely is the reason why the proportion of Hindu women living in widowhood begins to get excessive in the fourth decade of life."

Rao Saheb Mahipatram Rupram.—I think it is absurd to institute any comparisons between English maids and widows and their Hindu sisters. English country life is very pure, but in the towns of course, where "wealth accumulates and men decay," temptations abound, and extremes of riches and poverty produce those "silent crimes of capitals" of which we have all heard. But we have heard of them so much because the English live in glass-houses, so to say, because they are not given to nursing their diseases, and propagating them among their brethren, and handing them down to their posterity. It is always easy to pick out the specks and blemishes of others—but we ought also to "see ourselves as others see us", and not vindicate early marriage "as the only safeguard", to use Professor Wordsworth's words, "against universal sexual license", for every right-thinking Hindu ought to admit that this argument is "a confession of moral incompetence", as the learned Professor puts it, which no people with any self-respect should advance.

As to Hindu young widows, without going the length of charging one and all with wicked conduct, I can safely say that a large number of them go astray, and the consequences are horrible. Attempts at procuring abortions, which in some cases terminate in death, and murder of pregnant widows by their relations are the results. No English woman is old at thirty. Life is not a blank for her even when past forty. I would say, with the poet,

"Life has its bliss for these, when past its bloom.
As wither'd roses yield a late perfume.
Serene and safe from passion's stormy rage,
How calm they glide into the port of age."

Can we say this of Hindu widows?

KUMAR P. BHUSHAN DEVA.—Premature marriage is not only a pernicious custom because it ages wives at thirty, or gives us virgin or unhappy widows—but because it leads to the deterioration of the race. This was admitted even by the ancient medical-science of the Hindus, the Ayur Vedas.

RAM SHASTRI.—The deterioration of the race can't be the effect of this custom, unless we suppose that every premature marriage is at once consummated. But I deny this most strongly.

DR. SAKHARAM ARJUN.—The truth is the baneful effects of early consummation have been so patent and far-reaching that men who would not budge an inch from their orthodoxy in other matters, now willingly defer it, in the case of their children to a pretty long period.

Mr. Hari Parsad Santokram.—In Maharashtra and Northern Canara, consummation is always put off. Hence the physique of the people remains unimpaired, and they are able to maintain their traditionary repute for activity and political agitation. In most cases in Gujarat and Kathiawar also, consummation is put off.

Mr. Gurshidapa Virbasapa.—I can say from my knowledge of the Southern Division of the Bombay Presidency, that consummation as a rule never takes place before the girl arrives at maturity.

Mr. Shrikrishna Narhar.—In the Berars, too, consummation is never or very seldom allowed before the pair attain full maturity.

Mr. Waman Narayen Bapat.—Consummation is not a day too early among us. That consummation which takes place just when the parties have arrived at the age of puberty is a direct call of nature, and cannot be early or late.

Mr. Gokuldas K. Parekh.—In cases of grown-up husbands marrying very young girls, the consummation takes place sometimes too early, and leaves a lasting effect on the girl's constitution.

Mr. P. Desai.—In Gujarat, according to the custom now prevailing, Hindu parents are often compelled to get their daughters married when they are scarcely six or seven years of age to boys of whom they know little or nothing. Shortly after their marriage, they are taken to the homes of their boy-husbands. At about twelve or thirteen, they become mothers of one or two sickly children, and their life is then necessarily spent in looking after household affairs, and often in performing, in the higher classes, trivial religious duties.

Mr. Lalshankar Umiashankar.—This is but too true. In Gujarat the real evil in the case of girls is the early consummation of marriage.

Babu K. C. Bhattacharji.—I can testify that ordinarily on our side, the marriage is consummated in the girl's tenth or eleventh year.

Mr. Gurshidapa Vibasapa.—But in India, you must, remember, owing to climatic causes, we have precocious maturity, and a girl of twelve in this country is not a child, but a young woman.

Mr. Gaurishankar Udeyshankar.—It is on this account, that I consider eleven to be a fairly good marriageable age for girls in India.

Mr. V. R. Katti.—Whatever Mr. Wordsworth may say, experience has shown that to leave girls and boys, long after their 12th and 16th years respectively, without their partners, leads to looseness of character and disease.

Mr. K. H. Desai.—True to my Hindu instincts, I, for one, am against keeping girls unmarried after they have reached their twelfth year. Even an Englishman, I mean Mr. Cordery, admits that the obligation of the tie makes the honour of the child respected by others, and by no means necessarily leads to premature consummation by the husband for whom she is safely reserved. Sir M. Melvill also says that premature consummation is not a necessary accessory of a premature marriage.

Mr. Lallubhai Nandlal.—The climate of India makes it desirable that girls should be married at from seven to ten years of age, and though at the same time it would be very much desirable that the consummation should begin a little later, I think to provide for this a remedy in checking marriage at the age above mentioned, is rather fighting against nature itself.

Mr. Manmohandas Dayaldas.—Girls should be married between the ages of 8 and 12. If it be desired to preserve public health then the best course is to drive away all prostitutes from cities. They are a source of immense mischief.

As to when our girls attain puberty, I say that in towns they attain it, generally speaking, between the ages of ten and twelve, and in the country, between fifteen and eighteen. As regards bearing children, nothing depends upon whether a woman has had natural or unnatural menstruation. It is my belief that a girl who has menstruated unnaturally will be a mother sooner than one who has menstruated naturally, as is the case with a mango graft fed with various manures and chemicals. But it is an indisputable fact that the fruit of such a graft never equals in quality a fruit naturally borne by a tree. Looking rather minutely into the matter, it appears that out of the children of the present generation, hardly two per cent can be said to be a fine set of children. It is my belief that every woman miscarries at least once or twice in the beginning. It is past human belief that the progeny proceeding from originally diseased wombs can ever be strong or healthy, since, according to medical science, unnatural menstruation is a disease.

Dr. Mohendralal Sircar.—I am afraid you are not quite consistent. You admit the difference between rural and urban girls, and the climate being the same, you ought to admit that climate is not the cause of the difference. Many of my friends here, again, confound pubescence with puberty. The commencement of the menstrual function is no doubt an index to the commencement of puberty. But it is a grave mistake to suppose that the female who has just begun to menstruate is capable of giving birth to healthy children. The teeth no doubt are intended for the mastication of solid food, but it would be a grievous error to think that the child the moment he begins to cut his teeth, will be able to live upon solid food. Our anxiety, on the contrary, should be that the delicate masticatory organs are not injured or broken by giving the child too hard food. So when we see a girl beginning to have the monthly flow, we should not only anxiously watch its course and regularity, but should also watch the other collateral developments of womanhood, to be able to determine the better the time when she can become a mother safely to herself and to her offspring. For it should be borne in mind that while early maternity results in giving birth to short-lived or unhealthy children, it at the same time seriously compromises the health of the mother also. I can speak positively on this subject from personal experience. A number of complaints from which our females suffer life-long, or to which they fall early victims, arise from the evils of early marriage, namely early pubescence and early maternity.

PANDIT BADRI DUTT JOSHI.—The other day I heard a native physician repeat a *sloka* from Susrut, stating that up to the age of 25 years in man and 16 in woman, the bones and vital fluids do not reach complete development, and consequently any wasting of the latter before this age should be discouraged.

PROFESSOR BHANDARKAR.—I believe that if a young man and a young woman begin to live as husband and wife in all cases when they are 21 or 22, and 16 or 17 respectively, the total physical effect will be better than at present.

MR. K. T. TELANG.—I, too, have no doubt that reform is most urgently called for in regard to the time of consummation, but not so much in regard to the time of marriage.

MR. M. G. RANADE.—But I have not yet heard it denied, by any sensible man, that early marriage leads to early consummation.

MR. VISHNU MORESHWAR MAHAJANI.—The Hindu girl reaches puberty (as popularly understood) at the age of thirteen or fourteen, and custom directs that the consummation should take place soon after. Her home-education, her surroundings, the talk among women, her sports, the proud celebration of the religious ceremonies attending the consummation, all work upon the imagination of the poor girl, and give an unnatural stimulus to her passion, which is certainly mischievous. A girl as soon as the consummation takes place receives benedictions from old women and from priests: "Be you soon a mother of eight sons"—and until she becomes a mother she has very little respect in the family. Her parents do not dine at her husband's until she gets a son. Under these circumstances, it is no wonder that consummation takes place at an age too early for her physiologically to become a mother.

Dr. Mohendralal Sircar.—Yes, the fact which demands serious consideration is that the minimum age of menstruation has, since the days of Susruta, become much lower. I have no doubt in my mind that high and luxurious living and early seeing and knowing of child-husbands and child-wives, favoured by the anxiety of fond parents to see their little ones become fathers and mothers, are the chief causes of this forced puberty. And its results are disastrous. As Dr. Smith said:—'The present system of early marriage panders to passion and sensuality, violates the requirements of nature, lowers the general standard of public health, lessens the average value of life, takes greatly from the general interest of existing society, and allows the present race to deteriorate both to its own disadvantage and to the detriment of future generations.'

Dr. Atmaram Pandurang.—I quite agree.

A Hindu Social Reform Missionary.—And every medical man agrees. Surgeon-Major Parekh tells us: "I see every day the dire results of early marriages on the constitutions of women and children who throng my hospital (the Gokuldas Tejpal Hospital). There is a great deal of sickness and mortality and difficulty in the act of child-birth, due to imperfect consolidation of the bones of the pelvis at the tender age......at which women in consequence of early marriages give birth to children. The heads of the children of young mothers are also unduly pressed upon, and so either the children die prematurely or grow feeble, both in body and mind, and turn out helpless idiots."

A lady doctor, Mrs. Mitchell, bears the same testimony. She came across cases of consummation—call it rather rape—at the age of seven, and the injury done, she says, was beyond repair. Dear friends, it was said of old: "Where women are honoured, there the deities are pleased: but where they are dishonoured, there all religious acts become fruitless".* Consider how immeasurable is our fall, and in God's name, impede not the elevation of woman to her proper rank, and her restoration to her old rights. Only the other day I came across a little book in Mahratti called the Vedokt Sanskara Prakasha, by a Pandit, Balaji Vithal Gaunvskar, which lays down as a Vedic rule that no consummation should take place until a girl menstruates 36 times, or before her sixteenth year. Contrast this precept with the present practice, and then say if it is not madness—if it is not worse than the very worst sin—to continue sinning in this fashion against our dearest and nearest, against ourselves, our offspring, our country, our God?

Secretary Jessore Indian Association.—This language is too impassioned to be logical. I represent an association which holds that early marriage weakens the physical strength of a nation, stunts its full growth and development, affects the courage and energy of individuals, and brings forth a race of people weak in strength and wanting in hardihood. This, however, according to our association, is but one side of the picture. Its other and brighter side, I am sorry to say, has been overlooked. Physically the institution is bad, but morally it is good. It is a powerful check against the wantonness of youth. Absence of free-will and choice creates no unhappiness, for this is more than compensated by the interest which guardians take in securing suitable matches. Selection by youths eager for marriage may be influenced by several transitory considerations,

* Manu III—56.

but the sober judgment of their guardians cannot be. Moreover, continuous association from their early years offers sufficient opportunities to the married parties, to be acquainted with each other's thoughts and traits of character, and by smoothing their differences and enhancing their reciprocity, teaches them to assimilate and live joint and peaceful lives. The Hindus are the only nation among whom matrimonial scandals, and disgraceful breaches between husbands and wives, are rarely heard of.

HON'BLE MR. NANABHAI HARIDAS.—Yes, this last fact alone ought to make us pause. Our conjugal relations, I am disposed to think, are on the whole more satisfactory than those among other people. Our domestic differences are certainly fewer, and when they arise we arrange them without having recourse to matrimonial or other tribunals. However unreasonable certain usages and customs in India may appear to foreigners, it must not be forgotten that to the people at large, among whom they obtain, they appear in another light, and that the fact of their having existed for centuries is in itself some evidence of their being adapted to the circumstances of the people.

BABU GOPAL C. MUKERJI.—Early marriage certainly cements love, and it does not come in the way of education or progress. Are not nine-tenths of our Bachelors of Arts and Law, Benedicts.

MR. C. SUBBARAYA AIYAR.—I also think that early marriages, brought about under the discriminating and fostering care of Hindu parents, have not failed to lead to happy unions, securing to the married couples social and domestic felicity. I have heard from my European friends that even in England and other civilised countries, where freedom of choice and liberty of action are enjoyed in the highest degree by the contracting parties, marriage is a lottery in which more blanks are drawn than prizes.

Mr. T. Pattabhiram.—If men of so much above the usual or average run of mankind, as Lord Byron, &c., fail in their choice, and in a society which allows free scope for many a private talk and personal intercourse between the young lovers, can there be any meaning in the high-sounding phrase 'liberty of choice'?

Babu P. C. Muzumdar.—We cannot afford to have love-letters, flirtations, rejections and amorous fancies in our households. If we can help it, we will not permit the importation of these usages. Premature marriages are doomed, but the problem of finding out suitable matches for over-grown young ladies is far from solution. I would advocate betrothals long before marriage. The parents, according to Hindu notions, should propose and arrange the matches, but the daughter or son shall have the power to veto the selection. But if the selection once meet with the approval of parent and child, the match shall never be set aside, unless either of the contracting parties show a physical or moral unfitness.

Mr. Varjiwandas Madhawdas.—I don't believe that, generally speaking, premature marriages are productive of discord between man and wife, after they come to live together, to a much greater extent, than would be the case if the marriages occurred at a later period of life.

Professor R. G. Bhandarkar.—There is no reason for supposing that the child marriages which do take place in Hindu society are ill-sorted. The parents of the bridegroom and bride belong to the same caste and same social condition, and from childhood, the girl and the boy are brought up in the belief that they are destined to be wife and husband, and that their mutual relation is as much the work of nature, and consequently inviolable, as the relation between brother and sister or parents and children. This belief enters into the formation of their character, and they grow up as wife and husband, and consequently become adapted to each other. Cases of child-marriage proving ill-sorted afterwards, are therefore extremely rare, and deserve no consideration. Though, therefore, I can't attribute ill-sorted matches to this custom I still think it productive of evil. A young man is too early burdened with the cares aud responsibilities of a family, and even when his parents, being alive, relieve him of the burden, the excitement and diversion of thought inseparable from a married life render a single-minded devotion to study, and to the improvement of the mind, all but impossible. The result is worse in the case of girls. The merest elementary education is all that can be given to them. Their being married when they are eight or nine years old, increases also the chance of their becoming child-widows. Hence the opinion I have already expressed.

Rao Saheb V. N. Mandlik.—I don't agree with you, Professor Bhandarkar. If a healthy mind in a healthy body may be accepted as good evidence, in order to judge of the results of unions in early life, I could produce the evidence of scores of families over at least three generations, producing men able to work at 50, 60, and ages yet higher. Those who mourn in these days of diseased constitutions, of weakened intellects and perhaps of perverted morals, of* those whom they cite in support of their contentions, must seek the cause of such unhappy results in quarters other than those of those early married Hindus who have been trained under proper family influences.

Secretary British Indian Association.—In the opinion of our association, early marriage is not the sole or the most important cause of the degeneracy of our race. Climate, food, hereditary predisposition to disease, injudicious selection in marriage, and other causes of arrested growth are potent factors in the case, and it is illogical to overlook them.

Ram Shastri.—It has been said that the earth is but the king's bride, and follows the king's moods. It has been also

* So in the original.

said that "the king is the cause of the time" and "the creator of the Krita, Treta, Dwapara ages, and the cause also of the fourth Yuga."* Ours is the fourth *Yuga*. The king has taken away the old landed hereditary incomes. Hence there are divisions in families, and every divided member has to maintain his own family. The real reason of our degeneracy is that, while formerly one member only of the joint family had to provide the maintenance of the whole, and the others led an easy and quiet sort of life, he cannot now so provide it. To earn a livelihood, the chief resource now left to the people is Government service which they can enter only after studying the English language and passing certain examinations. The trouble and anxiety consequent upon these tell upon the constitution of the younger generation who thus become weak and subject to disease. This is the cause of the people's weakness, and premature marriages have nothing to do with it.

GANGADHAR SHASTRI.—True, O Shastriji, true. You might have added that, when a girl is married in her childhood, the mind then being stable, her sense of respect towards her husband is strengthened by the advice of her elders who tell her to look upon her husband as her god, and there thus remains no possibility of her character being afterwards spoilt.

MR. NARAYEN PRABHAKAR PARASPE.—And you might add that the boy is saved from practising unnatural ways of satisfying carnal instincts.

MR. WAMAN NARAYEN BAPAT.—And you might further add that early consummation tends to make the husband more steady, more tractable, and even more studious, than he would be without it. Liberty of choice is a mere phrase. So long as human nature is not prepared to forget its high descent and lofty destiny, it cannot traffic in human flesh, with that utter oblivion of the demands of decency, with which it enters into other contracts. Hence in contracting marriages much

* Mahabharata Santiparvan, 2674-2693, Muir I-149.

will always be left to chance, and little to deliberation and choice. Our system has many advantages to recommend it. Children are naturally more exposed to observation than adults, and less likely to assist in cheating. In late marriages outward form carries everything, for adults have little patience for the exercise of cool judgment, and can hide their weaknesses from each other. Again, in child marriages you can chisel off many of the irregularities of temperament by a proper course of treatment; but in late marriages one cannot be a disciplinarian and at the same time a loving husband and wife. Every one of us has read Malabari's tirades and jeremiades. But another Parsi, Mr. Dinshaw Ardesir Taleyarkhan, bears testimony to the "marked harmony" of our homes. He says:—"If we have weakly children (I deny this) the homes at least are happy, contented, well-regulated, and economical. The boys and girls have no world of their own, which we delude ourselves by believing they would have as soon as we give it to them. They are the creatures of their parents, brought up in the time-honoured instincts, associations, and motives of caste organisms."*

Messrs. Bhaskar Rao B. Pitale and Nana Moroba.—Yes, our houses are very economically managed. In this indigent country, the practice of living together under one roof and under one head is a great boon to Hindus, and early marriages (not infant marriages) considerably contribute towards attaining this end, for adult marriages are sure to entail dismemberment of the family and the family estate.

A Hindu Democritus.—Yes, let us sing the praises of this system of premature marriage. What a fine specimen of our wisdom is this institution! How noble in its reasonableness! How infinite in its resources! In loveliness of form and moving unction how express and admirable! In active results how angelic! In apprehended results, how god-like! The beauty

---

* See Page 51.

of the Aryan world! The paragon of institutions! The quintessence of Purusha and Pradhan, of Ishan and Shakti, and the very yelk of Brahma's fat golden egg. What a pity it is that the Purusha Sukta, that mystic hymn in the Riga Veda, does not mention it along with curds and butter—the Vedas and the four castes—as one of the products of the Universal Sacrifice it celebrates. What a pity that no Vedic text calls lovely woman "a bundle of snakes." But what matters it? She appears to have been no better in ancient times than she is now. I beg your pardon, gentlemen: I mean she was a much worse creature than she is now, for have we not infant and child marriages now as her surest safeguard? It was woman that disturbed the Rishis' meditations of old, and they cursed her or blessed her, if you please, with premature marriage. You know who tempted Vishvamitra, though we ought to be thankful he was tempted, for if he had not been, there would have been no Shakuntala for Kalidasa and none of course for us. There is high authority, however, for holding that even Shakuntalas are "vessels of sin." Does not the Taittreya Sanhita say that female children are rejected and males are taken up?* And does not the Nidana Sutra say that "Women are irregular in their conduct", and the Shatapatha Brahmana say that Rakshas follow after women and a Brahmin's birth is uncertain, and Yajnavalkya say: "Who would mind his wife consorting with other men"? † Who, again, has not read or heard of that passage in the Mahabharata which tells how Sveteketu put an end to the custom of community of wives? Are there not texts also which sanction the levirate; and those twelve kinds of sons and eight forms of marriage mentioned by Manu, what do they not mean? Let us laugh, my dear Heraclitus, while we may. It is a mad world this, my masters, and true wisdom consists in letting it spin its whirling course, and enjoying the playful humour of the Creator.

---

*Muir I. 26 (Note.)

† Muir I. 136 (Note.)

A Hindu Heraclitus.—This earth, Oh frivolous philosopher, was made out of the tears of Prajapati—so it is said in a Brahmana.* And Prajapati wept, because he was alone—until impelled by desire, which has been truly said to be the bond between entity and non-entity,† he created woman. In the golden age of Aryan glory when the only *brahma* priest was prayer—the only *hotri,* Truth—the only *udgatri,* Immortality,‡ our ancestors used to say that a "wife is the half of one's self" and "the man who has no wife is unfit to sacrifice."§ Heaven's "last best gift" to the father of mankind—our great Manu—was Ida, his wife, our mother; and the Shatapatha Brahmana tells us that "whatever benediction he asked with her was all vouchsafed to him."‖ Then woman was held in the greatest esteem, and all lovely imaginings took her form. Uma Haimavati who told Agni and Vayu of the One Supreme was a woman.¶ Vách, the goddess of speech, the daughter of Brahma, his Divine Word, was figured as a woman. So was Gayatri and so was Shraddha,** the goddess of faith. Even in the Mahabharata, Brahma is made to say that he fashioned the first woman "faultless in beauty and in all her qualities," from "whatever was most excellent in the several members of different creatures.†† Woman was then a true *patni,* and was called Devi, and we still preserve these names though we have forgotten their significance. Turn, again, to the marriage ritual and mark the deep reverence which underlies it. Draupadi was told at her marriage: "What Indrani is to Indra—Sváha to the Sun—Rohini to the Moon—Damayanti to Nala—Bhadrá to Kuvera—Arundhatti to Vasishtha—Lakhshmi to Narayana—be thou to thy husband." And a similar verse is read at every

* Muir I. 29.

† Muir I. 32.

‡ Muir I. 41 Note.

§ Taitt Brahmana III. 3,35 Muir I. 25.

‖ Muir I. 184.

¶ Muir IV. 357 (first edition.)

** Muir V--346 (3rd edition)

†† Uttara Kanda 24 Muir I—121

Hindu marriage. What nobler ideals can ever be imagined? And the men who imagined them could not but have been chivalrous in the truest sense. And yet you quote a few fragmentary texts and legends relating to times outlived by the Vedic poets, or due to the absorbing passion of our Smriti writers for exhaustive enumeration and discussion, as proofs of a low estimate of woman by our ancestors. I say, read the ancient documents as a whole and not piecemeal, and you cannot escape the conviction that we are a fallen race, and to use a Vedic phrase, "our stars have dishevelled hairs."

A Hindu Democritus.—Dishevelled hairs! I protest they have no such ugly appendage. They are shining as brightly and merrily as of old when our fathers imagined their regent to be a polygamist with a harem of thirty-three wives. That beautiful Rohini who monopolised the devotion of the Moon and brought on consumption upon him as a punishment for his neglect of his other wives—that Rohini is still sporting in the sky, and I bet, despite what astronomers may say, she is as lovely to her Soma as before, and as lovely to us all. The light of Daksha's sprightly daughters is not yet quenched, believe me, and they are as much giggling in their sleeves (if they have any) as when Bhrigu's beard was singed, and Bhaga's eyes were torn out, and Pushan's teeth knocked off. This blue vault above us, with its myriad eyes and lips, has had its peals of laughter at our ways and at the ways of our gods before, and your lugubrious laments will not prevent it having many more. It laughed when the jovial Indra seduced the stainless Ahalya—the delightful Ruchi—and that pearl among Asura maidens, Vilistenga. It laughed when Varuna spirited away the beautiful Bhadra, betrothed to another. It laughed when Brahma embraced his daughter—and Yami wooed her brother—and the As'vins married their sister. It laughed when Agni fell in love with the wives of the Seven Rishis—when Svaha assumed the forms of all except the chaste Arundhatti, when Anasuya was asked by the Three to bare her body. It laughed when Surya bedded with his wife and mother Ushas—when Siva forgot his meditations in the arms of Parvati before the birth of Kartik—when Krishna ceased to think of Vaikunth in the presence of the lovely Gopis. And I say it laughed when Nahusha coveted Indrani—when Nala and Yudhishthira turned first-rate gamblers—when Ravana flew off with Sita, and Jayadrath drove off with Draupadi, and Krishna with Rukshmini, and Arjuna with Subhadra, and Anirudh with Okha. Talk not, therefore, friend Heraclitus, of your good old times. There was enough to laugh at before, and there is enough to laugh at now, and I say there is no choosing between the two.

A HINDU HERACLITUS.—Blasphemous chatterer, how can you talk so irreverently of our brightest ideals? Does it follow that we have not fallen because Rukshmini and Subhadra and Okha knew how to love and to be loved, or that Sita and Draupadi had severe trials and came out of them as pure gold? And as to our Aryan gods, do you not see that these very tales you mention betoken our degeneracy, for who does not know the difference between the Vedic deities and their travesties in the Puranic and post-Puranic times? It was a corrupt age most certainly which putrefied those lovely allegories and similitudes—the creatures of natural poetry and paradox—into loathsome and prurient legends. Interpret those allegories and similitudes aright—and you will be shocked at the unmeaning, vapid, and tasteless distortions which they have undergone. Was there any thing wrong, for example, in one poet imagining the Dawn as the wife of the Sun, and another as his mother? Will you conclude English society to be rotten if two English poets were to call Sin the mother of Death and the wife of Death respectively? You might as well conclude that patricide and matricide were not deemed sinful in the Vedic age, because the Vedic poets represented Agni as the child of the upper and lower pieces of wood still used by Agnihotris, and as the murderer of his parents immediately at his birth. Remember that the hymns of the Riga Veda were not written (or as the Vedic phrase goes, seen) by one man, and remember that the gods thus celebrated are impersonations of natural phenomena and the conceptions derived from such phenomena. Indra was Beneficent Might—the lord of S'achi (Power)—and tenderly devoted to her, for in a hymn in the Riga Veda it is said: "A wife, Indra, is one's home. She is man's dwelling......Thou hast a lovely wife and pleasure in thy house." * And the Vedic poets were as incapable of representing him a debauchee as of representing Varuna (their moral governor) a seducer. That great repository of legendary lore, the Mahabharata, is disfigured by numerous interpolations—some of which, as in the case of the second version of the story of King Shibi—the chapter of lies about places of pilgrimage—and the seduction of Kunti by Surya—in the Vanaparva—are on the face of them such, while others are not so easily distinguishable. The Brahmanas also contain several puerile developments and expansions and explanations of Vedic metaphors, paradoxes, and allusions—and these and the Mahabharata are responsible for almost all the foolish tales about the gods you have referred to. Can you imagine the simple poets who sang:

"Thou, Indra, art a friend, a brother,
A kinsman dear, a father, mother.
Though thou hast troops of friends, yet we
Can boast no other friend but thee.
With this our hymn thy skirt we grasp,
As boys their father's garments clasp.
Our ardent prayers thy form embrace,
As women's arms their lords enlace.
They round thee cling with gentle force,
Like saddle-girth around a horse,
With faith we claim thine aid divine,
For thou art ours and we are thine:"†

Can you imagine that the poets who sang of Varuna "The great one who rules over these worlds beholds as if h were close at hand......Whatever two persons sitting togethe

---

* Muir V—82.
† Muir V—136

devise, Varuna the king knows it (being present there as) a third......He who should flee far beyond the sky would not there escape from Varuna the king......King Varuna perceives all that exists within heaven and earth, and all that is beyond. The winkings of men's eyes are all numbered by him......May thy destructive nooses, O Varuna, which are cast sevenfold and three-fold, ensnare the man who speaks lies, and pass by him who speaks truth:" * I say, can you imagine that these poets could have desecrated these pictures with the foul and insipid imagery of the Puranas? I hold this is impossible. We have no end of paradoxes like that Aditi (Eternity) created Daksha (Spiritual Force), and Daksha created Aditi, or that Time (Kala) "is a formless form," or that "with sacrifice the gods worshipped Sacrifice", or that Indra was contained entire in Skambha and Skambha in Indra. But we have no gross fancies, no indecencies, and no vulgarities. And as for woman she is talked of as a priceless blessing, and the relation of husband and wife is always spoken of as a blessed relation. "With that great golden hook of thine which confers wealth, O lord of S'achi," sings a Vedic poet, "reach a wife to me who am longing for one."† Another beseeches Savitri, the Sun-god, to hasten to him "as cattle to a village, as warriors to their horses, as a cow to give milk to her calf, as a husband to his wife".‡ In a hymn to Váta (the Wind-god) it is said: "The gusts of the air rush after him and congregate in him as women in an assembly,"§ showing that women used to mix freely with men. Ushas to whom the most beautiful hymns in the whole Riga Veda are addressed is likened to a housewife and to a maiden, and you can see that the maidens of those days were not like the maidens of ours. "Like an active woman, Ushas advances cherishing all things; she hastens on, arousing footed creatures, and makes the birds fly

* Muir V—63-64.

† Muir V—87.

‡ Muir V—164.

§ Muir V—146.

aloft;......lively, she loves not to stand still."* "Like a maid triumphing in her beautiful form, thou, goddess, advancest to meet the god who seeks after thee (the Sun); smiling, youthful, and resplendent, thou unveilest thy bosom in front. Like a fair girl adorned by her mother, thou displayest thy body to the beholder.........As a woman who has no brother appears in presence of (another) man, as a man mounted on a chariot goes forth in pursuit of wealth, as a loving wife shows herself to her husband—so does Ushas, as it were, smiling reveal her form.........She displays her person like a fair woman—like one rising out of the water in which she has been bathing.........Wearing out the lives of men, the lady shines with the light of her lover (the Sun)." † This last expression we can now hardly translate into any modern vernacular, without marring its beauty, and yet you tell us there is no difference between our past and our present. No difference! Where are the old gods gone—the gods who represented various beautiful or sublime manifestations of the One Supreme—the gods with whom our early fathers could hold daily intercourse and be the better for it—the gods of the Aryas who protected the Aryan colour, then fair, now dark—who "subjected the black skin to Manu" and his sons—who quelled the pride of the Dasyus—who were fatherly and motherly, brotherly and sisterly—yes, those gods, where are they? Nature has now no significance for us. We have hardly a sense of the Beautiful or the Sublime. We do not ask, "What was the forest, what was the tree, out of which they fashioned heaven and earth"? We do not ask how all, except the sun of India, is set. We do not ask how we lost our fair complexion—our fair fame—our noble simplicity—our steadfast righteousness—our ancient sovereignty. We are content to be niggers in face and form, as well as in mind and soul, and yet you say there is no difference. As well say there is no difference between day and night!

---

* Muir V—182.

† Muir V—185-186.

A HINDU DEMOCRITUS.—And who says there is? Do you not know that Day and Night are sisters? Do not the Vedas say:—"They strain not, they rest not, the prolific Night and Dawn, concordant though unlike." * Our past and our present are also concordant though unlike.

AN ANTI-REFORMER.—That is a true word spoken. If our present is built on our past, it cannot but be concordant with it. As certainly as the Puranic pantheon had its archetypes in the Vedas, as certainly as the *gotras* of the present Brahmins are traceable to the old Rishis, so certainly our present institutions are derived from the Vedic. We are told our early fathers were "wise and righteous, and companions of gods in their festivities," † and the Vedic funeral hymn calls upon Agni to take our unborn part to the realms of these early Rishis. But I guess these same progenitors of ours were as much alive to the good of early marriage as we ourselves are. They longed for "stout sons" ‡, and they knew how to get them, for even modern science admits that "the children that are born by mothers during the prime of life are heavier and larger, and therefore probably more vigorous than those born at other periods." §

A HINDU SOCIAL REFORM MISSIONARY.—Yes, and the authority you quote also says: ‖ "The very poor and reckless, who are often degraded by vice, almost invariably marry early, whilst the careful and frugal, who are generally otherwise virtuous, marry late in life so that they may be able to support themselves and their children in comfort........With women, too, marriage at too early an age is highly injurious; for it has been found in France that 'twice as many wives under twenty die in the year as died out of the same number of the unmarried.' The mortality also of husbands under twenty is

---

* Muir V—188.
† Muir V—193.
‡ Muir V—186.
§ Darwin's Descent of Man.
‖ Darwin's Descent of Man, p. 174.

'exceptionally high'; but what the cause of this may be, seems doubtful." You are confounding premature marriage with marriage in the prime of life. I say, have the latter by all means—but not the former, and I challenge any one to prove that our ancestors practised the former.

AN ANTI-REFORMER.—Then how did we come to practise it? Are we not the sons of our ancestors? Have we not inherited their good and their evil? I say, it is most illogical to father this custom upon us and not upon our fathers. As for your fallacious French statistics—why, they prove as little as the statistics relied upon by temperance fanatics to prove that sobriety causes a decrease in crime, or by marriage fanatics to prove that marriage more than celibacy conduces to longevity. As Herbert Spencer points out, "some of the soberest nations in Europe yield a proportion of crime higher than" that in England, and it is not marriage that leads to longevity but the superior physique and the surplus of energy accompanying it which are generally evidenced by marriage.

A HINDU SOCIAL REFORM MISSIONARY.—Thanks, many thanks, for your correction, but your Herbert Spencer says, if you would only read him aright: "In all creatures of high type, it is only when individual growth and development are nearly complete, that the production of new individuals becomes possible; and the power of producing and bringing up new individuals is measured by the amount of vital power in excess of the needful for self-maintenance. The reproductive instincts, and all their accompanying emotions, become dominant when the demands for individual evolution are diminishing, and there is arising a surplus of energy which makes possible the rearing of offspring as well as the preservation of self; and speaking generally, these instincts and emotions are strong in proportion as this vital energy is great. But to have a large surplus of vital energy implies a good organization. So that in fact the superiority of physique which is accompanied by the strength of the instincts and emotions causing marriage, is a superiority of physique condu-

-cive to longevity." I would ask for no other blessing from the Almighty than that this passage should become true of India one day. "Instincts and emotions causing marriage"! Where are they in India! Superiority of physique evidenced by marriage! Why, in heaven's name, the greatest weaklings need not in India despair of getting this evidence. There were Aryas of old, whose arms were compared to the trunks of elephants. Show me a single Arya of that type, and I would then admit that we are truly the sons of our ancestors.

AN ANTI-REFORMER.—I don't know what you may be; but I know what I am. I care very little for your heroes with elephant-trunked arms. The "Tasmanian Devil", the English bull-dog, our common game-cock, are probably all superior to him. I have the authority of no less a person than Herbert Spencer for saying that even English fighting men are inferior to these. Civilisation does not consist in the development of one's sinews and thews, but in the development of the nerves and the "grey matter of the head." In this sense we are fully developed, for have we not beaten Englishmen at competitive examinations, and are our publicists and writers any way inferior to their English brethren? Look at our philosophical literature. Why, even Schopenhauer, the greatest pessimist of this century, confessed that our Upanishads had been the "solace of his life," and would be "the solace of his death." Look at our political gatherings—at our organizations—at our Bar—at our Bench—nay even at the army, and you find that we are no way degenerate. And as for our homes, why, read what Sir George Birdwood has written about our "perfect daughters, wives, and mothers, after the severely disciplined self-sacrificing Hindu ideal, the ideal also of Solomon, Sophocles, and St. Paul, remaining modestly at home as the proper sphere of their duties, unknown beyond their families, and seeking in the happiness of their children their greatest pleasure, and in the reverence of their husbands the amaranthine crown of a woman's truest glory." Our friend Hume bears similar testimony.

A HINDU SOCIAL REFORM MISSIONARY.—Yes, and yet he admits that on the whole the evil of this custom of child-marriage outweighs the good—that it is "fraught with grievous misery in too many cases" and that it is "a custom marked for extinction and daily becoming more and more an anachronism and more and more of an evil, taking its results as a whole." But let us suppose that all Englishmen consider this custom to be the very cream of excellence—will that any way alter the real facts as all candid Hindus know them? It is as natural for an Englishman to admire our customs as for us to admire his, for like always repels like and attracts unlike. It is to this law that we trace the Englishman's fondness for our art-wares and for Indian knick-knacks, and it is to the same law that the love of some of us for boots and pants and even for brandy and soda-water (if the accounts of the National Congresses are correct) is traceable. I blame Sir G. Birdwood as little for his ideal as I blame myself for mine. But letting alone all ideals and illusions, you and I and all of us here are interested in deciding whether it is a violation of the natural law to marry children before puberty, and whether such violation is not only sinful and criminal but suicidal.

AN ANTI-REFORMER.—This is mere moonshine.—Suicidal! Criminal! Sinful! A custom which cements the joint-family, prevents unnatural carnality, makes our students steady, and has no room for the "bow-wow" or the "cavalier servante," or the frivolities of fashion, can surely not be criminal or sinful or suicidal.

A HINDU SOCIAL REFORM MISSIONARY.—I say it is all the three. Ask Mr. Chiplonkar why he recommends that none but real bachelors should be Bachelors of Arts and Law. Is it because your custom makes the student steady? Ask Professor Bhandarkar and Sirdar Gopalrao Hari Deshmukh, why they would have the Universities rule, after giving five years' notice, that no married candidate shall be admitted to the Matriculation Examination. Is it because married candidates are very good students? Ask Messrs. Telang and Chandavarkar and the Tipperah Association, why they have no objection to all scholarships and prizes being confined to the single. Is it because the single are unsteady? Why, ask even Pandit Gattulal to say if he is not in favour of marrying boys between sixteen and twenty "or some time after that". I should like to know who among us is opposed to the old Brahmachari practice, and I should like to know why the Sanskrit word for choice and love is the same, why the word *kumari* means in Sanskrit a girl under sixteen, and in most of our vernaculars, a girl unmarried, and how the old Sanskrit word *wara* "chosen husband" has come to mean even a baby-husband, and the word *anuwara* which used to be formerly applied to the best man of the bridegroom is now employed, in Gujarat, to signify the duenna of a betrothed girl taken on festal occasions to her father-in-law's. Was the joint family in danger—was morality in danger—when no girl was married under sixteen, or when girls were allowed to choose their husbands? In Heaven's name do not confound separable accidents with *caused* effects, and do not tell us that physical strength need not go hand in hand with mental vigour, or that the full development of the heart or of the head is independent of bodily health.

Mr. Mahipatram Rupram.—Or that the mother-in-law is not a proverb among us for plaguing her dear daughter-in-law. I say if infant marriage solders the joint family, the mother-in-law and the daughter-in-law, between them, know well how to pull it to pieces.

An Anti-Reformer.—I am afraid it is you, gentlemen, who are confounding accidents with effects when you charge the system of parental choice with all the monstrous evils existing in your imagination. I say none properly brought up is at all the worse for this system.

A Hindu Social Reform Missionary.—Pray do not shift the issue. We are not concerned with this system of parental selection, but we are concerned with infant marriages, child marriages, premature marriages. You cannot defend the marriage of a child under ten, on the ground that the marriage of a child of ten or over ten will interfere with the rights of parents, nor can I imagine how the marriage of a girl of fourteen or of a boy of eighteen, can interfere with them. You ask the Government every year through your National Congress that you should have a right of interpellation in the Legislative Councils, and what we ask is that you should allow this same right to your children, by postponing their marriage to the minimum age of puberty, laid down by Indian medical authorities. If the concession you demand is not revolutionary, the concession we demand cannot be so.

An Anti-Reformer.—I am afraid you have "Infant Marriage" so much on the brain, that you cannot understand how a political reformer need not be a social reformer. Can you not see that we are not now grown-up children but grown-up men, and ought to be admitted to the councils of the sovereign? Our children on the other hand are but children, and we know what is good for them better than they do. At any rate you cannot deny that we love our children better than the Government loves us. We therefore require to be represented, and are entitled to have at least a right of interpellation, but our children want no representatives and no interpellators, for we can fully safeguard their interests.

A Hindu Social Reform Missionary.—But I say that you do not safeguard their interests when you marry them at an unripe age; that you are an enemy of your daughter, when by marrying her early you increase her chances of widowhood, and decrease her chances of education, and of maintaining sound health, and breeding vigorous progeny; that you are an enemy of your son, when you early engulf him into the vortex of sexual distractions, make him a victim to a most unnatural sensuality, and burden him with puny offspring; and that for these reasons you are an enemy of society, and an enemy of your own self. I say your "fostering care and discrimination" are all rot, so long as you choose to set the clear law of nature at defiance, and expect that premature marriage will not bring about forced puberty, that forced puberty will not bring about early consummation, and that early consummation will not produce sickly children and affect the health and strength of the married couple.

An Anti-Reformer.—You are making a mountain out of a mole-hill. At the very worst premature marriage is no worse than tight-lacing, and yet your civilised English ladies do not mind breaking their ninth ribs or compressing their livers, or even exposing the upper lobes of their lungs at fashionable balls. Nature is kind to all, and knows how to adapt herself. Let the modish belle do what she may, let her reduce her waist to eighteen inches, let her ruin her digestion and her nerves, boon Nature lets her daughter have full 25 inches of waist, and wreaks no revenge.

A Hindu Antiquary.—Just a word, friends. Is it not surprising that in our Sanskrit epics one of the commonest epithets of our heroines is "slender waisted"—and in one place there is a passage—very much like a well-known verse of Hafiz—in which the waist of the Hindu beauty is said to be "as nothing." Then as to balls, is it not surprising to find that Arjuna was an accomplished dancer, and had the hardihood, in the guise of a person of the neuter sex, to present himself before the king of Vrat, and say: "King of Vrat, I am a dancer and singer by profession, and wish to teach your daughter, Uttara, these accomplishments"? Imagine a speech like this addressed to a modern orthodox Maharaja. And yet the king of Vrat actually closed with the offer, and we find Arjuna for a whole year giving lessons to Uttara (his future daughter-in-law) and her female friends, in a dancing hall provided for the purpose.* Again, is it not remarkable that a Vedic poet should sing—"Ushas like a dancer puts on her gay attire; she displays her bosom as a cow its udder." †

* See the Vrat Parva of the Mahabharata.

† Muir V—185.

I conclude that the Hinduanis of old could dance and sing as they can even now in some parts of India. And they could love too, for even one of the Brahmanas says: "Women love a man who sings,"* and about the As'vins, it is said that they used to bring together two lovers—that they provided a husband for that old maid Ghosha, and were generally guardians of aged spinsters.† Again, who has not read that enchanting little scene of sweet Sagarika painting her lover's image under the Asoka bower, in one of our dainty Sanskrit dramas? I say, therefore, our women knew formerly to love and to sing, to paint and to dance, as much at least as our men knew the delights of flesh and wine. If you do not believe this last fact, just see the bill of fare provided by Draupadi for Jayadrath, and by Damayanti's father for Rutuparana, and recall to your mind how Agastya immolated bulls to the Maruts, and consumed meat at Vàtàpi's; how Vasishtha himself didn't mind living on mutton; how Vis'vamitra's wife and children used to take game brought by a Chandala prince; how a Puranic Rishi, Jalabi, used to kill an elephant once a year and subsist on its flesh; how when a guest came, the old Hindus, like the old Jews, used to slaughter a bull or a calf in his honour; how traces of this custom still exist in the marriage ritual; how animals were commonly used for sacrifices like the Ashvamedha and the Vrishabmedha; and lastly, how the Hindu anatomy is based upon the knowledge acquired by the dissection of such animals. The thirsty souls of our fathers also figured a paradise full of "ponds of clarified butter, honey, *wine*, milk and curds"‡, and it is curious to find that they had no objection to the use of skins, for Pushan was besought to maintain his friendship steadfast "like a skin without holes and well filled with curds,§" and Parjanya was besought to "open and invert his water skin."‖

* Muir V—263.
† Muir V—242-243.
‡ Muir V—308.
§ Muir V—172.
‖ Muir V—141.

They had, however, as great a horror of taxes as we ourselves have, for their Elysium was a place where they expressly state no taxes had to be paid. They came from a cold country with all the habits natural to their climate, and with fair complexions, and sturdy faith, and manly energy. The Vedic poets sang to Indra, very much like the primitive Jews to their Jahveh:

"And thou dost view with special grace
The fair-complexioned Aryan race,
Who own the gods, their laws obey,
And pious homage duly pay.
Thou giv'st us horses, cattle, gold,
As thou didst give our sires of old.
Thou sweep'st away the dark-skinned brood,
Inhuman, lawless, senseless, rude,
Who know not Indra, hate his friends,
And spoil the race which he defends.
Chase far away, the robbers chase,
Slay those barbarians black and base."*

I take it, therefore, that the old Indo-Aryans when they first came to this land were very much like Englishmen.

An Anti-Reformer.—Very well, and your conclusion, I suppose, is that we ought to take kindly to corsets and waist. laces and late marriages and hysterics, and give up what experience has shown to be better adapted to us, our vegetable diet, our abstinence from alcoholic liquors, our simple dress. Can you not see that, if the old Hindus were flesh-eaters and winebibbers, their new environment must have forced them to cease to be such? And how can you convince me that, though our unlikeness in these particulars has been thrust upon us by our struggle for existence in India, our deviation from the old marriage customs is merely a wanton perversity or an irrational fashion? I say this deviation is as justifiable and as wholesome as any other. Our fathers and mothers may have

* Muir V—138-139.

had their courtships and their love-meetings. But they found out, in course of time, as the English too will one day find out, that love is a distracting feeling which sane men ought to be free from as much as from anger or hatred. This was the conclusion to which the Greeks and the Romans also eventually came, and Swinburne in his Atalanta in Calydon makes Althæa say—

"But this most,
This moves me, that for wise men as for fools,
Love is one thing, an evil thing, and turns
Choice words and wisdom into fire and air.
And in the end shall no joy come, but grief;
Sharp words and souls' division and fresh tears
Flower-wise upon the old root of tears brought forth,
Fruit-wise upon the old flower of tears sprung up,
Pitiful sighs, and much re-grafted pain."

If you are not yet convinced, I say read Mrs. Mona Caird's letters, and judge for yourself whether our institution is not far better.

A HINDU SOCIAL REFORM MISSIONARY.—Why, Mrs. Mona Caird supports you as much as Herbert Spencer! If this lady is to be taken as an authority, her ultimatum is that "the principle towards which modern reforms in marriage ought to point is the frank recognition of the equality of all subjects, male and female, before the law, and also the recognition that every member of the community ought to be free to enter into what contracts he pleases, provided he injures no other individual, and does not interfere with the welfare of the community." The experience of centuries has shown that a marriage dissolvable at pleasure is a worse failure than a marriage not so dissolvable, supposing, for the sake of argument, that such marriage is a failure at all. And I say the experience of centuries has also shown that child-wives and child-husbands breed a race which cannot be independent, and cannot deserve independence, for open your history and just count the numerous foreign invaders and foreign rulers we have had. Darwin tells us:—"Obscure as is the problem of the advance of civilization, we can at least see that a nation which produced, during a lengthened period, the greatest number of highly intellectual, energetic, brave, patriotic, and benevolent men, would generally prevail over less favoured nations.*" This shows why we have survived as the fittest subjects of others, and such survival is no reason for self-congratulation.

A HINDU FATALIST.—What are you all talking about? There is no difference between subjection and independence to one having true wisdom. Do you not know what Krishna said to Arjuna: "A flowery doctrine, promising the reward of works performed in this embodied state, prescribing numerous ceremonies, with a view to future gratification and glory, is preached by unlearned men, devoted to the injunctions of the Veda asserters of its exclusive importance, lovers of enjoyment, and seekers after paradise. The restless minds of the men who, through this flowery doctrine, have become bereft of wisdom, and are ardent in the pursuit of future gratification and glory, are not applied to contemplation. The Vedas have for their objects the three qualities (Sattva, Rajas, Tamas, or goodness, passion, and darkness); but be thou, Arjuna, free from these three qualities. As great as is the use of a well which is surrounded on every side by overflowing waters, so great (and no greater) is the use of the Vedas to a Brahmin endowed with true knowledge."† And I say all your learning and all your deeds are of no greater use, and I beseech you all to have that true knowledge which says to all the phenomena of Maya—"Avaunt, I know your deceptive juggleries. I rest in Him Who knows not Time or Space, Who is above all appearances, and the only Real Substance."

A HINDU SOCIAL REFORM MISSIONARY.—This is all extremely practical and extremely hopeful. We have assembled

* Descent of Man, p. 180.

† Bhagvad Gita ii. 42 ff.

here to discuss a simple question, and to urge a moderate reform. We say with a great man that, a society "without the means of some change is without the means of its conservation"; that a change is desirable for our own welfare—a term which is quite distinct from happiness, but which includes it; that in carrying out the change, we should see that we are "not wholly new" just as we should see that "in what we retain we are not wholly obsolete," for "people will not look forward to posterity who never look backward to their ancestors"; that, therefore, upon the body and stock of our inheritance we should not "inoculate any scion alien to the nature of the original plant," but a scion which should assimilate with it, and that this assimilation can be secured by putting a stop to marriages under ten altogether, and discouraging marriages of girls under 14 and of boys under 18, and gradually increasing the marriageable age to the old limits of 16 and 20. English fashions and true knowledge have as much to do with this question as with the National Congress.

A Hindu Fatalist.—Then I will tell you how they are relevant. Our world, as geology teaches us, is not merely as old as the English civilization. There were other civilizations, but we have only faint memorials of them, for, as a profound philosopher has remarked:—"Time seemeth to be of the nature of a river or stream which carrieth down to us that which is light and blown up, and sinketh and drowneth that which is weighty and solid." Now I say that history repeats itself, that probably there was as good a civilization before in India as the English, that is, a civilization perfectly consistent with the existence of extremes of riches and poverty, with the existence of sweaters and millionaires, miserable workmen and bloated capitalists, fashionable ladies and dying street-walkers. And I say that the English may one day have to adopt what we have adopted—a caste system to prevent competition—a joint family system to preserve union and domestic happiness—and our philosophy that knowledge is greater than works to maintain mental equilibrium. The European renaissance was due to the study of Greek and Latin classics. But there will be a greater renaissance when Sanskrit classics are as much studied.

A Hindu Antiquary.—All this, of course, may be extremely probable to you. But pray tell me how it is that our Yuga is called the Kali Yuga and that our past is supposed to have been much better. This tradition is a hard fact. It is a part of the consciousness of every Hindu. It is recognised by all our ancient and modern records. The Vayu Purana, for example, says :—"The age is changed; through its baneful influence, the Brahmins have become feeble, and from the same cause the measure of everything has gradually declined, so that little is seen remaining. A part of the Veda consisting only of these ten thousand verses is now left to us from the Krita age ; vigour, fire and energy are diminished, and everything is on the road to destruction.*" So it is said in the Bhagavata Purana that Vyasa divided the Vedas, "perceiving with the eye of divine intelligence that disorder had in each Yuga been introduced into the duties proper to each, through the action of Time whose march is imperceptible, that the strength of beings formed of the elements had in consequence declined, that men were destitute of faith, vigour, and intelligence, that their lives were shortened, and that they were miserable."† Do not these passages suggest the evolution of all our evil customs, and with them our philosophy of deep despair, our doctrine that it is better to suffer than to struggle—a doctrine at which our first strugglers, the Rishis, would have stood amazed. Those who considered this world itself as the creation of divine desire, would never have abjured that 'progressive desire' which is the essence of modern civilisation.

An Anti-Reformer.—But surely our present doctrine must have had its roots in the old faith.

---

* Muir II. 40 (2nd Edition.)

† Muir II.—41.

A Hindu Antiquary.—I say no. Our present doctrine is not descended from the old faith but is the result of our departure from it amidst new surroundings, and that departure has given us the tradition of the four Yugas. Just transport yourself to the age when the Aryans first came to the land of the Seven Rivers, with the thoughts, the feelings, the views common to them, the old Persians, the Greeks, the Latins, and the Germanic races. They are an imaginative people, quite unlike the humdrum prosaic Hindus of the modern times, and

> " ......meadow grove and stream,
> The earth and every common sight"

appear to them,

> " Apparell'd in celestial light
> The glory and the freshness of a dream."

They people the rays of the Sun with the pious, and the stars with the lights of the righteous or with the eyes of Varuna; and they feel Fire as a link between the Earth, the Atmosphere, and the Heavens, and call it the Calf of Prithvi, the Falcon of Dyaus, " the brilliant banner of all sacrifices." To them the Dawn and the Hours before the Dawn appear as Ushas and the As'vins, the Winds as Vayu, Rudra and the Maruts; the lightning and thunder as Indra; the Moon as the Sun's son-in-law with the constellations as his brides; the showers of rain as Parjanya, the Waters as Apas, the Forests as Aranyani. All these are to them living powers—male or female—with wives and husbands and children, and all these beneficent deities are the guardians of the Aryas in the strange land of their sojourn, and do not disdain to share their festivals and sacrifices, and drink the Soma juice and eat the roasted meat. But even the Sun sets, the trees grow sear, and the loved ones die, and, thoughts of a hereafter forcing themselves upon their bright natures, they imagine a world beyond, where their good fathers dwell, and imagine a Ruler at Whose command Day and Night run their appointed course, and Life and Death visit this earth. Gradually they perceive a Supreme Unity in all physical phenomena, and adore it in its various phases and under the names of Savitri (the Producer), Tvashtri (the Artificer), Visva Karman (the All-shaper), Skambha (the supporter), Kala (the Time), Kama (the Desire), Prana (the Life), Prajapati (the Creator), Aditi (the Eternal Mother). But the faculties of imagination, curiosity and memory which first led them "to believe in unseen spiritual agencies, then in fetishism and polytheism, and ultimately in monotheism" infallibly lead them also "to various strange superstitions and customs" such as the sacrifice of animals, "the trial of innocent persons by the ordeal of fire, witchcraft, &c."* Nevertheless, so long as they are a militant people, they are an united people, with erect forms, and eyes looking up to the great Father for guidance and help. They are all Brahmins, that is prayer-offerers; but some can offer poetic and prophetic prayers, and these eminent men often fight side by side with their less gifted but more warlike brethren, just as later on the Brahmins, Drona and Ashvatthama, fought by the side of the warriors, Bhisma and Karana. The women of these men of active, ardent, vivid faith, and strong, unsuspecting, unsophisticated natures, are heroines worthy of them—heroines who could number Vasishtha and Visvamitra among their sons—heroines whose daughters later on gave us Rama and Arjuna—heroines whose sisters in other climes gave birth to those great epic characters which the world has not yet forgotten. This was the real Krita or Satya Yuga—the age when truth was felt to uphold the Earth as the sun the sky†, when goodness (Sattva) was the regulating principle of life‡, when "duties did not languish, nor the people decline," when all the classes were "unceasingly devoted to one deity, and used one mantra, one rule and one rite."§ But gradually the settlements of the invaders

---

* Darwin's Descent of Man, p. 69.

† See Riga Veda quoted in Muir V—158.

‡ Vishnu Purana quoted at p. 90 of Muir's first volume.

§ Vana Parva 11240—12245.

spread, the eminent prayer-offerers became an important class, the Riga and Sama Veda hymns and the ancient medical and magical formulæ preserved in the Yajur and Atharva Vedas form the heirloom of this class, the simplicity of former worship and sacrifice is overlaid with superstition by the Brahamanas, the simplicity of the former creed and code of morals is replaced by the profound speculations of the Upanishads and the detailed rules of conduct embodied in the Smritis and the old half-mystic, half-poetic conception of the Unknowable is resolved into the triad of Brahma, Vishnu, and Siva, and further resolved into a Being with Nama and Rupa (Name and Form) as his two brooding wings. The initiated and the uninitiated, the thinkers and the formalists, alike remember and revere the Vedas as the fruitful gift of godlike men, and to exalt their vocation, imagine themselves to be sprung from the mouth of Brahma with a special tutelary God, the Brahamanaspati, and trace the descent of the military, the commercial, and the menial classes that have naturally * come into being with Aryan conquest and colonisation, to the arms, the thighs and the feet of Brahma. These classes, however, are not yet castes, and intermarriages take place as in the case of Vasishtha with Akshamala, Mandapala with Sarangi, Agastya with Lopamudra, Rúshiashrangha with Shánta, Rachik with Satyavatti, Chyavan with Sukanya. The old environment is, however, changed. The conquerors rule over a subject population, and have numerous serfs whose low status reacts upon the free people as it has reacted everywhere. Some of the female slaves are kept as handmaidens and concubines, and marriages with the aborigines or low-class women, as in the case of the ancestor of the Pandavas and the Kuravas, are not uncommon, though probably not so frequent as in Yudhishther's time, for he could say to Nahusha: "Birth is difficult to be discriminated in the present condition of humanity on account of the confusion of all castes. All sorts of men are continually begetting children on all sorts

* See Max Müller's Chips from a German Workshop, Vol. II.

of women."* This intermixture of blood heralds the Treta age, for the old Aryan usages are no longer pure and undefiled, but interwoven with many a custom of the aborigines and many a new superstition. The last of the native rebels was probably Ravana, a convert probably to Brahminism, but a haughty upholder of the rights of his race. The Aryans, after his fall, are no longer afraid of any insurrection, and they parcel out the country into various principalities, and dynasties like the Solar and the Lunar reign on in peace. But there are various influences at work in this transition age between the Satya and the Dwapara—the influence of the priesthood—the influence of power—the influence of wealth—the influence of the contact of the Aryas with the indigenous people. The ambition and the cupidity which impelled the first conquests are still alive, and the Aryan victors soon turn their arms against one another just as their brethren in Greece, Rome, and Persia did. These internecine feuds culminating in the great war celebrated in the Mahabharata distract the Dwapara age. The Brahmins have become more exclusive and assumed enormous privileges; superstition has made immense progress; vices like those of gambling and lechery have increased; the slaves are sometimes cruelly treated, and it is not perhaps uncommon to burn them at the funeral pyre of their owner that they may serve him in the next world, for just remember that Kichak's relations proposed to immolate Draupadi in this manner in order that Kichak, her lover, might at least enjoy her after death, though not in his lifetime. But Draupadi dies in the Himalayan snows; Nakul and Sahdeva, Arjuna and Bhima, follow their faithful spouse; Parikshit reigns at Hastinapur, and at the sunset of his life beholds the Kali Yuga already on earth, and his son Janmejaya, like us all, turns his longing, lingering look towards the past that is gone, and delights in nothing so much as the recital of the Mahabharata. The Aryan glory is fading away; the Aryan princes are disunited and weakened; the Aryan priests are corrupt and addicted to the sale of

* See Vanaparva.

indulgences ; the Aryan religion is a vast congeries of penances, for which gifts to Brahmins may be substituted, and of ritualistic observances out of which the soul is gone ; and the Aryan pantheon has multiplied with Aryan misfortunes, and includes many a hero worshipped as an *Avatar*. There is a reaction against the old freedom, against the old individualism, against the old catholicity, and the classes are petrified into castes, and castes into sub-castes. The rule of endogamy within the caste or sub-caste, comes into operation; and leads to female infanticide among the Rajputs. The frequent emigrations from one kingdom to another owing to insupportable tyranny, give rise to the numerous subdivisions of sub-castes named after their place of residence. These subdivisions are impressed with the old tendency to exclusiveness—a tendency strengthened by the inconvenience and expensiveness of intermarriages with the parent sub-caste living in a remote town. This exclusiveness in course of time affects the status of women both where their number is larger than that of males and where it is smaller; in the former because they become a source of keen anxiety to their parents and their birth is a calamity; in the latter because they become merchantable commodities, and Asura marriages become common. Under both these conditions there would be keen competition, and to escape it early marriages and, in course of time, infant marriages would be resorted to; and such marriages—the effect of exclusiveness, would, like all social factors, confirm their cause and further degrade woman. Buddhism would better her position for a time, would inflict a severe blow on the old superstitions and on the caste system, would create a deep prejudice against the use of meat and probably of wine, and eventually being itself the result of the gloom overhanging the Aryan world, would leave it in a deep calm, but in the calm of deep despair. The old creed would lose all its brightness and hopefulness, and become a dismal fatalism. Its interpreters would be the Purans, and its priests idolators, and its stronghold the caste. Society thus "cabin'd, cribb'd, confin'd, bound in" to caste regulations and restrictions, would have but blunted sympathies and a most lethargic life. It would care very little whether it was under an Aryan ruler or a foreigner, and patriotism would by degrees cease to mean anything, except allegiance to the narrow platoon of a caste section. Such a decayed society would fall an easy prey to invaders from without or within, and would slavishly imitate its kings and its priests. Such evil practices as *Suttee*, the shaving of widows, the pardah, the worship of demons, human sacrifices to Kali, the murderous procession of the Jaggernath Car, the Karnal at Kasi, the Bherav Jap at Dwarka, the swinging with hooks through the air before the image of Khandoba, came then into vogue. Every idol would have its Mahatam, the chronicle of its miraculous production and its achievements. Every evil usage would have its justifiers and propagators. Every vestige of a different state of society, and every record of the *ancien regime* would be tampered with or explained away, and new authorities would be cited as binding on the people in the Kali Yuga to the exclusion of all others. The interpolation in the Vedas themselves for the vindication of *Suttee*, the forgeries direct or exegetic in the Code of Manu for the exaltation of Brahmins, and the legalization of new usages like that of premature marriage, the concoction of apocryphal Smritis, and the insertion of false legends in the Mahabharata to give countenance to Brahminical pretensions, or sanctity to places of pilgrimage or to tone down unpalatable facts—are all traceable to the reaction against Buddhism and the final triumph of Brahminism. The celibate Sadhus of the numerous sects that have since arisen are responsible for some of the most unmanly and unmannerly attacks against the gentler sex, and what with their false diatribes against woman written in some of the holiest books, and what with the Brahmins reciting at every marriage the spurious text of Parasara recommending marriage at eight, one need not be surprised at the spread of this institution of infant marriage. Moreover, the old caste sub-divisions and the unbridled lust of some of the new rulers, their satraps, and their satellites, made the custom a necessity, as is clear from the fact that wherever these causes did not operate it did not exist. Among several large undivided castes there are men even now living, who can swear that the custom is foreign to them, and has come into fashion within a generation or two among their rich men suffering from a plethora of wealth, and anxious for that phlebotomy of money which an infant marriage supplies. The old order is changing day by day, "giving place to new"; for, Providence in His mercy has once more confronted us with Aryan customs, and enlarged the sphere of our vision, and encircled us with the descendants of those who at one time lived together with our ancestors "within the same fences." "The Hindu," says Max Müller, "though perhaps the eldest, was the last to leave the central home of the Aryan family. He saw his brothers all depart towards the setting sun, and then turning towards the south and east, he started alone in search of a new world," and the great savant should have added, that the Hindu not only found a new world, but, in the fulness of time, his brethren also. My dear friends, let us eschew all jealousy of the Englishman, for the Celt, the German, the Greek, the Italian, the Slavonian, and the Parsi are all our Aryan brethren, having more or less the habits and customs which characterized our ancient fathers. "There is no authority whatever in the hymns of the Veda for the complicated system of caste. There is no law to prohibit the different classes of the people from living together; no law to prohibit the marriage of people belonging to different castes; no law to brand the offspring of such marriages with an indelible stigma. There is no law to sanction the blasphemous pretensions of a priesthood to divine honours, or the degradation of any human being to a state below the animal."* These are the words of one who has spent a lifetime in the study of our books, and if we act upon them, there is no reason why we should not stand shoulder to shoulder with other Aryas in the onward march of

* Max Müller's Chips, Vol. II.

progress, and one day live under the canopy of heaven as an united family of nations, just as the forefathers of us all lived of old as an united family under the Central Aryan sun.

A Hindu Lawyer.—This is a long rigmarole, and I don't quite see its relevancy or utility. Our religion, our morality, our social institutions may require as much revision as our political and economical status. But I think what requires revision and reconsideration the most is that part of Hindu law, or rather the Hindu law as interpreted by our judges, which bears upon woman's rights, I mean her concrete, and not her abstract, rights. I hate, for instance, the new ruling that a wife refusing conjugal society to her husband can be sent to prison for her refusal, and I hate all those customs which are not sanctioned even by the fourth abridgment of Manu we now have, but which are nevertheless enforced by the courts although they are opposed to the spirit of all our institutions. "The Vyavahara Mayukha declares," say Messrs. West and Bühler, "that the very practice given by Gautama as an example of one that usage could not establish—the marriage of a maternal uncle's daughter—is sanctioned by custom in the Deccan."* And "in the South, marriage with a sister's daughter is common even amongst Brahmins."† Rao Saheb V. N. Mandlik testifies to the existence of these and kindred customs, so detrimental to physical well-being, and so diametrically opposed to our Shastras. Again, Steele tells us :—"Persons negotiating a marriage, if successful, often receive from 100 to 1,000 rupees, according to the difficulty of the case, and the circumstances of the parties." ‡ Now this is a custom which no Hindu with any particle of self-respect can say a word in favour of. In England marriage brocage contracts are void, and so I suppose they will be held here, unless some judicial luminary falls in love with this custom, just as other lights of the law have shed

---

* See their Digest, 3rd Edition, p. 868.

† Ibid p. 1031.

‡ See his work on the Customs in the Deccan, p. 334.

their benign influence on Asura marriages condemned outright by Manu, but prevailing in the teeth of Manu in even Brahmin castes. The opposite evil of purchasing bridegrooms flourishing among the Kulins and some other communities is equally detestable and equally forbidden. All these baneful customs are due, I take it, to caste subdivisions, to caste narrowness, to caste stupidity, and to the supposed religious necessity of marrying girls early lest they should go astray. This is a horrible fallacy. Natural history teaches us that "the female, with the rarest exceptions, is less eager than the male." "As the illustrious Hunter long ago observed, she generally requires to be courted; she is coy and may often be seen endeavouring for a long time to escape from the male." * As a rule, the female is less sensual than the male, and more faithful. But the fools who deprived woman in India of the right of saying her say, in books, about man, and even of the right of reading the Veda, have thought fit to represent her as more sensual and less faithful—a representation which I make bold to say is a huge lie and the foulest slander upon their own mothers and wives, daughters and sisters. This is a rotten error which we ought to expose until it crumbles to pieces, and until justice is rendered to woman. I say the injustice we have been doing her is almost unparalleled in the history of civilized nations. Manu says it is better for a damsel to "stay at home till her death" than be given in marriage "to a bridegroom void of excellent qualities." But Sir M. Westropp says:— † "Minors, idiots, and lunatics are by Hindu law unable to contract; yet not only are the marriages of infants upheld, but it has been distinctly laid down that the marriage of a Hindu lunatic is valid." In other words, there are lunatic parents who, instead of finding out good husbands for their daughters, are not ashamed to marry them to ninnies and boobies, and the law sanctions such outrageous lunacy. Our old institutes lay down that an unchaste widow should be

* Descent of Man, p. 273.

† Sidlingaha vs. Sidava I L. R. 2 Bom 628.

deprived of her inheritance from her husband; but our High Courts say she should not be, because (and here is the sting of the ruling) by adopting the old rule "not only will a fruitful cause of domestic discord be largely extended, but a motive will be afforded, to say the least of it, for publishing and bringing into court the most deplorable scandals." How complimentary to us! So then there are "most deplorable scandals" about widows apparently! A decision like this, based mainly on this reason, is not supposed to shock native opinion, but a decision that a remarried widow by her remarriage is not to lose her inheritance, is supposed to be one which "would certainly be a severe shock to native opinion." In other words, we prefer unchastity to remarriage, and this is what is called administering the Hindu law. Manu says:—"Let mutual fidelity continue to death. This in a few words may be considered the supreme law between husband and wife",* and this supreme law has become so one-sided that, while the husband is at liberty to violate all his promises solemnly sworn at the marriage altar, the wife is severely punishable for neglecting them. He may remarry during her lifetime, but she cannot, even after his death. And our loving High Courts have chosen to extend the rule even to those among whom caste would dissolve marriages for valid reasons, for the fiat has gone forth that even a Sudra wife allowed by her caste to remarry owing to the idiocy or impotency of her husband, must prove a divorce by her husband or go to jail for bigamy and adultery. On the one hand we have customs enforced among the higher castes which are utterly repugnant to their best traditions—and on the other hand we have customs thrust upon the lower castes which are utterly unsuited to their constitution and to their institutions, and in either case it is woman that mostly suffers. Why, even her ordinary ancient rights are gone in most places. Our law of inheritance tells us that by marriage she becomes a sapinda of her husband. In Western India this word *sapinda* has one meaning, while in Bengal it has quite

---

* IX.—101.

another, and, in the latter province, although Brihaspati is admitted to have said that the wife was half the body of her husband,* she cannot adopt a son to her worse half after his death, even to rescue him from *put*. So she is held also incapable of inheriting property without a special text in her favour†, for, it is said by the Bengal jurists that the text of Manu—"What was given before the nuptial fire, what was given in the bridal procession, what was given in token of love, and what was received from a brother, a mother, or a father are considered as the sixfold separate property of a married woman"‡—is comprehensive, and no other property can be the separate property of a woman, unless an express exception can be cited. So, in Bengal, the unmarried and the widowed daughters always go to the wall, and the married, especially those who have children, are preferred as heiresses. Even elsewhere, the old text—"To the unmarried daughters by the same mother, let their brothers give portions out of their own allotments respectively; ....let each give a fourth part of his own distinct share, and they who refuse to give it shall be degraded§"—is set at naught, and, parents therefore, hasten to get their daughters married in their own lifetime.

SECRETARY, JESSORE INDIAN ASSOCIATION.—This is what our association consider as a principal cause of infant marriage.

A HINDU LAWYER.—Whether it is a principal cause or not, I don't know. But, then, the fact is that we do not choose to follow those texts of Manu which are favourable to woman, and enforce mostly those which are adverse to her. "Let him choose for his wife a girl," says old Manu, "whose form has no defect; who has an agreeable name; who walks gracefully like a phenicopteros or like a young elephant; whose hair and teeth are

* Colebrooke's Digest, Bk. V. T, 399.
† Mayne's Hindu Law S,361.
‡ Manu, IX., 194.
§ Manu, IX., 118.

moderate, respectively, in quantity and in size; whose body has exquisite softness." Just go to a Hindu marriage, and you will see whether the baby-wife walks "like a phenicopteros or like a young elephant." Why, she is hardly allowed to have a margin of nutrition before she is called upon to bear children; and woe unto her if she doesn't, and woe unto her if she does, but brings forth only daughters. I say the times are out of joint. I am afraid my little speech is also out of joint, and I am as guilty of talking nonsense as Old Antiquity here. But I would just conclude, like a lawyer, with an extract from a terribly learned judgment of Mr. West, bristling with authorities, in Vijiarangam *vs.* Lakshuman (8 Bom H. C. R. O. C. 244-256). He says:—"In the dim twilight of the early Vedic period, it is possible to discern some indications of a theory of perfect equality once subsisting between the parties to a marriage. These indications are not by any means uniform; but the prevailing notion appears to have been that of a free choice of her husband by the damsel, who was even dowered by her father. The married couple were enjoined to pass their lives in union and content. Yet by the time of the actual composition of the Vedas, a text could be introduced (just what you would expect), which, according to the interpretation of Baudhayana (Pr. ii., Kanda ii., 27) and Apastamba (Aph. Pr. ii., pat 6, K. 14) declared that 'women are not entitled to use the sacred texts or to inherit'. (How brutal!!) Thus the traces of generous respect were partly lost in the overgrowth of another stage in the national existence, (or rather death) and by the time when the Code of Manu was drawn up (I suppose the 4th recension) the sex had fallen to a distinctly lower position. A woman is never to seek independence; no religious rite is allowed to her apart from her husband; she must revere him as a god. (Manu V., 148, 154,155.) To the same set of doctrines must be assigned such texts as Manu IX. 185, 187 which, taken without the gloss of Kulluka Bhat, exclude wives and daughters from the line of inheritance." And Mr. West might have added such texts as: "It is the nature of women in this world to cause the seduction of men."* "Let no man therefore sit in a sequestered place with his nearest female relations."† "By a girl or by a young woman, or by a woman advanced in years, nothing must be done, even in her own dwelling-place, according to her mere pleasure."‡ "Women have no business with the texts of the Veda; this is the law fully settled; having therefore no evidence of law and no knowledge of expiatory texts, sinful women must be as foul as falsehood itself; and this is a fixed rule."§ Surely these cannot be the words of the righteous, chivalrous husband of Ida, nor his who said—"From the wife alone proceed offspring, good household management, solicitous attention, most exquisite caresses, and that heavenly beatitude which she obtains for the *manes* of ancestors and for the husband himself;"‖ nor his who said—"Where females are honoured, there the deities are pleased: but where they are dishonoured, there all religious acts become fruitless."¶ My dear friends, the very fountains of Hindu law have been corrupted, and I say to all practical Hindus to take up the reform of the Hindu law first of all, to keep a sharp eye on the High Courts, and, to especially help poor Hindu women ignorant of law.

BABU MENULAL CHATTERJEE.—An excellent suggestion this. I know widows who are robbed by means, fair and foul, of their purse and *stridhana*, as in the case of the Natore family. Their husbands' relations annoy them in various ways, turn out bitter enemies, and drive them to commit immoral acts.

PANDIT N. K. VAIDYA.—I can cite several such cases.

---

* Manu ii-213

† Ibid-215.

‡ Manu v. 147.

§ Manu IX, 18.

‖ Manu ix-28.

¶ Manu iii-56.

An Anti-Reformer.—I have no doubt you can, as I can cite several cases of oppressed wives and widows even in civilised England; for instance, the recent Langworthy case. But all such cases are perfectly irrelevant, because, they furnish no sufficient data for a correct generalization. It is otherwise with such solid testimony as that of Mr. Denzil Ibbetson, who says that "unchastity and offences connected with women are conspicuously more frequent in the west of the Panjab where infant marriage is the exception, than in the east where it is the rule." Those also who say that infant marriage is the cause of our deterioration, have to explain how the Panjabis retain their martial vigour.

A Hindu Social Reform Missionary.—The testimony you quote is not altogether in your favour, for this official says, first of all, that "infant marriage, if it leads one way to immorality and suffering, in another way prevents it." It may be that in some places the existence of infant marriage coincides with the existence of chastity; but such coincidences or co-existences can never, of themselves, prove any causal relation: otherwise we would have to infer that the "Mahratta proper" ladies and the Nambudri Brahminesses must be unchaste. On the other hand, Sir C. Bernard tells us that in Burma, "young men and maidens make love and marry, usually with the parents' consent, any time between the ages of 15 and 23 for the maids, and 17 and 28 for bachelors;" that (1) the proportion of widows according to the census "is less than half the corresponding proportion in the rest of the Indian Empire;" (2) that "women occupy a happier, a more important, and a more respectable position in social and family life in Burma than they do in India;" (3) that "in Burma, 320 females in 10,000 are able to read and write as compared with 20 per 10,000 among the Hindus of India, and 16 per 10,000 of the Hindus of Bengal;" (4) that "the number of women in jail is only one per cent. of the total prison population, while, in the rest of India, according to the most recent returns available, the proportion of female to total prisoners was 5 per cent."; (5) that "suicides of women are extremely rare, and cases of infanticide are almost unknown in Burma, whereas both crimes are unhappily not uncommon in India." Now, these five coincidences speak more eloquently in favour of marriages at ripe age, than any that can be cited in favour of premature marriage. The truth is that in sociological questions, *á priori* reasoning must go hand in hand with observation and experience, at least as much as in political and economical problems, for otherwise no practical conclusion can ever be arrived at. Apply this reasoning to this question of infant marriage, or rather apply the proved conclusions of physiology, and you cannot doubt that such marriage is prejudicial to health and strength. Therefore, we should demand most cogent and convincing evidence before admitting that this institution has been proved by experience to be favourable to both. There is no such evidence forthcoming in the case of the Panjabis. On the contrary, the evidence is all the other way. They retain their martial vigour because they are not addicted to premature marriages, and not in spite of such marriages the Panjab Census Report says that throughout a large proportion of the country, infant marriage is the exception, and the Honourable D. C. Barkley says (1) that "such marriages are less prevalent among the illiterate classes than among the educated"; (2) that "there are considerable tracts of country in which the customs of the people are opposed to early marriages, and it is usually the higher castes and the people of best social position who consider them most necessary"; (3) and that "where they do not prevail, the physical characteristics of the people are evidently better than where they do." This is much more solid testimony than any that you can adduce.

RAI MULRAJ.—In the Panjab, most people have not the courage to refuse an offer of betrothal for their sons when it comes from the parents of a girl, for fear of getting a bad name among the community to which they belong. Others, again, hasten to get their sons betrothed because if a boy grows up unbetrothed, it is frequently considered to be due to some defect in the boy or in the family, and then it becomes difficult to get the boy betrothed afterwards. On the other hand, the parents of a girl are anxious to betroth her as soon as possible, for if they wait till the girl grows up, they rarely succeed in finding a suitable match for her, all the boys of well-to-do families having been betrothed beforehand.

A HINDU SOCIAL REFORM MISSIONARY.—All this might be true of your caste and some others. But you cannot say that all this is true of a large part of the Panjab, for the Panjab is not so caste-ridden or priest-ridden as Bengal or Gujarat or even the Deccan. What you say, however, proves how little "fostering care and discrimination" are exercised.

MR. M. T. PILLAI.—Fostering care and discrimination indeed! A man approaching the grave can easily secure a maid of nine or ten years for his partner, provided he makes up his mind to pay a handsome price for her. A leper even can secure the hand of a fair maid for money.

H. H. THE THAKORE SAHEB OF MORVI.—What horror!

BABU KEDARESAR ROY.—It is worse than a horror, when the old sinner leaves his wife a widow in her teens. There are many people, I am sorry to say, who give their daughters to the highest bidder.

MR. RAMANUCHARI.—Like goods at an auction-sale without reserve.

PANDIT GATTULAL.—This practice is very sinful, as it is contrary to the Shastras. It seems necessary that a law in conformity with the Shastras should be made, in order to vindicate them.

PROFESSOR BHANDARKAR.—To marry a girl of 11 or 12 years to an old man of 50, whom it is impossible the girl should like for her husband, with the certain prospect of a lifelong widowhood for her, after a few years of distasteful and unhappy married life, is unfeeling cruelty. This wilful and wanton condemnation of an innocent girl to a life of misery, comes, in my opinion, within the legitimate scope of law. The Hindu religious law and respectable Hindu opinion condemn the practice, but have become powerless.

BABU K. C. BHATTACHARJI.—I regret to say that, in spite of the social degradation that attaches to the selling of brides, the practice is rather common all over Bengal, and cruelly oppresses certain sections of the community.

MR. HIRANAND KHEMSING.—Among the Amils of Sind, it is the bridegrooms that are sold, and not the brides, and the evil is equally demoralizing.

MR. NAGINDAS TULSIDAS.—In certain castes in Gujarat and Kathiawar, when two women are in the family way, they agree with their husbands' consent that, if the issue of one is a male child and that of the other a girl, the two unborn children are to be regarded as married. With this understanding, the two mothers go through the ceremony with balls of flowers in their laps. If the issue of both is male or female the ceremony goes for nothing. Such is the absurd extreme to which the system of infant marriage is carried on. However, there is this to atone for it, that remarriages are open to females as well as to males in these castes.

A HINDU LAWYER.—Not to the females, unless they have a *chor chithi*, or a *farghati*, or a regular divorce deed from their husbands. A caste decree is not enough.

MR. GOKALDAS K. PAREKH.—There is another practice equally repugnant to the notions of orthodox Hindus. I mean the very abominable system of exchanges. The family of A can only get a bride for one of its boys from B's family, on condition of A's family giving one of its girls to a boy in B's. This practice has gone so far that sometimes when the bride's family has no present necessity for a girl, there are conditions made to the effect that the future female issue of the marrying girl should be at the disposal of the members of her parents' family, for the purpose of procuring in exchange girls for boys that might be born in the family. In some castes, no bride can be had except on condition of exchange.

A Hindu Lawyer.—And often there is a regular chain of exchanges. For example, in one case A's parents in order to get a bride for A from D, had to give A's sister to B, and B had to give his sister to C, and C had to give his sister to D. Let us call A's wife Ganga, B's wife Shivi, C's wife Jamna, and D's wife Gomti. They were all married while infants; but, according to the custom of the caste, they remained with their parents until they became pubescent. Shivi unfortunately was afflicted with a loathsome disease, and her husband's parents did not send for her, and would not have her. As a natural consequence, Jamna, Shivi's exchange, was not sent to C. Gomti had attained her pubescence before Shivi, and had been sent to her husband D, and so also Ganga had been sent to A. Now A was found impotent, and Ganga eventually refused to go to A. So also Gomti's brother not having received his bride, Gomti was sent for and prohibited from going to her husband. The disconsolate husbands assembled the Panch, and the Panch in solemn conclave extricated the parties from their embarrassments by dissolving their marriages, and giving them liberty to remarry or to provide fresh exchanges. Two of the parties entered into fresh agreements. Shivi remained without a husband, while Ganga and Jamna were married to other husbands. Thereupon Ganga's first husband was instigated by some enemies of her second husband to prosecute her for bigamy, and her second husband for abetment of bigamy, and of course, the criminal court following several High Court decisions, refused to recognize the caste decree and sent both to jail! Here was an evil custom for which the people had provided a palliative. But the courts, while not interfering with the custom, interfered with the palliative.

Mr. Shantaram Narayen.—This is scandalous. But the whole administration of Hindu law is, in fact, based upon a legal fiction, and it affords a signal example of the fact that our customs are already being regulated by judiciary interference of a sort. And to the Hindu people, such interference is as effective as legislative interference, for the Sarkar, whether sitting in the majesty of justice, or the Sarkar proclaiming laws from the throne, is to the Hindu alike paternal, and may be held equally liable to be complained against as meddlesome. Those, therefore, who think that there is no State interference now with our religious practices or social customs, are either not aware of the real state of things, or are ignoring it.

A Hindu Social Reform Missionary.—What is urgently needed is, if I may say so, State interference with its own interference. The State should, at least, redress the grievances caused by its own tribunals and its own laws.

Mr. K. Krishnaswamy Rao.—I think that, in India, the protection of the interests of minor girls who are often victims of the caprice, and sometimes of the avarice, of their guardians, renders it necessary that some restriction should be imposed.

Mr. S. Subbramania Aiyar.—The most orthodox, I take it, cannot deny that the evil is a real evil having a most degenerating influence on the social, moral, intellectual and physical well-being of society.

Mr. Trimalrao Venkatesh.—Infant marriages, I say, have already ruined Indian society to a very great extent, and unless put a stop to, will do more harm. It is the parents, and especially the mothers, sisters, and other female members of the infant brides and bridegrooms, that really wish that their infant children were married, not so much for the purpose of getting them married as for the sake of enjoying the fun and pleasure of going through the ceremonies attendant upon the marriages.

Mr. Munmohan Ghose.—I look upon the system of child marriages as the greatest curse of our country.

Mr. Navalram Lakshmiram.—So do I.

Mr. S. N. Tagore.—It is a canker that eats into the vitals of our national existence, and if not removed in time, may lead to the degeneracy and decay of the whole race.

Mr. Keshavlal Madhavdas.—Just so.

Sirdar Gopalrao Hari Deshmukh.—I consider it a most pernicious custom. Hindus have, owing to it, hardly strength to become soldiers, or to cultivate land, or go for trade to foreign countries. They are unfit as colonizers. Every man has a family. Even little boys are burdened with wives and children. A girl cannot be kept unmarried beyond ten years, hence parents are very anxious to get her wedded even to an old man or a sickly youth. The race is thus gradually deteriorating. Children die soon, and there are more widows now than there were fifty years ago. The evil is very great, and is corroding the very vitals of the nation. At present women have no status in society, and they are made to give a silent consent to all cruelties.

An Anti-Reformer.—This is news to me! One gentleman says it is women that bring about infant marriages. Another says women have no status in society. I don't know whom to believe. A third talks of sundry diseases, and concludes that because they exist in certain castes they exist throughout India. A fourth talks of disparity between the age of the bride and the bridegroom, as if such disparity is unknown in England or France or Germany or Russia or America, as if that old story of January and May is not typical of certain marriages, as if there are no cases in other societies of old women like the Baroness Burdett-Coutts marrying young men, and young women marrying old men. All such vapid and vaporous talk proves nothing.

A Hindu Social Reform Missionary.—I agree with you so far that every one of us should avoid "the falshood of extremes." But I say, nevertheless, that baby-brides and baby-husbands are a disgrace to India, and to India alone.

MR. M. G. RANADE.—I think that after making all allowances, it cannot be denied that Hindu society contrasts very unfavourably with all other civilised races in these social matters. Nor can it be denied that early marriage leads to early consummation, and thence to the physical deterioration of the race, that it sits as a heavy weight on our rising generation, enchains their aspirations, denies them the romance and freedom of youth, cools their love of study, checks enterprise generally, dwarfs their growth, breeds weaklings and sickly people, and lastly that it leads in many cases to all the horrors of early widowhood. How to achieve reform may be open to question, but the fact itself cannot be denied, even by those who take the extreme view, that some remedial action is possible or desirable. With those who are so wedded to the existing arrangements as to maintain that they are the best possible that can be conceived, it is useless to argue, for they ignore history, they ignore their best traditions, they ignore the dictates of their most solemn religious texts, they violate their natural conscience and their sense of the fitness of things. They ignore history, traditions and religious texts, because they know full well that the existing arrangements are later corruptions. They violate their natural conscience and their sense of the fitness of things because, while they mumble the old rites and pronounce the old declarations, they virtually trample them under foot, and while the men reserve to themselves all manner of freedom, no such measure of liberty is allowed to the poor women, even when widowed in childhood. These men virtually place themselves out of court in these discussions.

A HINDU SOCIAL REFORM MISSIONARY.—"Widowed in childhood"! Are not these words which should burn into the inmost core of our hearts? Is not every one of us ashamed of the connotation of the vernacular word for widow? Listen to the sad words of Pandit Ishwar Chandra Vidiasagar—a man who has spent almost the whole of his life to secure justice to widows, and failed. He says :—"How many hundreds of widows unable to observe the austerities of a Brahmacharya life, betake themselves to prostitution and fœticide, and thus bring disgrace upon the families of their fathers, mothers and husbands...... Unfortunately, man, the stronger sex, arrogates to himself rights, which he is not willing to concede to weak woman. He has taken the Shastras into his own hands, and he interprets and moulds them in a way which best suits his conscience, perfectly regardless of the degraded condition to which woman has been reduced through his selfishness and injustice. A sight of the wrongs of the women of modern India is really heart-rending. To respect the female sex, and to make them happy are things almost unknown in this country. Many men who consider themselves wise, and are esteemed so by others, take a pleasure in the degraded state of their females. I beseech you to think seriously for a while upon the subject, and then to say whether we should continue slaves to such a custom.........Woman! in India thy lot is cast in misery." Now, there may be some exaggeration in this picture; but its outlines are perfectly true, and it is a shame to us that they are true.

Mr. Kalianrao H. Desai.—I don't think widows are as badly off as you suppose. In all household and family matters a widow as such enjoys a far greater authority than a married woman. She directs the whole house, as she has more leisure for such duties, and in almost all matters relating to family or caste customs, she, especially if grown-up, is always looked upon as a final authority. Of course, her position as a widow excludes her from the performance of such religious ceremonies as require the presence of woman on auspicious occasions. As to any other social wrong to which widows as such are compelled to submit, I humbly submit, I fail to discover any, after a lifelong experience of my community.

A Hindu Social Reform Missionary.—Then pray confine your proposition to your community. The testimony of

Vidiasàgar is as to Bengal, an d there is abundant testimony to the same effect as to other provinces. But of course there are exceptions.

MR. KRISHNASWAMI RAO.—I think that, if widows have unredressed grievances, their existence is entirely due to their reluctance to bring them to public notice.

BABU P. C. MOZMOODAR.—It seems to me, friends, a wise economy of Providence that quite an appreciable number of men and women among every civilised people, whether in the shape of the widowed or the unmarried, should remain disentangled from the anxieties and trials of matrimony, for the ministry of sorrow and suffering and other wants of general society.

A HINDU SOCIAL REFORM MISSIONARY.—That may be, but I don't know if it is also an economy of Providence that a widow's head should be shaved, that every "sensible warm motion" in her should be made a "kneaded clod," and that

> "The weariest and most loathed worldly life
> That age, ache, penury and imprisonment
> Can lay on nature"

should be a paradise to what she fears of her lot.

MR. RANGRAO V. PURANDHARI.—You are making a gross mistake. No widows are forced to shave their heads, but the shaving of a widow's head being a religious practice, widows get their heads shaved of their own accord, and lead a single life.

A HINDU LAWYER.—As religious a practice I suppose as the marriage of idiots, which is of course a sacrament, or a marriage within prohibited degrees which also is equally a sacrament. Cropping a widow's hair is, I conceive, another sacrament, a religious "trapping and suit of woe", which requires a filthy barber's services every month.

Rao Saheb V. N. Mandlik.—This is mere impertinence. To become a widow is a misfortune. There is no balm to a soul so wounded, except the one obtained by entering into a higher kind of life.

A Hindu Social Reform Missionary.—And shaving her head.

Rao Saheb V. N. Mandlik.—I say except the one obtained by entering into a higher kind of life, abnegating one's self on the altar of duty, and sacrificing self to a higher self, in a manner recognized by the highest religious sanctions as well as by the sanction of society, and by training the body and mind so to live in this world, as to qualify one's self for a higher. This is the accepted doctrine and practice of the Hindu Shastras, which the highest minds have adopted and still pursue more or less successfully. What does the actual condition of the people disclose? The simple but effective Savitri Upakhyana which is religiously observed throughout Hindustan, shows that the second marriage of a woman is opposed to Hindu religious convictions. The Savitri day or days are the holiest festivals for females in India. My authorities are from the Mahabharata down to the Vrataraja.

A Hindu Antiquary.—Savitri, however, was not an infant bride. She chose her own husband, and would not give up her first love although she was told by no less a Muni than Narada, that he was destined to die within a year. He did so die, and Savitri pursued his soul into the regions of Yama, as Orpheus pursued his Eurydice; and Yama, unlike Pluto, rewarded her fidelity by restoring her husband to her unconditionally, and giving her several other boons. This is the story of Savitri in the Mahabharata, and I fail to see how it justifies the horrors of widowhood. On the contrary, it shows that self-choice and marriage at a ripe age produce such lovely examples of conjugal devotion as that of Savitri. I should very much like to know in what authoritative Shastra the shaving of widows is enjoined.

A Hindu Social Reform Missionary.—Dear Mr. Wordsworth said at one time :--"Human nature is marvellously plastic, and a state of life, which many women deliberately adopt, and which extrinsic circumstances impose on a multitude of others in all civilised lands, cannot be without compensating consolations. In those cases where it is sweetened by domestic affection, sustained by religious devotion, or fortified by intellectual passion, I have no doubt that the lives of those who, from choice or necessity, adopt it, are neither unprofitable nor unhappy." And he compared Indian widows to Italian nuns. But even he had not a word to say in justification of child-widowhood. On the contrary, he wrote :—"I need hardly say that I consider the existence of the Hindu child-widow one of the darkest blots that ever defaced the civilization of any people, and it is the direct and necessary consequence of infant marriage." I don't know if Mr. Wordsworth still thinks that widows other than child-widows have many compensating consolations in castes in which they are shaved. But in my opinion it is perfectly truthful to say that, "all the voyage of their life is bound in shallows and miseries."

Mr. Govindrao B. Joshi.—The educated men of the present day often hold forth on this subject, and say :—" The poor helpless widowed girls are absolutely undone, their distresses and hardships are horrible even to contemplate. The butcher cuts the throat of an animal but once, and the consequent pain and torture are over in a moment once for all, but the unceasing sufferings of bereaved widows are lifelong ", and a deal of talk of this kind. Should, however, early widowhood become the lot of one of their own daughters of tender years, not a single one of them hesitates to wipe off her *kanku*, to break her bangles, and get her head shaved. Thus matters have come to a mournful pass. We are really in a helpless state of infancy, and need guidance by the State.

An Anti-Reformer.—This is a gratuitous slander upon educated natives.

Mr. Joterao G. Phullay.—I can't say if it is, but my own experience is that the widow is stripped of her ornaments, is forcibly shaved by her near relations, is not well fed, is not properly clothed, is not allowed to join pleasure-parties, marriages, or religious ceremonies. In fact, she is bereft of all worldly enjoyments, nay, she is considered lower than a culprit or a mean beast.........I established a foundling house in my own compound in Poona for the Brahmin community. From its commencement up to the present time, 35 pregnant widows have come to the house, and been delivered of children of whom five are living, and thirty died from injuries done to them while in the womb by the poisonous drugs which the mothers must have taken to conceal their pregnancy. Many beautiful and helpless ignorant young widows of respectable Brahmin families have turned out private and public prostitutes, on account of this wretched system.

Mr. Trimalrao Venkatesh.—There is no doubt that several widows are virtuous; but the rest practise a good deal of immorality. I do not think that one-fourth of the offences of the latter are ever brought to light.

Mr. Mahipatram Rupram.—It is but too true that Hindu society prefers to wink at the crimes of the widow rather than allow her to remarry. No notice is taken of well-known irregularities of conduct; proved abortion and desertion of infants are pardoned, and even conviction in a court of justice does not exclude a widow for ever from caste and society. But the marriage of a widow, even with a member of her own caste, is considered a more heinous crime than all these put together.

Mr. K. T. Telang.—Would you wrest the power of excommunication from the hands of the caste? That, I maintain, would be tyrannising over caste. As Sir Joseph Arnould said in the famous Agha Khan Case:—"In fact, in every community whether of a religious nature or not, whether church or chapel, caste or club, there must, as requisite for the preservation of a community and as inherent in the very conception of a community, necessarily exist a power, not indeed to be exerted except in extreme cases and on justifying grounds, of depriving of the privileges of membership those who persistently refuse, after due notice and warning, to comply with those ascertained conditions of membership to which by the very fact of being members of the community, they must be held to have given an implied, if not an expressed, consent." That is the doctrine which I hold, and paradoxical as it may seem, I hold it not merely as being what is demanded by considerations of justice, but also as being that which, under our present conditions, must accelerate the decline and fall of caste as a power hostile to progress.

A HINDU SOCIAL REFORM MISSIONARY.—The paradox is only intelligible if you mean, and as I suppose you really mean, that no efforts should be spared by means of energetic organizations to improve the caste from within, and to turn the weapons of caste against social abuses rather than against social reforms. If there are to be no such efforts your paradox is likely to prove a delusion.

MR. C. K. AIYAR.—If the Legislature rule that no girl should be treated as a wife before consummation, they will put a stop to that most cruel and heart-rending scene of every day's occurrence, viz. taking the betrothed (I say betrothed for I can't call her married) girl losing her husband to the burning ground on the first day, and again, on the tenth day, making her wear her jewels and good clothes and deck her hair with flowers and ornaments as the last day that she can use them or enjoy such luxury in her life, while all this time the unfortunate child is unconscious of the significance of the ceremony. Such a girl has nothing to do with the burning of the body, which is done, in a great majority of cases, by the brothers or father of the deceased. Such a girl, however young she may be, is denied the privilege of mixing with the betrothed girls of her age in singing, wearing ornaments, &c., and of doing all that betrothed girls are required to do on occasions of marriage or auspicious ceremonies at home and elsewhere. Such an infant girl is denied the privilege of going to temples on festive occasions, and enjoying the sight of a festival, as other betrothed girls of her age do. The most melancholy scene of all is the so-called widowed infant not knowing the reason of her exclusion, asking her parents how she had offended them or others, and why she was not treated as a married girl, and the parents then beginning to weep over the misfortune of the girl.

A HINDU SOCIAL REFORM MISSIONARY.—Why do they weep? Why should we wipe their tears or mix ours with theirs? Will not the wounded soul enter into a higher kind of life, abnegate herself on the altar of duty, and sacrifice self to a higher self? No hope may brighten her days to come, no "memory gild her past", but what does that matter? Society ordains it and the law allows it! The wise economy of Providence requires premature marriages and virgin-widows for the ministry of sorrow and suffering! What a cold, heartless philosophy! If widows are wanted for such ministry, why not widowers! Just rule that no young man should marry a second wife after the loss of his first, even though he might have lost her in infancy, and then you would have a taste of the ministry of sorrow by these young widowers!

MR. M. I. PILLAI.—It is a cruel and inhuman custom. I have known instances of respectable men—who were ornaments of Hindu society—having met with premature death, broken-hearted and unable to bear the misfortune of their beloved daughters. A Hindu family with a young widow is in perpetual misery, and gloom prevails in it. The consolation attempted by the orthodox Brahmins is in itself insulting. It is gravely said by them that a woman becomes a widow by the result of her *karma* in the previous births, and that it is a sin to allow her to marry again. This is something like misers preaching it to be a sin to help the indigent, who by the result of their *karma* are destined to be poor.

A Hindu Antiquary.—The Vedic poets held no such doctrine as that of the transmigration of souls. The speculations of Hindu philosophy were pushed to their extreme when we were enveloped in misery, and the result was Buddhism.

Mr. Venkut R. Katti.—And it is curious that no trace of a shaved widow could be found before Buddhism. That faith required the shaving of its religious persons, men or women. Such widows in those days as had no attraction for this world turned *sanyasis* of their own accord, by getting their head shaved and wearing red cloth, and went to live in Viharas or monasteries. This custom was regarded as a great improvement, as it granted equal rights to women with men in religious matters, and the astute Brahmins retained it, with the double purpose of making their own religion more attractive to the masses, and exposing the dark side of the banished religion to the world. But it is heart-rending to see a beautiful young face deprived of the ornament which nature has bestowed on it. What an abject spectacle must a shaved widow be presenting to the eyes of European ladies passing through the streets of Indian towns. Has man power to cut down the hair of a woman's head any more than her nose or ears ?

Mr. M. G. Ranade.—I say the desperate misery of infant widows is a scandal and a wrong which is a disgrace to any well-regulated society. There is really no choice allowed to the unfortunate creatures, who are disgraced before they feel the reason why such cruelty is practised upon them. It was on this account that I proposed a legislative enactment fixing the limit of marriageable age.

Sir T. Madava Row.—And I also am of opinion that such limit should be fixed. Even if it is fixed at ten it will do considerable good. It may be fixed at fourteen or fifteen for non-Brahmins.

An Anti-Reformer.—I oppose legislative interference altogether. I say that infant betrothals and marriages are not specially Oriental institutions, and "were well known in Europe at a comparatively recent historical period."* I say also with Mr. Hume that, infant marriage not being "an unmitigated curse should be left to die its own fate," and that "sporadic crusades to destroy particular evils are an utter waste of power."* And further I say with Mr. Wordsworth that, "a society divided as Hindu society is, and dominated as it is by religious tradition and priestly law, will never be reformed piecemeal and in detail." and that "religion and habit were not created and cannot be destroyed by logic."† I am if you please an out-and-out let-aloneist.

A Hindu Democritus.—And I am another. The quantum of good and evil, of happiness and misery, of wisdom and folly, and (if you please) of laughter and tears, is as fixed and invariable as the quantum of the seventy elementary substances out of which this whole universe has been built up. There is no annihilation and no augmentation, no *real* destruction, no *real* construction; but there is a great deal of transmutation, and there is a great deal of illusive jugglery. The best way, therefore, of enjoying life is to see how "the pairs of opposites" so often mentioned in our Hindu philosophy fight it out between themselves. "Polarity, or action and re-action, we meet" as Emerson says, "in every part of nature: in darkness and light; in heat and cold; in the ebb and flow of waters; in male and female; in the inspiration and expiration of plants and animals; in the undulations of fluids and of sound; in the centrifugal and centripetal gravity; in electricity, galvanism, and chemical affinity. Superinduce magnetism at one end of a needle, the opposite magnetism takes place at the other end. If the South attracts, the North repels. To empty here you must condense there. An inevit-

---

* See Chapter I—65, of this book.

† See Chapter IX.-58.

able dualism bisects nature, so that each thing is a half and suggests another to make it whole: as spirit, matter; man, woman; odd, even; subjective, objective; in, out; upper, under; motion, rest; yea nay;" and he would have added if he had lived in India, Malabari, Mandlik; A. O. Hume, Sir Auckland Colvin; the National Congress, the Patriotic Association; radicalism, conservatism; pure theism, idolatry; reformation, *deformation*. Yes—reformation, *deformation*, for who does not know what came in the wake of the religious reforms introduced by Chaitanya in Bengal, Nanik in the Panjab, Sahjanand in Gujerat. Why idolatry of a subtler form! And as for your European civilisation, I say it is as bad as barbarism; for, if barbarism is bad, national drunkenness is at least equally bad. It was not long ago that England drew a third of its revenue from drink, and it was said by an English paper: "Drink pays our Army and Navy, and it pays the interest on our Rule Brittania Debt." Look at the English poor-houses, at the English public-houses, at the English jails, at the English lunatic asylums, and then say if the English civilisation means any increase of goodness, of happiness, or of wisdom. And as for other European nations, why take a stock only of their armaments and note their ways of warfare, and compare them if you please with the military code of the Pandavas and the Kauravas, and you see at once that European civilisation is but another form of barbarism with a thin veneer. Yes, certainly, there are schools and hospitals and other make-believes of progress; but as Herbert Spencer has shown, some of the most-educated men turn out the greatest scoundrels, for they can make their villainy a fine art or, if you please, an elaborate science. And as for hospitals, the same philosopher tells us that "as fast as more and more detrimental agencies are removed or mitigated.........there arise new destructive agencies. Let the average mortality be diminished by more effectually guarding the weak against adverse conditions, and inevitably there come fresh diseases." Your drainage-fanatics and sanitation-fanatics who have inoculated so many of our municipalities with their fads, and burdened the people with so many taxes, ought to lay this profound observation to heart. What then has European civilisation done? I forget it boasts of its newspapers; but do the newspapers do more good than harm? The editors seem to say—as a fine parody makes them say—

> "Now about our task we'll go,
> In the poisoned slander throw,
> Hubble, bubble, toil and trouble,
> Lies and shams and sneers we double."

Their lying advertisements, their unscrupulous attacks, their unconscionable flatteries, their prurient scandals, their sensational monstrosities are a curse to the people. The little girl in *Punch*—my favourite weekly—offers "a penny for a paper with three orrid murders in it, and two fires with people burnt to death, and some drownings and an earthquake and a shipwreck and a few bad robberies; and please", she adds, "if you ain't got one with enough of orrers in it, mother says I'm only to give a 'a penny." I say this is nothing but savagery in disguise. It is certainly not civilisation! You talk of your physical conveniences, but forget the moral and intellectual harm they have done. You talk of your intellectual achievements, and forget the physical harm they have done. You talk of the destruction of superstition, and forget how many new fetishes we have set up. "Nodding crucifixes and melting blood", says a clever writer, "went out with the Reformation, nor do I think that those kinds of pious frauds have returned. But in their place we have charity-balls, shilling-subscriptions, charity-bazars, public dinners, and public meetings." Haven't we a host of such pious frauds? Are they not as plentiful as black-berries? Are not most of your philanthropic institutions the result of so many pious frauds? Read Carlyle and you will see how many humbugs there are in civilised England, while this horrible word is simply untranslateable in any ancient language. And

English humbuggism of all sorts is running rampant in our own land also. To give the most recent instance, Sir Auckland Colvin's letter about the Congress is charming humbug, and Mr. Hume's is another. The former talks "of India under education, of India compelled in the interests of the weaker masses to submit to impartial justice; of India brought together by road and rail; of India entering into the first-class commercial markets of the world; of India of religious toleration; of India assured, for terms of years unknown in less fortunate Europe, of profound and unbroken peace; of India of the free press; of India finally taught for the first time that the end and aim of rule is the welfare of the people and not the personal aggrandisement of the sovereign." The latter talks, on the other hand, of India under foreign rule and foreign institutions; of India compelled in the interests of Great Britain to submit to a bleeding process which is every year draining her life-blood; of India brought into contact with England like the famous earthen pipkin with the brass pot; of India exporting more than is good for her, to pay her tribute, and getting the exchange heavily against her; of India of religious decadence; of India assured, for terms of years unknown in more fortunate Europe, of poverty, without even a Famine Relief Fund to mitigate its extreme; of India of the free police and perjury—encouraging law-courts; of India of compulsory drunkenness; of India disarmed and emasculated; of India with her necessaries taxed; of India taught most convincingly that beautiful laws may not be well administered, and beaurocracy and circumlocution are not specially desirable blessings." Both are right and both are wrong, and a man who is both right and wrong is the biggest humbug in the world. Our fore-fathers believed that the Creator had produced Maya for his amusement, and I say she is also for the amusement of all true philosophers. Watch the play of antagonistic forces, and you will soon know what is meant by my new science "the statics of dynamics." It discovers the face of Maya in all sorts of places and in varying phenomena, and those who understand it most, care very little whether they have sanitation and education and adult marriages, or filth and ignorance and baby marriages; for they know that the law of life, to quote Spencer, will soon assert itself and produce a merry rhythm. Truly, "Men are but the sport of circumstances when circumstances, seem most the sport of men."

A HINDU HERACLITUS.—Yes, indeed, the law of life produces a rhythm, though not often a merry rhythm. The mole chooses to burrow underground, and the law of life, depriving it of eyes, adapts it to a darkened existence. The hermit-crab, avoiding the struggle of its species with waves and rocks, chooses to live in the whelk of a mollusc, and the law of life, shrivelling up its fourth and fifth pair of limbs, and attenuating the thick shell on its abdomen, compensates it by developing the extremity of its tail to enable it to hold on to its borrowed house. The dodder chooses to suck its food-supply at ease from the stem and branches of adjacent plants, and the law of life takes away its organs of nutrition, and makes it a "pauper of nature." Read Mr. E. Ray Lankestar's book on Degeneration, and you will have many more examples of such "merry rhythms." "Any new set of conditions," says this great scientist, "occurring to an animal, which render its food and safety very easily attained, seem to lead as a rule, to degeneration; just as an active healthy man sometimes degenerates, when he becomes suddenly possessed of a fortune; or as Rome degenerated when possessed of the riches of the ancient world. The habit of parasitism clearly acts upon animal organization in this way. Let the parasitic life once be secured, and away go legs, jaws, eyes, and ears; the active highly-gifted crab, insect, or annelid may become a mere sac, absorbing nourishment and laying eggs."* The parasite is nevertheless happy in its own way, and, I suppose it is only mere perversity on the part of scientific men to class

* P. 33.

it as a low organism. It is also equally perverse to put man in a different class from the *amœba*, for this tiny organism knows how to feed itself and save its little body, almost as well as man. If the end of life is to eat, drink, and be merry, the *amœba* secures that end almost completely, and the slothful *coccus* or scale-insect fulfils it as much as the active busy ant. But is this really the end? If it is, the evolution of man from a structureless, jelly-like, but vital compound of carbon, hydrogen, oxygen, and nitrogen, is utterly inexplicable. Surely Nature has ever been travailing to produce greater and greater perfection and greater and greater life. The life of a tree is not the same as the life of a bird, and the life of a bird is not the same as that of a man. And yet the embryonic life of all the three is the same. This is one of the astounding discoveries of science. "The apple which fell in Newton's garden, Newton's dog Diamond, and Newton himself began life at the same point."* Every one of them grew out of a mass of protoplasm,† but the ancestors of each had exercised different activities, and each became differentiated accordingly. It is in the power of every organism to vary. Two of the four essential characteristics of every living being are, according to physiology, assimilation and spontaneous action. The frog, to which Brahmins are likened in the Riga Veda, has, by continual efforts to breathe air direct from heaven, succeeded in acquiring lungs, while his fellow-dwellers in the waters who have made no such efforts, continue to retain their gills. The true Brahmins of old—our true Rishis—our true Yogis—by similar continual efforts succeeded in acquiring spiritual lungs, in establishing an almost perfect correspondence with the Immutable, and living unto the spirit by dying unto the flesh. They were at least religious zoophytes, so to say, and not like us, religious epiphytes. Are we not such? Is it not true that our spiritual food and safety are matters of no concern?

* Henry Drummond in his "Natural Law in the Spiritual World."

† See Huxley's Lay Sermons, 6th Edn., p. 127.

Is it not true that every one of us considers them easily attained? We have only to bolt into our mouths the formulæ of a Hindu cult, or fill our ears with certain Mantras and Tantras, and lo, we are saved! We have only to shelter ourselves under the accommodating roof of a particular Hindu doxy, and our salvation is of course ensured! There are deities innumerable, who are obliging enough to give us board and lodging, free of charge, and the result of their cruel kindness is that we are the spiritual parallels of natural parasites. Is not this religious parasitism a most mournful thing? But alas! our downward fall has not stopped here. Intellectually, the majority of us are no better than parasites. Have we not plenty of Sanskrit-educated parasites who suck our ancient literature like "industrious bugs," and produce what the bug produces? Have we not plenty of English-educated parasites, mere walking dictionaries of quotations from Milton and Shakespeare, Bacon and Burke, Austin and Bentham, Darwin and Spencer? But fortunately, the intellect of the country has been, for the last half century, steadily struggling to free itself from this crushing parasitism, and it is the resultant independence and the resultant good secured by the struggle, which make us hope that a similar struggle will wean us from spiritual parasitism and from social parasitism. Do you think, my brethren, that we are not social parasites? Can you deny that woman, who is in most advanced countries still a semi-parasite, is among us, with the exception of some classes, almost a complete parasite? She has had scant justice even in Europe. The professions are generally closed to her, and any attempt on her part to compete with men in their avocations is generally considered unwomanly. But in Europe such notions are becoming gradually obsolete, while in India we still continue to believe that the great end of a woman's life is marriage, and we still continue to enforce the ordinance of the Smritis that she is always to live in a state of dependence. And yet none in these scientific times can deny, that the child of a parasitic mother and an unparasitic father is a lower organism, that is, has lesser possibilities of future perfection, than the child of an unparasitic couple. This is a truth which is self-evident to every thinker, though it has not yet been brought home to the masses. What, however, we have to lament in India, is not only that woman, except among the lower, and a few of the upper, classes, is no better than a parasite, but that even man, her lord and master, is no better than a slave in social matters. The priest and the *pandit* now-a-days do not rule our spiritual and intellectual life so much as the caste rules our social life. Almost every detail of such life is settled for us. Caste has "for infancy, pupilage, and manhood its ordained methods of sucking, sipping, drinking, and eating; of washing, anointing; of clothing and ornamenting the body; of sitting, rising, reclining; of moving, visiting, travelling. It has its laws for social and religious rites, privileges, and occupations; for education, duty, religious service; for errors, sins, trangressions; for intercommunion, avoidance, and excommunication; for defilement and purification; for fines and other punishments. It unfolds the ways of what it calls sins, accumulating sin, and putting away sin; of acquiring, dispensing, and losing merit. It treats of inheritance.........of bargains, gains, loss, and ruin. It deals with death, burial, and burning; and with commemoration, assistance, and injury after deatq. It interferes, in short, with all the relations and events of life, and with what precedes and follows, or what is supposed to precede and follow life. It reigns supreme in the innumerable classes and divisions of the Hindus, whether they originate in family descent, in religious opinions, in civil or sacred occupations, or in local residence; and it professes to regulate all their interests, affairs, and relationships. Caste is the guiding principle of each of the classes and divisions of the Hindus viewed in their distinct and associated capacity"*. Caste prescribes the age of marriage and the conditions of cohabitation.

* Modern Hinduism by Wilkins, p. 125-126.

It exacts a fixed quota of dinners on auspicious and inauspicious occasions. It has a code of its own and a court of its own. Its main commandments are :—"Thou shalt not cross the black water;" "Thou shalt not marry a widow even if she is a virgin-widow;" "Thou shalt not inter-dine or intermarry with another caste." These are its capital crimes, for their punishment is death unto the caste, death unto one's family, death unto one's dearest and nearest. Such despotism—despotism unfortunately not tempered by enlightenment—kills all individuality, arrests growth, and hastens decay. There is a "pair of opposites", one of which uplifts those who put themselves in a position to rise, while the other drags down those who do not care to rise as they find it so easy to fall. Yes, there are thousands and tens of thousands in the organic world, who find it easy to fall. Life is to their west, to their east, to their north, to their south, above them and below them, and in closest contact with them on every side,* but they see it not, neither do they hear it, they taste it not, neither do they even touch it. The inorganic elements which are absorbed by every organism have a tendency to topple lower and lower, while the vital force which builds them up into plant and animal has a constant tendency to soar higher and higher. But to utilise this upward tendency, to become more and more alive, the organism must bestir itself and attempt to drink deep draughts of the life around, while to utilise the downward tendency, no such attempt is necessary. Hence it is that we find so many *lazzaroni in nature* with the doom of death on them. Hence it is that spiritual and intellectual and social parasites, suffer a slow but sure atrophy of their souls and intellects and individuality. This law of life which fixes the conditions of re-generation and de-generation, is not a mere phrase or a figment of science. It is as hard a fact as our Penal Code, but unlike it, it requires no Criminal Procedure Code and no Evidence Act to supplement it; for, he who breaks it

---

* Adapted from the "Ganapati Atharva Sirsham."

is his own policeman, his own prosecuter, his own judge, his own jailer. It is given to us to know the law itself, but not its why and wherefore. The stars in the milky way can be seen by us; but the eye, fortified with the best telescope yet invented, is not able to fathom the depths of nebulosity behind them. None can yet say why Variety should mean Growth, or why Uniformity should mean Decay. But there is no doubt as to this meaning. And there is equally little doubt that those who follow the law of life are masters of their fate, and those who do not, are the sport of circumstances. It is thus that we have fallen, and it is thus that we shall fall still lower, unless we once more utilize that vital force, primarily impressed on all nature to succour self-help, to conquer evil, to "make for righteousness". My dear brethren, there is hope for us all if we will but awake and arise. We are all very fond of reminding our rulers that "righteousness exalteth a nation"; but shouldn't we occasionally administer this reminder to ourselves also ? May I recall to you those noble verses in Manu which we have so much disregarded ! "Giving no pain to any creature," says the great Rishi while prescribing man's duties, "giving no pain to any creature (far less, therefore, to one's own flesh and blood), let him collect virtue by degrees, for the sake of acquiring a companion to the next world, as the ant by degrees builds his nest; for, in his passage to the next world, neither his father, nor his mother, nor his wife, nor his son, nor his kinsman will remain in his company: his virtue alone will adhere to him. Single is each man born; single he dies; single he receives the reward of his good, and single the punishment of his evil deeds. When he leaves his corpse, like a log or lump of clay, on the ground, his kindred retire with averted faces; but his virtue accompanies his soul. Continually, therefore, by degrees, let him collect virtue, for the sake of securing an inseparable companion, since with virtue for his guide, he will traverse a gloom, how hard to be traversed" !

A Hindu Fatalist.—But tell me, my profound philosopher, if your virtue will save you from being born again. Why need an inseparable companion at all? Is it not a nuisance to have an inseparable companion? I say, have true knowledge, and virtue will take care of itself. If there is life around us and in us, it will take good care of itself and of us. Is not this the only true knowledge? Why then trouble yourself with vain fantasies? Does not our Shâstra say: "By works, a creature is bound; by knowledge he is liberated; wherefore devotees gifted with perfect insight perform no works. Through works a creature is born again, after death, with a body (of one or other) of sixteen descriptions; by knowledge he becomes the Eternal, Imperceptible and Undecaying. Some men of little understanding eulogise works, and so embrace with delight the entanglements of corporeal existence. But those who have reached the highest intelligence and a perfect comprehension of righteousness, do not commend works, as a person drinking from a river thinks little of a well. The results which a man obtains from works are pleasure and pain, prosperity and adversity; by knowledge, he gains that condition in which his griefs are at an end, in which he dies not, in which his birth is not repeated, from which he does not return, in which that Supreme Brahma exists Imperceptible, Unchanging, etc., etc."*

A Hindu Lawyer.—I think this is an excellent doctrine. Let us all practise it; let us give up our professions; leave the National Congress as well as the Social Conference to its fate; retire quietly into the closet of our own consciousness, and contemplate ourselves from the navel upwards, and starve ourselves, if need be, into euthanasia. It is really absurd to make any effort to improve our condition in any way, for "Life's best is that it leads to Death."

An Anti-Reformer.—I suppose you do not believe that Christ was a Vedantist or a Yogi, and yet he is reported to

* Mahâbhârata XII. 8,810 p. p. Muir V.—327.

have said: "This is Life Eternal that they may *know* Thee; the only true God"*. It is in this sense that knowledge is contrasted with works in the passage quoted by our friend. As one of our Upanishads says: "All this is Soul. He who perceives this, thinks this, knows this, delights in Soul, sports with Soul, takes pleasure in Soul; he becomes self resplendent."† And this old doctrine is also the latest result of Western thought. Turn to that thoughtful work "Natural Law in the Spiritual World", and you find that the author, a scientific man and a Christian, says, after quoting Herbert Spencer's definition of "perfect life:"‡ "There lies a something at the back of the correspondences of the spiritual organism, just as there lies a something at the back of the natural correspondences. To say that Life is a correspondence, is only to express a partial truth. There is something behind. Life manifests itself in correspondences. But what determines them? The organism exhibits a variety of correspondences. What organizes them? As in the natural, so in the spiritual

---

* John XVII.

† Chandogya Upanishad VII. 2—52, Muir III.—173.

‡ "It is manifest á *priori*, that since changes in the physical state of the environment, as also those mechanical actions, and those variations of available food which occur in it, are liable to stop the processes going on in the organism; and since the adaptive changes in the organism have the effects of directly or indirectly counter-balancing those changes in the environment, it follows that the life of the organism will be short or long, low or high, according to the extent to which changes in the environment are met by corresponding changes in the organism. Allowing a margin for perturbations, the life will continue only while the correspondence continues; the completeness of the life will be proportioned to the completeness of the correspondence, and the life will be perfect only when the correspondence is perfect" Principles of Biology, p. 82. Again, "Perfect correspondence would be perfect life. Were there no changes in the environment but such as the organism had adapted changes to meet, and were it never to fail in the efficiency with which it met them, there would be *eternal existence* and *eternal knowledge*."

there is a Principle of Life... .....The relation between the spiritual man and his environment is......a filial relation. With the new spirit, the filial correspondence, *he knows the Father, and this is Life Eternal.* This is not only the real relation, but the only possible relation.........It takes the Divine to know the Divine, but in no more mysterious sense than it takes the human to know the human. Such being the quality of the new relation.........it contains the guarantee of its eternity. Here at last is a correspondence which will never cease......... It, and it only, will stretch beyond the grave, and be found inviolate,

> "When the Moon is old,
> And the Stars are cold,
> And the books of the Judgment Day unfold."

Thus the latest phase of enlightened Christianity is exactly the oldest phase of Hindu Yoga.

A HINDU SOCIAL REFORM MISSIONARY :—Granted. But what is your conclusion? Is Yoga within the reach of all? Can a complete filial correspondence be established without works or intellectual advancement? Can man become Divine in less time than it has taken him to become a man? This organism of ours which has not yet succeeded in adapting itself to a tithe of the changes of the natural half of its environment, cannot at once become perfectly *en rapport* with the spiritual half. True, there is Life all around us, and we are at liberty to drink as much of it *as we can.* But *can* we drink it without a capacity to drink it? Can we have such capacity without advancing higher than the low plane of our existence? And can we so advance without any effort? Did man evolve mind, did man evolve language, did man evolve a will, without trying at all? Had he not always an Actual and an Ideal, and is not his life-history nothing more than a series of struggles to rise—a series of progressive Actuals and progressive Ideals? Has he not always had an Ideal far in advance of his Actual, and has not every expansion of his

Actual—every increase in his correspondences with his environment—every accession of more life, meant the attainment of a longed-for Ideal, and has not every such attainment been but a prelude to the burst of a higher Ideal on his vision? "The situation", says Carlyle, "that has not its Duty, its Ideal, was never yet occupied by man. Yes, here in this poor, miserable, hampered despicable Actual, wherein thou even now standest, here or nowhere, is thy Ideal; work it out therefrom: and working, believe, live and be free." Is not this exactly what our own classic Rishi, Mudgala, said and practised? Does not the Christian Paul say the same thing—"Work out your own salvation"? Can salvation be worked out without working out self-purification, and can we work out self-purification without self-denial and without righteousness? There may be higher types of man whose store of hereditary purity, accumulated by the self-denial and self-sacrifice of generations of ancestors, or whose store of self-acquired purity, due to the favourable influence of their spiritual environment, may fit them at once for the higher plane of ideal ethereal life, without any troublesome preliminary apprenticeship to the Actual. But such men—the prophets and saints of all lands—are very few. They are the salt of the earth, and help us to grow by their example. The rank and file of humanity have still to work their way to higher goals, by realising their conditions, by utilising their surroundings—surroundings vital with a Heavenly Presence—by acting well their part on earth—by hoping for a higher life—and by that 'divine discontent' which has always been the fore-runner of progress. Icarus could not fly like a bird, but a modern balloonist, by utilising Nature, can soar high into space, and unlike a bird, can even take a companion or two with him into the higher regions. The old astronomer in the fable, with his eyes turned towards the stars and his feet going astray, terminated his studies in a cold well, but the modern astronomer, well knowing that negligence is as great a crime as rashness, takes care both of his eyes and his feet, and, with telescope in hand, sweeps the heavens from his observatory in perfect security. Friends and brethren, let us not befool ourselves with idle phrases. Go to the root of the question, if you please; look into its ins and outs, and survey it in all its aspects; but you cannot get over the invincible truth that progress is impossible without effort. We are day by day curtailing our old inheritance, and doing next to nothing to improve our surroundings. And yet we have only to exert ourselves in right earnest, and the traditions of our race, the memories of our fathers, nay, their living presences around us—for good men never die—will infuse a new life into us, and make us better, purer, holier, happier. Every year, we make our offerings to the *manes* of our progenitors out of an ever-diminishing stock of righteousness, and every year, by walking after the stubbornness of our hearts in devious ways, we decrease the chances of a better progeny. We care as little for our ancestry as for our posterity; we listen neither to reason nor to authority; we worship forms without understanding, and, forsaking the fountain of living waters, "hew out cisterns, broken cisterns that can hold no water." How long, dear brethren, are we to disobey the clear laws of Nature, pervert our plain path, persist in our trespasses, and gradually make our old "heritage an abomination," and cur ancient "pleasant portion" a wild desolation? How long are we to continue this prodigal waste of hereditary vigour and virtue, in utter forgetfulness of the undying Nemesis that dogs the heels of every inordinate act, every inordinate omission? Is it not yet time for us all to awake from our sleep of ages, and put our households once more in order? Is it not yet time for a combined, sustained struggle against our new vice of blood, against that fatal blight which so often nips our youth in its bud, or sears the flower of our manhood in its bloom, which turns tender maidens into women before their time, which fades their beauty, stifles their growth, eats into the roots of their life, and riddles them with untold maladies? Surely, my brothers, you do not believe that the Almighty Lawgiver is dead! Surely, you do not believe that his police or his judiciary is less efficient than ours! Surely, most surely, we are being punished for our transgressions, punished to be schooled into a better life, but to be schooled only if we will learn. Every child-widow in India means a crime against Nature, a sin against God. Every consummation during pubescence, every marriage entailing such consummation, means the curses of the children to be born, a failure of our duty to our past, to our present, and to our future! Do you think that such failure of duty is a thing not to be ashamed of? Is it not equivalent to moral insolvency? And is such insolvency less disgraceful than pecuniary insolvency? Far be it from me to say that we are all moral insolvents. But so long as we choose to turn a deaf ear to the reproofs of our own back-slidings, so long as we do not break the yoke and burst the bands of the evil customs which hold us in thrall, so long as we strike no blow for our own freedom from their tyranny, we deserve no better fate than that of moral insolvents and parasites and slaves.

A Hindu Antiquary.—And no better Yuga than the Kali Yuga—the Yuga of Kalhi—the Age of Misery. Read, my friends, the sixty-fourth Adhiaya of the Adiparva of the Mahâbhârata, and you find that in the Satya Yuga, men knew not women before their full prime, that children never died in infancy, that sterility was the lot of none, that disease was unknown, that woman was not a

"Poor thing of usages! coerced—compelled,

Victim when wrong, and martyr oft when right,"—

that health and holiness went hand in hand, and vigour and virtue were inseparable companions. We have long divorced them by this brutish and foolish usage of premature marriage and the demoralisation it has entailed, and I propose that we solemnly swear, each of us, to rest not and to pause not until we succeed in bringing the old Satya Yuga back again, at least in this essential respect.

A HINDU ANTI-REFORMER.—And pray how are you going to bring it back, dear old man? Are you going to apply to the prosaic British Government for this boon?

A HINDU ANTIQUARY.—I mean to try my own people first, and when I despair of them it will be time to apply to the Government.

A HINDU LAWYER.—Bu t how are you going to try your own people first?

A HINDU ANTIQUARY.—Well, I will join my friend, the missionary here, and implore each caste to reform itself. I will entreat my educated brethren to become missionaries like us, and shame them into establishing at least one indigenous mission which may compare favourably with the 800 foreign missions we have amongst us. I will ask the public to support it at least as well as the Countess of Dufferin Fund, for the object of the fund is curative while ours is preventive. I will devote the remaining few years of my life to this work, for I feel that not a single earnest word, not a single honest effort, is ever wasted. My God, my Father, will bless my poor endeavours, and enable me to sow at least a seed which may one day germinate and grow into a goodly tree. This is my simple old-fashioned faith, and I mean to act up to it.

> "We live in deeds, not years; in thoughts, not breaths;
>
> In feelings, not in figures on a dial;
>
> We should count time by heart-throbs. He most lives
>
> Who thinks most, feels the noblest, acts the best."

M. G. RANADE.—I wish every one of us had your faith and every one of us acted up to it.

A HINDU LAWYER.—It is not difficult to act up to it, if one can only understand that the best selfishness lies in unselfishness. I am afraid I can't become a missionary, but though I can't spare my time, the mission is welcome to my money.

AN ANTI-REFORMER.—But I don't yet understand what this new-fangled mission is wanted for.

A HINDU ANTIQUARY.—Well, if you can't understand that self-help is essential to our progress, that progress is necessary for perfection, that perfection should be the aim of every human being; if you can't conceive any higher ideal than that of personal happiness, you can at least understand the great disparity which premature marriage is creating between the two sexes. It has been well said that this practice "shortens the period of pure and joyous maidenhood," and that "the child is thereby forced by an abrupt and violent transition into the woman. It is only the joylessness of a people, that could have made the *Nautch* a pleasurable mode of passing an evening. This result is a direct consequence of India having withdrawn, from the commerce of society, the element which Nature has provided to brighten, purify, and elevate it; and Nature, indignant at the affront, has retaliated by the infliction of the *Nautch* as the great national amusement." The Greeks had their *hetœrœ*, and we have our Naikins, and the origin of the latter is the same as that of the former. Is it, I ask, conducive to happiness, for the husband to be well educated, and the wife to be-ill-educated or not educated at all? Then is it conducive to happiness or even to sensual gratification, to mate an unripe girl to an unripe boy? We are in this respect more kind to our mares and horses, our cows and oxen, than to our own kin, our own sons and daughters. Again, is it conducive to happiness, to have a feeble or unhealthy family? Lastly, if intellectual pleasures are superior to physical pleasures, and if such pleasures are desirable, do you expect that so long as this barbarous custom overshadows our life, we can ever have good poetry or excel in art? Read the sorry stuff turned out every year, and then say if chivalry is not its own reward. Read any of our modern dramas or novels, and you will find them uninteresting, unless they deal with our past, or borrow from European sources. A Gujarati graduate and poet has tried recently to depict modern Hindu home-life, as attractively as possible. But all the attractions arise from what modern Hindu life sadly lacks. Even the name of his heroine—Kumudsundari—has a classical turn. She is certainly a loveable ideal, but no reality. Where is the Hinduani, wise and pure, who can quote Sakuntala and the Merchant of Venice, play on the *sitar* and the *sarangi*, and sing divinely? Every educated Hindu would like to have such a Kumud—such a lotos—lovely maiden—for his wife. But where are these "phantoms of delight" in Hindu society? They exist in the brains of those who have read Kalidas and Shakespeare, but otherwise we know them not. And yet, alas! there was a time when they were not unknown, when they adorned Aryan homes, and inspired the highest poetry and the highest art. But now, truly, the age of Aryan chivalry is gone! That of canting sophists, and heartless calculators, has succeeded! Our true seers are dead; our blind guides of the blind remain!

> "The seer from the East was *then* in light.
>
> The seer from the West was *then* in shade.
>
> Ah! *now* 'tis changed. In conquering sunshine bright
>
> The man of the bold West now comes arrayed.
>
> He of the mystic East is touch'd with night."

SIR T. MADAVA ROW.—Let us hope, however, that a brighter day is in store for us. There is no community which suffers more from self-inflicted, or self-accepted, or self-created and therefore avoidable, evils, than ours. Let us hold provincial conferences, and caste conferences, and send delegates annually to the Central Social Conference, to keep alive a constant agitation against social abuses. Let us employ our own missionaries, to create public opinion in favour of social reform, and let us all band ourselves like brothers, and work together in harmony, and shrink from no self-sacrifice until our end is achieved. Let us, my brethren, deserve success, and then, under God's providence, we are not likely to be baulked of it.

A HINDU LAWYER.—Yes, let us put forth our best energies and have an effective organisation. We must tackle the castes in right earnest, and induce those, which are ahead of the rest, to form themselves into registered associations, so as to be able to enforce their penalties for violated pledges through a court of law. We should move the Legislature to amend that disgraceful provision regarding the age of consent in cases of rape. We should keep a watchful eye on our judge-made law, and spare no efforts to protect the rights of helpless women.

DEWAN BAHADUR RAGHUNATH ROW.—And what is to become of the child-widow? Is nothing to be done for her immediately? Do you not know, gentlemen, what a life she leads in our parts—privation of food, of clothing, and of even necessary comforts, observance of fasts which at times extend to 72 hours, enforced absence from every scene of festivity; the enduring of execrations heaped upon her if she unwittingly or unfortunately comes in front of a man, a priest, or a bride; these, I say, become the daily experiences of her life. I say you must agitate for the re-marriage with full Vedic rites of such widows at least. I have watched your discussion in silence, but I can't let it close without putting in a word for the child-widow.

A HINDU ANTIQUARY.—Become a missionary like me, my friend, and devote yourself to her cause, and you will not fail.

Sir T. Madava Row.—I don't think there is any one here that has a word to say in favour of child-widowhood. But let us cut at its very root, and concentrate our efforts on the removal of its cause.

A Hindu Social Reform Missionary.—And now, dear brethren, allow me to offer a humble prayer to the Giver of all Good, for guidance and help. May He, Whose work is all Love, yet all Law,* teach us to fulfil His Law, and fill us with His Love! May He, "Whose Essence is Sacrifice,"† "Who sacrificed himself in created things, and created things in Himself",‡ may He inspire us with self-sacrifice, and turn it into power for good! § May He Who is full, Who remains full even if a full be taken from Him,‖ may He give us a part of His own fulness of life, and help our unborn part to rise higher and higher, by good deeds, and pure thoughts, and holy communion! O Holy One, Who art Brahma, Vishnu, Rudra, Indra, Agni, Vayu, Surya and Soma—O Mighty One, regenerate our being, preserve our true life, deaden us unto sin, bountifully shower Thy grace upon us, warm us with Thy loving kindness, breathe into us a breath of Thine own purity, illumine us with Thine own light, and upheave us with Thine own force! Holy, All-merciful Father, guide our erring footsteps, as Thou didst guide our fathers' of old—forgive our backslidings, and incline Thine ear unto our cry for help! Help us, oh Light of the World, oh Life of Life, to do Thy will, to check the ebb of our national glory, and to spread Thy sunshine in our darkened homes! Spirit of the Universe, Lord Supreme, accept our lowly prayer and bless Thy little children! Shánti!

All—Shánti! Shánti! Shánti!

---

* Browning.

† Muir I.—495.

‡ Muir IV.—25.

§ Muir IV.—52.

‖ Muir IV.—219.

CHAPTER I.

STATEMENTS OF FACT ON THE SUBJECT OF INFANT MARRIAGE.

SECTION I. MADRAS PRESIDENCY.

1. A. SANKARIAH B. A. PRESIDENT, HINDU SABHA, MADRAS.—Freedom to marry girls and widows at any age is not denied now, and was not denied at any time, and the agitators are not just and even honest in interfering with those who do not religiously, or socially, approve of that freedom.

2. K. KRISHNASWAMY RAO, CHIEF JUSTICE, TRAVANCORE.—The existence of the evils of infant-marriage and enforced widowhood......cannot be denied.........................

In countries where marriage is a matter of contract, and the bride has the right of choosing her own partner in pleasure and in sorrow, there will be no necessity for placing any restriction on the right to marry, but in India the *protection* of the *interests* of minor *girls* who are often victims of the caprice and sometimes of the avarice of their guardians, renders it necessary that some restriction must be imposed.

The practice of marrying boys to girls older than themselves seems to be confined to a very small section of low classes, in certain districts, among whom marriage after puberty is not prohibited. Marriage of girls being compulsory and the difficulties of procuring husbands of proper age of the same caste as that of the girl, seem to be the sole reason of the existing practice.

3. H. H. RAMA VARMA, MAHARAJAH OF TRAVANCORE.—I do not for a moment doubt that the majority of these sensible men now consulted, will express their decided opinion against these horrible causes of much misery and 'biting afflictions', to their poor sisters and daughters.

4. C. Ramchandra Aiyar, Sub Judge, Madura.—From my experience of 23 years of several districts in this Presidency, I am in a position to assure the Government that in spite of liberal education, and a painful consciousness on the part of the educated men of the evils of all sorts arising from it, infant marriage has become more numerous than ever, and I should say it has become the mania of the people at large. Even graduates of the University and educated men generally have been disposing of their infant girls of two or three years by marriage, simply from an apprehension that they could scarcely get rich boys or sons of rich men at a future time.

The fashion of the day is that infant girls of rich men are forced upon the sons of rich men with dowry of great value, and that, in a competition of this kind the boy's parents choose the infant who brings them the largest sum as dowry. That a reform in this direction is certainly needed, has been admitted on all hands; but nothing can be done and will be done by the Hindus, if they be left to themselves, even for a century to come. A few of the educated Hindus no doubt take real interest in effecting a reform in this matter, but their exertion is not enough to override the powerful opposition of the masses under the influence of their priests. To substantiate my assertion, I would respectfully ask the Government if there is today any graduate or educated man who as a father of infant girls has not got them married, while they were infants, or if there is any graduate or educated man who has had the moral courage of keeping his daughter unmarried till she had attained her puberty and then getting her married. No one will come forward to say that he has done so............

To render a gift made by a Brahman valid, his wife should sprinkle water on the betel which her husband passes to the donee. During the performance of religious ceremonies his wife is required to stand by, touching him with a holy grass. During the performance of Yogam, a sacrifice of sheep, cow &c., one end of the husband's cloth and one end of the wife's cloth are knit together, and they both move together wherever and on whatever purpose they may move. For all these purposes a betrothed infant girl is considered unqualified, till she attains her puberty, and her marriage is actually consummated.........

If we go today to a college in any district we can hardly find unmarried Brahman boys of 12 or 13 years.................

The belief that a girl attaining puberty before betrothal or marriage loses her caste...............has no legal basis. To show that it is so, I have to refer to the community of Nambudri Brahmans of the West coast, among whom infant marriage is rare, and I should say never takes place.............. In any illom or house of a Nambudri having such unmarried girls, the Patter Brahmans of Pal Ghat, as well as their brethren of the East coast, sit in a line with the Nambudris and take meals which are prepared by such girls.

A majority of boys (in colleges and schools) are Brahmans, and infant marriage is greatly among them, and to a fearful extent, and this vice has been copied by other caste people who try to imitate them in every respect.

5. C. Subbaraya Aiyar, B.A., B.L., Third Judge, Appellate Court, Ernacollum.—Referring to the census statistics of 1881, it will be found, on a comparison of figures, that the custom of early marriage is prevalent specially among the Brahmans. To quote from the census report, "some are married before seven and nearly all are married before 10." The figures suggest that between 6 and 7 is the average age of marriage for females among Brahmans. This has the natural result of a high percentage of widows, and we find that nearly 1/3rd of the Brahman women are widows......Out of a total of 80,000 widows under twenty, 60,000 belong to the Brahman caste, and 20,000 only to other castes.

Early marriages, brought about under the discriminating and fostering care of Hindu parents, have not failed to lead to happy unions, securing to the married couples social and domestic felicity...........I have heard from my European friends that, even in England and other civilized countries, where freedom of choice and liberty of action are enjoyed in the highest degree by the contracting parties, marriage is a lottery in which more blanks are drawn than prizes.

6. S. Subbramania Aiyar, Vakil, High Court.—To be brief, Mr. Malabari has not exaggerated the evil effects of the pernicious practice of marrying boys and girls before they attain proper age, now obtaining among a large section of the Hindu community. The most orthodox cannot deny that the evil is a real evil having a most degenerating influence on the social, moral, intellectual, and physical well-being of society. It is however gratifying to find, that there is a strong reaction in the minds of the educated classes in this matter, and the percentage of such marriages is on the decrease.

7. Chentsal Rao, Superintendent of Stationery.—According to custom which is regarded, I think, erroneously, as the law, every girl has to be married before she atttains her puberty, and if she is not so married she loses her caste. Girls in this country usually attain puberty at 12 or 13, and sometimes even so early as 11, so that the latest period up to which a girl can be safely kept unmarried is 10............................ In my humble opinion it is far better that a boy of 16 or 17 marries a girl of 8 or 9, than that a youth of 21 or 22 years marries a girl of 9 or 10.

As regards marriages of infant girls with old men, I certainly think it is a matter in which Government can interfere, without provoking the slightest suspicion in the minds of intelligent natives. I have known cases in which girls of 8 or 9 years have been given in marriage, for the sake of money, to men of 60 years, but such cases are so very few that the interference of Government is hardly called for. If Government is to interfere at all, it must be by legislating that such marriages are illegal.

In this part of the country, there are but very few cases in which older girls are married to younger men, and the matter hardly calls for legislation. I have heard of such marriages among the Goundens of Coimbature.

8. M. TILLAINNAYAGAM PILLAI, DEPUTY COLLECTOR, MADURA.—Infant marriage is largely practised more among the Brahmans than other castes. Komattis and high caste Vellalas have followed this example of the Brahmans. Early marriage is however almost unknown to the low caste Sudras, among whom remarriage of widows is also permitted...... ....

When 9 per cent is the average of widows in the European countries, 21 is the percentage obtaining in India, and 31 the percentage among the Brahmans..........................

Instances are not wanting where young men have been spoiled by early marriage. Many have given up their studies, unable to find time for the same, having been burdened with the cares of conjugal life. They lose their spirits, and are bound down to their houses, and in fact become less useful to society than they would otherwise be. Early marriage is therefore an obstruction to the progress of society. I have heard a highly talented candidate for the University examination tell his friends that, he would have answered some of the questions better had he not been anxious about the condition of his sick child. If this is the case even with grown up men a raw youth married early and blessed with children, must fcol worse under the circumstances. Besides, early marriage affects the general health of the married couple, and their progeny, and the result is, we have a weak and imbecile nation.

....

A man approaching the grave can easily secure a girl of 9 or 10 years for his partner, provided he makes up his mind to pay a handsome price for the creature. A leper can in the same way easily secure the hand of a fair maid for money.

9. T. PATTABHIRAM, HEAD SERISHTADAR, TRICHINOPOLY COLLECTORATE.—Among all castes of Hindus other than Brahmans and Komattis, infant marriages are rare and exceptional and not the rule.......................................

The Brahmans bear the percentage of 4·94 to the whole population of India as detailed in the margin.

Census Report Vol. I p. 308.

Madras	Presidency...	3·94
Bombay	"	...4·83
Bengal	"	...6·06
		3)14·83
		4·94

The Brahman female population for the whole of India is 6,606,000; of this 31 percent or 2,047,860, are widows, and 21⅔ per cent or 1,436,805 are unmarried.

Thus both unmarried and widowed females of the Brahman class come up to 52⅔ per cent of the female Brahman population, while in Europe the single and widowed females come up to 67 per cent of the total female population there, or 14⅓ per cent more (Census Report p. 94 Vol. I.)

SECTION II. BOMBAY PRESIDENCY.

10. MAHIPATRAM RUPRAM, C.I.E. PRINCIPAL, TRAINING COLLEGE, AHMEDABAD.—Now and then we see an infant girl married to a rich old man, for the sake of his money, and, in some castes, especially the Patidar caste in the Ahmedabad and Kaira Collectorates, and the Anavala Desai caste in the Surat Collectorate and Gaekwad territory in Southern Gujarat, a boy of 6 or 8 is frequently married to a girl of 12 or 16, though, seldom, I believe, from any wicked designs. Generally such marriages are contracted from family pride. In other castes disparity of age also prevails to a more or less extent. Bridgrooms are several years younger than their brides. Little girls are sometimes married to old men also........................

The harm done by the custom of infant marriage is really great, and Mr. Malabari has not at all overstated the mischief arising from it.

11. NANDSHANKAR, ASSISTANT JOINT ADMINISTRATOR, RAJPIPLA.—The baneful effects of early and ill assorted marriages, are in some cases felt and acknowledged even by the uneducated mass of Hindus; but so powerful is the hold which the doctrine of fatalism or predestination has on their minds that,

unfortunate marriages are regarded rather as the inevitable decrees of fate, than the result of their own folly or indiscretion.

The custom is almost unknown among the aborigines of Gujrat; and among the upper class of Rajputs, the anxiety evinced by the parents to secure husbands for their daughters of a class higher and nobler than themselves, operates in some cases as a check upon this practice. Marrigeable girls among some sections of the Shravak Community, and a few sub-divisions of Brahmans, are regarded as marketable commodities, whose value rises with age. Girls 13 or 14 years of age are, when they are with their parents, regarded as a "bundle of snakes," whose presence is attended with more or less risk, and hence their eagerness to keep them with their husbands, before their passions are developed................

So long as the Hindus consider it an act of merit or honour to give away their daughters in marriage before they arrive at the age of puberty, so long as they are anxious to consummate marriage before their constitution is developed, so long as they are solicitous of marrying their sons in boyhood, and of taking part in the frolics and festivities attending the marriage of their sons and daughters, during the precarious terms of the lives of themselves or other aged members of their families, and so long as parents are eager to make money out of the marriages of their daughters, it is almost impossible to devise measures calculated to discourage child-marriages or ill-assorted unions, without offending the moral susceptibilities of the orthodox portion of the Hindu community.

Prolonged virginity among Hindu females is not visited with excommunication.

12. Lallubhai Nandlal, Native Assistant to the Commissioner, Northern Division.—There is no such thing as marrying two infants together except on very rare occasions ....
Among the higher caste people, girls are generally married from

between the age of 7 to 10, the bridegroom being a little older. It is among the people of the middle caste, that infant betrothal is carried on to a certain extent.

13. GURSHIDAPA VIRBASAPA, DEPUTY COLLECTOR, BELGAUM, (A LINGAYAT.)—From my knowledge which extends only to the Southern Division, I find that infant marriages are of rare occurence now-a-days, and that child marriages too are becoming scarce, as people have begun to understand that such marriages end in unhappiness. By child marriage I mean marriage celebrated before a female child is 11 years old. In India owing to climatic causes we have precocious maturity and precocious old age, while this is not the case in Europe and other cold countries. A female child generally arrives at puberty at the age of 12, and a girl arriving at the age of 12 cannot be called in this country a child, but she is at this age a young woman.

It may be noted here that, however early the marriage may take place, consummation, as a rule, never takes place before the girl arrives at maturity, and that the husband of the girl is always older than the girl by some years. Moreover child marriages do not affect those classes in which widow marriages are allowed.

14. NARAYEN BHIKAJI, DEPUTY COLLECTOR, NASIK.—I am fully acquainted with the customs obtaining in the Deccan and Carnatic. Marriages..................of big grown up girls of 12 to 15 years of age, betrothed to boys of 8 to 10 do not occur therein. An elderly woman is considered in the light of a mother, and therefore the boy's age always exceeds that of the girl by 3 to 6 years In *very rare* cases it is equal, but in no case less than that of the girl, in the Deccan and the Southern Mahratta country.

While employed in the Ahmedabad District, I had a Magisterial case before me in which a big grown up Kunbi girl having been betrothed to a small boy, he was poisoned by the friend of the girl when she arrived at maturity. Cases of this kind occur sometimes in Gujrat, but not in the Deccan and Karnatic.

15. K. C. Bedakkar LL. B. Deputy Registrar, High Court.—Mr. Malabari's complaint against the parents of boys of tender age married to elder girls, is a gratuitous slander upon Hindu society. Such marriages, so far as I know, are more common in the section of the caste of the Surat Anavlas called Desais. With this community I am well acquainted, and I assert, without fear of contradiction, that it is not guilty of the criminal arrangement insinuated by Mr. Malbari. Rare instances of misconduct may be found among Desais, but they will also be found elsewhere.

16. Trimalrao Venkatesh, Inamdar at Dharwar.—It is true that infant marriages have already ruined Indian society to a very great extent, and unless put a stop to, will do more harm.

Boys and girls, under the age of 10 years, have no idea of what marriage means, and what its consequences will be, and do not express any wish to be married. They only know that they are well-dressed, and fed, and led through several processions of music, dances of dancing girls, fire-works &c., and that they are married. It is the parents, and specially the mothers, sisters and other female members of the infant brides and bridegrooms, that really wish their infant children were married, not so much for the purpose of getting them married, but more for the sake of enjoying the fun and pleasure of going through the ceremonies attendant upon the marriages.

Infant marriages take place mostly among the rich, and not to that extent among the poorer classes.

17. Venayek Vasudev.—According to my information, there is now a considerable decrease in the number of infant marriages compared with past years.

18. Hariparsad Santokram, Desai of Bhavnagar.—What actually takes place in most cases in Gujrat and Kathiawar, is that the parents of the brides select a suitable person, and go through the ceremony of Veshval or betrothal. The actual marriage is usually deferred to a future date convenient to both

the parties. It often happens that in the meantime the brides and the bridegrooms grow up. If however they have not come of age, the actual consummation is put off a few months or years as circumstances require, and when the time is ripe, the ceremony of Ana Valva is performed, and from that time the pair live as man and wife.................................

In the Maharashtra and northern Canara, which form the other part of the Bombay Presidency, marriages are celebrated early, but the day of consummation is put off sometimes one, two, and even four years, to allow the pair to attain maturity. Their physique therefore remains unimpaired, and they are able to maintain their traditionary repute for activity and political agitation.

19. HURRICHUND SADASIVJI HATE A.M.I.C.E.—Early marriage is undoubtedly a great social evil in the native community. It tends to the physical deterioration of the race, to retard intellectual progress, to sap the foundation of mental and moral energies, to check the spirit of travel in foreign lands, and enterprise, to bring about ill-matched alliances, to produce evils of over-population, to burden one too early with the cares and responsibilities of a family, and in cases of girls to enforced widowhood.

20. BHASKARRAO BALKRISHNAJI PITALE AND NANA MOROBA.—We beg to observe that in the higher castes of the Hindu community only, the system of early marriages and that of widow celibacy exists.

In this indigent country, the practice of living together under one roof and under one head, is a great boon to Hindus, and early marriages (not infant marriages) considerably contribute towards attaining this end.

A woman introduced into the family at the age of about twenty, will not easily yield to the orders, wishes, whims and caprices of the old ladies of the family. She will have no sympathy for them, nor will they have any for her, while a young girl at the age of 12 or so, introduced into the family will soon be attached to it. Sympathy for each other will reciprocally be generated in both. On the other hand, in the case of a woman, the chances of a rupture are imminent. This will entail dismemberment of the family and of the family estate.

21. BHAWOO MANSARAM, NAIK, POONA.—The custom of early marriages is gradually dying out of itself.

22. PREMCHAND ROYCHAND.—A Hindu girl while she is but eight or ten, is joined to a boy who is equally ignorant of the world. Even in his minority he becomes a father. We are eyewitnesses to innumerable instances of sickly children, with poverty staring in the face of their parents.................I am aware of many instances of promising youths, leaving off their student life, and ready to be employed on any insignificant post. The reason is obvious. The boy not having means to command a liberal purse for the maintenance of conjugal feliciy, is driven to suffer any kind of humiliation to be able to earn something. It is then that, in the eyes of his relations, he is regarded as a man of the world. As time passes, he becomes the head of his family. He is thus ushered into the world at an unnatural age. Mr. Malabari's picture of the state of a Hindu bridegroom is in fact no exaggeration. The area of my experience may be limited, but so far as Gujrat communities are concerned, I can distinctly point to instances of men dying under the pressure of such suffering.

23. VEERCHAND DIPCHAND.—As regards Infant Marriage this practice has been in existence in India for ages in all sects, including Parsis and Mahomadans.........The principal obstacle in the way of the suppression of such practice is the caste system among Hindus, which divides the community into innumerable ramifications, each in a tangent of its own, and which seriously contracts the area of selection, the more so as intermarriage among blood relations is prohibited with a few exceptions.

24. Mahadeo Wasudeo Burve, Poona.—The system of early or infant marriage no doubt leads to painful results......... Such marriages do take place in some of the higher classes of Hindu Society even up to this day; but as compared with the number of such cases 30 years back, they are now comparatively less, and the tendency of the general public is much opposed to them.

Instances of another form of objectionable marriages viz. of a girl 12 to 15 years old with a boy of 8 to 10, are rare occurrences in the Deccan and Southern parts of the Bombay Presidency.

25. Karsandas Valabdas.—Being a member of a community, in which both the above evil customs are in vogue, I am really so much horror-struck at the disastrous results thereof, that I am almost inclined to suggest to Government to lose no time in suppressing these long existing evils, which have been the source of detriment to social and domestic happiness, and physical deterioration of my country men, by the powerful aid of law...............But I am prevented from doing so by the fact that, under the present circumstances, legal measures in such matters will prove a source of terror and tyranny among the poor and ignorant classes. I therefore cordially approve of the remedies proposed by Mr. Malabari.

26. Diwan Bahadur Manibhai Jusbhai, (Diwan of Cutch.)—There is no doubt that the evils pointed out by Mr. Malabari do exist..............It may, I think, be safely assumed that the educated Hindus, as a class, regard the custom of infant marriage and enforced widowhood as baneful, and that the necessity of adopting some remedial measures in that connection, is fully recognized.....................

In the Kurdva Kanbi caste marriages take place at an interval of 12 years, the custom being based on a supposed oracle of the goddess. Amongst some other castes, it has been customary to celebrate marriages at certain intervals, with a view to ensure a saving of expenditure connected with caste feasts. Some castes again are very limited in extent, and, in some, the number of girls is extremely small. Moreover Hindu parents generally do not keep their daughters unmarried beyond 12 years, and education has as yet made so little progress that in the struggle which the proposed restriction must give rise to, between marriage on one side and higher education on the other, the former will in most cases he preferred to the latter.

27. VURJEEVANDAS MADHAWDASS.—Marriages of boys and girls under the age of puberty, prevail undoubtedly to some extent in this country; but I do not believe that generally speaking they are productive of discord between man and wife, after they come to live together, to a much greater extent than would be the case if the marriages occurred at a later period in life.

28. M. G. RANADE, POONA.—I had good reason to hope that as the result of several meetings held here, a sort of general agreement would be arrived at, among the leaders of native public opinion who were consulted on the subject. So far as the proposal to push on the age limits for boys especially, and also for girls is concerned, I am glad to see that such an agreement has been arrived at............

There can be no doubt that the evils complained of, are not so general nor so great as at first sight they appear to be, nor can it be said that there is no other side to the question. At the same time the statistical argument may be pushed too far, and may serve to blind, when it is intended to enlighten, the vision. Granted that the evils of "Infant Marriage and Enforced Widowhood" affect a much smaller number of individuals, and affect them less rigorously, than Mr. Malabari is inclined to admit, it does not follow that this circumstance in any way diminishes the gravity of the evil as far as it is admitted to exist, or lessen the responsibility of timely and sedative action on the part of those who are called upon to lead social movements in these matters.

After making all allowances, it cannot be denied that Hindu society contrasts very unfavorably with all other civilized races, in both the points noticed so prominently by Mr. Malabari. It is also not denied that early marriage leads to early consummation, and thence to the physical deterioration of the race, that it sits as a heavy weight on our rising generation, enchains their aspirations, denies them the romance and freedom of youth, cools their love of study, checks enterprise, and generally dwarfs their growth, and fills the country with pauperism, bred of over-population by weaklings and sickly people, and lastly that it leads in many cases to all the horrors of early widowhood. All admit that in both these respects reform is desirable. How to achieve it, may be open to question, but the fact itself cannot be denied, and is not denied, even by those who take the extreme view, that some remedial action is possible or desirable. With those who are so wedded to the existing arrangements as to maintain that they are the best possible that can be conceived, it is useless to argue, for they ignore history, they ignore their best traditions, they ignore the dictates of their most solemn religious texts, they violate their natural conscience, and their sense of the fitness of things. They ignore history, traditions, and religious texts, because they know full well that the existing arrangements are later corruptions.........These people violate their natural conscience and their sense of the fitness of things because, while they mumble the old rites and pronounce the old declarations, they virtually trample them under foot,and while the men reserve to themselves all manner of freedom, no such measure of liberty is allowed to the poor women, even when widowed in childhood. These men virtually place themselves out of court in these discussions,and although they are strong in numbers and prejudices, their number will not avail them, and their prejudices are not entitled to much sympathy.

29. Venkat Kango Katti.—I and my brother were joined at the age of 12 by our father, who was a Shastri, to girls who had yet to complete their 7th year. This was the type of marriage in those days, (i.e. 40 years ago); a girl was scarcely allowed to complete her 8th year

without being married. An unmarried Brahmin girl of 10 was then looked on as a shame to her parents, who always tried to conceal her age. This state of things no longer exists. In most of the present marriages the age of the bride is from 8 to 10, and that of the bridegroom from 13 to 15 .... I have a son who will complete his 16th year in September next; he is yet to be married and I have selected for him a girl of 12, (the daughter of a Shastri) with his approval ....I am told however that infant marriages are much in vogue in Gujrat.

30. Rao Bahadur Bholanath Sarabhai.—There s an association here the members of which have taken a pledge not to marry their sons before the age of 16, or if they are to be married before that period, to see that their brides are 5 years younger than they. But on account of difficulties thrown in its way by caste, the association has not been able to fix any age for girls.

It is admitted by all enlightened Hindus that early marriages and unequal matches are mischievous. They believe that early union leads to the production of unhealthy families, and ultimately to the moral and intellectuald eterioration of the whole race.

31. Sakharam Arjun.—Infant marriages as such having reached their crisis are happily now on the wane...........I am aware that Gujrat and parts of the mofussil, far too much removed from the beneficial influences of western culture, occasionally indulge in the suicidal and demoralising luxury of infant marriages; but this very fact rather proves the exception than the rule...........We have therefore to deal not so much with infant marriages as with early marriages..............The baneful effects of early consummation have been so patent and far reaching that, men who would not budge an inch of their orthodoxy in other matters, now willingly defer the consummation of marriage in the case of their children to a pretty long period.

32. S. H. CHIPLONKAR.—Mr. Malabari appears to be under the impression that, the system of infant marriage prevails very largely amongst the Brahmins especially, whereas the truth is that the system is least prevalent amongst the Brahmins, as compared with the non-Brahminical sections of the Hindu community. The system in question is also not confined to the Hindu community only, but is more or less prevalent among the Mahomadans and other native communities, even Parsis not excepted.

As a general rule no Hindu girl is married before she has entered upon her 8th year, and nothing can therefore be more incorrect than to describe all these marriages as infant marriages. I may even add, that, except in Gujrat and the adjoining Native States, infant marriages in the proper and literal sense of that term, are almost unknown. And even there, this system is principally confined to one section of the Hindu community viz. the Kadwa Kanbis, among whom the marriage season comes once in a period of 10 or 12 years............The larger and more predominant caste almost invariably sets the fashion, and thus the contagion spreads. The extent of the evil, for I yield to none in regarding it as an evil all the same, is very limited, and so we must not allow our minds to be carried away by any exaggerated notions on the subject.

During the last 20 years, a good deal has been effected in the direction of discountenancing early marriages, so much so that, as justly observed by the learned writer of the Baroda Census Report, the average marriage age for girls among the Hindus is now between 10 and 11, whereas only 20 years since it was quite different..................During the next 10 or 20 years we shall see a still greater change in the same direction, if the Hindu mind, which is very conservative, and impatient, nay suspicious, of all external influence, does not undergo any revulsion of feeling in consequence of any outside pressure, however benevolent in itself...............I fully agree with Mr. Secretary Mackenzie in the sound advice he has given to Mr. Malabari, who would do well to re-read and specially study the

Chapter on Spain in the second Volume of Buckle's History of civilization in England..

In conclusion I have only to add that, this system of early marriages, which is now prevalent among the Hindus, is an institution of only modern growth. It originated with the last years of the Peishwa dynasty, and received abnormal development in the early years of British administration, so far at least as this part of the country is concerned. Soon after the establishment of schools and colleges, and immediately after the close of the mutiny of 1857, the early pioneers of social reform directed their attention to this among other subjects, and they and their successors have been silently working in the proper direction, with considerable success thus far, and with the prospect of a still greater success in the immediate future.

In this Presidency the average marriage age for Hindu girls is between 10 and 12, or to be more accurate about 10 certainly. Now let us see if this average age at which marriages take place, not only in the Presidency, but as a general rule in all parts of India, can in any sense be said to be very backward, when compared with the minimum marriageable age which is fixed by the English law, and which is considered by that law to be sufficiantly high for giving legal validity to the consent of the contracting parties. The following extract speaks for itself. "The next disability is want of age. This is sufficient to render voidable other contracts, on account of the imbecility of judgment in the infant who contracts; *a fortiori*, therefore it ought to avoid this the most important contract of any. Therefore, if a boy under 14, or a girl under 12 years of age, marries, their marriage is only inchoate and imperfect, and when either of them comes to the age of consent aforesaid, they may disagree, and declare the marriage void, without any divorce or sentence in a court. This is founded in the Civil law. But the Canon law paid a greater regard to the constitution than the age of the parties; for if they were *habiles ad matrimonium* it was a good marriage, whatever their age might be, and in our law it is so far a marriage that, if at the age of consent the

contracting parties agree to continue together, they need not be married again" (Broom's Commentaries on the Law of England Vol. I. page 526)

The following figures are quoted from the last Census Report by this Gentleman.

PROVINCE.	HINDU BOYS.		Percentage.	HINDU GIRLS.		Percentage.
	Total number under 10 years.	Total No. of married and widowed		Total number under 10 years.	Total No. of married and widowed.	
Bengal	6,442,284	357,890	$5\frac{1}{2}$	6,453,697	896,286	14
Berar	329,925	13,632	4	340,726	74,095	$21\frac{3}{4}$
Central Provinces.........	1,107,442	28,727	$2\frac{1}{2}$	1,104,772	88,169	8
Madras	3,523,896	28,467	$\frac{4}{5}$	3,637,908	163,555	$4\frac{1}{2}$
North-Western Provinces	5,075,867	121,596	$2\frac{2}{5}$	4,762,291	258,325	$5\frac{1}{2}$
Punjab	940,722	10,467	$1\frac{1}{9}$	839,893	29,228	$3\frac{1}{2}$
Bombay	1,678,675	42,779	$2\frac{1}{2}$	1,653,495	172,892	$10\frac{1}{2}$

BOYS.	HINDU. GUJERATHI.	GIRLS.
287,261	... ...Under 10 years single... ...	250,113
106,067	... ... 10 to 14 " "	47,833
393,328	... ... Total of Single	297,946
17,587	... ...Under 10 years married... ...	36,582
41,458	... ... 10 to 14 " "	65,812
740	... ...Under 10 " widowed... ...	1,145
1,480	... ... 10 to 11 " "	2,432
61,265	... ...Total of married and widowed... ...	105,971
454,593	... ... Grand Total under 15 years	403,917
14 per cent. ...	...Proportion of married to Total... ...	27 per cent

KONKAN.

Boys		Girls.
318,848	... ...Under 10 years single... ...	293,769
105,337	... ... 10 to 14 „ „ ...	35,137
424,185	... ... Total of Single	328,906
3,798	... ...Under 10 years married... ...	24,047
13,770	... .. 10 to 14 „ „	58,825
98	... ...Under 10 „ widowed... ...	489
359	... ... 10 14 „ „	2,287
18,025	... ...Total of married and widowed... ...	85,648
442,210	... ... Grand Total under 15 years	414,554
4 per cent.	... ...Proportion of married to Total... ...	21 per cent.

DECCAN.

Boys		Girls
643,291	... ...Under 10 years single... ...	594,849
256,678	... ... 10 to 14 „ „	76,250
899,969	... ... Total of Single	671,099
10,936	... ...Under 10 years married... ...	63,077
52,843	... ... 10 to 14 „ „	168,718
525	... ...Under 10 „ widowed... ...	1,453
2,045	... ... 10 to 14 „ „	5,995
66,349	... ...Total of married and widowed... ...	239,243
966,318	... ... Grand Total under 15 years	910,342
7 per cent.	... ...Proportion of married to Total... ...	26 per cent.

WESTERN CARNATIC.

Boys		Girls
286,357	... ...Under 10 years single... ...	252,519
147,185	... ... 10 to 14 „ „	54,406
433,542	... ... Total of single	276,925
6,930	... ...Under 10 years married	39,535
26,959	... ... 10 to 14 „ „	89,532
713	... ...Under 10 „ widowed	2,154
3,671	... ... 10 to 14 „ „	7,988
38,273	... ...Total of married and widowed... ...	139,209
471,815	... ...Grand Total under 15 years	416,134
8 per cent.	....Proportion of married to Total... ...	33 per cent.

SIND.

Boys.		Girls.
47,702 ...	...Under 10 years single... ...	42,180
16,442 ...	... 10 to 14 „ „	7,661
64,144 ...	... ... Total of Single	49,841
328 ...	...Under 10 years married... ...	889
1,628 ...	... 10 to 14 „ „	4,067
3 ...	...Under 10 „ widowed... ...	11
26 ...	... 10 to 14 „ „	70
1,985 ...	...Total of married and widowed... ...	5,037
66,129 ...	... Grand Total under 15 years	54,878
3 per cent. ...	...Proportion of married to Total... ...	9 per cent.

BOMBAY CITY.

Boys		Girls
52,437 ...	...Under 10 years single... ...	47,173
21,606 ...	... 10 to 14 „ „	3,087
74,043 ...	... Total of single	50,260
1,101 ..	...Under 10 years married	3,432
5,849 ...	... 10 to 14 „ „	15,666
10 ...	...Under 10 „ widowed	78
71 ...	... 10 to 14 „ „	294
7,031 ...	...Total of married and widowed	19,470
81,074 ...	...Grand Total under 15 years...	69,730
8 per cent. ...	...Proportion of married to Total... ...	28 per cent.

BOMBAY PRESIDENCY.

Boys		Girls
1,635,896 ...	...Under 10 years single... ...	1,480,603
653,315 ...	... 10 to 14 „ „	224,474
2,289,211 ...	... ... Total of Single	1,705,077
40,690 ...	...Under 10 years married... ...	167,562
142,517 ...	... 10 to 14 „ „	402,620
2,089 ...	...Under 10 „ widowed... ...	5,330
7,652 ...	... 10 to 14 „ „	19,066
192,948 ...	...Total of married and widowed... ...	594,578
2,482,159 ...	... Grand Total under 15 years	2,299,655
8 per cent. ...	...Proportion of married to Total... ...	26 per cent.

33. Rao Sahib Vishram Ramjee Ghollay.—Female children from 7 to 16 years old are commonly married. The girls of high caste Marathas called Maratha proper, remain unmarried in very many instances till 20 or more years. The Brahmins are bound so to speak, to get their girls married before they arrive at the age of puberty, that is about their 12th year, but some girls above that age are to be found unmarried amongst Brahmins also. The average ages at which boys and girls are married amongst us varry from 16 to 20 years in the case of the former, and from 10 to 12 in the case of the latter.

34. R. G. Bhandarkar, Professor of Sanakrit, Deccan College.—Why should we suppose the child marriages, that do take place in Hindu society, to be ill sorted. The parents of the bridegroom and the bride belong to the same caste and same social condition, and from child-hood the girl and the boy are brought up in the belief that, they are destined to be wife and husband, and that their mutual relation is as much the work of nature, and consequently inviolable, as the relation between brother and sister, or parents and children. This belief enters into the formation of their character, and they grow up as wife and husband, and consequently become adapted to each other. Cases of child marriage proving ill sorted afterwards, are therefore extremely rare, and deserve no consideration............The earliest age at which a boy begins to live as husband is 18 or 17, and the girl as wife is 14 or 13, and ordinarily I believe it is higher. It is however extremely rare that a girl begins to bear children before she is 16.

Overpopulation is another evil effect attributed to early marriage; but I believe if we compare an average case of this with a similar one of late marriage, we shall not find the fecundity of the former to be greater.

Though, therefore, I cannot agree with Mr. Malabari in attributing such woeful results to child marriage, I do think that the custom is productive of evil. A young man is too early burdened with the cares and responsibility of a family, and even when his parents, being alive, relieve him of the burden, the excitement and diversion of thought inseparable from a married life, render a single minded devotion to studies and to the improvement of the mind all but impossible. The result is worse in the case of girls. The merest elementary education is all that can be given to them, under the present circumstaces. Their being married when they are 8 or 9 years old, increases also the chance of their becoming child-widows. And I believe that if a young man and a young woman begin to live as husband and wife in all cases when they are 21 or 22 and 16 or 17 respectively, the total physical effect will be better than at present. But I would not avoid the evil, and secure the good, by a legislative measure.

35. Gavrishankar Udeyshankar, (Bhavnagar).—As far as my knowledg extends, infant marriages are not common among the bulk of the Hindu population, but are confined chiefly to a few among the upper classes, such as Brahmins Kshatrayas and Wanias. The prohibition against the remarriage of widows also operates among nearly the same classes, as well as the more respectable of the Rajputs, Grassias, and Patidars.................

I consider 11 years for girls and 15 to 17 for boys to be fairly good marriageable ages for the two sexes, in a tropical country like India.

36. Nagindas Tulsidas.—When there are too many sub-divisions of castes, with strict injunctions against intermarriage outside the sub-division, it is natural that parents become anxious to secure for their sons and daughters suitable wives and husbands, as soon as possible. This has been carried to such an absurd extreme, that in Gujrat and Kathiawar, infants a few months old are married in some castes, where marriages are allowed to be celebrated at certain long intervals. In these castes, even unborn children are married. This is managed thus. When two women are in the family way, to whose children's marriage there is no hin-

drance on account of consanguinity &c., they agree, with their husbands' consent, that if the issue of one is a male child and that of the other a girl, the two unborn children are to be regarded as married. With this understanding, the two mothers go through the ceremony with balls of flowers in their laps. If the issue of both is male or female, the ceremony goes for nothing. Such is the absurd extreme to which the system of infant marriages is carried on. However there is this to atone for it, that remarriages are open to females as well as males in these castes...

The evil (Infant marriage) exists not only among the Hindus but also among the Mahomedans, and even among the Parsis, and to some extent among the uneducated classes. The hot climate has also to answer for the evil to some extent.

37. PANDURANG BALIBHADRA.—With regard to infant-marriages, there cannot be two opinions that they are baneful in the extreme. They sap the foundation of all physical, intellectual, and moral growth. They enfeeble the individual. They degenerate the community. They impoverish the country. But strongly as I would condemn the practice of *infant marriages*, the question is whether *such* marriages are at all frequent or common at the present day.......................So far as my experience goes, I think that the practice has become almost obsolete...................The married couple do not cohabit till they attain the age of puberty. In the Prabhu caste, to which I belong, infant marriages are very rare indeed. Within the last decade I have not seen or heard of any.......................

Most parents find it difficult to secure suitable husbands for their daughters, unless they promise and can afford to pay a good round sum of money (seldom below Rs. 1,000) to the intended bridegroom or his parents. It is now become almost a fashion for one side to demand, and for the other to submit to this payment, as a condition precedent to marriage. The result is, children of poor parents who cannot pay the heavy price, grow up to a mature age, without the chance of marriage.

38. Lakhmidas Khimji.—The picture of evil and disastrous consequences of infant marriage and enforced widowhood drawn by Mr. Malabari in his paper is, in my opinion, true in all its sense, and not at all imaginary, and the evil consequences from these long continued practices among the Hindus are even more than what Mr. Malabari has described.

39. Lalshankar Umiashankar.—Twelve years ago an anti-early-marriage-association was formed at Ahmedabad, of which Mr. Ambalal Sakarlal Desai and myself were secretaries. After a good deal of discussion, it was found that the greater evil was in marrying a boy in his infancy, and that the increase of age in the case of boys would, of itself, lead to improvement in the case of girls. Accordingly the following affirmation was fixed to be the qualification of a member.

"1. That I shall not celebrate the marriage of my son before he completes his 16th year, or that I shall seek for his wife a girl who is at least 5 years younger than himself.

2. That I shall try to delay my daughter's marriage till as high an age as is not objectionable, according to the Shastras."

More than 200 persons from different castes and places in Gujrat became members. Monthly meetings were held, and tracts were issued. A few marriages took place under the rules, but several broke the pledge, saying their caste members in the association being few they were unable to follow the rules. After a few years, some of the energetic members left the place, and the progress became slow. The pamphlets were discontinued, and the association is now only a name. The above experience showed the necessity of making an attempt with one entire caste. While at Sholapur, I found that in the Lingayet community, which consists of more than 5000 inhabitants of the place, and which though commercial, is very backward in education, marriages were taking place at an extremely young age, sometimes while in cradles, and a good deal of useless expense was incurred on such occasions. I discussed the subject with the intelligent leaders of the community, and they adopted some rules.........and got them sanctioned by the whole caste. I am glad to say that some of the rules have immediately come into force, and I hope all will be followed as occasion arises...........

In the Deccan, where there are not so many subdivisions among Brahmins as there are in Gujrat, the sphere of selection is wider and the evil is less. In Gujrat too the evil is not so much in the castes in which the brides are scarce. In families that are considered 'Kulwan,' and in castes where the number of girls is greater than that of boys, the evil is much spread. It therefore seems to me that leaders of castes should be persuaded to introduce the reform in their castes, by making rules according to their requirements.

40. Chaturbhooj Morarji.—Among the Aryan people marriages are celebrated between the 8th and 12th year......... This is just. Some persons marry their daughters before the latter have completed their 6th year. But this is contrary both to the Shastras and usage, because they cannot enjoy connubial happiness.

41. Ram Shastri Dikshit Apte, of Poona.—In the times of former governments, marriages of boys and girls were performed in the same way as they now are, but the people then possessed strong bodily constitutions and lived long. In those times, there existed the undivided family system, and only one member of a family had to look after the maintenance of the whole family, while the others led an easy and quiet sort of life. This state of things was possible, as in those times the people enjoyed landed hereditary incomes, but such not being the case now, one man cannot provide for the maintenance of the whole family. Families have thus been divided, and every man has now to bear the burden of maintaining his own family. To earn a livelihood, the chief resource now left to the people is (government) service, which they can enter only after studying the English language and passing certain examinations. The trouble and anxiety consequent upon these, tells upon the constitution of the younger generation,

who thus become weak and subject to disease. This is the cause of the people's weakness, and infant marriages have nothing to do with it, because though infant marriages are now celebrated, the same are not consummated, until both the husband and the wife have attained the age of maturity. The difference between the ages of the two is also in many cases not inconsiderable. (Gangadhar Shastri gives the same opinion at page 165 of the Selections.)

42. MANMOHANDAS DAYALDAS.—Girls in towns attain puberty, generally speaking, between the ages of 10 and 12, and those in the country between 15 and 18. As regards bearing children, nothing depends upon whether a woman has had natural or unnatural menstruation. It is our belief that a girl who has menstruated unnaturally will be a mother sooner (than one who has menstruated naturally), as is the case with a mango graft which is fed by various manures and chemicals. But it is an indisputable fact, that the fruit of such a graft never equals in quality a fruit that has been naturally borne by a tree. Looking rather minutely into the matter, it appears that, out of the children of the present generation, hardly two per cent can be said to be a fine set of children. It is our belief that, every woman miscarries at least once or twice in the begining. It is past human belief that, the progeny proceeding from originally diseased wombs can ever be strong and healthy, since, according to medical science, unnatural menstruation is a disease.

43. GANGADHAR SHASTRI DATAR OF POONA.—When a girl is married in her childhood, the mind then being stable, her sense of respect towards her husband is strengthened by the advice of her elders, who tell her to look upon her husband as her god, and there thus remains no possibility of her character being afterwards spoilt. When marriages are, however, performed at a late age, the mind being unstable, it is possible the character may be spoilt.

44. PANDIT NARAYEN KESOW VAIDYA.—Of late infant marriages have become a curse to the Hindus ....

Among the higher classes of Hindus especially, girls are married to boys sometimes in their teens, and to old men of 50 or 55.

45. Pandit Guttulal.—The institution of child marriages, that is, marriages in which the bridgroom and the bride are children, and have not attained the marriageable age, is now prevalent in spite of its being opposed to the Shastras and to reason.

46. Gokuldas Kahandas Parekh.—In some cases there are apparently no sub-divisions, but there are degrees in the caste positions of different members, and there is then on the part of parents a strong desire to marry their children, and particularly daughters, in the highest families available. ....In some castes, marriages between members of the same gotra, or between persons otherwise within the prohibited circle of relationship, though prohibited by law, are recognized. The custom of marrying within prohibited degrees is of recent origin; such marriages are in my opionion of doubtful validity. Another practice equally repugnant to the notions of orthodox Hindus, which has arisen from the difficulty of getting a sufficient number of eligible girls, is the very abominable system of exchanges. The family of A can only get a bride for one of its boys from B's family, on condition of A's family giving one of its girls to a boy in B's. In many cases, there is no bride to be got, unless there is a bride for exchange. This practice has gone so far that sometimes when the bride's family has no present necessity for a girl, there are conditions made to the effect that the future female issue of the marrying girl should be at the disposal of the members of her parent's family, for the purpose of procuring in exchange girls for boys that might be born in the family. In same castes no bride can be got except on condition of exchange.

47. Honorable V. N. Mandlik.—There is no enforced widowhood in India, at present. Nor is there any such a general early marriage system prevalent, as can be remedied by Government action, either executive or legislative.

If evidence is of any value, I could cite at least ten times more cases of happy unions in early life, some even beyond the dreams of such writers (as Mr. Malabari). But I refrain. If a healthy mind in a healthy body may be accepted as good evidence, in order to judge of the results of such mrraied life, I could produce the evidence of scores of families over at least 3 generations, producing men able to work at 50, 60 and at ages yet higher. Those who mourn in these days of diseased constitution, or weakened intellects, and perhaps of perverted morals.........must seek the causes of such unhappy results in quarters other than those of these early married Hindus, who have been trained under proper family influences.

48. HIS HIGHNESS THE THAKOR SAHIB OF MORVI.—The evil consequences resulting both directly and indirectly from infant marriages, are very numerous and disastrous.............. Here in our part of the country where the evil is growing as any where else, the most galling of all the results is the growth of sickly generations, and the consequent early old age and grave. These marriages are a stumbling block in the way of study. Of late, I have noticed, with heartfelt regret, several instances, in wich infants that promised to turn out the brightest jewels in their infancy, have had the edges of their intellect and energy blunted, by their being married to brides of equal age at an early age, when they were to find full scope and development. I think there are not, and cannot be, in these days of western civilisation, two opinions as to the enormity of this evil, and that it ought to be put a stop to ....

An old man of 60 or 70 verging on the grave is married, and that too with impunity at present, to a tender girl of 10 or 12, for sheer sake of money.

What horror is this?

49. SHANTARAM NARAYEN.—Statistics have been cited to shew that, the customs complained against apply to a limited section of people. I should say to this, in the first place, that even if the evil is limited in extent, that is no reason

why it should be tolerated, merely because it does not prevail more largely. In the second place, it should be remembered that, in this country, the lower classes regulate their social procedure by the example of the higher classes. Widow marriages being disallowed among the latter as sinful, the lower classes though excepted from the ban, intuitively as it were learn to look upon it with some prejudice, and in illustration of this, one could mention non-Brahmin communities, among whom widow marriage was allowed and prevailed formerly, but who, within living memory, declared themselves against the custom ....
I must further point out what has struck me all along in noticing the several comments made upon his (Mr. Malbari's) paper that, none of his hostile critics has attempted to show that what he calls an evil is not an evil..............This is a point which deserves special notice, as showing that, generally speaking, most agree or feel forced to agree, most, that is, of those who are enlightened, that infant marriage and enforced widowhood are evils. That they are......not only social but economic evils is the best argument that can be used to show that, the State has an interest in mitigating their influence, and in preventing their mischiefs, so far at least as that influence and those mischiefs tend to deteriorate the physical capacities and morality of the communities concerned, and breed.........mischiefs of an economic nature............

50. Jaswantsing, Thakore Sahib of Limbdi.—The baneful consequences of infant marriages have begun to be felt, and other circumstances, such as the poverty of the people &c. are, though imperceptibly, helping the cause of reform by the difficulties thrown in the way of such marriages.

SECTION III. BENGAL PRESIDENCY.

51. C. H. Tawney, Director of Public Instruction.—A large body of medical opinion was collected by the late reformer, Babu Keshub Chandra Sen, to the effect that that limit

(i.e. of marriageable age,) should be 14 years, and it is now the law of the land. There seems to be no doubt that, if a Hindu omits to give his daughter in marriage before the age of puberty, he brings damnation upon 3 generations of ancestors. But there seems to be considerable uncertainty as to the definition of the period of puberty......On the whole it seems to be clear:—(1) That according to educated native opinion in Bengal 14 and 20 are the proper ages for the marriage of women and men respectively. (2) That marriages generally take place before these ages. And (3) that such marriages constitute the evil denounced by reformers as infant marriage.

Several students have already banded themselves into associations, and bound themselves by pledges to remain single until they attain a certain age. The influence of educated, parents is tending in the same direction.

52. C. T. Metcalfe, C.S.I., Commissioner of the Orissa Division.—In Orissa, the evil is less than in Bengal, for here young children are only betrothed, and a second ceremony takes place when the wife is old enough to cohabit with her husband; but in Bengal the infant proceeds at once to her future home. Among the Kandaets and Kurrans of Orissa, infant marriage is not practised at all, and girls and boys attain the age of 16 and 20 before they think of marriage. In some places, such as Tajpore, whole communities are to be found, who do not marry till the girls are 16 and the boys are 20.

53. A. Smith, Commissioner, Presidency Division.—As to the existence of the evils described by him (Mr. Malabari), there can be no doubt. As regards infant marriages, there is a consensus of opinion, as to the limit of marriageable age having been raised, with the progress of education and the widening influence of a healthier public opinion.

54. F. M. Halliday, Commissioner, Patna Division.—The evils of early marriage and enforced widowhood are admitted on all hands, but the means proposed for their removal are generally considered to be neither practicable nor desirable.

55. Babu Kedaresur Roy.—There are people who, if I may so term it, give their daughters in marriage to the highest bidder, who may be too old to marry a girl of 10 or 12 years of age, and depart this life long ere the girl reaches her mature age.

56. Babu Kailash Chandra Bhattacharji, Head Master, Zilla School, Noakhally.—The whole question of 'infant marriage' turns upon the unanimous injunctions of the Shastras to marry girls before the age of puberty........... Generally, the seeking of a bridegroom begins with the girl's slipping into the 7th or 8th year of age, and ordinarily the marriage is consummated with her 10th or 11th year. The feelings of the educated guardians in all communities are against the custom; but no one is, in his own case, prepared yet to put up with the social ignominy, attaching to the departure from a deep-rooted and time-honoured custom, enjoined by the Shastras.

In spite of the social degradation that attaches to the selling of brides, the practice is rather common all over Bengal, and cruelly oppresses certain sections of the community.

57. C. N. Barlow, Commissioner, Bhagulpur Division.—Some of the leading gentlemen, belonging to the orthodox party, make a distinction between the two cases, and suggest that the proposals of Mr. Malabari, involving direct interference by the State with infant marriages, which are not inculcated by the Shastras, might be attempted; but they decline to approve of anything being done to assist the remarriage of widows, as they view the prevailing system upon this head as supported by the sanction of religion.

58. Babu Peary Mohan Sircar.—A Hindu girl generally attains her age of puberty, after she passes her 12th year and before she reaches her 14th; but there is no knowing when such an event will happen. Consequently a Hindu parent is obliged to marry his daughter, at or before the age of 12.

59. Babu Gopal Chunder Mookerjee.—He says "that early marriage cements love from the tender ages of the married people." In his opinion early marriage in boys leads

to no obstruction of their education and progress. To prove this he states "that 9/10 ths. of the University graduates are led through the hymeneal altar."

60. **Babu Hori Mohun Chandra.**—He quotes the following statistics from Mr. Bourdillon's report on the census of 1881 in Bengal.

Statement showing, for children from 5 to 9 years of age, the proportion borne by the married and widowed to every 100 children of that age.

Religions.	Males.		Females.	
	Married.	Widowed.	Married.	Widowed.
Hindus............	10.31	.29	27.12	1.14
Mahomedans	2.26	.06	16.03	.70
Christians	1.40	.02	2.14	.17
Buddhists	·8	.04	2.96	.18
Aboriginals.........	2.27	.04	4.44	.26
All religions	7.32	.20	22.56	.96

Statement showing the number of the married in every 100 persons between 10 and 15 years of age.

	Males.	Females.
Hindus...	23.35	66.59
Mahomedans	9.90	68.59
Christians	4.19	14.87
Buddhists	3.16	23.03
Aboriginals	9.55	26.12
All religions	18.50	65.74

Mr. Bourdillon writes.........."It may be assumed that no marriages take place during the first quinquennial period...... Among that people (i. e. the Hindus) more than 10 boys in every 100, between 5 and 10 years old, are bridegrooms while of the girls 28 in 100, or more than 1 in 4, are wives or widows at an age when, if they were in Europe, they would be in the nursery or the infant school.

The following statistics are also quoted.

Total number of Hindu males and females in all India and the percentage of males and females of different ages from 1 *to* 60 *years.*

	Males.	Females.
Single	39,738,477	25,076,102
Married	40,351,930	40,486,641
Widowed	4,405,808	16,117,135
Total ...	84,496,215	81,679,878
Unspecified	11,513,012	10,248,345
GRAND TOTAL ...	96,009,227	91,928,223

Ages.	Hindus. Males.	Hindus. Females.
0 to 9	26·77	27·29
10 „ 14	12·20	10·11
15 „ 19	8·21	7·69
20 „ 24	8·14	9·12
25 „ 29	9·12	9·36
30 „ 34	8·98	8·96
35 „ 39	5·92	5·38
40 „ 44	6·51	6·53
45 „ 49	3·47	3·25
50 „ 54	4·40	4·73
55 „ 59	1·63	1·61
60 and over	4·65	5·97
TOTAL...	100·00	100·00

Percentage of population of different ages from 1 to 60 years.

Ages.	Italy.		England.	
	Males.	Females.	Males.	Females.
0 to 4	Both sexes 13·82		13·90	13·22
5 „ 9	11·01	10·76	12·41	11·84
10 „ 14	10·16	9·90	11·10	10·49
15 „ 19	8·73	9·31	10·03	10·59
20 „ 24	8·63	8·82	8·80	9·12
25 „ 29	7·63	7·84	7·77	8·00
30 „ 34	7·11	7·25	6·65	6·79
35 „ 39	6·19	6·22	5·89	5·97
40 „ 44	6·14	6·34	5·33	5·45
45 „ 49	5·19	5·13	4·33	4·53
50 „ 54	5·20	5·12	3·84	4·02
55 „ 59	3·33	3·22	3·02	3·18
60 and over	8·97	8·64	6·93	7·80

Male and female population in Bengal and their percentages at different ages from 1 to 60 years.

Ages.	Hindu males.	Hindu females.	Percentage of males.	Percentage of females.
0 to 9	22,578,544	22,874,262	28·47	28·5
10 „ 14			11·15	8.9
15 „ 19			7·70	7·3
20 „ 24			7·37	8 3
25 „ 29			8·99	9·4
30 „ 39			15·16	14·5
40 „ 49			10·2	10·0
50 „ 59			5·9	6·4
60 and upwards...			4·87	6·5
		Total...	99·81	99·8

Mr. Bourdillon also writes: "In point of fact, every member of the female population is given in marriage as soon as she has reached a marriageable age, and the figures representing unmarried females above the age of 15 years, are really largely composed of the prostitutes who form a separate and distinctly definite class, in every district of these Provinces."

61. British Indian Association.—The Committee readily admit that, under certain circumstances, in some castes and certain places, considerable harm is done by the practice of early and ill assorted marriages. Infant marriages, i. e. marriages of girls under 5 years of age, have become exceedingly rare, and the average age of marriage for boys and girls has risen to a marked extent. Enlightened popular opinion...... has already begun to assert itself. The expensiveness of marriages, and the hard struggle for existence, are also affecting the age of Hindu girls, in the same manner. The Committee......... deny that it has been proved that early marriage is the sole or the most important cause of the degeneracy of the native race. Climate, food, hereditary predisposition to disease, injudicious selection in marriage, and other causes of arrested growth, are patent factors in the case, and it is illogical to overlook them.

62. Jessore Indian Association.—We hold that early marriage weakens the physical strength of a nation; it stunts its full growth and development, it affects the courage and energy of the individuals, and brings forth a race of people weak in strength and wanting in hardihood. This is but one side of the picture; its other and brighter side has been overlooked. Mr. Malabari has considered the institution physically only... Its moral influence he has not taken into consideration. It is a most powerful check upon our youths against deviating in wantonness and vice. We are often told that early marriages are likely to be unhappy, on account of the absence of free-will and choice in the married parties, but in our opinion there is very little truth in this assertion. The Hindus are the only nation, among whom matrimonial scandals, and disgraceful breaches between husbands and wives, are rarely heard of. The absence of choice and discretion in the Hindu husbands and wives, is more than compensated by the interest, which their guardians take, in uniting them to suitable matches. The selection by the youths eager for marriage, may be influenced by several transitory considerations, while the sober judgment of their

guardians is above them. Moreover continuous association from their early years, offers sufficient opportunities to the married parties to be acquainted with each other's traits of character and thoughts, and by smoothening their differences, and enhancing their reciprocity, teaches them to assimilate and live joint and peaceful lives.

63. KUMAR PRAMOTHA BHUSHAN DEVA, RAJA OF NALDANGA.—That it (Infant marriage) leads to deterioration of the race, and physical suffering to the young wives and their children, is admitted even by the ancient medical science of the Hindus the Ayur Vedas.

SECTION IV. NORTH-WEST PROVINCES AND OUDH, THE PUNJAB, CENTRAL PROVINCES, BURMA, ASSAM, COORG, HYDRABAD (DECCAN) &c.

64. CHIEF SECRETARY TO GOVERNMENT N. W. P. AND OUDH.—The betrothal of infants, no doubt, gives rise to incompatible unions, and excluds that individual freedom of choice, which Englishmen are accustomed to think essential to happiness in the married state. But this view is not shared by all Western nations; and very many who are opposed to child marriage seem prepared to admit that, the real injury to the community at large is due to premature cohabitation, and not to early betrothal. The Lieutenant Governor and Chief Commissioner is not disposed to underrate the drawbacks of infant marriage. Besides its own peculiar evils, it is responsible for the existence of a large number of widows among the higher castes, and it is entirely reponsible for that form of widowhood in which women have never been wives or mothers.

65. C. K. HAWKINS, DEPUTY COMMISSIONER, AMRITSAR.—I would first observe that infant betrothals and marriages are not specially oriental institutions. They were well known

in Europe at a comparatively recent historical period. They have now disappeared, without any special action on the part of any State.

66. HONOURABLE D. C. BARKLEY, MEMBER OF THE LEGISLATIVE COUNCIL OF THE PUNJAB GOVERNMENT.—The case of the marriage of a girl to a boy who is her junior need not arise from any criminal motive, and when it does, all that can be done is to punish the crime when committed and proved.

In the Punjab at least, early marriages are probably less prevalent among the illiterate masses than among the educated. There are considerable tracts of country in which the customs of the people are opposed to early marriages, and it is usually the higher castes and the people of best social position who consider them most necessary. Where they do not prevail, the physical characteristics of the people are evidently better than where they do.

67. DIWAN RAM NATH, DISTRICT JUDGE, HOSHIARPUR.—No sensible man will deny the truth of Mr. Malabari's remarks, and I will further add that infant marriage is not only fatal to the physical and moral interests of the young couple, but it is to some extent ruinous to the girl's parents, who to please the other party, spend money beyond their means, and thus involve themselves in debts and everlasting troubles.* One of the causes of indebtedness of the agriculturists, jagirdars, and old families is *kurtoot*, or anxiety to get a great name on the occasions of marriage &c., and if a father of a high caste girl does not show his *kurtoot* beyond his means on such occasions, he is sure to expect the displeasure of his daughter's parents-in-law, and his daughter will, during her infancy, receive the hints of the failure and ill-treatment.

68. DENZIL IBBETSON, DIRECTOR OF PUBLIC INSTRUCTION, PUNJAB.—I agree with much that the writer (Mr. Malabari)

* Heavy expenses are not ordinarily made when the marriages are performed of adult males and females, because in such cases the parents of the bridegroom are rather anxious to get their son married, and the son himself rather wants a wife than money.

says of the great evils caused by these two customs. It must be remembered, however, that neither of them is by any means universal in the Punjab. Throughout a large proportion of our area, infant marriage is the exception (Census Report 1881 paragraphs 688 to 690); ....And it must be remembered that infant marriage, if it leads in one way to immorality and suffering, in another way prevents it. Unchastity and offences connected with women are conspicuously more frequent in the west of the Punjab, where infant marriage is the exception, than in the east, where it is the rule................

The form of marriage by which a woman is for purposes of cohabitation the wife of A, while her children by him, are for purposes of inheritance reckoned as the children of B in the next generation, is common enough among semi-civilised races, and is by no means necessarily criminal or immoral. But where it is the exception, it probably does lead to immorality. Our law, however, provides punishment for adultery, and I do not think we can profitably do more.

69. RAI MULRAJ M. A., EXTRA ASSISTANT COMMISSIONER GURDASPUR, PUNJAB.—There cannot be any manner of doubt that infant marriage is a serious evil. It is the cause of many of our social grievances; it goes to increase the number of widows, and has a very injurious influence on the development of both the body and the mind of the nation. Perhaps not a single good word can be said in its favour these days. A large section of my countrymen both Hindus and Mahomedans, would be glad if infant marriage could disappear from the country...

In the Punjab, it is the custom among almost all classes to betroth boys and girls when they are mere infants. Most people have not the courage to refuse an offer of betrothal for their sons, when it comes from the parents of a girl, for fear of getting a bad name among the community to which they belong. Others again hasten to get their sons betrothed, because if a boy grows up unbetrothed it is frequently considered to be due to some defect in the boy or the family, and it then becomes difficult to get the boy betrothed afterwards. On the other hand, the parents of a girl are anxious to betroth her as soon as possible, for if they wait till the girl grows up, they rarely succeed in finding a suitable match for her, all the boys of well-to-do families having been betrothed beforehand. In that case, it becomes necessary always to be on the look-out for a widower of comfortable means, or the girl is given in marriage to a boy of poor parents.

Such considerations induce the parents of boys and girls to betroth their children while mere infants of one, two, or three years.........Parents at the time of betrothing their children are in many cases sincerely of opinion that they will marry their children at a ripe age. But when the girl grows up to the age of 13 or 14 years, she attains the age of puberty , and her parents think it necessary to give her in marriage. But as boys do not attain the age of maturity as early as girls do, the father of the boy finds that his son at the age of 13 or 14 years is a mere stripling, and, if a man of education, he is opposed to the marrirge. He recalls to his mind his declared opinions against early marriage, together with all the evils which follow in its train, but he finds himself powerless, as the parents of the girl press for immediate marriage. He has, therfore, to give his consent against his will, and in spite of his education and conviction. He has to hang down his head before his fellows in thought, who, however, are compelled by the early betrothal of their own sons to play the same part when their turn comes.

Again early marriage increases the chances of widowhood, and has to answer for being the cause of the most miserable class of youthful widows, who have perhaps never even spoken to their husband or seen his face.

70. Chief Commissioner, Central Provinces.—The native gentlemen, both official and unofficial, assert that not a few of Mr. Malabari's statements are exaggerated and sensational; that they are not of universal application; that he fails to correctly estimate the influence which the spread of

education has already exercised both on Hindu men and women; and that the remedies and steps proposed by him are ill-considered, and are likely, if adopted, to work mischief.

71. CHIEF COMMISSIONER, BRITISH BURMA (MR. BERNARD).—Among the people of Burma, whether Burmese, Karens or Talaings, we have no infant marriages. Young men and maidens make love and marry, usually with the parents' consent, any time between the ages of 15 and 23 for the maids, and between 17 and 28 for bachelors. Marriages and remarriages also occur between older parties. Unions between elderly ladies and young men are almost unknown. But comparatively elderly men on remarriage often take wives much younger than themselves. Occasionally a wealthy old man may take a young girl for his second or third wife. But though a plurality of wives is allowed, the feeling of respectable Burman society is against a man who takes more than one wife, unless he be a king or some very highly placed personage, or unless his first wife is childless,

The figures on pages 86 and 91 of Mr. Plowden's Census Report for India, bear out what has been said in the foregoing paragraph. They show that the proportion of widows to the total female population is about the same in Burma as it is in Southern Europe, is less than half the corresponding proportion in the rest of the Indian Empire, and is little more than 1/3rd the proportion for the province of Mysore. Whether it be the result of, or whether it be only coincident with, Burman marriage customs, it is a fact to which Indians as well as Europeans who know Burma will testify, that women occupy a happier, a more important, and a most respectable position in social and family life in Burma than they do in India. In Burma 320 females in 10,000 are able to read and write, as compared with 20 per 1,000 among the Hindus of India, and 16 per 1,000 of the Hindus of Bengal. In Burma the number of women in jail is only 1 per cent. of the total prison population; in the rest of India, according to the most recent returns available, the proportion of female to total prisoners was

5 per cent. Returns of suicides according to sexes for the different provinces of India are not available. But it may be stated that suicides of women are extremely rare, and cases of infanticide are almost unknown in Burma, whereas both crimes are unhappily not uncommon in India.

These contrasts are drawn not to magnify the merits of the Burmese, but because these satisfactory social phenomena are coincident with, though they may not be wholly due to, the absence of infant marriages and of enforced widowhood among the Burmese. Men and women in India, and social reformers in India, may be encouraged by the experience of their sisters and brothers on the east of the Bay of Bengal, to struggle against these ordinances which do so much to blight social life and family happiness among the upper and middle classes in India.......................

It may perhaps be doubtful whether infant or early marriages are......responsible for over population. Very early marriages are more common among the wealthier classes, the great landholders, and the nobles of India, than amongst the cultivating classes and the poor. Sterile marriages are much more frequent among the former classes, and large families are more often seen among the latter classes. The truth probably is that adult marriages would be more likely to, and actually do, yield larger families than infant marriages. Therefore in so far as the multiplication of children may cause over-population, this result is due to adult rather than infant marriages. The circumstance that reproduction occurs more frequently, and a new generation follows the old more rapidly, under a system of infant maariages, does not appreciably affect this position. The Census statistics show that among adult-marrying races, such as the people of Burma, and the aboriginal tribes of the Central India uplands, children are more numerous and the increase of population more numerous, than among the infant-marrying races of Mysore and the Gangetic Doab.

72. CHIEF COMMISSIONER, ASSAM (MR. G. ELIOTT).—Quotes the following from the Assam News.—"As regards infant

marriage, it is almost unknown in the Assam Valley. No girl of any other caste than Brahman is married before she arrives at the age of puberty, and even Brahman girls are seldom disposed of in marriage while under 12 years of age.

73. T. J. Clarke, Chief Commissioner, Coorg.—I find it stated in a small Manual entitled "Coorg Civil Law," published in 1871, that, while in former days among the Coorgs no girl was given in marriage till she had attained the age of puberty, this rule or custom had in recent years become relaxed, and occasionally marriages of girls of 8 years of age, but not less, have been allowed. This statement is confirmed by tho Commissioner of Coorg, who has reported that, while adult marriages prevail generally among the Coorgs and the Gowdas of North Coorg, this practice of infant marriage "has come into vogue within the last 40 years, chiefly to secure a certain provision for daughters," and there is the further reason that the Coorgs have not been superior to the temptation of following the example set by the Brahmins, Rajputs and other caste races, who have come to settle among them in increasing numbers.

While the evil, so for at least as it arises in allowing the consummation of marriage at too early an age, is acknowledged almost universally among educated natives, it is not too much, I submit, to hope that they will in time find means to check and even repress it, by associating themselves together for such an object

74. Lieut. Colonel H. C. A. Szczepanski, Deputy Commissioner, Wun District.—There may be objections to infant marriages, but there are also advantages. The system suits the country, and the late census shows that the results are sufficiently satisfactory, as far as population is concerned; the various races are not deteriorating, every woman is to a certain extent provided for, although in consequence there are many virgin widows. Yet, on the other hand, if it were not for these infant marriages, there would be many unmarried females, and the result from a moral point of view would probably be worse.

........In the present state of female bringing-up and debasement, it would be unsafe to leave girls after a certain age without legitimate means of fulfilling what, to their understanding, is the aim and object of their lives.

75. Luxmon G. Rishi, Deputy Educational Inspector, Basin District.—The objectionable form of marrirge referred to in the concluding portion of Mr. Malabari's note I, (marriage of grown up girls with boys) obtains nowhere, except among Hindus of Northern India who keep the zenana system. Among them the girl cannot be seen by the parents or relatives of the boy, the would-be husband of the girl : and if the boy be the son of a well-to-do person, the parents of the girl purposely conceal her real age, to secure the match and a well organized father-in-law's house for her, no matter if she be older than the boy.

76. Narayen Prabhaker Paraspe, Head Master, Anglo-Vernacular School, Raja Deulgaon.—It is true that a boy, if married before 12, is prevented from prosecuting his studies just 4 or 5 years after the wedding, when the girl generally becomes a woman. It will at the same time be admitted that, native boys feel a desire for sensual enjoyment at the age of 17. When a boy exceeds the 17th or 18th year without means of enjoying carnal pleasure, he is driven to practise an unnatural way of satisfying his desires for sexual congress. The means adopted by the boys are the most detrimental to their health. The most pernicious habit I speak of, is very common among the school boys and the college students. The girl too is supposed to get the menses from 12 to 16, the first and the last years being rare cases of the first appearance of the menses. ....If a girl, especially a Brahmin girl, remain a virgin when she has menstruated, no one will accept her for a wife, and the consequences would be such as to render her life single. Similar difficulties are not found among the Mahrathas and other classes of Hindus, and their girls can be allowed to remain unmarried till they are full grown.

77. Vishnu Moreshwar M. A., Head Master, High School, Akola.—Infant marriage does often entail enforced widowhood,.........Of the two most objectionable forms of in-

fant marriage which Mr. Malabari has noticed, *i. e.* of a young girl with an old man, and of a grown-up girl with a boy younger than herself, the second is pernicious ; but I do not know how it can be prevented. It does not prevail in Maharashtra but, I learn, prevails in certain limited castes in Gujrat. As often the ill-assorted marriages are held for want of boys of proper ages as for the illicit purpose mentioned by Mr. Malabari, and it would be hard for Government to distinguish between the two cases.

78. BAJABA RAMCHANDRA PRADHAN, EDUCATIONAL INSPECTOR, HYDRABAD ASSIGNED DISTRICTS.—Ten years ago it was very rare to find a girl above the age of 8 years, who was not married. There are now many unmarried girls of 10 and 11 years in respectable families. Some of the girls married last year among the Brahmins and the other higher castes were, I know, 13 and 14 years old..............It will be a mistake to suppose that any reform adopted by the higher castes, will not be taken up by the lower and less educated classes of the people.

79. SHRIRAM BHIKAJI JATAR B. A., DIRECTR OF PUBLIC INSTRUCTION, HYDRABAD ASSIGNED DISTRICTS.—I believe that his (Mr. Malabari's) discriptions of the evil effects of early marriage and widow celibacy have been overdrawn; but as the customs he criticises are undoubtedly pernicious, nothing is gained by going minutely into the observations and saying that the evil is not so great as he represents. All reasonable men admit the urgent necessity of some steps for the removal of the evil.

80. WAMAN NARAYEN BAPAT, TAHSILDAR, CHANDUR TALUK.—Even in the present state of things, every good has almost its inseparable factor of evil, and all that humanity is capable of, is to consider both the credit and debit side of every good and evil, and strike the balance if it can...........

In India, for climatic reasons, women and men arrive at the age of puberty much sooner than elsewhere, and the average limit of puberty for women may be fixed at 13, and that for men at 16. All marriages below this limit may be classed as infant or improper marriages.

(This gentleman's elaborate arguments may be represented as follows :—

Evils of infant marriages according to Mr. Malabari.	REPLY.
1. Enforced widowhood.	Infant marriage not responsible for the widowhood of those who have the misfortune of losing husbands of 16 and upwards.
2. Absence of free-will.	The evil has small proportions. Mr. Malabari himself says "The argument of absence of the exercise of free-will may not commend itself readily to all practical reformers"
3. Hobson's choice owing to endogamy in the caste or sub-caste.	"If castes and sub-castes are to exist, one does not perceive how late marriages will prevent these evils."
4. Physical defects or moral taints.	"So long as human nature is not prepared to forget its high descent and lofty destiny, it cannot traffic in human flesh, with that utter oblivion of the demands of decency, with which it enters into other contracts. Hence, in contracting marriages, much will always be left to chance, and little to deliberation and choice......Children are naturally more exposed to observation than adults, and less likely to assist in cheating.
5. The out-growing of husband or wife	"Due care is generally taken to prevent this."
6. Husbands becoming fit for the grave when the wife becomes fit for his home.	These are "rare cases and few and far between."
7. Total or partial absence of physical adaptability or temperament.	"Married life has seldom a complaint to make on the score of physical adaptabili-

ty. As to disparity of temperament, in late marriages outward form will carry everything—adults have little patience for the exercise of cool judgment–and can hide their weakness from each other. In child marriages you can chisel off many of the angularities of temperament by a proper course of treatment. In late marriages one cannot be a disciplinarian, and at the same time a loving husband or wife. Mr. Malabari himself observes that infant minors turn out happy in a large majority of cases."

8. Social alienation.

9. A too early consummation of marriage and its consequences.

"Too early" is vague. No consummation takes place before puberty. Marriages are so arranged, that by the time the boy is 16 the the wife is 13. "That consummation which takes place just when the parties have arrived at the age of puberty, is a direct call of nature, and cannot be early or late. Nature is generally credited with being unerring and perfect. In cases especially when she writes in legible characters, and where it is impossible to misunderstand her, it is not always possible to disregard her. If she is opposed or slighted she knows how to have her revenge. It may be less direct, longer in coming, but it is none the less certain. In these timely consummations if it is nature that calls, we cannot be presumably wrong in res-

10. Breaking down of constitution.

11. Ushering in of disease.

12. Birth of sickly children.

13. Necessity of feeding too many mouths.

14. Poverty.

15. Dependence.

16. A disorganised household leading to sin.

17. Premature death.

18. Unprotected infants.

19. The giving up of studies by the husband

20. Over-population in poverty

21. Contracting of debts to solemnize marriages with eclát.

ponding to her. Hence, we should be disposed to argue that if Hindu children are comparatively more sickly and less robust, it should be the effect of causes other than these wrongly called untimely consummations. It will not do to forget that a strong physical constitution is the product not of one or two, but of several causes combined. Climate, food, habits, and a host of other things go to form it as much as consummations do.''

Consummation not a day too early. Therefore it tends to make the husband more steady, more tractable, and even more studying, than he would be without it.

" Begin early and end early, is a law of nature. If you begin early in begetting children, you must end it early also. Over-population is not yet one of India's standing grievances. If it is, it is the direct result of every well ordered Government, which disturbs nature's operations to restore equilibrium, by either preventing wars. famines, diseases &c., or by minimizing their mischief. In countries where marriages are late, progeny is more numerous, longer lived, and spreads far and wide and like a fig tree.''

Overpopulation and poverty do not go together. England is over populous but not poor. The Sahara Desert is poor, but not over-populous. Over-population is a fear, a danger, a reality, only when the whole habitable world is taken into account. Marriage is rather the occasion than the cause of this spending. Ignorance and not marriage is the root of this evil.

81. RAGHUNATH B. TALVALKAR, B. A., HEAD MASTER, HIGH SCHOOL, AMRAOTI.—No doubt the custom of child marriage prevalent among the Hindus and some other races in this country, leads to many evils, and its abolition would greatly contribute to the progress of the people, material and moral......

It appears from the report of the last census that, among the Hindus the proportion of boys married under 10 years of age to the total number of boys under that age is, in Bengal 5.5 per cent., and is higher than that in other provinces. In Berar that proportion is 4, and in Bombay, 2-5. Similar proportions for girls under 10 are14 per cent. in Bengal, 21·7 in Berar, and 10·5 in Bombay. The Central Provinces, Madras, North-Western Provinces, and the Punjab, show these proportions for boys and girls comparatively lower than those of Bengal, Berar, and Bombay. The precentage of girls married under 10 in Berar, it is to be observed, is the highest. Early marriages in some sections of the Gujrati Brahmins are very rife; but this is only an exception. Now, if these Brahmins are excepted, the number of boys married under 15, in the Bombay Presidency, is 6 per cent., while that of girls married under 15 is not more than 30 per cent.

Our *Shastra*, or caste, requires only, that girls should not remain unmarried after puberty; and, for obvious reasons, this rule is salutary, until education enlightens our females......... I am not sure if over-population is an evil attendant upon early marriage. But surely progeny at early age makes parents dependent, and involves them in cares earlier, and certainly enhances their misery, howsoever caused. The most enormous evil of early marriages or rather of early consummation of marital troth, is, indeed, physical degeneration of parents and their offspring. Family cares deprive a man of his independence and spirit of enterprise, and the earlier these cares beset a man, the sooner he becomes helpless and grovelling. Youth is a formative period of life, and in a country wherein its youths are not free to enjoy their independence a long time, there is no hope of the growth of enterprising and energetic characters. That country must remain far behindhand in the race of material and moral advancement...........

SECTION V. EXTRACTS FROM OPINIONS GIVEN TO MR. MALABARI.

82. HON'BLE J. GIBBS C.S.I., C.I.E.—The former (child marriage) is a practice not confined to Hindus, but is practised by Parsis and Mahomedans also. And having watched it carefully for many years, I am convinced that it results in great physical as well as moral evils. I was first struck with the results of early marriage when I was serving in Gujerat, about 30 years ago. And the inquiries I then made, led me to the conclusion that the physical consequences were very injurious to both sexes. Young mothers became stunted in growth, and often became invalids for life, while children were too often puny and weak. But it was during my residence in Bombay in 1860-62, when I first met poor Karsandas Mulji and heard from him the result of his inquiries, which went much farther than mine had done, that I found my own view terribly confirmed.

83. THE MARQUIS OF RIPON (AUGUST 1886.)—I trust that the day is not far distant, when the reforms which you advocate will be accomplished, and I do not hesitate to say that *the effect of their adoption upon public opinion in England will be of the best kind.*

84. A. MACKENZIE ESQ., SECRETARY TO GOVERNMENT OF INDIA:—I wish you a hearty god-speed in your compaign against these two monstrous evils, which have so long been sapping the morals, the mind, and the physique of India.......... It is quite true that, with much that is hopeful, there is much to discourage those who would fain see India growing. Many of my native friends who were sound enough is theory on the subject of infant marriage, failed when the question came to personal and practical issues. They could be pilots of others, but sank themselves to be castaways. It is because I think such a movement as you desire to inaugurate, would strengthon the knees of such feeble folk, that I especially wish you success

85. SIR STEUART BAYLEY.—That they are both serious evils, no one can doubt, and I believe the evil of them to be generally recognised among the educated Hindus.

86. MANOMOHAN GHOSE.—I look upon the system (of child marriages) as the greatest curse of our country, and entirly agree with you in all that you have said.

87. S. N. TAGORE ESQ., C.S.—The pernicious custom of child marriage ought especially to engage our attention. It is a canker that eats into the vitals of our national existence, and if not removed in time, may lead to the degeneracy and decay of the whole race.

88. DINSHAW ARDESIR TALEYARKHAN.—When girls are scarce in any caste, a grown up youth or an ederly man will not grudge to have the smallest girl in marriage. In fact she would not be within reach, without a large dowry. In a railway train, some time ago, I came across a high caste Hindu gentleman, certainly much over thirty, in company with a girl hardly eleven who was his wife, thin and pale beyond description and a figure of lean flesh and nominal bones, which folded up and fell into deep slumber as soon as the carriage moved. It perplexes me often to know how a renovated spirit can be inwardly induced, to mitigate premature womanhood, and not omitting such manhood too...

And yet it is a wonder, how this nation has succeeded, for ages, in preserving such a marked harmony of their homes. If we have weakly children, the homes at least are happy, contented, well regulated and economical. We must be careful in not losing this natural feature, while we cautiously attempt to bring about a new good......................................

Our English ideas actually jar with their sympathies, their antipathies, and all the important affections of their heart and head. The boys and girls have no world of their own, which we delude ourselves by believing they would have, as soon as we give it to them. They are the creatures of their parents, brought up in the time-honoured instincts, associations and motives of caste organisms.

89. Rao Bahadur Sirdar Gopalrao Hari Deshmukh, late Member of the Legislative Council, Bombay:—With regard to early marriage, I consider it a most pernicious custom which makes the nation very weak. It is necessary that in a country, there should be a number of bachelors who would venture upon enterprize, foreign travel &c. What makes Hindus so feeble, is the custom of early marriage. They have hardly strength either to become soldiers, or to cultivate land, or to go for trade to foreign countries. They are unfit as colonizers. Every man has a family. Even little boys are burdened with wives and children. A girl cannot be kept unmarried beyond ten years: hence parents are very anxious at any cost to get her wedded, even to an old man or a sickly youth. The consequence of this is, that the race is being gradually deteriorated. Children die soon, and there are more widows now than there were 50 years ago. The evil is very great, and is corroding the very vitals of the nation.........At present women have no status in society, and they are made to give a silent consent to all cruelties.

90. N. C. Biswas First English Teacher, Government Model School, Calcutta.—In Bengal, infant marriage is countenanced by low caste Hindus. This abominable custom,

I am happy to say, does not nowadays suit the taste of the upper ten of the Hindu community.

91. Rao Bahadur Madhav W. Shirgaonkar, Joint Administrator of Miraj.—I condemn infant marriages, not because I think that they afterwards prove unhappy—which statement I will not accept unsupported by statistics—but because such marriages increase infant widows, and the issues of such unions are not such as they otherwise would be, if marriages take place in mature age.

92. Col. E. W. West, Political Agent, Kathiawar.—I know well the miseries of these infant marriages. I have seen often puny striplings, the fathers of still more puny and feeble offspring, and I have, on various occasions, tried to impress on my native friends, that the reason for the energy of the Teutonic races may be found in the practice which Tacitus remarked many centuries ago, "Sera juventum venus adeoque inexhausta pubertas." I have known many cases of old men marrying girls not yet emerged from childhood, and it needs but little knowledge of human nature to realise the misery, during the husband's life time, and of Hindu ways, to realize the misery, after his death, of the girl. When I have referred to such cases in conversation with native friends, they have always been ready to acknowledge the wretchedness that such customs produce, while they invariably deplore their inability to deviate from custom.

93. Keshavlal Madhavdas Esq., (Rutlam.)—Early Marriages are a novel institution, which is not observable except in the East. It makes the whole nation altogether weak and unfit for enterprise.

94. Ramanujchari, m. a., b. l., Vice-Principal Maharaja's College, Vizranagram.—The thing complained of, is the practice of the selling of girls by their parents or other near relatives, and it has become so rife in these parts of the country, that girls are disposed of in marriage to the highest bidders, like goods at an auction sale without reserve, every other consideration being subordinated to that of money.

Girls are married, as a rule, before they attain their 8th or 9th year—an age when they are utterly incompetent to comprehend the character of the contract they enter into; unmarried maidens of ten or eleven form an exception, the circumstances giving rise to such an exception being the absence of suiters willing to pay the price demanded, coupled with a strong hope on the part of the guardians of girls to realize larger sums by the postponement of the marriage..............

It is thus evident that maiden-owners are determined upon deriving a pecuniary advantage, present or prospective, as the case may be......................

The evil custom of marrying young girls whose ages range from 6 months up to 12 years.........obtains among all classes of the people, especially among the Brahmins in Southern India.

The connection existing between the disposal of maidens in marriage to the highest bidders, and slavery, has been strangely overlooked. The practice above alluded to, involves 1st the selling outright of a girl for a pecuniary consideration, 2nd absence of will on the part of the subject, the very elements which enter into the composition of slavery. As pecuniary consideration is generally permitted to over-ride every other, the highest bidder, though he may be subject to grievous mental or bodily defects, is sure to carry the day, in spite of the feeble voice of opposition, raised occasionally on the part of the infant victim.

94. Surgeon Major D. N. Parekh, Chief Physician, Gokuldas Tejpal Hospital Bombay.—I fully and most cordially and actively endorse your views. I am placed in a position where I can be a daily witness to the misery of the children of the poor and of their infant parents, if I might use that expression. I see every day the dire results of early marriages on the constitutions of women and children, who throng my Hospital ....Of all females of the lower classes to be met with in India, the Hindu female is the gentlest, the meekest, the least complaining, and the most unmercifully trodden down creature,

and therefore the most deserving of the sympathy of right thinking men.

I consider that, in India, no woman outght to marry under the age of 15, and no man under the age of 20, looking at it in a healt h point of view. What is good for the individual's health is good for the health of the community, and indirectly beneficial to the State. There is a great deal of sickness and mortality and difficulty in the act of child-birth, due to imperfect consolidation of the bones of the pelvis at the tender ages at which women, in consequence of early marriages, give birth to children. The heads of the children of young mothers are also unduly pressed upon, and so either the children die prematurely, or grow feeble, both in body and mind, and turn out helpless idiots. There is a greater amount of sickness and mortality due to poverty of blood, caused by want of food, the necessary consequence of the struggle for existence; and the greater the number of children, the greater the tax on the physical constitution of the parent, and on the poor purse of the working parent. No sight is more pitiable than that of a young half-starved mother with one child at the breast sucking away her very life, and three or four others worrying away her life; and such a sight is by no means a rare one; it is a very common one. No sight more grotesque, but by no means any the less pitiable, therefore, than that of a poor student struggling for university honours, who wanting his thoughts concentrated on his infinitesimal calculus finds them wandering away, and lighting on his baby's teething troubles, and his other children's school fees, or marriage ceremonies. And yet such a sight is not unfamiliar to those who move in Hindu society.

95. P. Desai.—According to the custom now obtaining amongst us, Hindu parents are often compelled to get their daughters married, when they are scarcely six or seven years of age, to boys of whom they know little or nothing. Shortly after their marriage, they are taken to the homes of their boy-husbands. At about twelve or thirteen they become mothers

of one or two sickly children, and their life is then necessarily spent in looking after household affairs, and often in performing, in higher classes, trivial religious duties.

96. PANDIT BADRI DUTT JOSHI, POLITICAL PENSIONER, ALMORA.—It was scientifically proved by medical men in India, in the days of yore, that infant marriage proves injurious to the physical constitution of both parties, as well as to their progeny. The other day talking to a native physician in my neighbourhood on this subject, I heard him repeat a *sloka* (verse) from Soosroot (a work on medicine), stating that up to the age of 25 in man, and 16 in girl, the bones and vital fluids do not reach complete development, and consequently any wasting of the latter before that, should be discouraged. He further told me that Slokas of this nature are found scattered all over works on medicine by Soosroot and others. Besides this, the law books of Manu and Jajnavalk, for whom our Hindus have great respect, and consider them as the highest authorities on the Shastras, do not enjoin early marriage, nor do the Vedas, the most sacred books of the Aryans.

How does it (the Native Press) expect that a native gentleman of 25, weakened by the wears and tears of a couple of wives and half a dozen children, would leave home to go to the North-west frontier or the Soudan, and there command a division fighting with the enemy of Her Majesty the Empress of India?

I am very sorry to see and hear of many men who don't hesitate to dine at Hôtels, use English hats and pantaloons, English soap, biscuits, and brandy, and thereby lose religion, nationality, money, and respect, and call this reform, which they are spreading in the country. But what would be a real reform, they have thrown into the background, and quite neglected.

97. HON'BLE MR. KASHINATH T. TELANG, M.A., L.L.B.—Those conclusions may be thus formulated. First that neither caste nor Shastra, as popularly understood, exacts anything

more than that girls should not remain unmarried after attaining puberty. Second that neither caste nor Shastra, as popularly understood, has anything to say in the matter of consummation of marriage. And third, that reform is most urgently called for in regard to the time of consummation, and not so much in regard to the time of marriage.

Upon these conclusions, the question arises–If caste and Shas tra are alike out of the way, what is it that stands in the way of the reform here pointed out? My answer is, that the obstacle is in the family.........The man who wants to initiate this reform finds his difficulties neither in the Shastras, which are only imperfectly, if at all, understood, nor in the caste, which, as such, has not claimed to exercise jurisdction in the matter, but in those dearest and nearest to him, in his family, and among his relations. To many of these, the proposed new departure is distasteful, first, because it is a new departure; secondly, because it is looked upon as calculated to defer the enjoyment of the great blessing of having a son; and thirdly, though this perhaps only to a small extent, because it is calculated to interfere with the *eclàt* of the celebration of the "second marriage."

98. NAVALRAM LAKSHMIRAM, PRINCIPAL RAJKOT TRAINING COLLEGE.—I look upon early marriage as the curse of Aryavarta, which deteriorating its noble race, has contributed so greatly to its complete effacement as a nation from the political world. Its disastrous influences are still at work in almost every family, in one form or another, throughout the length and breadth of Gujarat* at least, as I can testify from my own personal knowledge. The evil is of course more prevalent in towns and among the upper classes, but any where it will be a real phenomenon to see a girl of 14 who is not already married. Generally all classes give away their daughters, in marriage before they have completed their 11th year...........The com-

* When I say Gujarat I don't include Kattywar, where the marriageable age or both sexes is a little higher; the Rajputs also form a noteworthy exception in many respects.

mon saying "my children were betrothed while in their cradle yet," is the proud expression of the completely satisfied aspirations of a Gujarati parent. I am afraid of being disbelieved by a foreigner, when I say that sometimes betrothals are made even before the children are born, but such is the actual fact, of which any can convince himself by a little inquiry at Ahmedabad, or some other place where Kadwa Kunbis (who have this peculiar custom) are congregated in any large numbers.

99. G. E. Ward Esq., Collector, Jhansi.—There are probably among those interested in the cause many barristers and pleaders of ability. It will be a suitable task for them to examine the existing law, so far as it affects the institutions you seek to destroy, and use their efforts to secure justice in individual cases, and to obtain definite rulings upon points which are at all obscure. I have known cases in which the husband of a woman married for the second time, has been refused redress under S. 498 I.P.C. on the ground that the second marriage was not celebrated with the ceremonials prescribed for first marriages. In my opinion, this was a decided error, but the point is one upon which a trained advocate might have much to urge. What I wish to point out is, that when the effect of the existing law has been tested by the action of the courts after a systematic exposition of the arguments best calculated to forward your object, and by the accumulation of specific cases in which you are of opionion that the existing law in any way supports the institutions you condemn, or does not act harmoniously with the wishes of the best informed social reformers, you will be in a far better position than you are now to recommend any change in the law, and at the same time public opinion will have been much influenced in your favour. I trust that your national association for social reform may soon be established, and that it may be truly national.

100. G. H. R. Hart Esq., Private Secretary to H. E. Sir James Fergusson, Governor of Bombay.—Sir James Fergusson's own opinion upon the questions discussed in your papers is that held, he supposes, by every European, that infant

marriages do violence to nature itself, set at naught the rights of women as human beings, and are calculated to produce manifold evils; while enforced widowhood entails undeserved misery and frequently leads to crime.

101. A. O. HUME ESQ.—Most entirely do I agree with you that much misery results from these customs (infant marriage and enforced widowhood), that in the present day (whatever may have been the case in times long past) the evil generated by them far outweighs any good with which they can justly be credited—that yearly this disproportion will increase, and that their abolition is even now an object in every way worthy to be aimed at.................... ....

Though I admit that the evil does on the whole outweigh the good, it is not fair to our people to allow it to be supposed that they are so helplessly blind, as to cling to institutions which are utterly and unmitigatedly bad. In the existing state of the native social problem, no really impartial competent judge will, I believe, deny that, in many cases, these institutions, even yet, work fairly well. There are millions of cases in which early marriages are believed to be daily proving happy ones, and in which consummation having been deferred by the parents (and this my friends say, is the usual case) till a reasonable age (I mean for Asiatic girls), the progeny are, so far as we can judge, perfectly healthy, physically and mentally,

A native friend writes to me.—"The wife, transplanted to her husband's home at a tender age, forgets the ties that bound her to the parental hearth, and by the time she comes of age, is perfectly naturalized in her adopted family, and though she is allowed no wifely intercourse with her husband until she attains a fitting age, still the husband and wife have constant opportunities of assimilating each other's natures, and growing, as it were, into one, so that when the real marriage takes place, the love they feel for each other is not merely passion, but is mingled with far higher and purer feeling. Misfortunes cannot alienate our wives, they have no frowns for us, even though we commit the most heinous crimes, or ill-treat or sin against themselves. Those ignorant of our inner life call this a vile subjugation, and say that we have made our wives our slaves; but those who live amongst us know, that it is the result of that deep seated affection that springs from early association and religious (if you will, superstitious) teaching. Where will you find a wife so true and contented as a Hindu's? Where more purity of thought or more religious fervour than in the Hindu women of respectable families? Our men alas! may be materialists, atheists, immoral, base, but our women are goodness in human shape, and why? Because they have been shown an object on which to concentrate the entire love and veneration of their natures, at a time when their pure hearts were unsullied by any other impressions or ideas, and taught to look up to their husbands, whose faces they could only look on after many solemn ceremonies, as their guardians, protectors, and gods."

Every thing in this world has its darker and brighter sides, and the blackest cloud has some silver lining; and though my friend in his happy husbandhood (for his has been, I know, a happy infant marriage) generalizes too enthusiastically from his own experience, still he has some foundation for his contention; and infant marriage (though fraught with grievous misery in too many cases, though a customs marked for extinction, and daily becoming more and more of an anachronism, and more and more of an evil, taking its results as a whole) has not yet become that unmitigated curse, unrelieved by redeeming features, which, forgive me if I say so, your vigorous onslaught would, it seems to me, lead the European readers to believe.

Do you remember Uncle Tom's Cabin?............But for Uncle Tom's Cabin, I fully believe that slavery would have been abolished before now, and without any civil war.

102. Hiranand Khemsing B. A. Hyderabad. (Sindh).—Gold is the chief motive of many parents in our

marriages; every other consideration of suitableness, age, education, and a fair face, being sacrificed to this powerful incentive. On account of extreme divisions of caste, and on account of reluctance or rather impossibility of our marrying from another caste, girls for marriage are generally scarce, and hence follows their sale to the highest-bidder. But it is quite the contrary with the Amil community to which I belong. Here we have a regular sale of boys to the highest bidder who has a daughter or two to dispose of. The reason is that the rules of the Amil Panchayat do not prevent them from marrying their boys with girls from other Hindu classes of Sind...........The Amils are thus free to import girls, but not export their own...........The number of girls and boys for marriage being out of proportion, a sale of boys follows.

103. LILARAM VATANMAL, SUB-JUDGE, KARACHI DISTRICT.—That the two vices you have so ably exposed do exist, even to the extent shown by you, is a fact that every educated Hindu of some experience will acknowledge inwardly, if not outwardly.

104. W. WORDSWORTH.—I consider infant marriage an irrational practice, and one which must seriously hamper any society that adopts it. I believe that this opinion is held by Hindus who have learned to exercise their reason freely, and that even among the followers of the old learning, there are some who hold it. I listened with keen interest, the other day, to Mr. Raghonath Row's lecture on this subject, and to Mr. Ranade's impressive appeal to his countrymen to accept the platform proposed by the lecturer. It seemed to me that his audience were, on the whole, agreed that infant and early marriages were undesirable, but that their agreement went no further................................

How far Indian society has suffered and how far it has gained, if you will concede that it has gained any thing, from its peculiar marriage customs, is a poblem which no one is in a position to solve. I believe that those customs are inconsistent with the new life, into which India is daily being impelled, and that the new ideas of that life no less than its material circumstances and conditions, must tell inevitably against them*

105. HON'BLE MR. DYARAM JETHMUL.—It may be taken for granted that infant marriages are a monstrous evil.

106. HON'BLE MR. C. P. ILBERT, C.S.I.—That the social position of women is one of the surest tests of civilization, and that the institutions of infant marriage and enforced widowhood are incompatible with the position which women ought to occupy in a perfectly civilised society, these are propositions which command a ready assent.

107. RIGHT HONOURABLE LORD HOBHOUSE.–I quite concur in the importance which you attach to infant marriages, and believe them to be a serious obstacle to the improvement of Indian society.

108. HON. SIR RIVERS THOMPSON.—The subject, in both its aspects of restraint of infant marriages and of enforced widowhood, has been for some time under my consideratian officially, and I am happy to be able to give you the assurance that so far from anything like hostility or indifference to your efforts, the common opinion of every officer whom I have cnnsulted, is in strong support of your endeavours to accomplish what would be the greatest social reform ever effected in India.

---

* In a minute recorded by Mr. Wordsworth as Chairman of the Rukhmabai Defence Committee, he wrote "I am quite willing to believe with Mr. Telang that, domestic virtue and conjugal felicity are not incompatible with infant marriages, and I join with him in insisting that our committee should not so enlarge its scope as to embrace any direct attack on that system, or even formally to pronounce any opinion about it. Personally, I hold strongly that no great social or political improvement can be looked for in Hindu society, so long as it adheres to that system. For one thing, it seems to me simply incompatible with any marked advance in female education, and I cannot hope that Hindu society will ever emerge from what I consider its present feeble civilisation, which must condemn it in the future as it has condemned it in the past, to be the servants of manlier and more energetic races, so long as Hindu mothers remain in their present bondage of ignorance and superstition

CHAPTER II.

CAUSES OF INFANT MARRIAGE.

SECTION I. MADRAS PRESIDENCY.

1. C. Ramchandra Aiyar, Sub-Judge, Madura.—The Courts created by the British Government, so far back as 1805, without thoroughly investigating into the question when raised, and without acquainting themselves with the forms and ceremonios constituting infant marriage, but relying upon the statements of the old priests, whose prejudices in those days were deeper than the prejudices of the orthodox Brahmins of the present day, recognized in a betrothed infant girl the status of a widow. I feel sure that it can be shown, to the satisfaction of the Government, that the term 'widow' has through misapprehension, error, and ignorance, become perverted from its original signification, so as to apply even to a babe in the arms of her mother......................As Sub-Judge I have had experience of Ganjam, Vizagapatam, Cocanada, Bellary, Palghat, Calicat, Tellicherry, and I have attended innumerable marriages...........The Palghat Brahmans, and the Brahmans of the East coast, do perform the tail, tying ceremony and Sapta pathi on the first day, and on the fourth night they make the infant couple sleep on one mat in a room, which is only a symbolic consummation, or a symbol of actual consummation, which is essential to the completion of a marriage. The same practice is observed even to this day in all the Brahman families of Travancore and Cochin, and in some of the Brahman communities of Tanjore, Madura, and South Arcot Districts. Among the Telegu Brahmans of Northern Circars, Masalipatam, and Bellary, on the 4th day of the infant marriage, the infant couple are made to sit on one mat, and they are made to exchange betel and nut and chew, which is only a symbol of consummation. I call it symbol, because the first thing

that a husband and wife do on the date of actual consummation of marriage, as soon as they retire into the bed chamber, is to exchange betel. This practice is observed invariably on the 4th day of marriage by all classes of Brahmans................ This mock consummation proves beyond doubt that child marriage, which was not so common, is only a later graft on the ancient marriage after puberty.

Apart from the unfounded nation that a girl attaining puberty before betrothal loses her caste, the difficulty of obtaining young boys suited to the girl as to age and position at a future time, as the girl grows as old as 12 or 13, engrosses the attention of the parents, and they begin to negotiate for the boys from the very moment of the birth of the girl. The boy's parents receive thousands of offers of the kind, with rich dowries, and they choose................

The next thing that encourages infant marriage, is the cursed astrology in which the uneducated women and the educated men alike confide............Every one believes that the country will get on as pre-ordained by Brahma...........No Brahman betrothment takes place, without an astrologer's opinion of the coincidance. in every respect, of the horoscopes of the infant boy and girl to be betrothed, and the chief thing that the astrologer is asked to ascertain is that the girl will not lose her husband, and become a widow. If the astrologer says that the horoscopes agree, the parents of the girl think that they have made the best selection imaginable.............. Palmistry by which gipsies in England indulge in fleecing young girls by predicting their future, is made a criminal offence. Astrology has been breediny more mischief in this country.

2. C. Subbaraya Aiyar.—The restrictions which religion, as at present understood, or more properly, caste rules, impose upon the marriage institutions of the country, naturally tend to circumscribe within narrow limits the field for selection, and leave, the parents no option in the matter

but to select, at the earliest opportunity, the best girls available for marriage to their boys. The narrower the field the keener the competition, and hence infant or rather early marriages are brought about.

3. T. PATTABHIRAM.—I do not deny that young men in India get themselves married earlier than those in the European countries, and so are the Mahomadans and Christians in this country. That is because of the climatic and other influences, and it cannot I think be saccessfully counteracted by any rules............Sir Comarasamy of Ceylon Mr. Mutha Krishna of Madura, Mr. Sabapathi Aiyah of Hydrabad and his brother Meenatchi Aiyah of Bangalore, are so many instances of enlightened men acting up to their convictions, and losing all chance of serving their community.

When the circumstances of the state of society among the Brahmins in the Smriti and Puranic periods are taken into consideration, one cannot but come to the conclusion that, in the lawless state of the country at the time,......the patriarch considered it desirable to secure a guardian and protector to the girl before she bloomed into womanhood. While the future husband was certain of the virgin purity of his wife, the girl herself had the double protection of her father's and husband's families, against seduction or mistakes which will embitter and poison her wedded life. Subsequent to the Vedic period (a period when the female had enjoyed the privilege of giving herself away to any young man she chose, after her years of discretion), the patriarchs would seem to have introduced the rule of marrying girls before puberty, in view to keep the blood pure, and eliminate all impurities from the Brahman stock..............Weak as the Brahman class is in physique as compared with the other classes of the Hindus, the superiority of their intellect as a class is most prominent and noticeable. This I believe is mostly due to the old patriarchal rule, which kept their blood and stock pure and untainted ....

This inhuman practice (marriage of girls to old men for money) is also prevalent among certain sections of the Brahmans (Kaniyalars and Aiyangars) in the Madras Presidency.

SECTION II. BOMBAY PRESIDENCY.

4. NANDSHANKAR.—Hindu parents generally believe that, their first and principal duty towards their children is to get them married. A long standing custom, coupled with some injunctions in what are commonly regarded as Shastras, enjoins that girls under 10 years of age should be married. Then, again, the desire of parents to partake of the pleasure of seeing their children united in bonds of matrimony at an early age, to enjoy the marriage festivities which are looked forward to with a keen interest, to see them m arried in their own life-time or in that of some old members of the family—these and other considerations, lend support and countenance to this practice.

5. HARI PARSAD S ANTOKRAM.—The Hindu marriage is a religious sacrament. It therefere takes the form of a gift of the daughter by a father to the intended son-in-law, and certain sentiments of purity operate to make it neeessary that the gift should be complete before her attaining the age of puberty.

6. VENKUT RANGO KATTI.—Girls in India arrive at maturity much earlier (generally in the 12th year), than those in Europe, or in any other temperate climate.

Experience has shown again that to leave girls and boys long after their 12th and 16th year s respectively, without their partners, leads to looseness of character and disease. Add further, the extreme tenderness for children cherished by Hindu fathers who consider it their final duty to their children, to see " two hands turned into four ", and also the difficulty caused by caste of finding a good and respestable matrimonial alliance, particularly in the case of girls............The custom of spending as much money as one can afford in the celebration of marriages, has its own part to act. A poor old father, seeing the difficulty of his son's or daughter's marriage after his death, is thus naturally tempted to finish it in his life-time, even when the child has not yet left its cradle.

7. Runchorelall Chotalall (Ahmedabad).—In a Province like Gujrat, where the Hindu community is divided and subdivided into so many small castes, it is very difficult to rule that girls should not marry before a certain age. It is possible that, in a small caste, all available boys may be married away if the parents of girls were to wait until a fixed age; and as they cannot give in marriage their daughters to boys of different castes, they are obliged to marry their daughters at such a time as may be most convenient to them.

8. Bholanath Sarabhai (Ahmedabad).—The origin of this custom (early marriage) can be sought in the division and sub-division of society into numerous castes, and ignorance of the spirit of the Hindu Shastras which never enjoin early marriage either for a male or a female...........These divisions are more in number in Gujrat and Kattyawar than in the Deccan.

9. Jagjivandas, (Surat.)—In this country, clubs, hotels, and boarding houses or schools are not as amply and conveniently provided as in Europe and America. On the other hand, Hindus on account of their caste prejudices cannot resort to them as freely as Mahomedans and Parsis. Accordingly the assistance of females is urgently needed for the management of domestic affairs in almost every family. In agricultural and several other avocations such as weaving &ca., the assistance of females is also as useful as that of males. The parents of a boy therefore consider it to be their main duty to see him provided with a suitable match, as far as the means at their disposal permit.......................

Amongst Parsis a great change has however already taken place in this direction, without any legislative or government departmental measure..............

Many Parsis bitterly complain of the change, on the ground that when infant marriage was much prevalent amongst them, respectable unions could conveniently be effected without large expenditure in the shape of dowry, but now a father of a girl is required by the intended husband to pay an exorbitant sum for the marriage, and in the event of his refusal or inability to meet the demand, the results are often very unsatisfactory in many respects.

10. SAKHARAM ARJUN. (BOMBAY.)—Taking human nature as it is, bearing in mind the climatic influences on the native physique, and the enervating effect of social customs, recognizing the fact that the mental culture, the basis of self restraint of the community, particularly the female part of it, is at best only partially developed, and must continue to be so for years to come, all these facts considered, I am fully persuaded that our system of marriage is most wholesome under present circumstances, whatever our English friends may think of it, and is eminently adapted to prevent those dread contingencies to which late marriages are exposed.

11. VISHRAM RAMJI GHOLLAY, ASSISTANT SURGEON POONA.—The primary object of early marriages, in India, where the climatic influences bring on an early development of sexual proclivities, is to get a girl married just about her minimum age for maturity viz 12 years, and a boy about the age of 17 or 18 years, so that they may not go astray, and that the male youths may be saved from the pernicious effects of masturbation, an evil which exists to a great extent among the boys of the higher castes. The primary object is greatly abused by the people of late, owing to the peaceful times which they enjoy, and the custom has been allowed to preponderate more to one side than the other. Hence it has become an admitted evil to some extent among us—but the people have now become quite sensible of its pernicious effects on our moral physical and social constitution, by the dawn of Western civilization and education, which has penetrated the innermost parts of our society.

12. LALSHANKAR UMIASHANKAR.—The following appear to me to be the chief causes (of Infant Marriage).

1. Family pride. The sooner a boy is married the nobler is considered his family.
2. The parental duty to marry their children to continue the progeny is considered so supreme, that they (the parents) try to relieve themselves of this duty as soon as possible.
3. The fear that if any bodily or mental defect is found in a boy at an advanced age, it would be difficult to get a bride for him.
4. The desire of ignorant parents that before their death they should see their children married, and enjoy the pleasure peculiar to infant marriages.
5. The notion of social disgrace to keep a girl, after puberty, unmarried.
6. On account of castes and sub-divisions therein, the sphere of selection is very narrow. It becomes narrower in the case of elder girls. The difficulty of finding out a suitable husband thus increases with the age of the bride; every parent therefore tries the earliest opportunity to find out a suitable bridgroom. Infant marriage is the result of this competition.
7. In cases where a bride is in fact sold for money, her guardians, often, to make their gain sure, celebrate the marriage as early as possible.

13. GOVINDRAO BABAJI JOSHI OF BARODA.—It does not appear from the Hindu Law books that the custom of early marriage existed in ancient times. If it were, therefore, asked as to how the custom originated, it appears to me that it must have come into vague under the Mahomadan rule. In these times, journeys to distant places were attended with dangers, and people must have been obliged to give their daughters in marriage in their own or neighbouring villages, instead of

seeking alliances for them in remote parts of the country. In course of time, the anxiety on the part of the parents to secure suitable matches for their sons and daughters in their limited communities, may have led to the practice of early marriage, which gradually moving along the stream of time, has extended to our own period.

14. GOKALDAS KAHANDAS PAREKH.—The causes (of Infant Marriage) are as under.

(*a*) Non-calculation of the effects, and in, difference to the results of early marriages.

(*b*) Very small caste subdivisions, limiting the number of brides and bridegrooms for one's selection.

(*c*) Gratification of vanity in reference to the caste by the betrothal and marriage of the children while mere infants...... A large number (even in a subdivision of caste) would be unavailable to a person for marriage by being related in the agnatic line, however distant, or by being within the sixth degree in the cognatic line.

The circumstance that a man's son is betrothed while yet a baby in the cradle, is considered popularly an indication of his high position in the caste, and that another man was not able to get his son betrothed so early is an indication to the contrary.

SECTION III. BENGAL PRESIDENCY.

15. BABU KEDARESSUR ROY, SMALL CAUSE COURT JUDGE, DACCA.—A father dies leaving his son, who in consequence becomes helpless; the widowed mother seeks for redress in a suitable marriage of the boy, that her son may be placed under the guardianship of a fathor-in-law, who may be able to educate him. This is also done during the life-time of a father, who is unable to bear the expenses consequent on the education of his son. Numerous instances of this nature may be found in all the Government Colleges and Schools.

16. KAILASHCHANDRA BHATTACHARJI.—There is generally no anxiety on the part of the parents to marry their boys too early, say under 10 years, except under very peculiar circumstances, arising out of two rather extreme causes viz too much poverty or too much riches.

17. JESSORE INDIAN ASSOCIATION.—The Hindu law of succession does not allow the daughter to inherit her paternal estate, when she has her brother. She has to live entirely on the mercy of her brother for support, and if she incurs his displeasure, her position is extremely miserable. This anxiety always broods in the mind of her father, who, therefore, considers it his prime duty to unite her to a deserving husband in his own life time.

18. KUMAR PRAMATHA BHUSHANVA, DEVA, RAJA OF NALDUNGA.—The paralysis of social organism in India, is due to the fact that, whilst education has done and is doing much to elevate the minds of our men, the women portion of the community is well nigh where it was, centuries back. Women wield great power in domestic relations, and so long as their minds are not elevated by education to appreciate our refined ideas, any radical social change is the last thing that we can hope for.

SECTION IV. NORTH-WEST PROVINCES AND OUDH, THE PUNJAB, CENTRAL PROVINCES, BURMA, ASSAM, COORG, HYDRABAD (DECCAN.) &c.

19. HONOURABLE D. G. BARKLEY, MEMBER OF THE LEGISLATIVE COUNCIL, OF THE PUNJAB GOVERNMENT.—In the Punjab such marriages (of girls to boys who are their juniors) may arise from either of two causes. The caste of the girl's parents may be such that they have found it difficult to obtain what they consider a suitable match for their daughter, and they may therefore have to agree to marry her to a boy of proper caste who is younger than the girl, rather than leave her

unmarried. Or the girl may have been betrothed to an elder brother who has died, and popular opinion may be so strongly in favour of the claim of the family of the intended husband, when there is a younger brother to whom the girl could be given, that the parents may feel it impossible to resist the claim..

20. Dewan Ramnath District Judge, Hoshiarpur.—Public interference of any kind will not meet generally with satisfaction, as long as the idea prevails that it is a sin to keep a girl *unmarried,* after she is 10 years of age.

21. Kanwar Bekrama Sing Bahadur, Ahluwalia, C.S.I.—With regard to the question of early marriage, I beg to state that its prevalence is to be ascribed to the general feeling among the people, that it is one of their great responsibilities to get their children (especially daughters) settled in life, to save them from all future anxieties about having a proper home. But no doubt it sometimes happens, that the death of an infant husband comes as a great calamity.

22. Rai Mulraj M. A., Extra Assistant Commissioner Gurdaspur, Panjab.—It is no good denying the fact that many Hindus marry their girls at an early age, because they think that their religion requires them to do so. Most people however marry their sons and daughters at an early age, because they think it is required by the custom of the country. Almost all Hindus have a dread of a girl arriving at the age of puberty, before marriage...........Early marriage is not unfrequently the necessary and unavodable result of infant betrothal.

23. Bajaba Ramchandra Pradhan, Educational Inspector Hydrabad Assigned District.—The custom of early, marriages among the Mahrattas does not seem to be of a very ancient date. It had its origin in the times of their prosperity and became general during the latter days of the Peshwas. It attained its height in the early years of British rule in Western India, when the people first tasted peace........when education had not taken root, and the disturbing ideas of reform were not known.

SECTION V. EXTRACTS FROM OPINIONS GIVEN TO MR. MALABARI.

24. KESHAVLAL MADHAVDAS, (RUTLAM.)—At one time, there was great prosperity in India and abundance of food so that no one cared for increase in the number of family members. This gave rise to the custom of early marriages as well as numerous holidays, festivals, and caste dinners.

25. PANDIT BADRI DUTT JOSHI, POLITICAL PENSIONER ALMORA.—Your idea "that it (infant marriage) may have been forced upon the people under the first Mahomedan invasion" is likely true, but I am rather inclined to think that, the physical weakness produced by the evil led to the Hindus losing their country.................Previous to the time of the coming of the Mahomedans, there must have been a time at which disaffection in the country, or rather civil war among the different classes of people to make each influential over another, may be thought to have taken place, and with it the violation of the codes and precepts......................which by the time the Mahomedans came, must have so deteriorated the Hindus as (sic) led to their yielding to the invaders without the least opposition.

26. RAI H. C. SETH, (JHANSI).—In fact, so much internal pressure and adverse influence is exercised that sometimes with good reasons, educated Hindus have to submit and give up their laudable enterprise in despair. This mischievous impulse comes mostly from the females, who always have an extraordinary influence in directing family affairs. Such is not the case in India alone, but all over the world.

27. HON'BLE MR. DAYARAM JETHMUL.—I hear even now several infant marriages are being negotiated among families of standing and position. I also informed you in a former letter of the fearful expenditure required for these marriages, and a regular chain of transfers of bridal presents, which contributed mainly, if not solely, to early marriages. (Vide also this gentleman's opinion in chap. IV.)

CHAPTER III.

THE LAW ON THE SUBJECT OF INFANT MARRIAGE.

SECTION I. MADRAS PRESIDENCY.

1. K. Krishnaswamy Rao, Chief Justice, Travancore.—The plea of religious necessity which many an old and sickly man puts forward to justify his marriage with a girl fit to be his grand daughter rather than his partner, is perfectly untenable, for the marriage of a widower is not a religious necessity, and Sri Rama, than whom there is no higher Hindu authority, performed many *Aswarnada Yagoms*, with the gold image of his departed wife (Sitha), to supply the place of a wife in such ceremonies. I would not raise my voice against the marriage of an old man to an infant, if he marries under a *real* conviction of religious necessity *i.e.* to keep *agnihotram* (fire), but not one in a hundred old men who marry ever dreams of keeping *agnihotram*, and much less keeps it.

2. R. Ragunath Rao.—Infant marriages and enforced widowhood are not sanctioned by the Hindu Shastras, nor were they in use in India a few hundred years ago.

On the contrary the marriages of undeveloped girls are in a way prohibited by them, and widows are recommended by the Vedas and Smritis to remarry.

No girl who is a minor, that is, who has not attained the age of discretion, or an age which entitles her to express her consent to cohabit with a man, viz 10 years (vide I. P. C. Section 375) can according to the Hindu Law, be *married*. There can therefore be no widow who is a minor.

SECTION II. BOMBAY PRESIDENCY.

3. Trimalrao Venkatesh, Inamdar at Dharwar.—The general Hindu law, as expounded in the Dharma Sindhu

is that, the "Moonji", or the religious thread-girding ceremony should be performed on Brahmins, or boys of the priestly class, between the ages of 5 and 8 years. Under extraordinary and unavoidable circumstances, it might be postponed up to 16 years of age, but such cases very rarely or never occur. When the Moonji is performed, the boy becomes a Brahmachari, *i.e.* he is entitled to perform religious ceremonies. This state is to last for 12 years, during which be should study the four Vedas, six Shastras, 18 Puranas, Bharat, and Ramayan a, or at least portions of them. He then becomes fit to be married.

Among Kchetrias or the warrior class, the Moonji is to be performed ordinarily between the age of 11 and 12 years. In unavoidable cases, it may be postponed up to 22 years. In the cases of Vysias, the ceremony is to be performed between 12 to 16 years of age, it being allowed to be postponed till 24 years in unavaidable cases. In both the classes of Kchetrias and Vysias, the state of Brahamachary is to continue for 12 years after the Moonji is performed.

In ordinary cases the marriageable period of a male Brahman is about 20, that of a Kchetria 24, and that of a Vysia 28 years ....

As regards girls, the proper age prescribed for the marriage of Brahmin, Kchetria, and Vysia classes is between 6 to 8, but never under 6 years of age. To get them married between 9 and 10 years is middling, and between 11 and 12 undesirable.

A girl is called *gowri* or a young girl up to 8 years, and *kannika* or marriageable virgin up to 10, and above that period she is known as *Rajaswala* or as having entered womanhood... ....A girl attaining her puberty before being married, is considered to be Vrishala or a Sudra woman.

4. Bhikaji Amroot Chobhe.—The sale of a girl among the Hindus is an act looked upon as sinful in the highest degree. It is as heinous as using the flesh of the sacred cow.

5. Mahadeo Wasudeo Barve.—Early or infant marriages are not specially enjoined or prescribed by the Hindu Shastras. They simply permit them, and it was only in well-to-do classes that these were resorted to, more out of fashion than as a necessity.

6. Nanabhai Haridas.—With the Hindus, marriage is a religious sacrament (Sanskara) according to all the authorities on the subject, its performance in the case of a girl cannot be delayed beyond a certain period, and according to some authorities its performance a year or two before is most meritorious. That period is puberty, which is generally attained in India at the age of 12. So long, therefore, as the masses of the people continue to pay respect to these authorities there is not much hope of the maximum age for a girl's marriage being raised.

7. M. G. Ranade.—The Grihya Sutra texts, the earlier Smritsi, and the great epics, all contemplate and illustrate a state of society, where both men and women attained mature age before they took upon themselves the resposibilities of a married life. Women were educated, and sent to school, being eligible for the Upanayan or initiation ceremony. The boys had a twelve years' school course (Asvalayana Sutra) during which they were required to observe a self-denying course of life, in which abstention from sexual intercourse occupied a prominent place (Apastamba Sutra). The declarations made at the marriage celebration by the bride and the bridegroom, the significance of certain of the rites themselves, especially the fourth day ceremony, all tend to show that these rites and declarations were not meant for children in their teens. Marriage itself was a voluntary condition to be assumed when its necessity was realised. The woman married once by pledge of word, or gift of hand, was open to the choice of marrying again, under certain contingencies, equally with the man. These occasions were so numerous, in the first instance, that they had to be cut down to five contingencies. All this history is plainly spread before us, and it shows the

greatness of our present fall from a time, which, with strange inconsistency, we still regard as our venerated and ancestral past.

8. VENKUT RANGO KATTI, KANARESE TRANSLATOR E. D. THE DHARMA SINDHU SAYS:—"From the fifth to the 8th year of a girl's age is the proper period for her marriage. The two years after the 6th are the best. A girl should not be married before the 6th year, as Soma (the moon) Gandharva (a celestial singer) and Agni (fire) claim her each for two years from her birth. Marriage in the 9th and 10th years is neither good nor bad. In the 11th year it is mean, and in the 12th and succeeding years it requires prayaschittu (purification) ....

If a girl comes to puberty before marriage, her father, mother, and brothers fall in hell, the girl becomes Shudri, and so does her husband. In such case, the following is the mode of purification. The giver of the girl should give away as many cows as the number of times she was is her monthly course, or one cow, or he should feed Brahmins according to his means, and be fit to give the girl in marriage. The girl on fasting 3 days, and then drinking cow's milk, and giving to a Brahmin's daughter an ornament, with jewels set in it, becomes fit for marriage. The bride-groom will not be guilty if he marries her after offering libations of gourd to the fire. When a girl arrives at puberty before marriage for want of a giver, she should wait for 3 years, and then choose her own husband.

9. RANCHORELALL CHOTALALL, (AHMEDABAD).—There is no religious objection whatever to keeping a boy unmarried until 20 years or any later period.

It is a general feeling among the Hindus that, girls should not be allowed to remain unmarried beyond the age of 10 or 12 years. This practice is based upon the authority of certain texts of the Shastras, and upon the idea that it is not safe to allow a girl to remain unmarried after 12 years, lest she might go astray.

10. BHOLANATH SARABHAI, (AHMEDABAD).—The illustrious and primitive Hindu Law-giver Manu enjoins that a man aged 30 years should marry a girl of 12. According to Hindu Shastras, after being invested with the sacordotal thread, one should pursue the study of Vedas at least for 12 years....................During the Vedic period, girls were allowed to make self-choice of husbands.........From the hymns uttered at the marriage ceremony, and from the wording of the promise made by the husband to his wife, it is quite clear that a girl of 8, 9 or 10 years' age cannot understand the meaning of the promise.

11. SAKHARAM ARJUN.—Sufficient evidence can be adduced to prove that there was a time in the history of the Hindus, when marriage was performed at an age when the parties were capable of immediately consummating it, and the only safe inference that can be drawn from those texts of the Vedas which give directions about the mode of consummating the marriage is, that the marriageable age contemplated therein must have been a considerably advanced one; for these instructions would be unintelligible and meaningless to parties in whose especial behalf they were laid down, if they happened to be of tender years.

12. S. H. CHIPLONKAR.—There is nothing in the Hindu religion, to compel parents to marry their daughters before the 10th year on penalty of excommunication. According to the Hindu Shastras the bride must invariably be younger than the bridegroom.

13. GUNPATRAW C. SASTRI (KASWA).—I am of opinion that it is an infringement of the dispensations of the Shastras to marry or betroth children so soon as the people are now in the habit of doing, and I consider it an infringement of the physical laws to saddle the rising generation with the burden of children, while they are yet in their teens.

14. GAURISHANKAR UDEYSHANKAR, (BHAVNAGAR).—The Nirnaya Sindhu, a modern work of recognized authority on the law and customs of the Hindus in this Presidency, enforces

marriages proper on a girl at 10 years of age, but extends the limit to 11 under a penance, if it be found inconvenient to solemnige it at the age of 10. The Dharma Sindhu, another modern work on Hindu law, says :—" For girls,nine and ten are middling good ages, eleven a bad age, and twelve is one requiring the observance of penance to wipe away the sin." (See chap. iii). Further on the author of the Dharma Sindhu says :—"If a girl resides under the roof of her father unmarried up to 12 years of age, her father commits the sin of killing an unborn child. The girl at that age should marry herself without tho intervention of her father."

15. RAM SHASTRI.—A reference to the Shastras (1. Nirnaya Sindhu 2 Sanskar Mayukh, 3 Sanskar Kaustubh, 4 Prayog Parijat, 5 Mitakshara, 6 Smrityarthsar, 7 Madan Parijat, 8 Parashar Madhao, 9 Sanskar Ratna Mala, 10 Kalanirnya, 11 Purushartha Chintamoni, 12 Asharadinkarodyot, 13 Piyashadhara, 14 Jyotirinband &c.) shows that a boy can be married after he is 11 years old and till youth lasts ; and that for the marriage of a girl, the 5th and 6th years of her age are not proper, that the 7th, 8th, 9th and 10th years are proper, that the 11th and 12th years and the further period till the appearence of the menses are improper, and that they cannot be married after the menses have appeared. " The girl who sees the menses in her father's house (before marriage) is impure ; her father is guilty of *bhorunmahatya* that is killing of the embryo. She is considered to be a *vrishali* or Shudra female. The Brahman who marries her is weak in intellect ; no trust should be placed in him, and nobody should dine with him, and he should be considered as the husband of a Shudra woman."

The Shastras do not sanction the marriage of an old man with a girl. Youth and good health are the chief requisites of a bridegroom. It is stated in the Prayaschitta Hemodari that a man above 50 should not marry. The bride should always be younger than the bridegroom ....

16. PANDIT GUTTULAL.—Many wise persons believing that the real menstrual period commences from the 11th or the 12th, year consider the 10th as the latest marriagiable year. In support of this, there is the following in the Purans. "A girl is called a *Gowri* in the 8th year of her age, a Rohini in the 9th year, a *Kanya* in the 10th year, and after that a *Rajasvala*, that is one having the menses.

The menses are found in women in their 11th or 12th year. If the flower does not disclose itself out, still it exists within. One goes to the *Nak* world by giving a *Gowri* in marriage, to the *Vaikunth* by giving a *Rohini*, to the *Brahma* world by giving a *Kanya*, and the *Raurav* hell by giving a *rajasvala*."

In the Brahma Puran, in the Gautami Mahatmya, it is stated: "a father should try his best to perform the marriage of his daughter from the 4th year of her age upwards, till before the completion of the 10th year".........Still the marriage of a girl should not be performed before the completion of her 6th year, as there is a prohibition against it in the following and other verses.

"A girl should not be married before she is 6 years old, because in the first two years of her age she is enjoyed by the god Som, in the next two years by Gandharv, and then in the next 2 years by Nal."

Manu says.—"A man aged 30 should marry a good looking girl aged 12 years, and a man aged 16 should marry a girl aged 8 years. By marrying a girl before this time, a man neglects his religion."..

The time for a man's marriage is not assigned with the same precision as that for a girl's marriage. The thirty years' age &ca., mentioned is not suited to be carried into practice in the present times. It is objectionable, if the present period of man's life be taken into consideration..............................

There is every possibility of there being occasions for a man's fall on account of the breaking of the abstinence vow, by the time the age has approached. It seems reasonable therefore that a man should marry after he has commenced the 16 year of his age, and before the 20th year, or some time after that.................

The marriage of a girl, both according to the Shastras and according as it stands to reason should be performed after the girl has commenced the 8th year of her age, and before she has completed the 12th. The marriage of a girl performed as is some times now the case, in her very young age before she has commenced the 6 year of her age is against the majority of the Shrutis and the Smritis, and is also not consistent with reason.

SECTION III. BENGAL PRESIDENCY.

17. Babu Kedaressur Roy, Judge Small Cause Court, Dacca.—A girl at the age of 8 years is considered by the Hindu Shastras as marriageable, and the act of making her over to a bridegroom is thought as attended with virtues to her parents, similar to those which attended the making over of Gauri (Doorga) by her father to *Siva*; and the age of 12th year of a girl is considered as the age of puberty before which she must be married, or perdition shall befall her parents and ancestors. A deviation from this rule may sometimes he observed among the Brahmin Kulins of Bengal who marry their girls either earlier than 8th or later than 12th year of their age, when they find it difficult to procure conveniently a bridegroom descended from a family with whom inter-marriage is allowed by the laws of Kulinism, but such instances are rare, and tolerated as being according to the popular and time hallowed laws of Kulinism.

18. Babu Hori Mohun Chandra, Personal Assistant to the Commissioner Rajshahya District.—In chap. iii (of Manu) which deals with every minute detail of the marriage ceremony of the twice born, I nowhere find the marriageable age of males fixed.

In verse 89 chap. IX, I find that a "damsel though marriageable may stay at home till her death, if a suitable bridegroom cannot be found."

We find that this custom is frequently observed in the present age by many families unable to get bridegrooms of suitable position, or .... when they are unable to meet the demands of the bridegroom's parents or guardians.

Verse 90 says. "Three years let a damsel wait, though she he marriageable; but after that term, let her choose for herself a bridegroom of equal rank".................

In verse 93 I find the following sentence. "He who takes to wife a damsel of full age &ca." The words in the original text for a "damsel of full age" mean a girl who has begun to menstruate. Here it appears that a girl may be married after she menstruates.

19. KUMAR PRAMOTHA BHUSHANA DEVA, RAJA OF NALDANGA.—Of all the female characters delineated in the great Epics, none appears to have entered into matrimonial bonds, before she had attained the age of discretion. The first symptom of deviation from this most healthy social practice is observed in the..............Manava Dharma Shastra. This Sanhita does not countenance early marriage of males, but girls, according to this Shastra, should be married before puberty...........The father being considered as only *blameable* in the event of his failing to marry his daughter before puberty, it is evident that the Hindu population at that time had become sparse, owing to pestilence, civil war, or foreign invasion, and that the Hindus had been obliged to have recourse to early marriage for the speedy multiplication of species........ No Shastra attaches *religious* blame to the party marrying after puberty.

6

SECTION IV. NORTH-WEST PROVINCES AND OUDH, THE PUNJAB, CENTRAL PROVINCES, BURMA, ASSAM, COORG, HYDRABAD (DECCAN.) &c.

20. LUXMON G. RISHI, DEPUTY EDUCATIONAL INSPECTOR, BASIN DISTRICT.—Infant marriage, especially of the girl—for a man can marry at any age—is not enjoined by Hindu religion; and the Hindu girls of Northern India, nay even the hhig caste Brahmin girls on that side, grow to the age of 20 or 30 before they are married, or lead a life of celibacy till they are fit for the grave; and no priestly class puts them or their parents under the ban of excommunication. If the Shastras enforce marriage proper on a girl when she is 12 years of age, or at least before she sees her menses, why, as stated above, are the Hindu girls of Northern India and their parents not excommnnicated?

SECTION V. EXTRACTS FROM OPINIONS GIVEN TO MR. MALABARI.

21. M. RAMPRASAD TIVARI, MUNICIPAL COMMISSIONER (MYSORE).—The propositions by the Madras Association headed by the talented Diwan Bahadur Raghunath Row, are quite reasonable and allowed by early authorities viz, that we should not marry a girl under 10 years and a boy under 15 years, and that a girl can be remarried if she unfortunately loses the betrothed before consummation.

22. PROFESSOR MAX MÜLLER.—That infant marriage has no sanction whatever from either Sruti or Smriti I told you from the very first, and I see that no pandit now ventures to gainsay that. Manu wishes a young man to marry when he may become a Grihastha *i. e.* when he is about 24 years of age. As to the girl, she is to marry when she is fit for it, and that

may vary in different climates. But an engagement between infants is never contemplated by any legal authority, much less are the sufferings of widowhood contemplated by Sruti or Smriti, on a girl whose polygamous husband dies before she has even seen him. That argument has been treated with so much learning by your own scholars and lawyers that nothing more need be said on it. The study of Sanskrit, even by so called *Mlekkhas* like myself, begins to bear fruit. You remember how in the case of Suttee, the Shastris quoted passages from a lost Sánkhâ of the Veda, intended to show that widows should be burnt with their husbands. They actually tampered with a passage from their own sacred Veda, and not till I published the passage from the Asvalayana Grihya Sutras, forbidding widow burning, would they become silent. With regard to the proper age for marriage, I published the important passages in my Hibbert Lectures in 1878 p. 352-3, and as these lectures are being translated under your auspicies, I doubt whether any Shastri *now* will dare to invoke either Sruti or Smriti in support of infant marriage. But, of course, they will invoke the authority of Akara or Desadharma, unless they remember that custom and local law have no authority whenever they conflict with Sruti or Smriti.

CHAPTER IV.

REMEDIES PROPOSED TO PUT AN END TO INFANT MARRIAGE.

SECTION I. MADRAS PRESIDENCY.

1. K. Krishnaswami Rao, Chief Justice, Travancore.—I would prohibit the marriage of males after the age of 50.

The legislation I propose has the support of the Shastras, for according to them none who is more than 50 years old should marry.

2. C. Ramchandra Aiyar, Sub-Judge, Madura.—I would respectfully suggest that a simple prospective legislation be passed, providing that a betrothed infant girl losing her husband before consummation of the marriage or nuptials, shall not be considered a widow, and shall not be entitled to claim the rights of a widow under the Hindu law, but shall be treated as a maiden of her parents having all the rights as such under the Hindu law..............................

I would further suggest the renewal of the old Hindu law now considered by the Hindus as obsolete, that a boy should marry after passing through the period of studentship.

3. S. Subramania Aiyar.—I do not think that Government will be well advised to interfere actively with such usages by legislation. At the same time I do not see any objection to indirect encouragement on the part of Government. I certainly think with Mr. Malabari, that the restriction to confer university honours to unmarried men will have a deterrent effect on early marriages. I would even go a little further, and recommend that no boy under 16 be allowed to appear for any university or public examination, if he is married.

4. R. Ragunath Rao.—I am sure the government would not sanction anything against Hindu law, if they prohibited marriages of girls of less than 10 years, and encouraged those of developed maidens.

The Sastras of the Hindus do not sanction marriages of elder women to younger men. Government may prohibit such marriages also.

5. T. Pattabhiram.—Until caste becomes a thing of the past, there is no hope of preventing the marriage of girls before years of discretion among Brahmans..........................

An enactenent laying down a rule that money received from the (aged) bridegroom, save and except that which is paid for the marriage expenditure, should be safely deposited in the bride's name and exclusively for her use, will, I believe, not only be a great boon to the poor infant victim, but will also serve as a wholesome check against inhumane parents thus sacrificing and selling their female children for their own benefit. It is a fit subject for the interference of Government.

6. MAHIPATRAM RUPRAM.—I beg to suggest the enactenent of a Marriage Act, which shonld contain the following points.

1. Compulsory registration of all births in municipal offices in cities and towns, and in the Taluka Local Boards' offices in the villages.

2. The Municipal and Taluka Local Boards' offices to give certificates of birth to each party, containing the names of the child and parents.

3. No marriages to be allowed to take place without a license from Municipal authorities in towns and cities, and from Local Fund Boards in the villages. These boards to give marriage certificates.

4. Certificates of births to be shown along with an application for a License.

5. The Municipal and Local Fund Commissioners to be authorized to fix the minimum ages of brides and bridegrooms before which no license can be given, and to raise the same from time to time as they may think proper.

6. Nominal marriages such as take places among the Kadwa Kunbis in Gujarat at an interval of 12 years, in which a girl is married to a bunch of flowers &c., may be exempted from the age rule, but in such cases all second marriages must take place under the rule...

The Hindu law forbids the taking of money or any other gratification or reward by parents or guardians, from bridegrooms or their relations, for marrying their daughters. In this respect some legislative action may be taken to protect the interests of infant girls.

7. JOTEERAO GOVINDRAO PHULAY.—Government should rule that, boys under 19 years of age and girls under 11, should not be allowed to marry. In case they do, some reasonable

tax may be levied on the parents of the parties married, and the money thus obtained should be used in the education of the middle and lower classes of Hindus.

8. NARAYEN BHIKAJI, DEPUTY COLLECTOR, NASIK.—I beg to state that the marriage system among the Hindus does require a little reform, and shall be glad to see an act passed by Government :—

1stly. That no boy before the age of 16 and no girl before the age of 11 be betrothed, on pain of a fine not exceeding Rs. 1000, recoverable with distress and sale of the offenders property. This ruling is not opposed to the present custom followed by the educated men, and therefore will not be objected to.

2ndly. That no old man, that is a person about 40 years of age, should marry a girl below the age of 12, and then too (*i.e.* at 12) without her written consent recorded before Punch to be appointed for the purpose. Girls of the age of 12 have sense enough to express their assent or dissent about the husbands selected for them by their parents. (This law to be made applicable to towns and villages on application of the inhabitants.)

9. K. C. BEDARKAR.—If India has to wait till public opinion is sufficiently educated to be able to effect radical changes, it may have to wait till Doomsday.

Under the peculiar circumstances of India, I think, that the interference of the State, where it advances general welfare, would not be out of place, and legislation tending to check infant marriages will undoubtedly advance general welfare.

As to whether State interference should be direct or indirect, I am decidedly of opinion that it should be direct........

The interference of the State, I think, may safely go to the extent of their enacting that no marriage of a girl under 13 or of a boy under 17, shall be legal in any part of British India in any caste or community. An interference to this extent will neither be violent, nor abrupt, nor open to serious religious objection. I dare say a storm will be raised at first, but it will soon subside, leaving the social atmosphere clearer and healthier. In castes in which infant marriages are most frequent, and in which infants of the most tender age are married, instances can be found of girls remaining unmarried till 14, and sometimes 15, and I can think of no authenticated instances in which they have led to excommunication. And as to instances of boys remaining unmarried till 20, they can be found in the best and wealthiest families all over India.

10. TRIMALRAO VENKATESH.—Nothing short of stringent legislative enactments can stop infant marriages and all the attendant evils.

Enactment proposed by this gentleman.

I. No boy, until he is 20 and no girl until she is 12 years old, shall marry or be married.

II. No man shall during the life-time of his first wife marry another woman, unless the first wife has not borne any children up to 10, or has borne only girls up to 12, or all of her children have died up to 15, years from the time of her commencing to live with her husband, or it is proved that she has committed adultery. Even then, he is to make full provision for the maintenance of the first wife &c.

III. No man who may have one or more sons, and whose wife has just died, and who has passed the age of 45 years, shall marry a virgin girl, unless he leaves a written permission, permitting, in case of his death, his new wife to remarry some other person, if she is minded to do so, provided that he may remarry a widow of any age.

No amount of education, persuation, and lecturing will be able to improve matters. Uuless the legislature takes the matters into its own hands, and makes suitable provisions, matters will continue to remain as they are at present.

11. HURRICHUND SADASIVJI SATE.—Government might show its disapproval of the practice (Infant Marriage) in strong terms, and even go further, and legislate that no

marriage contracted can legally be binding, before the age of 12 in case of girls and 17 in that of boys. This measure will meet with general approval.

To check the inhuman practice of the marriage of an infant girl of 9 or 10 years with an old man of 50 and upwards-Government may well follow the excellent suggestion of, Mr. Malabari.

12. Ranchodlal K. Desai.—The government may without detriment to the efficiency of the Police or the Military service, be pleased to rule that candidates for employment in either of these Departments shall generally be selected from those who have remained unmarried until the completion of their 21st birth-day, and have preserved their good character till then.........................

In my humble opinion the best course for checking this obnoxious practice, is to lay down that the marriage of a minor girl with an old man of 40 and upwards, is an offence, and that the money paid by the bridegroom in consideration of such a marriage is recoverable back.

As the guardianship of all minors is by law vested in the principal Civil Court of the District in which the minor resides, the parent or brother of the minor girl may justly be restrained in their improper actions in giving away the minor in marriage, by the Government or by the principal Civil Court, and consequently the Government will, I humbly think, be justified in taking a direct step to check the evil.

13. Kalianrai H. Desai, of Broach.—The only thing that is, in my humble opinion, calculated to effectually check the evil, is the observance of the Brahmachari Ashram, by those on whom the Shastras strictly enjoin it after performance of the thread investiture ceremony. As regards those who are debarred from their very birth from undergoing this ceremony, it is only sufficient that the boys should remain unmarried till they complete their 17th year.........................

True to my Hindu instincts, I, for one am against keeping girls unmarried after they have reached their 12th year, and I think that boys would, without an adequately vigilant discipline, inevitably fall into dangerous and vicious habits, if kept single for a long time after the completion of their 16th or 17th year.

14. PREMCHUND ROYCHUND.—Let a law be made that no girl under 13 should be married, and that there should be a difference of at least three years between the ages of the bride and the bridegroom, the latter having the seniority of age.

15. NARAYEN GANESH CHANDRAVARKAR.—There is no fear now that action on the part of Government in any shape whatever may be misunderstood and may give rise to political dangers, for with the diffusion of knowledge, on one hand, and the gradual displacement of the older people by a new and more enlightened generation of natives, on the other, the Hindu community have come to perceive the evils of the custom of early marriage.......................

What seems to me a better and more practicable modification of Mr. Malabari's proposal is that, Government might begin for the present, by declaring that *all scholarships and prizes with which the universities, colleges, and schools are endowed* should be held by and awarded to none but the unmarried. Such a declaration is not likely to offend any one. It will be a safe and good beginning to make.

16. DIWAN BAHADUR MANIBHAI JUSBHAI.—I recognize the general principle that in a social matter like marriage, legislative dictation is undesirable. I propose to obviate this difficulty, by providing that legislative action should come into play only on due application from the community concerned. There is ample warrant for this procedure; the Parsi Matrimonial Regulations and the Khoja Successation Bill were all conceived in this spirit, which might well be applied to the case of a Hindu Infant Marriage Law. There is however one particular in which a difference will have to be made in the

case of special legislation for Parsis and Khojas, and that proposed for the benefit of the Hindus. The former was I conclude based on applications made at the outset by the communities concerned; as regards the Hindus they are split into so many castes that no combined action, within a given time can be expected. The way in which I propose to overcome this drawback is that the legislature may at present pass an Act on the basis of Act XXVI of 1850, "an act to enable improvements to be made in Towns."..

The special Act need only be a brief one. It should prescribe the minimum marriageable age and lay down working details. The recently appointed Local Boards and Municipalities can be well utilized in this connection....................

It will be premature to say much on the question of age at present..............What I would do is to prescribe three classes, leaving it to the people to apply to be placed in any one they may be prepared for. The third or the last class should be that in which the minimum age for the marriage of children of both sexes should be 10 years*. In the second class the age of the girl should be 11, and that of the boy 14; in the first class the age of the girl should be 12, and that of the boy 16.

* I say 10, as that is most consonant with the prevalent ideas on the subject.

16. M. G. Ranade.—There are among the friends of reform those who think that the evils are gradually disappearing, and for their total abolition we must depend exclusively upon the growth of education, or upon a change in our public opinion, or upon a revival of our religious spirit, and that nothing can be done by direct State action. I am fully alive to the force of these considerations. I set most value upon the revival of the religious spirit among us, for till such a renovation of the heart is accomplished, men will never learn to be fully in accord with their best natures, and will not be inspired with the warmth which it is necessary to feel on such matters, for practical action to result in good. I set no less value upon the spread of education and the growth of public opinion. These

are necessary and indispensable factors, without which State action will always be futile. One reason why State action is now urgently called for, is that these agencies have been working for a considerable time past, and they have prepared the ground sufficiently to make State action intelligible and beneficial. These agencies are undoubtedly working for us, and they are likely to work greater results in the future, if they are concentrated, emphasized, and properly directed by corporate State action. The scattered forces will thus be brought into a single focus, and in their united strength will bring about the desired end earlier and with far less expenditure of national energy, with a very limited help, than without it......

The State is the nation itself, as represented by those who are its leaders in thought and action...........Social reform, so far as it is confined to the fixing of minimum limits of age, when men and women can do acts for which they are held responsible, implies a social compact or agreement among the leaders of society, and this circumstance has been held to justify the State in fixing the age of civil majority, as also the responsible age for certain classes of offences.

But it is asserted that we have no right to force our views upon an unwilling majority ....The thinking and responsible portion of the community press this reform, on the same grounds that justify the enactment of all coercive law, civil or criminal. The majority are not unwilling, they are inert, and their inertia encourages the evil doers to break the rule with impurity. If this argument be valid, it would put an end to to many useful practical reforms set on foot in our administrative machinery. A large number of people do not like sanitation or vaccination, and they do not like to be taxed for schools and roads, and yet we do not comply with their wishes. Even in the most free countries, the final power of choice and action does not rest with the numerical majority but the majority only determines the choice of those individuals to whose guidance it will submit. These few leaders can never have force with them. They must appeal to higher principles of justice, of expediency and right, and if these principles warrant a certain course of action, they must act with their best lights.

But it has been said all this may be true in free countries where people have choice of their rulers, and can have no application to a country subject to foreign rule as India is .... This argument however cuts both ways, for I think if the fact of foreign rule is to shut us out from all corporate action, we may at once cease all our activities. Where the interest of foreignors clashes with ours, this caution may be necessary and justifiable, but in this case the interests do not clash, and I maintain that the distinction of foreign and native rule has no place............To look upon the ruling body as a separate entity with hostile interests, and to shun their good services, is as foolish as it would be for a man with a deceased heart to shun the doctor, because be was not of kin and kith with the patient. In these matters the State in its executive and legislative capacities, is only the minister to give formal expression and legal validity to what the best, the wisest, and the purest minded men are inclined to support. I grant that the Legislative Councils as at present constituted, can not grapple effectively with these questions. A more liberal representation of native interest is desirable, and in a matter like this the State will be but too willing to convene an assembly of our notables, and listen to their representations in the way it has already done for Parsis, and proposes to do for the Khojas. A commission of inquiry, and a conference held under State auspices would be preliminary steps, and we should agitate for them, but it will not do for us to fold our hands, and say that, as long as we are under foreign rule, no reform of our social arrangements shall be undertaken. India cannot hope to be the master of its own destinies for centuries to come, and till then I do not see that it is either manly or wise to sit still and let things take their course........ ....

If our society had a self-regulating power in any of its relations I could have certainly understood the hesitation felt in respect of State action...........The religious texts which are supposed to regulate our life are immovably fixed, and we cannot adopt them, or change them, nor better them to suit changing conditions. Our civilization has been smothered by this bondage to past ideas. The only way in which our emancipation can take place, is to withdraw one by one these fetters of so called religious injunctions, and turn them into civil restraints which are more amenable to change and adaptation. This is the weakest point of our social system, and I do not see how we can get rid of it, if we are to abjure all State help in such purely civil matters as fixing the age when a man or woman may be bound in the tie of marriage. The jurisprudence of every other nation, ancient or modern, has always regulated these limits of age, and we must do likewise, if we wish to secure progress in these matters. It is not in fact putting on new chains, but removing old ones, or rather substituting flexible for inflexible bonds, that we seek in advocating interference in the regulation of age limits.

It may be fairly contended that State action can lead to no great results. This is however not a drawback against, but a recommendation for change No sudden elevation of age is desirable or possible. We have a slow progress to make in this matter,if our progress is to be sure. It is only necessary to put the stamp of general approval upon the best of the existing usages and customs. Such an approval will strengthen public opinion, and will secure the growth of education, otherwise so heavily handicapped by the existing customs. We shall also promote true religion, and, above all, we shall really make no innovation, but return to the best traditions of our race, and rehabilitate the mostvenerated texts. For the present it has been ascertained that 10 to 12 for females and 16 to 18 for males is a common age limit, and is not opposed to the Shastras, and is sufficiently in advance of existing usage to justify its adoption as a general law, subject to exceptions in particular castes and localities.

I would not in the first instance go further for the present. I would allow time to develop the action of the other forces at work, before any further change is to be thought of. No practical incovenience will follow from the general enforcement of these moderate limits.

As regards the practical method of proceeding, I would humbly suggest that a commission should be appointed to enquire into local usages, to receive evidence, and to formulate recommendations. I would not make the age limits compulsory in the sense of annulling marriages contracted before the age had been reached. I would only leave the parties concerned freedom to question their binding character when they come of age, unless they have in the meanwhile consummated the marriage. This freedom has been allowed by law in the Parsi Marriage Act. I would appoint non-official gentlemen of position, Municipal and Local Board Commissioners, Honorary Magistrates and Inamdars &c., as authorities with power to certify as to age, and would lay a small penalty for celebrating marriages without such certificates I would make over the fines to the heads of the castes for their caste purposes, or to Local Boards and Municipalities, whose members, elected by the people, may safely be honoured by the trust of the power of certifying to the age qualification. This arrangement would serve as a self-acting check..............Our people are naturally so law-abiding, that, few would run the risk of celebrating marriages without license. Some difficulty will at first be felt in ascertaining the ages, but this difficulty will not be great as the experience of similar regulations elsewhere is favourable, and it will gradually disappear when men become used to it. Simultaneously with this, the educational authorities may work in their own fields, and after a reasonable notice, confine their honours and distinctions to those, who in addition to their other qualifications, voluntarily submit to the qualification of single life during their college or school course. Such a restraint would be in keeping with the Brahmachari or student's tradition, and people will soon get used to it...........

Our medical texts lay down 16 as the limit of age for females, and 24 for males, before legal consummation can take place. I would lower these limits to 14 and 20, and amend the penal law to that effect. Such an amendment might be inoperative in a few cases, but on the whole it will not fail to produce the best results.

In regard to ill assorted marriages, I would lay down 45 as the limit of age for men after which they may not marry young virgins, and the marriage of young husbands with older wives should be strictly prohibited, as being unnatural and mischievous in many respects. In regard to polygamy, the Hindu law imposes certain permanent disqualifications on the first wife which must be fulfilled before a man can marry a second wife during the life time of the first. I would revive these restraints, and give them the force of law.

17. VENKUT RANGO KATTI.—The imposition of double fees on (married) candidates when they appear for the matriculation and other examinations, will be, in my humble opinion, a sufficient indication of the contempt with which Government regard early marriage. The suggestion that Government officers should evince personal interest in the matter seems to be too good to be practicable.

18. MOTILAL LALBHAI.—The creation and spread of a healthy public opinion is the duty of all educated men in this country, and Government can encourage and help them by bestowal of honours and titles on reformers; by inducements in the shape of prizes and scholarships to male and female students, by money contributions to associations for social reformation, and by establishment and support of institutions for the requisite education of the people. Beyond this no Government interference is, I think, desirable or advisable, except perhaps to show their disapproval of the evil customs under reference, by ruling that no suit will lie for possession of a wife before she is 16 and the husband is of 20 years of age, and by giving some special privileges to remarried widows of approved character.

But of all the means to be adopted for eradicating the evils in question, the most effectual will be a proper education of women.

19. RUNCHORELALL CHOTALAL.—I think the first attempt at reform should be to limit the marriageable age of males to 15 or 16 years..............The people of all castes may be invited to show reasons against the increase of the marriageable age.........and their objections might be duly considered before the enactenent of the law. In my opinion the measure would be approved of by almost every intelligent person...............

Taking everything into consideration, I am of opinion that Government should not interfere about the marriageable age of girls.

20. BHOLANATH SARABHAI.—1. Female education. 2. "Associations should be established in different parts of India, opening branches in chief towns. They should be encouraged by local authorities by attending the meetings and showing their sympathy with the noble cause." 3. Lessons in school books.

21. SAKHARAM ARJUN.—What is wanted is the separation of the marriage (*i.e.* betrothal) and the consummation into two distinct ceremonies...........The great aim of reformers should be, I think, to unite their efforts to get people to regard marriage and consummation as two essentially distinct ceremonies, and to make them defer the latter till the married couple arrives at maturer years..

It may be observed here in passing that, if, on the one hand an ordinary native confounds his social customs, which are a combination of personal hygiene and law, and mistakes Hindu Dharma (Hindu religion) for Dharma Shastra (code or science of duties or law), Government, on the other hand, in my humble opinion, have complicated matters by not yet making carefully a proper differentiation between Hindu law, religion, and custom. If a rigid distinction had once been made by the legislature between the Hindu law, religion, and custom, a great many difficulties, which now stifle the growth of reform, might have been easily removed. If Hindu law is dissociated from Hindu religion, as it properly should be, its absurdities and barbarities are sufficiently glaring to number its days.

If Government is not prepared to directly interfere in the matter, I think, it can safely tread on the lines indicated by the late Lieutenant Governor of Bengal..........................

"There was one thing, however," said Sir William Muir, "which the law might do, and that was to stipulate that the betrothals made in tender years by third parties should not be enforced as contracts demanding specific performance, unless there was a ratification of the betrothal by the principal contracting parties, after they had arrived at maturer years."

22. S. H. Chiplonkar.—As regards the first suggestion (viz.) that the Universities should rule that they would confer their degrees on unmarried students only, I should think it to be quite practicable, and one which our Universities might reasonably be expected to adopt. I do not think there is much force in what Mr. Lee-warner says about such a suggestion being outside the legitimate province of their functions. Until very recently, English Universities did impose such a condition in respect of their fellowships and degrees, and I further understand that a few of them do even now impose such a restriction. If my imformation be correct, I fail to see how it would be *ultra vires* of our Universities following the same example.

23. Ragunath Narayen Khote.—Approves the suggestion that married students should be excluded from University examinations.

"A student ought to be exclusively a student. He should be free from the trammels of family life and its cares. The Universities are interested in seeing that they give the country, men *qualified* to lead and enlighten the public."

24. R. G. Bhandarkar.—I am of opinion that the University might, on giving 5 years' notice, rule that no married candidate shall be admitted to the matriculation examination.

Hindu public opinion among the classes to which the candidates for matriculation belong, has, for some time, been gradually coming to recognize the advisability of keeping boys unmarried till about the age of 17, which is the average age at which boys matriculate.

To marry a girl of 11 or 12 years to an old man of 50, whom it is impossible the girl should like for her husband, with the certain prospect of a life-long widowhood for her after a few years of a distasteful and unhappy married life, is unfeeling cruelty. This wilful and wanton condemnation of an innocent girl to a life of misery comes, in my opinion, within the legitimate scope of law. The best way to deal with the matter would be to render a marriage penal, when the disparity between the ages of the bridegroom and the bride amounts to 30 years. This will not prevent an old man's marriage with a grown-up widow, but will put a stop to his taking a girl of 12 to wife. Such an enactment will invest with strength the Hindu religious law and respectable Hindu opinion which condemn the practice, but have become powerless, and therefore cannot be reasonably complained of ....

The propsals that he (Mr. Malabari) makes in connection with early marriage, have for their object the raising of the age in the case of boys only. But it is equally important that the age of girls also should be higher. There is no religious objection against the former, but there is against the latter. But the sin that a man incurs by keeping his girl unmarried till after a certain physical occurrence can, according to the Shastras, be wiped off by doing a prescribed penance, which is not heavy, so that the religious objection is not insuperable. What is therefore necessary is to create such a feeling against the marriage of girls before 12, as will embolden parents to keep them unmarried till a later age, and do the prescribed penance.

25. HINDUMAL BAL MUKUND OF POONA.—Voluntary associations may be formed under the leadership of different religious preceptors. I would ssk the Sarvajanik Sabha to

adopt the wise plan of sending expert agents to the different parts of the Presidency, as itinerant preachers, to deliver interesting and impressive addresses.........before large gatherings, and to point out the evils from infant marriage and enforced widowhood.

26. NAGINDAS TULSIDAS.—It is only through the orthodox priests that something can be effectually done, if anything can be done at all. So if Act XV of 1856 be extended, and inter-marriages among the numerous sub-divisions of one large class be encouraged, much relief will be given. At present, such inter-marriages are not illegal, but it is the tyranny of the caste in the shape of excommunication that makes such marriages virtually illegal.

27. LAKHMIDAS KHIMJI.—This gentleman wants a *direct* legislative measure for putting down the evil, on the ground that the British Government interfered in putting down evil customs, "found to be incompatable with reason, humanity, good order, or good government in the following instances."

"The practice of Suttie.

" " Infanticide.

" " 'Bherav Jap' at Dwarka (a leap into the sea from some projecting crags.)

" " Kasinoo Karval (or being sawn alive into two at Benares.)

" " being crushed beneath the car of Jagannath

" " buying of male children by Jain Gorjis (or priests) for the purpose of making them disciples.

" " thuggee, sacrificing human beings to Kali Bhovani.

" " fastening hooks into the bodies of infants and men, and then whirling them through the air, for some time, in fulfilment of a vow made to the God Khandaba.

The prejudice against vaccination.

I believe that if the marriageable age be fixed at 12 for the female, and 16 for the male—and, that in any case the difference between the ages of the bride and bridegroom as regards minors shall not be less than four, and as regards a minor female and a grown-up male, it shall not be more than 15 (the evil would be prevented.)"

28. LALSHANKAR UMIASHANKAR.—I believe the social efforts will be much strengthened by co-operation and moral support of Government in the following particulars:—

1. Lessons showing the evils, in various forms, should be introduced in all vernacular text books teaching the 3rd and higher standards.

2. Essays, tracts, and books on the subject should be largely used as prize books.

3. District officers should use their moral influence, and assist the associations in persuading people to introduce the reform; and to express their disapproval, should not attend any infant marriage party or procession.

4. Till 18 years of age, an unmarried boy should be preferred to a married one, in awarding scholarships.

I am also of opinion that, the State should adopt legislative measures to remove this evil, as soon as possible. There are persons who say that, social reform should take place from within, and that the State should not interfere in it, unless essentially necessary. But this applies to social questions that have no direct bearing on the public welfare.......... .... Even purely social practices when they become detrimental to others, come within the province of legislative action. For instance, custom would allow the use of indecent expressions on Shimga Holidays, but law would stop it. The criterion of legislative assistance is thus, not whether a thing is connected with social reform, but whether it affects public welfare. I believe no reasonable man will deny that the effects of infant marriages on society are disastrous..............................

Considering the present State of society, I think, the minimum marriageable age of bridegrooms only should at present be fixed at 18 years by law...............I would therefore suggest some provision like the following in the Minors' Act (Act XX of 1864) which already vests the care of persons of all minors in the Bombay Presidency in Civil Courts.

1. No guardian, whether appointed by the Court or not, shall without written permission of the Civil Court, celebrate the marriage of a male minor before he has completed his 18th year.

2. On the application of a guardian or friend of a male minor, the court, under special circumstances, after recording its reasons, may, permit the marriage before the age prescribed in the above clause.

To make these rules effective, some penalty should be prescribed for those who are concerned in the celebration of a marriage contrary to the law. The real evil in the case of girls is in the early consummation of marriage. This evil is likely to increase when big boys marry infant girls. To remedy this, the age of 10 years mentioned in section 375 of the Indian Penal Code should be raised to 12 years. To receive money for giving a bride is condemned both by Shastras and public opinion. Such a practice should therefore be made penal. This will to a certain extent prevent a young girl being given to a very old man.

29. Govindrao Babaji Joshi.—Some of the persons engaged in the discussion of the subject (early marriage) have already seen sons of their sons. Though such is the state of things, yet it is extremely lamentable that they do not seem to think seriously of making any improvement with regard to this evil custom, in the case of the marriages of their own children.

Nor is the condition of our widows any better.

The educated men of the present day who think it highly desirable that the practice of widow marriage should be introduced among the prohibited classes, while addressing meetings of people, say: "the poor helpless widowed girls are absolutely undone; their distress and hardship are horrible even to contemplate; the butcher cuts the throat of an animal but once, and the consequent pain and torture are over in a moment once for all, but the unceasing sufferings of the destitute widows are life-long" and a deal of talk of this kind. Should, however, early widowhood be the lot of one of their own daughters of tender years, not a single one of them hesitates to wife off her *kunka*,* to break her bangles, and get her head shaved. Thus it will be soon that matters have come to a mournful pass.

*The auspicious mark of red powder on the forehead of married Hindu women.

Why is this difference between our word and deed.

Children in their first endeavous to walk frequently meet with falls, and at such a time, their parents holding the little ones by the hand, teach them to walk. Similarly this country is at present in a helpless state of infancy.

From very ancient times preceding the British rule, the course of Government in the country has been this, that the king shows the way, and the subjects simply follow it. And this is the reason why the people of this country are so much attached to their sovereigns, and pay them divine reverence. I admit that by the spread of western knowledge among our people, a small portion of them are now beginning to distinguish, in a small measure, between the rights of the crown and the rights of the people. Still we are not yet so far advanced as to act for ourselves in all things. Therefore interference from Government seems desirable to guide us aright.

The wiews of Mr. Byramji M. Malabari on the subject in question are sound and considerate, and, therefore, Government will be pleased to assist us in the way recommended by him.

30. Dr. Atmaram Pandurang.—If the University could be prevailed upon to withhold from granting prizes and

scholarships to married students, I believe it may do good, without hindering the progress of education itself.

31. Utamram N. Mehta.—The following remedies are suggested by this gentleman for preventing infant marriage and introducing widow marriage:—"(1) The formation of associations for the consideration of this subject and of the means to be adopted to prevent these practices, (2) the co-operation of the Hindu church, (3) and of the Hindu States, (4) the moral support of those who are in authority, (5) the efforts of the educated, the influential, and the wealthy, (6) the great spread of education among the males and females."

In order to find out whether the progress of social reform is slow or rapid, he suggests entries to be made in all school registers and in Educational Reports of the numbers of married and unmarried students. He also suggests that District Officers should preside or attend at Social Reform Meetings.

32. Manmohandas Dayaldas.—The meaning we attach to the words "Infant Marriage" is marriage contracted in a state of ignorance. Whatever the age of a girl or boy may be, it is still an infant marriage, if the contracting parties are ignorant of what marriage or love is, how that feeling is created, what woman is intended for &c. The best means of preventing infant marriage is to impart instruction in these subjects through books &c. Besides, parents should also behave well in the presence of children.

33. Pandit Narayen Kesow Vaidya.—There have been lectures given from the platform, essays written which carried away splendid prizes, sermons preached from the pulpit, but practical action has been *nil.*

That can be achieved by legislation, and that only......... It is desirable that Government should legislate, and fix the respective ages of boys and girls at 16 and 11, which in my opinion, considering the climatic circumstances of the country, appear to be neither too high nor too low.

34. PANDIT GUTTULAL.—There exists a practice according to which parents and others, with the object of getting money, marry their daughters &c., to very young and sometimes to very old persons. This is a very sinful practice, which is particularly disapproved of by the people, and by the Shastras, and should in every way be put a stop to; because great blame attaches to the selling of girls..........It seems necessary that a law, which would be in conformity with the Shastras, should be made, in order that this great principle of religion may be strictly observed.

35. GOKULDAS KAHANDAS PAREKH.—Influential movements should be organized, each including all such castes as are of the same social standing and mix at dinner, for the purpose of removing all restrictions against marriage, when the parties, though not belonging to the same caste or subdivision, belong to castes which mix with each other at dinner. If these movements fail, then my proposal is that, in the event of a man marrying the girl of a person belonging to another caste or subdivision of the same caste with whom the members of his caste mix at food, the legislature should restrain the caste of the husband from excommunicating him, and of the parents of the bride from excommunicating them. By restraining I mean, that the legislation should declare such action on the part of the caste illegal, and visit it with a small fine. In most cases the castes and subdivisions of caste, that mix in food, are off-shoots of one original caste.

I consider it necessary to state why, when in my opinion the proposal that I make would be acceptable to a large majority of the people, they should not arrange this among themselves, and why a necessity, under certain circumstances, for invoking the assistance of the legislature is anticipated. The reason is abvious. This movement cannot be a movement of one or two castes, but of all castes of the same grade united: the combined castes form such an unwieldy and massive body that their opinion could not be obtained. As regards individuals, they are afraid to be severed from their relations by the action of the caste, who cannot sanction any movement of its members in this direction, so long as they are not sure that they would be reciprocated by the other castes. As regards those few people who would not care for the caste, their joining together will confer no good, as they would thereby be merely adding a new caste to the large number that exist. In my opinion, if there is a legislative measure of the kind I propose, all difficulties may be got over. I also think that it would be good, if the legislature makes all contracts of exchanges of girls void and unenforceable.

In cases of grown-up husbands marrying very young girls, the consummation takes place sometimes too early. This leaves a lasting effect on the girl's constitution. I propose that, the definition of the offence of rape may be so modified as to render intercourse with the wife, before she completes her 12th year, or in the case of her reaching puberty before the completion of the 12th year, before her reching puberty, illegal. The punishment for the consummation between the 10th and 12th year might be lighter than that of consummation when she is under 10 years of age, but it is necessary that such a consummation should be declared illegal and punishable.

36. His Highness the Rao of Cutch.—I do concur however in Mr. Malabari's suggestion as to moral support being advantageously accorded by the State, with a view to promote the object in view.

37, His Highness the Thakor Saheb of Bhavnagar.—These customs (infant marriage and enforced widowhood) involve the religion of the Hindus, whose feelings are likely to be injured by any forced measures. Consequently I do not think it wise or safe, to have recourse to any of them in such a way as to excite their feelings. To my mind, the remedies for the proposed reforms lie in the voluntary movement adopted by the unanimous voice of the community concerned, and this might only be expected by further spread of education, which will, I believe, make the majority in the various sections to appreciate, themselves, the necessity of any such reforms, as occasions may arise.

38. HIS HIGHNESS THE THAKOR SAHIB OF MORVI.—Direct interference of the State by way of legislation will have no salutary results, so long as rigid observances of caste distinctions continue with all their might and main. But, I think, Government can safely and rightly adopt other indirect means suggested by Mr. Malabari in his said notes, and approved of by many, for aiming a blow at the evil.

As to marriages of old men with young girls, the Thakor Sahib wishes for immediate interference. He says "These marriages which are the primary causes of grievous widowhood, and which add to the number of *young* widows on one hand, and which discourage widowers from accepting widows however young, beautiful, and noble they may be, as their wives, *ought to be stopped by authority.*

39. JAYASING RAO, REGENT OF KOLHAPUR.—At this rate the state of things will never improve. Let the so called leaders of society set an example themselves, and the rest are sure to follow.

40. SHANTARAM NARAYEN.—I am then humbly an advocate of legislative interference in the matter of infant marriage. All civilised Governments have dealt with the question of marriage, of the mutual relations between men and women, as one of which the State has a right and is bound to take cognizance. For instance, in Germany, the marriageable age fixed by law for men is 18, and for women 14; in Belgium 18 and 15; in Spain 14 and 12; in France 18 and 15; in Greece 14 and 12; in Hungary (for Protestants) 18 and 16 and (for Catholics) 14 and 12; in Portugal 14 and 12; in Russia 18 and 16; in Saxony 18 and 16; in Switzerland 14 and 12; in Austria 14 and 14 respectively.

Even in India, it has been from the ancient times a recognized principle for the law-giver to fix the marriageable limit of age for both men and women, and Diwan Bahadur Raghunathrao, one of our best Sanskrit scholars and leading social reformers, has shown that according to the Shastras infant marriages, as they now prevail, are not legal, and that they are of modern growth. Then again, the State is bound to protect the rights and interests of minors as their *parens patriæ*. Looking upon the question in this light, I do not see why the Government in India should not make laws on the subject of marriage. It is said that by making such laws the Government, not being an indigenous but an exotic one, would be departing from the principle of religious or social neutrality to which it had wedded itself in the administration of the country. But have not Government abolished Suttee, and legalised the marriage of widows, made laws for the management of religious endowments, fixed the age of majority by means of the Indian Majority Act, rendered the *Shesha* ceremony punishable under the Indian Penal Code? Some people argue as if the State or Sirkar has not yet interfered with our social customs. What do we witness every day in our Courts of Justice? We have a Hindu Law, it is true, but is not that law involved in confusion, and is it not a fact that our courts are expounding it as best they can, and bringing into vogue, in effect, new adaptations which Hindu lawyers of a bygone age would have probably stared at? The whole administration of the Hindu law is, in fact, based upon a legal fiction, and it affords a signal example of the fact that our customs are already being regulated by judiciary interference of a sort; and to the Hindu people such interference is as effective as legislative interference, for the Sirkar, whether sitting in the majesty of Justice, or the Sirkar proclaiming laws from the throne, is to the Hindu alike paternal, and may be held equally liable to be complained against as meddlesome. Those therefore who think that there is no State interference now with our religious practices or social customs, are either not aware of the real state of things, or are ignoring it.

I therefore respectfully submit that, it is the duty of the State and the State alone, to fix a reasonable standard of age for marriage. The question is as much political as it is social. All civilised governments have so regarded it, and whoever knows anything of Hindu society may rest assured that it will not move in the matter, unless the lead is taken by the State. The nation, I believe, is degenerating in a palpable degree, and since it is not capable of helping itself, it is the duty of the State to send us help from without.

41. H. H. JASWANTSING, THAKORE SAHIB OF LIMBDI.—It (Government) has a right to say that the public service shall not be open to people, who may have been married before a certain age. Such people may be excluded from higher University honours. Local Municipalities may be asked to lend their aid to the good cause, by introducing a system of registration, and the granting of licenses for marriage, under certain restrictions and so on...
It is the female that, in India, directly or indirectly, offers the greatest resistance to the cause of social reform. To train her mind, to prepare it to receive enlightened notions, should be the first care, I think, of every reformer, and much of the difficulty he now feels in his laudable endeavours would be removed. If, therefore, Government, in its parental regard for the interests of its people, renders female education, in a manner, compulsory, as elementary education, I am told, is in England, it will confer a great boon on the people of India.

SECTION III. BENGAL PRESIDENCY.

42. E. E. LOWIS, OFFICIATING COMMISSIONER, DACCA DISTRICT.—The Secretary of the People's Association, Burrisaul, states that the Association approve of Mr. Malabari's suggestion that the Educational Department should give a few chapters in its school books, describing the evils of infant marriage in various forms.

43. J. F. K. HEWITT, COMMISSIONER, CHOTA NAGPUR DISTRICT.—What is really wanted is that the people should learn and know that the Shastras do not enjoin either custom,

and that the priests and leaders of opinion, in the country, and the districts in which they live, are in favour of such customs being abolished. Let this be done by publishing a monthly paper in which these opinions are translated into the vernacular of the District to which the paper is to be sent, and let men of position be called on to declare "for" or "against," and let the names of the former he published. Branch associations should be formed to aid in this work, and every case of a widow marriage, or of first marriages when the ages of the parties were above the limit which the association might fix at which marriages are desirable, should be published under that head, for there is nothing after all like example in such matters. It is the bold ones who first lead the way, the timid ones will then soon follow. The association might include membership on the condition of each member pledging himself to carry on the objects of the association as far as lies in his power, by discouraging infant marriages and encouraging widow marriages. Government might aid the association with funds.

44. Kailash Chandra Bhattacharji.—There ought to be, in all chief centres of population, associations of guardians pledging themselves to act in concert, for the purpose of raising the limit of marriageable age of girls. Correspondingly there should be associations of boys' guardians also, to promote and co-operate with the former..................................

Among the priestly castes, there are to be found at present several Pandits of enlightened and liberal views, whose sympathies and co-opertion may be enlisted by a little management, and thus a good deal of orthodox opposition may be warded off, and the fear of social ostracism minimised.

45. Mr. Beadon, Collector of Dinagpore.—Government might now help in the growing feeling against these practices. The seed has been sown, the soil was not prepared at the time, and the young plant has raised its head under all the disadvantages of having to contend with the deeply rooted weeds of prejudice, timidity, caste oppression, and phy-

sical desire. Left entirely to itself it *may* grow up strong and well, but it may also be of very slow growth, and result in only a sickly and dwarfed shrub. Assisted by Government on judicious lines, the result will undoubtedly be speedier, and the growth firmer.

46. Babu Syama Mohun Chuckerbutty.—Education will take centuries to make the people conscious of the injurious effects of infant marriage, and to finally put a stop to them. When the evils are so great and should be speedily removed, it is but just and proper that the legislature should interfere, and frame such a law as will meet the desired end.

47. Babu Hori Mohun Chandra.—Some of my country men are of opinion that, direct legislative action should be taken in the matter, and it appears to me that such a course would be quite consistent with the Institutes of Manu...........

The question is not whether it (Infant Marriage) is a religious ceremony or a social usage—though it is undoubtedly more of the latter than the former, but is the custom an outrage on humanity? Is it productive of great evils in the community? Is it in short contrary to sound reason and morality? If so the Government should be true to its pledge as parent, and protector of society, and fall back on the wise and statesmanlike minute of the Marquis of Wellesley "that it is one of the fundamental maxims of the British Government to consult the opinions, customs, and prejudices of the natives, but only when they are consistent with the principles of humanity, morality and reason."

The objection on the score of religion would probably never he heard of, if our Government were a Hindu Government.

An Act might be passed making education of males compulsory up to a certain age, varying according to the social grades of the pupils, and prohibiting marriage until their education is finished, exception being made in cases in which the Municipal, District, Local or Union Board certifies that to fulfil the complete period of studentship would entail difficulties on the individuals or their families.

48. INDIAN ASSOCIATION.—The Committee, after giving their best consideration, find that they can safely make one practical suggestion for discouraging infant marriages. The educational authorities can pass a rule declaring married students ineligible for senior and lower scholarships, a senior scholarship once obtained not being liable to forfeiture by subsequent marriage.

49. UTTERPARAH PEOPLE'S ASSOCIATION.—Approve three of Mr. Malabari's suggestions viz (1) the formation of voluntary associations of graduates &c., (2) the introduction of chapters describing the evils of early marriage in school text books, and (3) his scheme of a national association.

50. RAJ SHAHYE ASSOCIATION—It is desirable that the practice of selling girls under the name of marriage to the highest bidder, irrespective of all consideration of suitableness of the match, should be put a stop to by Government.

51. MYMENSING ASSOCIATION.—Approve of Mr. Malabari's suggestions regarding giving greater publicity to the Remarriage Act, and regarding the formation of a national association.

52. TIPPERAH PEOPLE'S ASSOCIATION.—Recommend a rule to the effect that unmarried students only shall be eligible for *Government scholarships.*

53. BALASORE NATIONAL SOCIETY.—The society approve of the recommendation that the money received from the bridegroom—the price of the girl disposed of—is not to belong to the seller, the parent or relation of the victim, but to be safely deposited in her name and for her exclusive use.

54. KUMAR PRAMATHA BHUSHANA DEVA, RAJA OF NALDANGA.—The practice of selling girls, regarded equally by the Shastras and the respectable Hindu Community as a despicable action, may very well be put a check to, by ruling......

that the money received from the bridegroom is not to belong to the seller but to the girl.

55. BABU MENULAL CHATTERJEE.—Though Kulinism is on the decline, yet few marriages in Bengal take place, without imposing on the father of the bride a heavy fine for the sin of giving birth to daughters. Many a wealthy family in Bengal, which occupied once a conspicuous position in the front rank of society, and which was in fact the pride of the country, has by the mere accident of birth of daughters, been ruined and reduced to pauperism in consequence of their expensive marriages and the incidents which follow them .... The three superior forms of marriage contemplate a gift of the bride only, and nothing more than a declaration of the legislature that demands other than the gift of the bride will be illegal and treated as extortion and will not be countenanced by a Court of Justice, will materially help in checking the evil. There is room for legislation without offending the Shastras.

The demands of a father or other guardian of a bridegroom are very heavy, and comprise so many items that, on calculation, it is found to cover nearly all the costs incurred for the boy, commencing from the separation of the umbilical cord and ending with the last pice paid, up to the date of his marriage. These items or *abwabs* of the marriage are politely called *respects* for the family of the father of the bridegroom. This demand increases with the age of the bride. There are cases in which great difficulties are encountered in disposing of an aged daughter or sister.

Already cases are coming to courts for adjudication as to the legality of *pon* or price for the promised marriage, and such like matters. The highest court in the country is unable to put down attempts to make advantage of these contracts. It entertained doubts in decreeing a restoration of the *pon* even where the marriage broke off (I. L. R. 10 Cal. 1054.) In the absence of a prohibitory law, the Judges summarily regarded the custom of the country, and enforced a contract in every respect opposed to public policy..................... Matters have practically come to this pass that, secret contracts made with parents or other guardians whereby upon a treaty of marriage they are to receive a compensation or security for promoting a marriage or giving their consent to it, are passed under the guise of gifts or *stridhan*..

A Hindu Marriage Act would, like the Suttee Act of Lord William Bentinck, be productive of incalculable boon to the country, which will be treasured up in the memory of all the children of the soil as a precious monument of the benign rule of Her Gracious Majesty the Empress of India.......... Were the 12th year declared as the marriageable age of females, and all marriages under that age null and void by applying the principle of XIV. W.R. 403, the country would undoubtedly see the dawning of a better day.................. As it is in contemplation to make over registration of deeds and assurances to the Postal Deparment, and as Post offices are within an accessible distance, there could be no difficulty in procuring the attendance of a public officer to witness the marriage, and to take an inventory and enter in a register then and there, signed by the guardians of the married couple when both are infants.

SECTION IV. NORTH-WEST PROVINCES AND OUDH, THE PUNJAB, CENTRAL PROVINCES, BURMA, ASSAM, COORG, HYDRABAD (DECCAN.) &c.

56. C. R. Hawkins, Deputy Commissioner, Amritsar.—I should consider that the state should only show disapproval of such customs (as infant marriage.)—One means of showing this disapproval seems thoroughly practical and inoffensive. The State has certainly a right to prescribe the conditions on which any grant of money is made. Celibacy might be made a condition of all scholarships held by youths

under a certain age. Such a condition would be soon widely known, and specially tend to influence the rising generation. Any measure of this sort would be useful and unobjectionable.

The patronage of the State might be usefully given to societies (for the discouragement of early marriages and encouragement of the marriages of widows.)

57. HONOURABLE D. G. BARKLEY, MEMBER OF THE LEGISLATIVE COUNCIL, PUNJAB GOVERNMENT.—Several suggestions are made as to modes in which the State might indirectly show its disapproval of infant marriages. The only one of those which does not seem to involve undue interference with a practice which it is not expedient to prohibit by law is that, the Educational Department might draw attention to the evil in its school books. This would be simply assisting in educating public opinion on the subject, and if care were taken to introduce it in a way suitable for school books intended for children who can do nothing themselves to remove the evil until they come to maturer years, it would probably be unobjectionable ....

With reference to education of public opinion, Mr. Malabari seems to think that this must be confined to the small proportion of the population who have received elementary education. But this is not necessarily the case. After the annexation of the Punjab, much was done to create a public opinion opposed to female infanticide, by public meetings and conferences between leading men. The difficulties to be overcome were thus brought to notice, and efforts were made to remove these difficulties. Many of these arose from marriage customs, such as the feeling that a girl must be married into a superior sub-division of her caste, and in the case of Bedis, descended from the Guru Nanik, the absence of any caste accustumed to receive Bedi girls in marriage, as they had long ceased to be given in marriage. Agreements were come to with a view to reduce or remove these difficulties, and there is no doubt that amongst the Khatris a considerable reform was effected, though it has fallen short of what was hoped for at the time. Probably the great majority of those who took part in this movement, excluding the officials European and native, had no more elementary education than was required for the purpose of keeping accounts.

(Mr. Barkley also suggests, to discourage early consummation of infant marriages, an enactment to be made like Section 37 of Act XV of 1865, which runs as follows :—" Notwithstanding anything herein before contained, no suit shall be brought in any court to enforce any marriage between Parsis or any contract connected with or arising out of any such marriage, if at the date of the institution of the suit, the husband shall not have completed the age of 16 years or the wife shall not have completed the age of 14 years." But he would not pass any such enactment if not desired by a large proportion of Hindus.)

58. DIWAN RAMNATH DISTRICT JUDGE, HOSHIARPUR.—1stly. In provinces like Bengal and Bombay the learned classes of several castes and under-castes may be induced to ask the Government to pass an Act similar to the Parsi Marriage Act, and in that Act a provision might be made for the illegality of minor marriages. If an attempt of this kind were made in those provinces, it would partially encourage learned natives of the sister provinces to follow their example.

2ndly. The District and Municipal Board members should be now and then rewarded, who make an example in their own families againgst infant marriage.

3rdly. Pandits and Brahmans, Lambardars and Panches who strive to make people believe that infant marriage is a greater sin than allowing maidens to reach womanhood without marriage, should also be taken special notice of.

4thly. Brahmins be appointed by the Local Boards who would undertake to preach and use their influence for good, on this question.

5thly. Chairs be allowed before officers to the heads of the several tribes who effectually and heartily assist in the reform.

59. Kanwar Bikrama Singh Ahluwalia, C. S. I.—I would propose that parents be allowed to enter into betrothal contracts on behalf of their children, whenever they think fit to do so; but when the marriage takes place it should be registered in some Government office. Betrothals need not be registered, as the death of one of the betrothed parties does not debar the other from being betrothed again and married to some other person. The registration of marriage of boys under 14 and girls under 12, should be refused as unlawful, but the registration of marriage of boys and girls above the fixed age should be compulsory. But should parents or the married couple wish to have marriages registered after the couple attain the fixed age, they should be required to pay a larger fee by way of penalty, as in the case of unstamped documents produced in evidence. An unregistered marriage when disputed in a court of law should be regarded as inadmissible documentary evidence which is not stamped. This rule of registration will, in all probability, act as a preventive to early marriage.

60. Rai Mulraj m. a. Extra Assistant Commissioner Gurdaspur.—One of the great causes of why the sufferings of humanity in India have not been much removed in this direction, lies in the denational character of our reformers and the measures of reformation which are proposed from time to time. Our reformers attack everything at one and the same time. They assail religion, caste, and all that is dear to the Hindu when they propose any measure of reform, and they invoke the aid of Government in matters in which it should least interfere. The result is that they set the whole country against themselves and their measures of reformation, and make it impossible for the people to consider dispassionately the merits of the particular measure which is proposed for the good of the nation.

61. Chief Commissioner Central Provinces (Mr. Crosthwaite).—When a large number of Hindu women are educated, infant marriages and enforced widowhood will disappear.

62. Chief Commissioner British Burma (Mr. Bernard).—The Government and their officers, by their publications, by their utterances, and by their demeanour, may usefully show that they are on the side of reformers in these matters. Countenance can be shown, small grants of public money can be made, and local facilities can be given to reforming organizations such as Mr. Malabari describes.

63. Mr. Luxmon G. Rishi, Deputy Educatinal Inspector, Basim District.—It is most desirable that at least no girl under the age of 12, and no boy under 18 or 20, should be married........................It may be enacted, if necessary, that parents wishing to marry their daughter below the age of 12, should deposit in the Government Treasury a certain sum in her name, and for her exclusive use, that would pay an interest sufficient for her maintenance in after life, in case she becomes a widow. This would act as a powerful deterrent to the practice of infant marriage. In the same manner, no parents or guardians should marry a girl to an old man, or to one who is decidedly far advanced in age, or when great disparity of ages exists between the would-be couple ; but should they wish to do so the parents or guardians, as being the sacrificers of the unfortunate girl, should be obliged to make a provision similar to the above.

64. Gabusing, Special Magistrate Akot..—It should be enacted that the marriages of Hindu girls should be legally registered, making the contracts under the age 11 and 18 of the bride and bridegroom respectively objectionable, while the unregistered ones not only invaid but subject to some heavy fine.

The marriage of a girl with a man above the age of 40 should also be made subject to the production of a health certificate from licensed medical officers, in addition to the deposition of at least 2000 Rs. worth of estate in favour of the bride, distinctly apart from any claims of her relations during her life-time.

65. VISHNU MORLESHWAR MAHAJANI M. A. HEAD MASTER AKOLA.—All that the Government should do is to indirectly help the movement forward, and provided the aid does not assume the form of any restriction, it will be welcomed by a large section of the community. In this direction, district and other high officers can do much if they gain the confidence of the leaders of the native society...........We must make efforts.........We must form associations, and if we get the sympathy of our English friends so much the better.

66. SHRIKRISHNA NARHAR, EXTRA ASSISTANT COMMISSIONOR ELLICHPUR.—If however Government is at all minded to take part in this matter, the proper course would be to convene together all the spiritual heads of the Hindus, and ask their consent to a few and fundamental reforms. Persons should not be denominated heads merly because they have wealth or temporal power, but should be carefully selected from among those who really possess great religious influence over the people at large. Such, for instance are the Shankar Acharia, the Madhavacharya, the Ramanuyacharya, the Pandits of Benares, Nassik, Nagpur, Pandharpur, Poona, Mathura, and other places which are great Brahminical centres. If such an important diet were called into existence and proposals submitted to them, the legislation will have a very great moral support, and the populace will very easily acquiesce.........I am what Mr. Malabari calls a let-alone-is out and out, and put forward the above proposal only on the supposition that the Government of India are anxious to move in the matter.

67. SHRIRAM BHIKAJI JATAR, B. A., DIRECTOR OF PUBLIC INSTRUCTION, HYDRABAD ASSIGNED DISTRICTS.—I entirely agree with Mr. Malabari in what he says regarding the beneficial effects of "friendly sympathy" and "personal interest" on the part of the executive officers of Government. Of course no definite rules can be laid down; but much good is

likely to be done to the cause of social reform if men who evince moral courage, and break through a pernicious but long standing custom are especially encouraged by Government. If the conduct of such men be considered equivalent to meritorious services to the State and rewarded accordingly, the appreciation on the part of Government will be a great recompense to them for the social persecutions which they have to undergo.........

The suggestion made in the last paragraph regarding a "National association" has my hearty approval; but in my opinion the most effectual means for carrying out social reforms is the spread of education.

68. HARI MORESHWAR SHEVADE HEAD MASTER A. V. SCHOOL MALKAPUR.—The educated should before all others proceed to establish a national reform association, and enlist sympathizers. The agitation of public opinion by newspaper and monthly magazine writers, impressive representations from the chair and the pulpit, and the departments of education inserting lessons on the subject throughout the serial Readers, should be among the preliminary stps...........Our reformers must take the example of the Scottish Missionaries who are labouring so hard for the cause of Christianity all over this country.

69. WAMAN NARAYEN BAPAT TEHSILDAR, CHANDUR TALUK.—The most obnoxious of carly marriages are marriages of girls of 12 with dotards of 50 and 60. These can never be too sufficiently condemmed. They are brought about by wretches of fathers and mothers of viction girls from mercenary motives. Here you may strike as hard and deep as you can...In all such marriages Government should rule that the girls must be at-least 12. At this age a girl can choose and express her choice. Government should appoint a respectable *punch* in each caste to see that the girl consents of her own free will, and that such consent should be recorded.........Every caste is simply unanimous in its abhorence of these vile bargains and will go with Government, not against it.

70. RAGHUNATH B. TALVALKAR B. A. HEAD MASTER HIGH SCHOOL AMRAOTI.—Female enlightenment is an indispensable condition. The real obstacle to reforms of this kind is neither religion nor caste. Both have begun to loosen their hold upon us. It is in the family and among the relations.

SECTION V. EXTRACTS FROM OPINIONS GIVEN TO MR. MALABARI.

71. THE HON'BLE MR. J. GIBBS C.S.I. C.I.E.—Nothing but the constant hammering at all classes, but especially at the leaders of the different religious sects, can do good. The remedy in itself is easy. Let each leading man determine that he will not allow such marriages (child marriages) in his family, and in a few years the custom will die out.........You most bring public opinion to bear through the Press, and you must if possible, get expressions of opinion from men in high official positions as a background to work on.

72. MAHADEO GOVIND RANADE M. A. L. L. B.—Our deliberate conviction, however, has grown upon us with every effort, that it is only a religious revival that can furnish sufficient moral strength to work out the complex social problems which demand our attention. Mere considerations of expediency or economical calculations of gains or losses, can never nerve a community to undertake and carry through social reforms—especially a community like ours, so spell bound by custom and authority. Our people feel, and feel earnestly, that some of our social customs are fraught with evil, but as this evil is of a temporal character, they think that it does not justify a breach of commands divine, for such breach involves a higher penalty...........People find fault with us, even abuse us, for half-heartedness, for our apparent want of fire and enthusiasm. God only knows that in our household we are perpetually at war with our dearest and nearest, we struggle and strive to do our best, and have perforce to stop at

many points when we fear the strain will cause a rupture. This is our present situation. We do not think either Parsi or European philanthropists can make any impression upon our society. Empires come and go, dynasties change, but our society remains unconcerned. These are my views on the general question.*

As regards the two notes, I go in fully with you that time has now come for a determined effort to secure legislative and executive sanction to a moderate limit of minimum age being fixed, below which early marriages should be discouraged. Three years ago, we started a movement here (Poona) to fix the boys' age at 17 or 18 and the girls' at 10 or 11. These limits are not all that we should wish, but as a commencement we must carry the more cultivated sentiment of the people with us. Once this is done, we might by gradual steps raise the limit in due time...............I agree with you that in order to stimulate the discussion of the subject, a motion might be brought in the Senate of the University prescribing bachelorship as one of the requisite qualifications for the Matriculation Examination. The Educational Department might be also moved in the matter.

73. A. Mackenzie Esq., Secretary to Government of India.—You cannot scold or legislate the people at large into setting aside caste prejudices, but I do think you can make it to some extent "fashionable" to despise them. Get then, all the leading native gentlemen, whose education has already taught them the folly and wickedness of infant marriage and enforced widowhood, to band themselves into a national association for the propagation of sound ideas on these subjects. Education is after all the true and common basis for Indian nationality. Make it the object of the association to encourage and support all who hold similar views. Get all the leading official and non-official Europeans to affiliate themselves as sympathisers

* (This was written on August 18, 1884. The opinion given to Government is dated 12th February 1885.)

and well-wishers—Raise funds for compiling vernacular tracts on the subject, letting it be known far and wide, how influential the movement really is. Hold meetings periodically at all large centres to induce young men especially to join and pledge themselves to advance its aims; and you will I feel sanguine give a great and lasting impulse to the reforms you so much desire to bring about.

....

I have observed, with great interest and satisfaction, Mr. Justice Pinhey's Judgment refusing to import into Indian legal practice the English "order for restitution of conjugal rights" in cases of unconsummated infant marriages. When there has never been voluntary cession, no question of restitution can arise. If the decision is up-held in appeal (it was not) it will throw an effectual shield over many virgin—wives. There is however this practical difficulty—that few of them will be educated sufficiently to know their rights, and still fewer of them will care or venture to assert them.

74. Hon'ble Sir Auckland Colvin K.C.M.G.—The first thing to be done is to obtain from a large consensus of opinion amongst educated and influential natives a declaration hostile to these customs. If, as I understand from you, they rest on insecure legal bases, assistance should be given by natives interested in the matter, with the view of obtaining test decisions........... You need not to be reminded that, in matters of this kind, the Government cannot help you unless and until you help yourselves...

Try and get up, in each province, societies having for their aim the object you are advocating, encourage discussion, however bitter in its tone against you personally; and be no respecter of persons. Plain misrepresentations are best met by plain truths.

I am one of those who think, and have no hesitation in saying—that societies which will not make any combined effort to reform their own short-comings are not to be much trusted when they combine to reform public affairs. They lay themselves open to the suspicion that in the profession of public zeal, they find an agreeable cloak for the discouragement of private duty. It is because many native advocates of progress proclaim in public enlightened principles and urge liberal practices, the application of which to their domestic affairs they strenuously oppose, that I ventured in writing to you, to express the view that it was not the outside only of the platter, but the inner also, which requires attention.*

....

In India more than in many other countries the battle of social reform must be first fought by those whom it immediately concerns. They have always the Government behind and with them, as a reserve of strength, when the hour has come to employ it; but it is for them, by their efforts, to hasten that hour.

75. Hon'ble Sir Steuart Bayley.—At all events Government ought not to take the initiative. I think if a number of memorials from different associations all over the country, urging action and agreeing on a special line of action, were submitted, the hands of Government would be so far strengthened, that they might be justified in moving in the matter, and what I would suggest is that the associations all over the country which take an interest in the matter, be urged to adopt this method.........I suppose the most hopeful outlook on this question is that the guidance of caste feeling will gradually fall into the hands of educated men who will lend their influence, and thus that of the caste, in support of the object you have in view............................

---

* Mr. Telang in replying to Sir Auckland quotes the following from Herbert Spencer. "Submission whether to Government, to the dogmas of ecclesiastics, or to that code of behaviour which society at large has set up, is essentially of the same nature, and the sentiment which induces resistance to the despotism of rulers, civil or spiritual, likewise induces resistance to the despotism of the world's opinion."

All the more earnestly would I encourage you to labour on in the cause by means of local committies, societies formed for the purpose of advocating and *practising* the reforms, by pamphlets and speeches, and all the machinery of organization which in other spheres the natives of India have not been slow to adopt.

76. MANOMOHAN GHOSE.—An association of the kind you have suggested may do a great deal of good......A strong public opinion ought to be created, and our universities ought to be made to take the initiative.

77. S. N. TAGORE ESQ., C.S.—The only remedy possible is to educate public opinion. For my own part, I am not opposed to any well-considered law fixing a limit of marriageable age, but I fear that public opinion is not yet prepared for any such change.

78. B. N. PITALE, SUPT. HOME DEPARTMENT GOVERNMENT OF BOMBAY.—At present Hindu society is in a state of dormancy; it is by extraneous efforts of philanthropists whose hearts writhe in agony at the sight of customs so repugnant to human nature, that a beginning could be made. Happy will be the day in the social and moral history of India, when these dark spots are effaced from its pages.

79. DINSHAW ARDESIR TALEYARKHAN.—It is best to point out an instance or two of what innate forces have the power of effecting...........In certain parts of Kattywar, one of the Wania castes has bound itself by its own voluntarily framed rule not to give any girl in marriage before she is eleven...........Somehow or other the minds of these caste people were touched by a number of child girls having become widows before this caste *bandobast* was adopted. Again a sect namad Rackwal Brahmins, through the exertions of many of its influential and enlightened leaders, has recently entered into an agreement not to permit a boy being given in marriage until he is 16 and a girl unless she is 9. In the case of the

former there is an extra provision that the boy should have had an education up to a certain standard before the marriage would be allowed.

80. T. B. Dani, Editor of the Arya Vart.—This gentleman advocates, State interference on the ground that education will not remedy the evils in time. "It is impossible for education to spread to such an extent as to remedy the evils, before an utter destruction of the vitality of the whole community is made. It is a well-known fact that females have a greater voice in the matter of marriages, and that almost all females in the country are illiterate. There are millions and millions of males who are still illiterate."

81. Sirdar Gopalrao Hari Deshmukh.—Matriculation or degree examinations, would if limited to bachelors, go a great way to prevent early marriages.

(He also advocates the use of "political influence as far as it may be reasonable", and female education.)

82. Khan Bahadur Rustomji Karshedji Modi.—If we have not the bold administrators of the old times of Company Bahadur, who were habituated to taking the bull by the horns, we have none the less wise, less able, or less sympathetic men at the helm of our affairs now, and if as I take it, owing to the altered times, they desire that some august decree that they may shape should be "broad-based" upon the people's will let us by all the means in our power obey their call—let us move the whole country in such noble cause from one end to the other—send petition after petition, and show, in short, by ovewhelming proof what the will of the people really is. There is no doubt that legislation which is far ahead of the intelligence and active sympathy of a people, however righteous and well meant it may be, has many chances of turning out a failure. But on the other hand, there is equally little doubt that when the ideas and practices of a community have, of themselves and unaided, attained the desired goal, legislation is too late, useless or nearly so. As has been truly said

the ideas and practices of a few advanced spirits of today become the common property of a succeeding generation. The true function of legislation, I believe, is to discern the signs and tendencies of the times, and opportunely to put itself at the head of a movement, when it commends itself to the light of right reason; to so gently, if possible, yet none the less decisively, shape its course, smooth away difficulties, and generally guide its action, as to accelerate the attainment of the end in view. All signs tell me that the time is now ripe or nearly so for a decisive *coup de grace* to be given by our enlightened and merciful legislature to practices and customs which have no real foundation in Hindu religion, which are alike abhorrent to common sense and morality, are utterly prejudicial to the best interests of society at large, and which having already begun to give way and crumble under the silent but sure and powerful influence of public opinion, need but the necessary impetus of legislative condemnation to die the speedy death they deserve.

83. KESHAVLAL MADHOWDAS.—They (the Government) ought to make marriage legal for girls at any time of life beyond 12 years.

84. RUMANUJCHARI M. A. B. L., VICE PRINCIPAL MAHARAJA'S COLLEGE VIJIANAGRAM.—In all the other forms of slavery the law punishes both the seller and the buyer, and dissolves the relation originating from the unrighteous contract, but in the case of connubial slavery the real offenders are not looked upon as criminals at all, and the law is powerless to restore the enthralled to freedom by tearing asunder the fetters forged for her enslavement by the heartless greed of her parents. Can the infamous practice of selling infants be sanctioned under the cloak of matrimony? Can the sacred institution of wedlock, whose influence is highly beneficent and humanizing, be converted into a regular source of illicit profit, revolting to human feelings and brutalizing in its effects upon humanity..............................I cannot congratulate the

British nation upon having restored mankind to freedom by the complete abolition of slavery, so long as they permit the most aggravated form of it to continue under their very noses.

85. BABU P. C. MUZOOMDAR.—Against the evil of infant marriages there is a steadily growing public opinion.........The difficulty is with the girls. The tremendous difficulties of the vexed question of courtship present themselves as soon as you let the tender sex grow up to a certain age. Young ladies institute the most crucial tests of competency in admitting the claims of any human being to their affections, and, when they are good enough to fall in love they belie those tests so flagrantly as to provoke the strongest revolt against the infallibility of their choice. Parents are in great bewilderment, therefore, when they have a bevy of spirited undergraduate daughters. How you manage it in the Parsi community I should like to know. Infant marriages are doomed, but the problem of finding out suitable matches for over-grown young ladies is as far from solution as ever. I have already alluded to the puritanism of Hindu conceptions. We cannot afford to have love letters, flirtations, rejections and amorous fancies in our households. If we can help it, we will not permit the importation of these usages. What then, are we to do? I would advocate betrothals long before marriage. The parents, according to Hindu notions, should propose and arrange the matches, but the daughter or son shall have the power to veto the selection. But if the selection once meet with the approval of parent and child, the match shall never be set aside, unless either of the contracting parties show a physical or moral unfitness.

86. K. N. RANE.—A conservative people like ours do not care to profit by the signs of the times, and their thick skin could be pricked only by the stern hand of law.

87. K. VENCATRAO ESQ., FIRST GRADE PLEADER BELLARY.—It can be satisfactorily shown that the Shastras do not prohibit the postponement of the marriage of a girl till she

attains her 12th year, and of a boy till 16. As for caste or custom it does not seem to condemn the persons concerned in the marriage of a girl and boy aged respectively 12 and 16 or above. Hence it is clear that legislative interference in fixing the minimum of the marriageable ages of girls and boys, with penal clauses for punishing the parents or other guardians for violating the said law, will not shock the feelings of the people nor set in motion the torrent of reaction against the cause, nor be inconsistent with the non-interfering policy of Government in religious matters. As the people do not in 90 per cent of the marriages that now take place, adhere to the ages laid down in our Shastras, perhaps under the impression that those were the maximum ages permitted by our Hindu law, or for want of proper authorities to enforce the same, the necessity for securing legislative sanction for a moderate limit of minimum age, both for boys and girls, is very great. Those that deprecate legislation in such matters seem to hold that as female education advances, these prejudices perish of their own accord. If that be the case, there would have been no legislation on the subject in the civilised countries of Europe.........I think we are not without a precedent......The Indian Majority Act now determines the age of majority of a Hindu, and prolongs the period of nonage fixed by Hindu law. While the above Act interferes with the Hindu law of succession and contract as regards the capacity of the persons concerned, the one now asked for will merely declare the temporary incapacity of the persons entering into marriage life, or rather marital contracts.

88. HON'BLE MR. JUSTICE SCOTT JUDGE OF THE BOMBAY HIGH COURT.—I think you could not do better than adopt the rule that now obtains in most of the civilised countries of the world, which may be stated as follows: "A male person is enabled by law to consent to matrimony at the age of 14 and a female at the age of 12. Even though the male be under 14 or the girl under 12, the marriage is not absolutely void, but is only inchoate and imperfect. Either of the parties upon coming to the proper age, for his or her consent, may declare

the marriage void. This rule would provide for the Hindu system of betrothals, or rather it would substitute irrevocable betrothals for the present irrevocable infant marriage.

....

If you wait till individual Hindus take up and carry through single-handed, without outside aid, any great change in their social system, you will realise the fable of the countryman who sat by the river bank and waited for the stream to run dry before he crossed over to the other side. It is not in human nature to expect great changes to be effected in a society by its own members, when the advocates of change have to face family estrangement, social ostracism, and caste excommunication, as a probable result of their efforts. You must in such circumstances take some middle course. Mr. Melvill suggests a *Modus operandi*: "A few representatives of each caste" he says "must take the lead." I fully endorse that view, but I would add that the action these leaders must take is not on the lines of purely internal reform, but rather in favour of internal reform helped by a very moderate amount of Government interference. I believe that if a petition to Government were signed by all those leaders of native opinion who have already signified to you in one way or another their adherence to the reforms in question, the natural hesitation of those in authority to interfere with the religious or social institutions of those they govern would be removed. Deference and respect for native religion and usage is the basis of the English rule in India. But whilst the Government, steadily refuses to regulate belief or alter custom by law, it can still consistently and safely assist reform by cautious legislation, when the leaders of native opinion testify clearly to the wish of the people for progress..............

My experience of these things, gained in an Eastern country, though not in India, is that they are best done piece-meal. Every fresh change proposed disturbs a fresh set of prejudices and stirs up the animosity of special vested interests, and all your opponents combine, because each has a reason to suppress you.........................

If you confine yourself to this single reform (Abolition of Infant Marriages) you can have first the religious party, those who cling to the ancient ways more tenaciously than any others, on your side. Then secondly you must have all those who realise how the present custom undermines the vitality of the people. I have often thought that if it was only brought home to the minds of my native friends how fatal the progress must be to national degeneracy under the present system of premature marriage, every enlightened man in the country would be ranged on the side of this reform. I think, at any rate, you can find support enough to persuade the Government to help you, if you confined yourself to the infant marriage question. If that practice is abandoned, your other reform would incidentally be partially effected, for that class of widows who excite the most pity, the virgin widows, would disappear. But if you tried to carry the double reform, you might fail altogether from attempting too much—Do not forget the French proverb, Qui trop embrasse mal etreint.

89. HON'BLE MR. KASHINATH T. TELANG.—I am, however, prepared, although not without some hesitation and diffidence—to go as far as this. The university and the Government Educational Department may, I think, fairly lay down a rule that the scholarships and prizes awarded by those authorities up to a student's graduation shall be tenable only by unmarried men. ....

The object of the association (proposed by Malabari) should be, I think, to familiarize the people with the evils of the prevailing system, and to help anybody, be he a member or not, who is ready and willing to break through the system himself. If the members themselves break through it, well and good; the success of the association will be greater, more rapid, and more complete than in the other alternative. But I don't think that the success should be imperilled in advance, as it will be if a pledge is insisted on, which by the hypothesis we are not prepared practically to redeem I must add, too, that I have not much faith in the operative character of pledges of this sort ....

I agree that our ordinary school books should be made instrumental in this reform (i.e. prevention of early consummation); and carefully framed reading lessons on this and other social topics, if not made obtrusively didactic, might prove useful. I agree, too, that an association should be established for delivering popular lectures, and publishing short and cheap tracts, illustrative of the true views on these questions. I also concur to some extent in the opinion that officers of Government might do some service to the good cause by "evincing a strong personal interest" in it. One practical mode in which it will be in the power of all of them to do so is to decline to attend any of the *tamashas* which are taking place so frequently in Bombay, and on occasions, in the mofusil also, "in honour of" the weddings of little children. This will be one practical method of discountenancing the present mischievous system. And its effects, will not, I am persuaded, be quite insignificant. But I must say that the inclination of my opinion on these matters generally is such as would justify you in classing me with your friends the "let-alone-ists." My faith in "the education of public opinion," as a great social force, is unlimited. And I believe that in the long run the results of that education are not only more enduring, but what might seem paradoxical, more rapid than the results of such artificial remedies applied *ab extra* as are proposed in your note.

90. NAVALRAM LAKSHMIRAM.—I would require the sympathisers as well as the members to refrain from attending any marriage that is celebrated against the rules of the Association in the town. This looks a little puritanical no doubt, and will be found particularly hard by the natives, who are so fond of the nautches, the processions, and the grand '*tamashas*' that generally attend a marriage in a rich family.

91. G. D. B. Gribble, Retired C. S. Bangalore.—As regards encouragement to be given by the Universities and Colleges I see no objection to such a plan. The very name of Bachelor of arts implied an unmarried state, and there can be no doubt that early marriages act most detrimentally upon a scholastic career. This was long recognized by the English Universities, and until recently, a Fellow lost his Fellowship if he married.

92. Col. S. S. Jacob.—I quite agree with your suggestions that the State might offer special inducements to students who remain single (just as at our own Universities in England), also that University Graduates should form themselves into an association to further the project of reform, and that the money received from the bridegroom should be deposited in trust for the benefit of the wife. Nothing, I believe, would tend to draw together native and European—the best of each race, I mean, as reformation of this sort among the native race. It would command the sympathy of all good men, and when there is sympathy with one another, how easily all little differences and difficulties disappear. And what race or creed can have a higher motive for life and action than "love to God and love to man."

93. Dayaram Gidumal, C. S.—A short Act declaratory, if you please, of the Hindu law on the subject of marriageable age (since the Hindu law does not favour infant marriages) is all that is required. The age being settled, the easiest and the simplest way of enforcing it would be for the Courts to rule all marriages contrary to the statute to be illegal. Or better, far better still, a few sections may be inserted in the Act enabling the Government to call upon the people themselves to elect one or more Honorary Magistrates every year to whom births and prospective marriages should be reported and who should have the power to issue injunctions to prohibit marriages under the statutory age...............A law on these lines would be a boon much greater than that abolishing Satti or Slavery. It would produce much more good, as it would

arrest the deterioration of a whole race. It would involve no detailed interference, no administrative meddling—as its enforcement would be left to the people themselves.

The next best thing that the Government can do is to legislate whenever considerable communities call upon it to do so, for such communities—in fact in the same way that it gave a special marriage law to the Brahmos. Such legislation might have little symmetry, but it would be perhaps more welcome. It would entail an enormous labour on our patriots, but they are not worth their salt if they cannot carry on a successful campaign against Infant Marriage and induce the people to sign a prayer to Government for such legislation.

But if Government is not at present prepared to promise any such legislation, let it at least give us increased facilities for corporate action in social matters. It has passed an Act for the registration of Literary and Charitable Societies. Why should it not extend this Act to Social Reform Societies? This will enable such bodies to recover their subscriptions by an easy process, and give them at the same time an advantageous legal status. Then again, it is doubtful whether an agreement by a member of such a society with the society in its corporate charactor to do a certain thing or to abstain from doing a certain thing, will not be treated by our courts as an agreement without consideration and therefore void. On this point you should invite the opinion of your lawyer friends. If the weight of legal authority confirms my doubt, then I say it is high time for the Legislature to insert an exception in the Contract Act in favour of such agreements. This will enable us to recover penalties from seceders and indeed prevent such combinations as the Hydrabad panchayat from ending in a fiasco. It is mainly due to the English Civil and Revenue laws that the panchayats have lost their power, and I think it is but just to compensate us for the social sanction these panchayats formerly possessed by providing us with another enforceable by the courts.

94. A. O. Hume.—To me personally, the promotion of female education (using the word in its broadest sense) as neces-

sarily antecedent to the thorough eradication of the grievous evils you so forcibly depict, appears a more important and immediately pressing question than those selected by you.

95. REV DR. MURDOCH, (MADRAS.)—The Germans say "Whatever you would put into the life of a nation, put into its schools." What you would put into the *schools*, put into the *school books*.........The late Dr. Duff of Calcutta was one of the ablest and most successful educationists in India. His opinion about school books is as follows :—

" 'Give me' says one, 'the songs of a country, and I will let any one else make its laws.' 'Give me' says anothor 'the school books of a country, and I will let any one else make both its songs and its laws.' That early impressions—impressions co-eval with the first dawnings of intelligence, impressions made when a new world is opening with the freshness of morning upon the soul, are at once the most vivid and most indelible has passed into a proverb."

Throughout the whole school course there should be lessons in the reading books on social reform, adapted to the age and intelligence of the classes in which they are used.

In Government Reading Books caste could not be directly taken up, but the "brotherhood of men" might be taught. Probably Hindus would not object to the following quotation from the Mahabharata.

" Small souls inquire, 'Belongs this man
To our own race or class or clan.'
But larger hearted men embrace
As brothers all the human race."

96. CHOTALAL SEVAKRAM, PRIVATE SECRETARY TO H. H. THE RAO OF CUTCH.—The minimum limit should be 10 for girls and 14 for boys, and if a double standard of age be practicable, for instance that of 12 and 16 respectively, the same may be introduced, and a general law should be framed by Government providing that no children shall be married under the limit or limits of age fixed by the Legislature,

and that the benefit of the enactment shall be extended to those castes that would apply for it.

97. RAO BAHADUR TRIMALRAO VENKATESH (DHARWAR.) Infant marriages are not authorized by Hindu law. They are of modern growth and should be suppressed altogether. Boys ought not to be allowed to be married until they are 20, and girls until they are 12 years old.

98. DR. ATMARAM PANDURANG LATE SHERIFF OF BOMBAY.—I am afraid the efforts of reformers like you and of those that have preceded you, will not bear the desired effect until the education of girls is taken most earnestly in hand.

99. LALA BAIJNATH JUDGE OF AGRA, AT PRESENT CHIEF-JUSTICE INDORE.—I agree with you in thinking that a committee of Hindus, with yourself as its Secretary or even as its President, ought to be appointed to take active steps in the matter. This committee should :—

(1) Collect the opinions of pandits and the dicta of Shastras as to the legality or otherwise of infant marriage and the prohibition of the remarriage of widows.

(2) Collect and publish in book form all that has up to this time been written upon the subject since you initiated the discussion.

(3) See that *all* the former, and the main portion of the latter are translated into the principal vernaculars, and circulated freely amongst the masses.

100. NAVALRAI SHAUKIRAM, HUZUR DEPUTY COLLECTOR HYDERABAD SIND.—Your suggestion for the formation of a committee of representative Hindu gentlemen is a very good one, and will meet with the approval of all who have the interest of their country at heart. But I must beg of you to be the leading spirit of that Committee.

101. PANDIT BADRI DUTT JOSHI (ALMORA).—Your proposal to form a "committee of representative Hindu gentlemen" and to get collected "under the auspices and guidance of this committee" "all the opinions published during

the present discussion in a condensed form after careful and impartial editing" is an excellent one.

102. RAJA SIR T. MADAVA ROW K C.S.I.

(a) Though I have not been *demonstrative*, I have *fully* and *abundantly* sympathised with you in your noble efforts to bring about some reform as respects Infant Marriage and Enforced Widowhood.

(b) The great danger is lest *the present generation should, pass away in total inaction.*

(c) Legislation is indeed, difficult, but *not impossible.*

(d) The Hon. Mr. Ilbert will be here in a day or two and I'll see him and urge him strongly to take *some* action, however *moderate*. Our great aim should be to dislodge Government from the attitude of utter inaction. It must be made to move, however little.

(e) We should be content with a small instalment of legislation at the very first, as preferable to nothing at all.

(f) Once a movement begins all the rest will follow in due course.

103. SIR W. WEDDERBURN C.S.—You have plied the whip and spur with much vigour, and the steed is fairly aroused; but there is a danger of its getting out of hand altogether and going off the right track. What is now wanted is that it should be soothed and even coaxed by a hand and voice with which it is familiar.

The best plan seems, therefore, to be to approach each of these castes or local sub-divisions through their own natural leaders, seeking out those among them who are most reasonable and most alive to the evil consequences of the existing systems. In the more advanced groups such leaders would be found without difficulty. In the less advanced, it would not be so easy. But in all they would probably be willing to undertake the duty in preference to the present method under which their social system is attacked from outside, so that even the London *Times* discredits the whole Hindu Community on account of its social short-comings.

104. HON'BLE MR. DAYARAM JETHMAL.—I think the best thing would be for the Legislature to declare that marriage before a certain age (say 12 in the case of females and 16 in the case of males) will be null and void. I will not attach any penalty to an infringement of this rule such as imprisonment or fine, as proposed by Mr. Whitley Stokes. But I can not believe that any thing short of such legislative declaration will do good.

Education could not help you much. In the first place it will take a long time before education can effect a regular upheaval in society. In the second place, if there are some highly educated men who are thoroughly convinced of the evils arising from early marriage, they are powerless to prevent such marriage taking place in their families, either because they have elders who manage their affairs; or for fear that owing to the prevalence of the custom of early marriages among persons of position, suitable matches will not be procurable if the children are allowed to grow up; or because of the necessity they may be under, owing to limited pecuniary means, of getting presents on account of their sons to transfer them to their growing daughter. Supposing none of these obstacles exist, an educated man *may* set an example by postponing the marriage of his son or daughter, but the example is at the best of a negative character and will hardly act on others, At present, if you talk to any one here, he quite coincides with you, and wants others to do it, that is to say he wants a *Custom to be created*, and he will not be satisfied unless all belonging to his society follow a certain line of conduct. This is impossible to do by merely setting negative examples, especially when there are various counter-influences at work and in full force some of which I have hinted at above.

I think I have said enough to show you that it is no use relying on voluntary effort to effect the desired end. State interference or support is necessary, and I can see no other form for that support than a legislative measure.

105. KRISHNA BEHARI SEN M. A.—I wish there were a common method of action struck out among the reformers of the various provinces When you try to create political unity among the people why should there not be a unity in the programme of social reforms? I admit that it will be more difficult to reach unity in social opinions than in the political, still some co-operation is necessary, and it might have been attained in the present case.

106. HON. SIR M. MELVILL C.S.I.—The bill drafted by Sir M. Melvill is as follows.

"1. Whoever has social intercourse with a woman, who is above the age of ten but under the age of twelve years, shall be punished with imprisonment of either description which may extend to two years, or with fine or both.

2. Whoever being the lawful guardian of a woman, who is under the age of 12 years, knowingly permits her to have sexual intercourse, or does any act to facilitate her having sexual intercourse, shall he punished with imprisonment of either description which may extend to two years, or with fine or with both.

3. If the husband of any woman dies before she has attained the age of 12 years, the High Court or the District Court may, upon the application of such woman or of any person whom the Court may allow to appear as her next friend, declare the marriage to be null and void.

4. Before making such declaration the Court shall give notice of the application to, and shall hear any objections made by, the father, or if the father be dead, the mother of the woman by or on whose behalf the application is made.

5. Any person who, knowing that such a declaration has been made, does any act for the purpose of making it appear that such woman is a widow shall be deemed to have com-

mitted contempt of Court and shall also be liable to punishment under Section 188 of the Indian Penal Code.

6. Section 2 of Act XV of 1856 is repealed except in so far as it relates to maintenance."

" I do not think" wrote Sir Melvill " you can expect the Legislature to go so far, unless you can induce the leaders of Hindu Society to memorialise Government on the subject."

The following extracts are taken from Sir Melvill's letters.

" If it can be done without causing general discontent, I see no strong objection to declaring by law that the marriage of girls below the age of 12 is invalid. This might do some good though I fear it would give rise to a good deal of trouble and some vexatious litigation in cases in which family property was in dispute. In England baptismal registers are conclusive proof of age: but in India it is very difficult to prove a person's age. In suits involving questions of family property between a widow and her male relatives, I fear there would be frequent attempts to prove that the marriage was invalid, and there would be much hard swearing as to age. The young widow might be deprived of her property in consequence, and in this way the law might be productive of injury rather than benefit to women.

If consummation could be prevented before the age of 12, it would certainly be most desirable. But could the law effect this ? At present consummation of marriage before the age of 10 is punishable. But in the whole course of my experience, I have never known such a case brought before the criminal courts. Why is this ? The explanation must be either, that such cases do not take place, or that they are not discovered. The first explanation I think you do not admit and therefore you must fall back on the second. But if it is impossible to prove that the law is broken, when the girl is under 10, it would be equally, or even more difficult to prove it, when the girl was between 10 and 12. I say " more difficult" because the visible injury to the girl herself, would be less serious and less apparent. It seems to me that it would be impossible to enforce the law, except by means of an inquisitorial investigation of the most private affairs of domestic life which would be considered intolerable. In the absence of complaint by the wife (and she would never complain), how could any one be allowed to go into a man's house, in order to ascertain whether he had consummated his marriage before his wife was *apta viro*? And then there is the difficulty to which I have already referred, that in most cases it is almost impossible to prove conclusively whether a girl is 10, or 11, or 12 years old.

I cannot help thinking that a law against infant marriage would be unpopular. Premature consummation is bad, and the prohibition of the remarriage of virgin widows is bad; but these are not necessary accessories of Infant Marriage, and apart from these accessories, Infant marriage is not necessarily a bad institution, or at all events not so bad as to render legislative interference desirable.

As regards consummation, I should not be disposed to alter the provisions of $375 of the Penal Code......But I should not object to making it an offence, punishable with a milder punishment than that of rape, to have intercourse with a woman between the age of 10 and 12. This, I think, is the law in England.

107. H. H. Maharaja Syaji Rao, Gaekwar of Baroda G.C.S.I.—I do not doubt that your programme is a workable one, and although no hard or fast rules can be laid down to control tbe evils, the natural leaders of the community can lend the weight of their influence in discouraging such practices; and my firm belief is that before the general public can take such an advanced view, the female population particularly must be brought under the civilizing influence of the school. Though I am fully aware that it is difficult to increase the age, I would not like to see it under full thirteen for consummation.

108. Honorable Mr. Justice West,—Groups of enlightened and influential Hindus at the c hief centres of population

might unite to discountenance infant marriages by refusing to attend them and by exerting their social authority to prevent them. They might also diffuse a cheap and inoffensive literature exposing the evils of premature marriage. Individual labourers in ths same cause, may well employ themselves in trying to substitute a new set of conceptions in the mind of the people, for the gross realistic notions of which the existing marriage system is a natural outgrowth ....

The duty of a Government in such a matter is not violently to subdue the nature and instincts of its subjects to its own notions of propriety, but rather to watch for the rise of moral and beneficial tendencies, and then to foster their development by a process of natural growth and at the earliest fitting moment give them form and permanence in a law. This is why a marriage law as to infants and widows should be so framed as to admit of gradual introduction, according as different castes and classes gradually awaken to a higher perception of the moral elements of the matrimonial relations. Increased strength of character and purity of life amongst those brought under the improved law would make willing converts of crowds who would deeply and not quite unreasonably resent any compulsion.

Mr. West's draft of an act to remedy the two evils is as follows. He says that it is an endeavour to give a first formal shape to Mr. Malabari's views, rather than to his own. "I am not certainly indifferent" he writes, "to the great evils that arise from infant marriages and from the enforcement of perpetual widowhood, but in all that concerns the domestic relations, the proper and even the possible sphere of operation of the positive law is very restricted, in comparison with the field that must be left to popular morality, the general sense of what is right and becoming."

"AN ACT FOR THE PROTECTION OF HINDU INFANTS AND WIDOWS IN RESPECT OF MARRIAGE.

This Act shall apply to Hindu subjects of Her Majesty belonging to castes and classes whose desire in this behalf shall have been ascertained by the Government and notified in the *Government Gazette*, and to all acts and omissions on their part or in relation to them hereinbelow provided for, whether the same take place within or without British India.

A marriage of a female under 12 or of a male under 14 may, on the attainment of that age, be adopted or renounced either by the person attaining it or by the other party to the marriage.

The adoption or renunciation of a marriage may be declared before a judge, a magistrate or a registrar of assurances who, on being satisfied of the identity of the declarant, and of his or her mental capacity, shall accept the declaration and shall furnish a certificate thereof to the declarant, on payment of such fee as shall be provided by the law or by the Government.

A marriage susceptible of adoption or renunciation under this Act shall be deemed to have been renounced unless within three months from the attainment of the age of 14 or of 12 years it shall have been adopted by the parties thereto, as hereinbefore specified.

Consummation of a marriage between a male of 14 years of age and a female of 12 years of age or upwards, acting voluntarily, shall be deemed an adoption of any marriage duly celebrated between the same persons before such consummation and not validly renounced.

The right and duties subsisting between married persons whose marriage may be renounced as hereinbefore provided, on account of their infancy, shall not extend to conjugal society or intercourse.

In the case of a female married and under 12 years of age sexual intercourse with her by her husband shall have the same legal character, and, in the cases provided for by the Indian Penal Code or other law, shall be subject to the same penalties as if no marriage subsisted.

Abetment of sexual intercourse prohibited by this or any other law under a penalty shall be deemed abetment of an offence within the meaning of the Indian Penal Code.

In the case of a marriage subject to renunciation under this Act no right to maintenance or residence, nor any claim to money or things of value arises to one of two spouses as against the other, or the property of the other during his or her life, but in the event of the death of either the rights of the other as to inheritance and maintenance shall be the same as if the marriage had not been subject to renunciation.

A widow shall not, by remarrying, incur, with reference to her property derived from or through her deceased husband or her rights accrued in virtue of her marriage to him, any further or greater forfeiture or disqualification than she would incur by fornication committed with the person with whom she remarries.

Any person who, without her free, express and intelligent consent does any act towards the personal disfigurement of a female aged 12 years or upwards, by reason or under pretext of her being a widow, shall be answerable as for a civil injury in such damages as the court may award, *provided* that nothing herein contained shall be deemed to affect the provisions of the Indian Penal Code or other law in force relating to criminal force or any other offence thereby made punishable.

Whoever by threats, insults or menaces, or suggestions of divine displeasure or supernatural injury, endeavours to bring about or to prevent any marriage, contrary to the legal rights and discretion of the parties concerned, shall be subject to the penalties provided in Sections 506, 507 or 508 of the Indian Penal Code.

109. SIR WILLIAM MUIR.—I have always been strongly of opinion (and I think I expressed the same in the Legislative Council some 20 years ago) that the betrothal or marriage of minors should not be held binding at law unless consummated —that is—that specific performance of the contract made by

parents or guardians should not be enforced. Possibly court action for damages against these might be allowed. What the form and mode of repudiation should be, or the precise action of one or other of the parties indicating that he or she receded from the contract, would require more careful thought than I have time to give to the subject at present (for I am away from home in the Highlands.)

But beyond such a measure I certainly would not at present go. I agree with very much of what Mr. Melvill says. I do not think that the advocates of further legislation have at all appreciated how impossible it would be to enforce laws such as are advocated, in the present state of habit and feeling. How possibly could the executive spy into the recesses of family life and the Parda. Just think of the terrible handle it would give to enemies of a family and to the Police. I believe that any such laws would be utterly inoperative excepting in mischief and evil in the existing state of society, and would altogether fail of securing the results you are aiming at.

But that is no reason why you should relax your efforts to reform the national sentiment, and gradually to change its habits. *Macte Virtute.* Go on in your great work and may God grant you success in it.

110. Right Hon'ble Leonard Courtney, Deputy Speaker House of Commons.—Under a more aristocratic system there was greater readiness in imposing our ideas upon others, but whilst the democracy is ready enough to embody its ideas in domestic legislation, it has a real indisposition to govern other communities.

Your first and most difficult task is to influence opinion within India. You have recognized this and have set yourself to the labour, and I heartily wish you god speed in it.

Nevertheless having something of the older imperative temper, and feeling that in India, if anywhere, we have the responsibilities of power, I should like to see attempted such

legislation as Mr. Melvill and my friends Mr. Justice West and Mr. Justice Scott have suggested. Mr. West's draft seems to meet some of the objections Mr. Melvill had foreseen.

CHAPTER V.

FACTS ON THE SUBJECT OF ENFORCED WIDOWHOOD.

SECTION I. MADRAS PRESIDENCY.

1. Krishnaswami Rao Chief Justice Travancore.—As a rule widowed girls are allowed, until they attain the age of 18 or 20, to retain their locks, wear jewels and flowers, and to have meals, as their more fortunate sisters under coverture. But the strong but silent disapproval with which society looks upon these innocent enjoyments of the unfortunate young widow, and the example of others in her position, make her seek the miseries of widowhood, in preference to the comforts allowed to her by her loving parents and relatives. It is as a concession to the young widow's repeated entreaties, that the parents and relations often consent to the performance of the most melancholy rite of tonsure. I do not deny that there are bigoted men, who in their religious fervour have subjected girls, 7 or 8 years old, to all the miseries of perpetual widowhood, but their number was never large and is now dwindling. I may even say that such men are now very rare phenomena.

The social ill usage to which Mr. Malabari refers, is always of a *negative character*, such as refusal direct or indirect, to associate with a married widow or her husband, or her active sympathizers in meals, religious ceremonies, and in social gatherings.

From what has recently passed in Madras in connection with the bulls of excommunication issued by one of the leading muttadipathis one might legitimately infer that priests in the long run would be not disposed to exercise the power of ex-

communication, if by the exercise of it they would lose a large number of their wealthy disciples..................................

I need hardly add that both the widow who remarries and her husband will for a long time to come be deserters of their families and that they would, therefore, require support until the innovation becomes popular.

2. C. RAMCHANDRA AIYAR.—In practice, even to this day it is a fact that a betrothed girl is considered unfit and unqualified to accomplish religious ceremonies or join her husband in their performance, before actual consummation of the marriage takes place.

The legislation I have above* proposed will have the immediate effect of putting a stop to the most cruel and heart-rending scene of every day's occurrence viz taking the betrothed girl losing her husband to the burning ground on the first day, and again on the 10th day making her wear all her jewels and good clothes and deck her hair with flowers and ornaments as the last day that she can use them or enjoy such luxury in her life, while all this time the unfortunate child is unconscious of the significance of the ceremony. Such a girl has nothing to do with the burning of the body, which is done in a great majority of cases, by the brothers or father of the deceased. Such a girl, however young she may be, is denied the privilege of mixing with the betrothed girls of her age in singing, wearing ornaments &c., and of doing all that married girls are required to do on occasions of marriage or auspicious ceremonies at home and elsewhere. Such an infant girl is denied the privilege of going to temples on festive occasions and enjoying the sight of a festival, as other married girls of her age do. The most melancholy scene of all is the so-called widowed infant girl not knowing the reason of exclusion, asking her parents how she had offended them or others, and why she was not treated as a married girl, and the parents then beginning to weep over the misfortune of the girl.

---

* *i.e.* that no betrothed girl should be treated as a wife before consummation.

3. S. Subramania Aiyar.—There can also be no question of the vast miseries caused by enforced widowhood, but it is hard to believe that an order of things affecting a considerable portion of the female population should have been the outcome of mere caprice of the stronger sex.

4. P. Chentsal Rao.—The real difficulty is the fear of excommunication which not only degrades the man excommunicated in the eyes of his fellows, but also puts him to very great inconvenience, since he cannot easily get caste servants and priests for the performance of ceremonies which cannot be given up without loss of caste.

5. M. Tillainayagam Pillai, Deputy Collector, Madura —The hardest heart has felt the evil of widowhood, but it has yielded to custom-a cruel and inhumane custom-that prevails in the caste. I have known instances of respectable men, who were ornaments to the Hindu Society, having met with premature deaths, broken-hearted and unable to bear the misfortune that befell their beloved daughters. A Hindu family with a young widow is in perpetual misery, and gloom prevails in it...

It is gravely asserted by the orthodox Brahmins that a woman becomes a widow by the result of her *Karma* in the previous births, and that it is a sin to allow her to marry again. This is something like misers preaching it to be a sin to help the indigent, who by the result of their *Karma* have been destined to be poor. No amount of argument can convince these men, even if they are really serious.

It is argued by some that though the widows in India are more than double those in Europe, yet the unmarried women in the latter are nearly double those in India............I must ask these gentlemen to consider the difference between the conditions of women leading lives of celibacy of their own accord, enjoying all the innocent comforts and pleasures of life, and those of the Hindu widows who are looked down upon

as inauspicious sinful creatures, destined to live miserably without the comforts and pleasures of life.

The Brahmin character is peculiar in this respect. He is prepared to overlook the commission of the greatest of sins ....but would not brook (that) his daughter or sister (should) marry after she obtains puberty, or see her married, even if she becomes a widow when an infant, and he is the cause of her misfortune. He associates freely with a Brahmin murderer, dacoit, perjurer, forgerer, adulterer, whore-monger, drunkard, or eater of animal food, provided the latter is liberal and opens his purse freely, but the Brahmin will not associate with one who marries a virgin widow or a girl who has attained puberty, though she may be his kith and kin, in whom all his hopes are centered. He has no scruples to live with a Brahmin woman who may be known to be unchaste, but he will not admit into his society the unfortunate virgin widow who chooses to marry herself to a second husband. I have mentioned this anomolous state of things in order to show the strong prejudice that unfortunately exists against the introduction of the re-marriage of widows among the most intelligent and powerful section of the Hindu community.

6. T. Pattabhiram Esq.—He (Mr. Malabari) speaks as if there are 40 million Hindu widows, while according to the latest census the figure is only 16⅛ (1,61,17,135) (Census of 1881 Vol. I. page 88.)

To a Hindu caste widow who makes up her mind to resume her married state at the risk of caste, religion, and the affection and society of her relations, there now exists no obstruction to marrying a caste Hindu, if she succeeds in finding one, who is willing, or a Christian or a Mahomedan.

SECTION II. BOMBAY PRESIDENCY.

7. Mahipatram Rupram.—Without going to the length of charging one and all young widows with wicked conduct,

I can safely say that a large number of them go astray, and the consequences are horrible. Attempts at procuring abortions, which in some cases terminate in death, and murders of pregnant widows by their relatives, are the results. These abortions deaths and murders seldom come to light. Pregnant widows are not unfrequently taken away to distant places, and there such crimes are committed. When such attempts fail, infanticide is resorted to. I have not seen these things myself, but such is the general belief among the people, and there is I have no doubt, much truth in it. The unfortunate miserable widows excite our compassion on account of the unnatural and unjust caste rules which permit a widower to take a second wife freely, but prevent the widow under all circumstances from taking a second husband. Breaches of all other caste rules and religious ordinances are condoned, but the prohibition of widow marriage is always enforced with extraordinary severity All the high castes combine against those who disregard it, and no penalties and no bribes to heads of castes and priests can mitigate its rigour. Hindu society prefers to wink at the crimes of the widow rather than allow her to remarry. No notice is taken of well-known irregularities of conduct; proved abortion and desertion of infants are pardoned; and even conviction in a Court of Justice does not exclude a widow for ever from caste and society. But the marriage of a widow even with a member of her own caste is considered a more heinous crime than all these put together. It is an unpardonable offence, and all possible means are adopted to persecute the unhappy woman and man who defy the prohibition, and all who keep social intercourse with them.

8. LALLUBHAI NUNDLAL.—I am inclined to think that widowhood falls rather heavily on minors, and it may be well to allow them to remarry by all means.

9. JOTEERAO GOVINDRAO PHULAY.—She (the widow) is stripped of her ornaments, she is forcibly shaved by her near relations, she is not well-fed, she is not properly clothed, she is not allowed to join pleasure-parties, marriages or religious

ceremonies. In fact she is bereaved of all worldly enjoyments, nay, she is considered lower than a culpirt or a mean beast.

One of my Brahman friends named Rao Sahib Sudashive Bullal Gowndey, who was an officer of the Inam Commission, employed in his house a Brahman widow as cook, whose name was Kashibai. The poor Kashibai was a well behaved and beautiful young woman of a respectable family. She was a chaste woman. She served several months in his house. But in his neighbourhood there lived a shrewd and cunning Shastri-boova of a Brahman caste who tried his utmost to mislead this ignorant woman. Kashibai at first resisted his inducement, but at last she fell victim to his desire, and immediately became pregnant. Afterwards by the persuasion of her paramour, she tried several poisonous drugs to commit abortion, but all her attempts failed. After 9 months were completed, Kashibai gave birth to a beautiful son, and for the sake of her disgrace she murdered the innocent infant with a knife, and the corpse was thrown into a well behind the house of her master. Two days after, she was arrested by the Police on suspicion, tried before the Session Court in Poona, and sentenced to transportation for lifs......... Although my means were not sufficient to defray my expense yet I was compelled to establish a foundling house in my own compound in Poona, for the Brahmin community, immediately after Kashibai's trial was over.........From its commencement up to the present time, 35 pregnant widows came to the house and were delivered of children, of whom 5 are living and thirty died from the injuries done to them while in the womb by the poisonous drugs which the mothers must have taken with a view to conceal their pregnancy. Many of the beautiful and helpless ingnorant young widows of respectable Brahman families have turned out private and public prostitutes on account of this wretched system.

10. Gurshidapa Virbasapa —I am a Lingayat and as such belong to a sect of Hinduism in which widow marriages are allowed.

The evils pointed out by Mr. Malabari do exist.

11. NARAYEN BHIKAJI, DEPUTY COLLECTOR, NASIK.—No woman below the age of 35 gets herself shaved voluntarily; she is forcibly shaved by her relations. In consequence of this dread of disfiguration, many commit suicide and others run away.

There is at present a Brahmam lady in Nasik the wife of a decsased 1st class Mamlatdar. She has not shaved herself on the ground that she does not want her body to be touched by another man. Her conduct is a model of morality. She has composed an essay to the effect 1stly that it is cruel on the part of man to disfigure women because their husbands happen to die, and 2ndly that it is shameful to a spirited Hindu who secludes his wife from society simply to keep her off the evil eyes of bad men, to allow his female relatives to be handled by the barbers.

12. TRIMALRAO VENKATESH.—Many poor people allow their girls to grow up to 12 or 13 years of age. They wait for the wife of some rich old man to die, and then virtually sell their girls to him for a sum equal to about the rate of one hundred Rupees for every year of the girl's age. If the girl happens to possess personal attractions, and the old man is rich the price is increased. For fear, however, lest the seller and purchaser might be punished, the one for selling and the other for purchasing the girl, the money paid to the girl's parents is not called *purchase-money*, but an ordinary present. The old man then marries the girl, and loads her with ornaments and fine clothes. Long before two or three years pass away, he dies, and the children of his former wife strip the young widow of their old father of all her ornaments and clothes, and put her out of the house. If the young widow be a virtuous woman she earns her livlihood by begging or working for hire as a menial servant, or sometimes sues her step children and gets a small maintenance. But if she be not virtuous, she commits adultery, becomes pregnant, gives birth to children and kills them. It is rarely that she is found out and punished.

....

In 1837 my father exposed the immoral and shameful conduct of a young Brahmin widow with her step-son at Shapur a village belonging to the Chief of Sangli, and concluded by saying that any provision that might be made by the Legislature to prevent such a state of things would be welcomed. The report was fully approved by the District Judge, and sent to the Indian Law Commission, through the Sadar Adawlat.

There is no doubt that several widows are virtuous. The rest practice a good deal of immorality. I do not think that one-fourth of the offences of the latter are brought to light and punished as they deserve. I will here give two instances of such offences without, however, giving the names of the parties. First a rich and influential landholder holding a very responsible public employment at S, had married four wives one after another. At the time of his death the fourth wife was a young woman. As she could not agree with the children of the first three wives, she left S, came to D, and lived in the house of a priest who also belonged to a most respectable family of the holy order. An illicit intercourse commenced between the widow and the priest, and she was far advanced in pregnancy. The priest took her to H, to get the pregnancy removed. The medicines given were of such a violent nature that soon after the abortion took place, she got dangerously ill and died. The bodies both of the deceased child and the woman were quietly disposed of. The matter got noised about in the town, but was soon hushed up. *Second*, the daughter of a rich merchant towards the extreme East of the Dharwar District, who had become a widow, some-how or other became pregnant, gave birth to a child, and murdered it but continued to live in her father's house. The townspeople came to know of the affair, and excommunicated the widow and her parents...... At last the mother went before the chief priest or swami of the caste, and he exacted a fine of 1,400 Rs. from the father of the widow, and re-admitted them into caste. Notwithstanding this no one up to now drinks any water or eats any food from the hand of the widow.

On a reference to the Imperial Census Returns of 1881, it appears that out of the total population of 16,454,414 souls in the Bombay Presidency 12,307,773 are Hindus.

These are as follows :

	Males.	Females.
Never Married	2,860,620	1,771,956
Married	3,095,205	3,120,142
Widowed	335,464	1,124,786

In the absence of actual figures, it might be assumed that three-fourths (of the widows) belong to Sudras and other lower classes, among whom widow-remarriage is permitted.

13. Venayek Wassudev.—The number of widow remarriages is slowly but steadily increasing, as prejudice gives way to the march of enlightement.

14. Bhikaji Amroot Chobhe.—From the (census) Report, the proportion of widows under 30 years of age per 1000 of the population is seen to be Hindu $11\frac{1}{4}$, Mahomadan $8\frac{1}{3}$, Christian $4\frac{1}{8}$, Jain $8\frac{1}{3}$, Parsi $5\frac{1}{3}$, Brahmo $12\frac{1}{6}$, and the proportion of widows of all ages per 1000 of the population is Hindu $85\frac{2}{3}$, Mahomedans $79\frac{9}{10}$, Christian $46\frac{7}{9}$, Jain $64\frac{1}{12}$, Parsi $73\frac{3}{5}$, Brahmo $47\frac{10}{11}$.

Remarriage of widows among the Hindus is the rule, and its prohibition the exception confined to small sections of the community as the Brahmans, some sects of the Banias, Sonars &c.

In the first remarriage among the Brahmins, the first on this side of India which look place some 14 years back in Bombay, there was excommunication. But I have not read or heard of a repetition of any such thing since, though several remarriages have taken place.

15. Ranchodlal K. Desai.—It is undeniable that a small proportion of widows would remain unmarried if the power of the caste to excommunicate were removed.

16. Kalianrao H. Desai of Broach.—In all household and family matters a widow as such, enjoys a far greater

authority than a married woman. She directs the whole house as she has more leisure for such duties, and in almost all matters relating to family or caste customs she, specially if grown-up, is always looked to as a final authority. Of course her position as a widow excludes her from the performance of such religious ceremonies as require the presence of woman on auspicious occasions. As to any other social wrong to which widows, as such, are compelled to submit, I humbly submit, I fail to discover any, after a life-long experience of my community..

With the exception of Brahmins, Khatris, and Wanias who form the upper cream of our society, all the other castes do freely admit of widow remarriages which are of every day occurrence among them.........Caste so far as it goes never uses violence or exercises any other oppression to prevent a widow from remarrying if she so wishes it.........A club or a society imposing certain rules of observance on its members has a perfect right to exclude any one who infringes them from the benefit of its membership This is exactly the case with caste the rules of which are more intricate, and consequently affect more intimately the social and religious interests of its constituents..............................

The death of a daughter is to a Hindu parent a lesser evil than her widowhood..

The learned doctor (Dr. Rajendrao Lal Mitra of Bengal) has conclusively exploded this pessimistic theory of Mr. Malabari (as to widowhood leading to crimes) by instituting a parallel between the condition of the widows of India and the maids of England, and has thus proved beyond a possibility of doubt that there is nothing in the nature of the thing to warrant the conclusion of a frightful increase of crimes consequent on the evil attempts of the widows and their relations.

17. Bhaskarrao Balkrishnaji Pitale and Nana Moroba.—We beg to observe that in the higher castes of the

Hindu Community only, the system of early marriages and that of widow celibacy exists..

We fully endorse the view taken by the Honourable Mr. K. P. Telang C.I.E., in thinking that the majority of widows will not listen to, but actually shun the company, nay, detest those sympathising philanthropists who would volunteer advice to young widows, for the sin of remarriage is too deeply engraven at present on their minds.

18. VEERCHAND DIPCHAND.—Remarriage of widows is not prohibited amongst all the Hindus, but amongst those who belong to higher classes such as Banias and Brahmins, who hardly number more than the lower classes.

19. MAHADEO VASUDEO BARVE.—Widowhood of the nature pointed out exists amongst Brahmins and other higher Hindu classes.........A change in the right direction is already working on the feelings of the parties concerned.

20. M. G. RANADE.—At present the condition of infant widows is the most pitiable, and their desperate misery is a scandal and a wrong which is a disgrace to any well regulated society, There is really no choice allowed to these unfortunate creatures, who are disgraced before they feel the reason why such cruelty is practised upon them.

21. VENKUT RANGO KATTI.—The Brahmin has ever been the law-giver to the lower classes. Whatever he practised as good was publicly or privately copied by other classes. Not to speak of the many amusing stories of imitation in former times, we see in our own days, when the Brahmin supremacy is fast fading away, several of such customs as were monopolised by Brahmins as their own birth-right heartily welcomed by other classes. For instance wearing the sacred thread, reciting the Sandhya or at least a show of it, and keeping holy (sic) at the time of taking meals, can be seen adopted by tailors and saddlers. Widow celibacy itself though apparently repulsive, has not escaped imitation. Shaved widows wearing red cloth can be seen in numbers among the Kamtis, the Kasars, the

Sonars and the Gingars. I have read a long letter in the last month written by a Lingayat priest of Hubli to one of the Canarese papers of Dharwar, in which the writer condemned remarriage of widows, freely availed of by his sect, as a stepping stone to hell, and invited his castemen to adopt widow celibacy which he praised in the most alluring terms. This shows the force of the influence exercised by Brahmin customs on other classes, when it is remembered that the Lingayats outwardly show antagonism to the Brahmins.

Is it not sufficiently heart-rending to see a beautiful young face deprived of the ornament which nature has bountifully bestowed on it? What an abject spectacle must a shaved widow be presenting to the eys of European ladies passing through the streets of Indian towns? Has man power to cut down the hair of a woman's head any more than cutting her nose and ears. British magistrates punish swinging by hooks before idols, self-torture to extort money, slavery and sale of girls for adultery, confining human beings and a host of such petty misdeeds against the human body. Yet they quietly pass by a widow, pitifully crying from her inability to protect her natural ornament from the razor of a barber.

22. SAKARAM ARJUN.—The beneficial effect of widow remarriage cannot be exaggerated. Experience has shown that its adoption in certain higher classes of widows has acted as an efficient safety-valve against unchastity and the horrible crime of child-murder.

23. S. H. CHIPLONKAR.—If Mr. Malabari or any of those who may agree with him in the views he propounds, will examine the advertisement columns of the Marathi newspapers for any given month, he will, I have no doubt, find ample material in corroboration of my statement that even divorce and subsequent remarriage, to say nothing of the remarriages of widows, are by no means uncommon among the lower classes of the Hindu Community..

Widow remarriages are more or less deprecated and discouraged by all nationalities and in all countries.

The higher the social or worldly status any particular section of a community occupies in the estimation of others as well as its own, the greater are the artificial restrictions imposed upon the widows of that section, no matter what the general law affecting the whole community may be. The tendency always is in the direction of imposing such artificial restrictions owing to the real or supposed moral and consequently social superiority which the willing or compulsory submission to such restriction necessarily implies.

I believe I am expressing the almost unanimous sense of all those to whom this movement (widow marriage movement) has an absorbing interest, when I say that it is altogether a discredited movement.

24. Narmadashankar Lalshankar.—These three doctrines of Sapindya,* fatalism, and transmigration of souls, acting and reacting on each other, make every average Hindu, whether a male or a female, contented and reconciled to his lot, whether it be high or low, happy or miserable, and surely that ceases to be an evil, which is willingly accepted, patiently suffered, and readily submitted to, through a high sense of duty and religious good.

25. Ganpatram G. Sastri.—The very fact that the higher castes among whom widow remarriages are not permitted, are in a superior moral, intellectual, and economical condition, as compared with the lower castes, goes a good deal to prove that its non-existense is neither a source of vice, nor otherwise a great evil as depicted.......................................

The Hindu widow performs now the functions of an European nun, as well as of a married lady. She watches over the formation of moral and religious development of the rising generation, over the cleanliness of the house, over the orderly

* *i.e.* "The connection arising from inheriting the corporeal particles of one body which is necessarily that of the highest ancestor."

arrangement of the furniture &c., and over the physical improvement of the members of the family among whom her lot is cast. She has been the means of impressing on the young, and in some cases old people, by her living example, those lessons of morality and patience, economy and self-sacrifice which form the character of the rising generation—an acquisition that serves to smoothen their path of life and to facilitate solution of the thousand and one difficulties they meet with in the struggles of the world. A person so useful and exercising such an influence, and suffering from a misfortune which no human ingenuity can avert, will naturally be looked upon as a "guiding angel" a most deserving object of sympathy rather than an object of oppression as Mr. Malabari would have the world believe.

26. Rao Sahib Vishram Ramji Ghollay.—It is universally known that enforced widowhood, cruel and unnatural as it is, is confined only to Brahmins, Parbhus and a few Brahminical castes, who form a very small portion of our society. Excepting these castes, all other castes allow and practise remarriage as it should be, and as it is practised in the civilized world.

27. R. G. Bhandarkar.—Though I believe Mr. Malabari's account to be greatly exaggerated, there is no doubt that perpetual widowhood as imposed by custom on all women who have the misfortune to lose their husbands is a great and a crying evil..... ....

28. Gavarishankar Udeyshankar.—It is true that widow remarriage obtains among Lowanas, Laitas, Kunbis, Barbers, Dhobies, Mochis, Darjis, Khumbhars, Kolis, and other Hindu castes. But I may say I have known of instances of evil results following such second marriages. I can say from my pretty long experience of life among these classes, that matches of this kind have been received with disfavour by the Hindu community in general. They have been designated Natras or ill-assorted marriages. When a widow remarries, her off-

spring by the first husband are left to take care of themselves. They are in many cases rendered almost destitute of protection, if the husband has no father, mother or other relations to keep a close eye upen them.

29. NAGINDAS TULSIDAS.—The most aggravating case is that of an unfortunate girl who has the misfortune to lose her husband after the wedding ceremony is performed, but before she has ever lived with him as his wife. Mere betrothal does not amount to such wedding as will inflict on her life-long widow-hood.

30. PANDURUNG BALIBHODRA.—Female Education is still in its infancy. During the few years that a girl goes to school ordinarily from the 8th to the 12th year, she merely learns to read and write and calculate up to the simple rule of three. When she leaves school, she carries with her but a very superficial and elementary knowledge. At home she imbibes the tone of thought and feeling pervading her father's or husband's family. If her elders happen to be, as in the majority of cases they are, of the orthodox faith, she turns out a disciple of the same school. Like them she follows implicitly the teachings of the Shastras as interpreted by the priest. Like them she adheres with unswerving faith to old customs and old practices, any departure from which would be little less than a sin and a profanation. She reads or hears the interesting stories of the Hindu mythology, and her heart is moved by the fascinating virtues of Shita or Dropadi. She reads and hears of Tukaram or Ramdass, and her soul catches their religious tone and devotional spirit. Her character is then gradually formed and moulded by the very same influences to which her fore-fathers were subject for generations past, and she learns to live and act just in the same way as they did.

31. RUNGRAO VINAYAK PURANDHURE OF POONA.—No widows are forced to shave their heads, but the shaving of a widow's head being a religious practice, widows get their heads shaved of their own accord and lead a single life.

32. Utamram N. Mehta.—The fact is that the masses of the high caste Hindus are practically against the remarriage of widows, though a great many of them speak in its favour. About 30 years ago the public opinion was so strong against it, that no one dared to speak publicly on the subject while they can do so now freely and without molestation. If things go on as they have in the course of the last 30 years, there is a hope that in course of time the reform now recommended will be carried out by the people themselves.

33. Ambalal S. Desai.—Speaking of Gujarat, I may safely assert that it (the evil of enforced widowhood) exists in a very small degree among the agricultural classes who form the main bulk of the total population. It is in the urban communities, the Brahmins, the Banyas, and the kindred classes, that widowhood is enforced as an institution. Even among them the number of cases of females that are condemned by custom, prejudice, social tyranny and the like, to lifelong misery and whose age may excite compassion is very small. I believe the census reports will bear out these remarks.

As things stand now, few, if any high class widows will think of complaining of the ill-treatment of them by their relatives or even strangers. There will be complaints, no doubt, but, I fear they will mostly be found to have proceeded from women of no character, acting from mean and selfish motives, whom it will be hardly proper to encourage by a free offer of State support.

It is not the priest that excommunicates, but the caste, the priest merely acting as its mouthpiece and executive officer.

34. Pandit Narayan Kesow Vaidya.—A government servant of very high standing and position, lost his first wife by whom he had a son. He married a second wife when he was of 48 years: by her he had children also. After his 55th or 57th year he was pensioned; his second wife died, and a few months afterwards he married a third, aged 10 or 11. He had, it is stated, paid some money for the marriage and

made provision for her too. Soon after he died, his heirs, it is said, caught hold of the keys of the box, did away with the documents &c., and the poor creature is now, I understand quite helpless and dragging a miserable life. This instance occurred in the district of Ratnagiri, where the Brahmin element is strong. I will cite a case which occurred in the neighbouring district of Kolaba. A man of considerable property, a widower, evidently in his 57th year or so, married a girl of 11 years. He had given her ornaments worth about Rs. 3,000, assigned a certain sum for her to go to Benares and other sacred places, given her permission to adopt a son, and in the event of any dispute or disagreement taking place between the adopted son and her, she was to have for her absolute use a certain amount annually. The old man fell ill of diabetes and his medical advisers told him to go for a change of air in the Deccan, where after a lingering sickness of 2 or three months, he died, leaving a will wherein the above intentions were duly provided. All, however, was unavailing. It is stated that the genuine document was substituted for by another ; and it was given out that the boy to be adopted by the lady had already been adopted by the dying man. The boy's father became *Vahivatdar*,* took hold of the keys, cash, ornaments and everything that could be gathered, and the widow was left to her fate with only Rs. 100 a year. Many other examples can be cited to show the fate of widows after the demise of their husbands.

35. GOKULDAS KAHANDAS PAREKH.—In the higher castes when a widow remarries she immediately loses her caste, and the decree of the caste deprives her of the company and association of her parents, brothers, sisters and others for whom she would have considerable love and affection, but no such result follows adultery, however clear and convincing be its evidence.

36. HONOURABLE V. N. MANDLIK.—There is no enforced widowhood in India at present......To become a widow is a mis-

* Manager.

fortune. There is no balm to a soul so wounded, except the one obtained by entering into a higher kind of life, abnegating oneself on the altar of duty, and sacrificing *self* to a higher *self* in a manner recognized by the highest religious sanctions as well as by the sanction of society, and by training the mind and body so to live in this world as to qualify one's self for a higher. This is the accepted doctrine and practice of the Hindu Shastras which the highest minds have adopted and still pursue more or less successfully. What does the actual condition of the people disclose? The simple but effective Savitri Upakhyana which is religiously observed throughout Hindustan shows that the second marriage of a woman is opposed to Hindu religious convictions. The Savitri day or days are the holiest festivals for females in India. Government may refer to authorities from the Mahabharata down to the Vrataraja.

I cannot, I regret, accept with complaisance the compliment which the present writer impliedly gives to the Hindus as being so utterly incapable of self-action. Such a supposition argues ignorance of history, past and present. The Hindus have never lost their originality through countless revolutions and varying cycles of time. Has the effect of English Education which has brought them into contact with Milton and Shakespeare, Wordsworth and Tennyson, Goldstücker and Müller and their worthy compeers in the republic of letters, so enfeebled their intellect as to make them forget their own Bhishma Bali—Vashitha and Janaka and other illustrious ancestors and lose their own self-respect. The Hindu Community may have its short-comings; but, with submission, it need not fear its detractors, whoever they may be. Leaving the past (the memory of which is scrupulously preserved by the daily practices of the people), if a modern Ahalyabai at Indore could dispense justice like Dharmaraja from behind the *parda*, could strike terror into the hearts of neighbouring princes by plain letters, and yet could so sanctify her life as to make her shrine an object of devotion to her votaries at the present day, the widows of India are in excellent company, and need no lecture from the present writer.

37. JASWANTSING, THAKORE SAHIB OF LIMBDI.—There is indeed no doubt that the system of enforced widowhood is a social evil, which it must be the endeavour of every true reformer to eradicate.

SECTION III. BENGAL PRESIDENCY.

38. C. H. TAWNEY, DIRECTOR OF PUBLIC INSTRUCTION.—Dr. Trailakya Nath Mitra observes in his Tagore Lectures for 1879 p. 211 that very few marriages have taken place among high castes under Act XV. of 1856, because the Hindu Community at large has not accepted Pandit Iswar Chandra Vidiasagar's interpretation of the Shastras as correct. "The movement would have succeeded better, if instead of an appeal to the Legislature, which is alien in its constitution, a grand congress of the Hindus, learned in the Shastras throughout the country, and representing all possible shades of opinion, had been held under the presidency of one of its respected teachers, and the orthodox nature of the measure had been established by the decision of such an assembly. Such a decision would have been among the Hindus what the decree of an œcumenical council is among Roman Catholics, and would have been accepted by the mass of Hindus as genuine Shastra and the social reform would have been carried out most successfully."

Babu Radhika Prusanna Mookerjia states that Raja Pramatha Bhushan Dev Roy of Naldanga in Jessore has come forward with his vast influence to tread in the footsteps of Iswar Chandra Vidyasagar. There is clearly a small but energetic party in Bengal working in favour of the remarriage of widows.

39. C. T. METCALFE, COMMISSIONER ORISSA DIVISION.—It is gravely argued that wives would poison their husbands to get rid of them, and so marry other husbands more congenial to them, if widows were at liberty to marry. Many other opinions expressed in the papers before me are so childish and foolish that the only remark necessary is that it is astonishing that, men who in other matters hold sensible views, can really believe the opinions they express.

40. BABU KEDARESUR ROY.—A Hindu priest is, unlike the priests of ancient Popedom, not competent to excommunicate any; it is the Hindu society which does so.

41. TIPPERAH PEOPLE'S ASSOCIATION.—The real difficulty lies in the fear of social excommunication, which is indeed a very terrible thing to a Hindu widow.

42. KUMAR PRAMATHA BHUSHANA DEVA RAJA.—In Bengal, society is led by rich men of the upper classes, the mass of the people following in their wake. The priests and the Pandits watch which way the wind blows, and shape their opinions accordingly. They have no power to excommunicate or persecute any body. The leaders of society upon whose patronization depends the means of subsistence of the priests and the Pandits, utilize their services to suit their own inclinations. The Pandits readily grant immunity to these leaders, even if they be guilty of gross violation of Hindu social or religious ordinances. Such being the position of the Pandits, they raised a hue and cry against the venerable Vidyasagar, and sheltered under the fangs of the social leaders, set up legions of obstacles to frustrate the noble object he had in view............But the aspect of things has changed during the last 3 or 4 years.........The Vernacular Press in Bengal have taken up the question, in right earnest, and are doing their best to popularise the cause.

43. BABU MENULAL CHATTERJEE.—In the present state of society, widows require special protection by the State. Often the relations of their deceased husbands annoy them

in various ways, turn out bitter enemies, and drive them to commit immoral acts. Their purse and *stridhan* which ought to be held sacred, are robbed by means, fair or foul (see the case in the Natore family). They are objects of panegyric and adulation so long as they have strength to attend to domestic duties and command of their wealth. They are turned out of the family as beggars when the purse is emptied, and their strength fails. Even maintenance which the Shastras' humanity ordains is denied to them.

Hindu husbands are disposed to make adequate provision in their testaments for their wives' comfort and maintenance. But the Judge-made laws upon wills have created uncertainties and difficulties in the mind of many, which neither the testators nor the beneficiaries ever anticipated. Then the procedure for obtaining a probate is complicated and not intellegible to the widows. The cost of obtaining probate is heavy. Nor is this all. Young widows are not allowed to walk out of the Zenanas. They cannot exchange thoughts with competent legal practitioners, and determine for themselves the right course to follow. They are not good accountants. The legal fiction that every one is presumed to know the law ought not to apply to their case. If they happen to know reading and writing the vernacular, they may at most make their intention known to the pleader retained for them. Their inexperience in forensic matters is taken advantage of by rapacious village demagagues and Muktars who guide them and build their own fortune at their cost.

SECTION IV. NORTH-WEST PROVINCES AND OUDH, THE PUNJAB, CENTRAL PROVINCES, BURMA, ASSAM, COORG, HYDRABAD (DECCAN.) &c.

44. Chief Secretary to Government N.-W.-P. and Oudh.—The extent to which the priestly re-action has been

successful in enforcing widowhood seems much more circumscribed than Mr. Malabari imagines. ¶ | That particular form of widow remarriage known as the Levirate practice of marrying a brother's widow, obtains special acceptance. Among certain castes, and under certain conditions, it appears to be a duty devolving on a younger brother to marry his elder brother's widow.........It may be assumed that any caste which allows a widow to remarry her brother-in-law will also allow her to remarry a stranger, if the family do not insist on its right over her.........

It is stated by some that those castes alone absolutely prohibit re-marriage, which are or profess to be of the twice-born class viz the Brahmins, Rajputs, Vaisyas, and such mixed castes as Kayaths, which claim a similar descent .... Perhaps a more practical distinction will be found by taking those castes which have not and those which have Panchayats. The former, it is generally believed, do not recognize re-marriage, but punish it by excommunication; the latter permit it. In fact the second marriage is a sort of civil contract ratified by the caste brethern or Panch, and though not accompanied by the religious ceremonies which accompany the first marriage, constitutes in their eyes a formal or legal union. Without the consent of the brotherhood the union only amounts to concubinage, by consent of parties...........

Besides the "twice-born" castes, and those with no Panchayats, there are some families and individuals who strive to imitate those whom birth or tradition has placed above them in the social scale; and, when they have risen in the world try to cut themselves off from their previous associates by adopting the habits of people to whom they have been taught to look up to...........Hence in a good many instances may be found some special sub-divisions or families repudiating a practice which the rest of the caste admit.................

There seems no doubt that the numerical bulk of the Banya caste do permit re-marriage, and it is only the Agarwalas and the other higher and wealthier branches who absolutely forbid it.........No Brahmins of these provinces appear to admit remarriage of widows, but it is said that one clan in Sindh does so..............Following the details of Caste Statement VIII of the Census Report fer 1881 (Vol. I) the following seem to be the castes which interdict widow marriage.

Caste	Number (both sexes)
½ Banya	602 065
Bhat	129 921
Bhuinhar	188 080
Brahmin	4655 204
Chauhan	99 807
Joshi	33 303
Kayath	513 495
Tagas	47 288
Bengalis	2 521
Kashmiris	1 794
Marwaris	1 854
Rajputs	3027 400
Total	10,404,347

The total number of Hindus in this provinces is 38,053,394; so that, rightly speaking, only a little over a fourth of the Hindu population prevent their widows from remarrying; and this fourth comprises the most wealthy educated and high-born classes.

Taking 15 as the age of puberty out of the whole female population of that age and upwards, the percentage of widows is 26·7 among Hindus, and 25·1 among Musulmans. An abstract of the figures for the population under 15 discloses the result that out of a total female population of 6,582,405 Hindu girls of 14 years and under, there are 25,574 or 0·38 per cent widows; and out of a similar total of 1,050,030 Musulmans, 2612 or 0·25 per cent. are widows. Or if the females aged from 9 to 14 alone be considered, it appears that out of 1820,134 Hindus, 21,417 or 1·2 per cent are widows; and out of 293,109 Musulmans, 2113, or 0·7 per cent are widows...... The explanation must be sought in social or physical conditions which are common to both the great religions of the country. These conditions can probably best be traced by a comparison with other countries.........Turning to England— it appears that out of every 100 females of 20 years and upwards, 25·80 are single, 60·60 married, and 13·60 widows. In the North-Western Provinces and Oudh, the corresponding per centages are

Single .... 0·81
Married .... 69·64
Widows .... 29·55.

Whatever may be the difference between the two forms of society, the general social effect and result must be detrimental wherein a large body of unmarried women exists, whether these be widows or spinsters. The position of a single woman is no doubt more tolerable in England from the greater freedom and securety and the much higher social consideration and sympathy that women of every status enjoy there. And the restriction which the *parda* places on the movements of all respectable women of the higher castes in India must aggravate the isolation of widows here. There is no doubt that these things greatly intensify the disadvantages and unhappiness to which all women are liable who are denied their natural place in a household ; but the ultimate conclusion is little more than that the position of women everywhere is imperfect and often very unsatisfactory.

The proportion of widowed Hindu females only begins to become excessive in the 4th decade of life. It is 6·39 per cent between the ages of 20 and 30, and rises to 17·06 between 30 or 40, and swells to 60·9 and 83·04 in the next two decades. In England the proportion of married women between 15 and 20 years of age is only 3·1 per cent ; in the North Western Provinces and Oudh it is 87·8; between 20 and 30, 47·5 per cent of English women are married and 92·4 of

Indian women in this province. In the next decade the proportions are more equal being in India 82·5 to 75·1 in England; and in the fifth decade and afterwards the English returns show a higher percentage of married females.

45. C. R. HAWKINS, ESQ., DEPUTY COMMISSIONER, AMRITSAR.—Obstacles to the remarriage of widows are not much felt in this part of the country.

46. DIWAN RAM NATH, DISTRICT JUDGE HOSHIARPUR.—Remarriage in another caste is greater misery for the widow than widowhood; for she gets separated from her parents and parents-in-law and their relations for ever, and is thrown on the mercy of the man who marries her, not for love, but for passion, and may any time throw her aside. Moreover to change a caste is not only ruin to a girl, but it ruins the good name of her parents in their society or brotherhood, and so much sacrifice the majority of respectable widows cannot generally dare to make.

47. DENZIL IBBETSON, DIRECTOR OF PUBLIC INSTRUCTION PANJAB.—A very considerable proportion of our population—probably something like two thirds of the whole—practise widow-marriage (Census Reports 1881 paragrah 685). This latter fact however greatly increases the tenacity with which the higher castes of Hindus cling to their objection against the custom, which is indeed commonly used as the test, and spoken of as the mark, of their superiority.

48. RAI MULRAJ M.A., EXTRA ASSISTANT COMMISSIONER, GURDASPUR.—Ask any ordinary Hindu his views about widow-marriage and he will tell you that widow marriage goes, against Dharma..........................Mr. Malabari perhaps does not know that against widow marriage the opinion of women among Hindus is even stronger than of men.

49. CHIEF COMMISSIONER, CENTRAL PROVINCES (MR. CROSTHWAITE).—Vide Chapter I, Section IV.

50. CHIEF COMMISSIONER, BRITISH BURMA (MR. BERNARD).—Among Burman races there is no prohibition against the marriage of widows or of divorced wives.

51. CHIEF COMMISSIONER, ASSAM (MR. ELLIOTT) QUOTES THE FOLLOWING FROM THE ASSAM NEWS.—The re-marriage of widows is not in vogue among the Brahmans only. Those of all other castes re-marry freely whenever they choose, while the austerities practised even by our Brahman widows who are not allowed to remarry are not half so severe as those which widows of any caste are obliged to undergo in other parts of India. The Assamese widows are free to eat and drink anything not forbidden to Hindus, except fish and flesh, and the observance of *Ekadashi*, which is the bane of the lives of widows in Bengal, is quite optional with those of our country.

52. LIEUTENANT COLONEL H. C. A. ZEZEPANSKI DEPUTY COMMISSIONER WUN DISTRICT,—As regards widowhood it is only enforced amongst Brahmins and the higher castes. The general opinion is that the rule should be so far relaxed as to allow the re-marriage of virgin-widows. The argument is that child-widows are suffering from some grave misconduct in a previous existence which can only be expiated by meritorious conduct in this—such as remaining a widow; but as men do not suffer in any similar way and are allowed to marry again, it is, as a native described it, like a cart with only one wheel.

53. BAPUJEE HARI HEAD CLERK OFFICE DEPUTY COMMISSIONER BULDHANA.—I do not mean to say that there are no widows in those countries where infant-marriage is never dreamt of. All I mean to say is that there are more young widows in India than in all other countries put together. India's widows are made martyrs, while widows in other countries are pitied and prayed for. Here they are shunned by their own kith and kin; there they are looked upon as objects of compassion. And all this for no fault of theirs. They are married in infancy and when unfortunate in losing their husbands, are loaded with all sorts of misery, sufferings, and pain.

54. NARAYEN PRABHAKER PARASPE HEAD MASTER A.V. SCHOOL RAJA DEULGAON.-The remarriage of my own sister, who

was deprived of her first husband when she was only 11 or 12 years old, has given me sufficient experience of the persecution of excommunication and of the influence of the religious authorities. The so-called civilized or Europeanized Hindus (I am one of them) are very small in proportion to those in favour of the old customs and manners, and the former carry little influence over the latter, Hence they always fail in removing the prejudices of the masses. What best the reformers can do under the existing circumstances is that they should keep up their energies and devote their attention to the mental culture of the Hindu mind; promote morality in particular; and when sufficient moral courage is gained and a portion of the old bigotry has disappeared, it will be the proper time for reformers to bring social reforms into practice.

55. Vishnu Moreshwar Mahajani M. A., Head-Master High Shcool Akola.—It is not the priest who is a tyrant—but the whole caste. The bulk of the people follow immemorial custom rather than the priest. The other day one of the Shankaracharyas,—the Pope of the Hindus—moved by some of the new reformers ruled that the Shastras were not opposed to intermarriages among certain sub-castes of Brahmins, and yet few people have availed themselves of the liberty. Why? Because they fear that if they intermarry, their children would be looked upon, to borrow an expression from natural history, as 'cross breeds,' and they could not then have as large a field for selection as they now have.

56. Shrikrishna Narhar, Extra Assistant Commissionor Ellichpur.—As a matter of fact though the ceremonious portion of the marriage take place early, the actual consummation never or very seldom, is allowed before the pair attain full maturity; and to this purpose, the ceremony constituting it is deferred two, and in some cases four years after one of the parties has grown up, to allow the other to complete his years of nonage..

His (Mr. Malabari's) ideas are derived from the social satires and appeals, and therefore tainted with the haziness and exaggeration which are but too common in those compositions.

57. SHRIRAM BHIKAJEE JATAR B. A., DIRECTOR OF PUBLIC INSTRUCTION, HYDERABAD ASSIGNED DISTRICTS.—In 1867 a meeting was held at Akola in order to excommunicate a Brahmin who had brought about the marriage of his widowed sister in Poona. Some one said (rightly or wrongly) that the meeting was illegal as Government had passed an Act for making widow remarriage legal. The meeting dispersed without arriving at any conclusion, but that did not prevent the man from being excommunicated in reality. He was not only not invited to dinner parties, but people refused to drink the water touched, by him. When the man retired and went to live in Poona he had to buy re-admission into the caste by paying a sum of money and feeding many Brahmins. I do not know how Government can prevent this.

58. RAGHUNATH B. TALVALKAR HEAD MASTER HIGH SCHOOL AMRAOTI.—Modern India has not deprived woman of any rights of which she was possessed in ancient times. She enjoys them still. Her status has ever been subordinate, but not much inferior to man who has been always her guide and guardian. The class of misguided widows is very small.

SECTION V. EXTRACTS FROM OPINIONS GIVEN TO MR. MALABARI.

---

59. DR. RAJENDRALALA MITRA C. I. E.—Your picture about the immorality resulting from widowhood is highly over-painted......Under the present state of human civilisation there must always be a large number of men who will not or cannot marry, and as the proportion of men and women of

marriageable age is all but exactly the same, there must always be large numbers of women who cannot get husbands, and nature must prevail in most of these and the result will be immorality. There is no escaping out of the difficulty. Every widow married takes away a husband from a maid, and your utmost efforts result in converting a number of maids into fallen women. The less the number of widows, the greater the number of maids who can never have husbands. You must not conclude from this that I am an enemy to widow-marriage : far from it ; I yield to none in advocating widow-marriage, but, advocate it on the broad ground of individual liberty of choice and not on account of immorality possible or contingent, You know well enough that in England maids number not by thousands but by hundreds of thousands, and you will not have the hardihood to tell me that all of them or the bulk of them are chaste or for the matter of that more chaste than our widows. Nor can you tell me that unchaste maids are better than unchaste widows.

60. J. D. B. Gribble Esq., C.S.—I have long been of opinion that there is an immense amount of unpublished crime which is mainly due to these two evils. My experience over 20 years as Magistrate and Sessons Judge has confirmed that opinion. Take, for instance, the case of reported suicides and deaths by drowning. I find that in this Presidency (Madras) about one in every 35 deaths is reported either as a suicide or an accidental death. These figures an appalling, but strange to say they seem to have attracted little or no notice.

61. Govind W. Kanitkar, B.A., L.L.B.—The victims of the agitation for widow remarriage..............are leading their lives in social alienation like converts to Christianity. They are considered as a caste by themselves. The faithless leaders of the agitation gradually proved false to the standard they had raised.

62. Vithal K. Shrikhande, of Hyderabad College.—At present the sufferings to which our widows are subjected are simply heart-rending and it would be sheer

cruelty to refuse relief to the wretched victims. The present condition of Hindu widows is a deep blot upon Hindu Society.

63. RAO BAHADUR SIRDAR GOPALRAO HARI DESHMUKH LATE JOINT SESSIONS JUDGE AND MEMBER OF THE LEGISLATIVE COUNCIL BOMBAY.—Within these fifty years many lower castes have given up re-marriage simply to approach the Brahmins. Ne reform can be carried out unless some political influence is brought to bear on it.

We see many parents not only content with imposing the vow of chastity upon their daughters (widowed), but they shave the girls at their tender age and deprive them of all ornaments and decorations and keep them half starved throughout life. They are particularly deprived of all privileges of attending marriage and other religious ceremonies. Their appearance on festive occasions is considered an ill omen. In all higher castes the treatment of widows is very cruel, especially among Rajputs, Khatris and Banias. They vie with Brahmins in treating widows with great cruelty. The wonder is that they do not think that it is cruelty, but they think it is virtue and piety. The widows are made to sit in a dark room for two or three years; and I have known of a widow who did not leave her room for more than thirty years and was considered a living Satti.........

It must not be forgotton that priests derive a very large benefit from perpetual widowhood. A widow thinks that her misfortunes arise from her not having attended to religious duties in former lives, and therefore she must devote her time and wealth to pilgrimages and so on. The wealth of most widows is devoured by priests. It is the widows rich and poor, who maintain priesthood in luxury.

64. SURGEON MAJOR D. N. PAREKH CHIEF PHYSICIAN GOKULDAS TEJPAL HOSPITAL.—In my professional capacity, I have had many opportunities of seeing Hindu widows, young and old, in Poona and Bombay. I invariably noticed that they were feeble, prematurely aged, looking pale, devoid

of all mental or bodily energy, and apathetic. They gave me the idea that they were all suffering from slow starvation. Though such of course could not really be the case in all cases, yet knowing what we do of the way in which Hindu widows are treated, I could easily account for their appearance which I have discribed above. They are said to be looked down upon ; they are said to be constantly worried by their mothers in-law ; they have no hope of happiness ; they are said to be perpetually taunted for their ill-luck as if they were the arbiters of their destiny in that respect ; they are said to be underfed and kept in close confinement. Now, I have some experience, as a Surgeon in Her Majesty's Service, of the manner in which Government treats the prisoners in Her Majesty's Jails as far ar food, clothing etc. are concerned, and if what is said of the Hindu widow's life is true, then I am constrained to declare the she is far worse off than a prisoner on the criminal side of Her Majesty's Jails.

65. PANDIT BADRI DUTT JOSHI.—Fourthly the virgin widows, whose milk teeth have not yet fallen, who have not even the least idea of what a husband means. For such miserable members of our society, I say I should like to enforce marriage on them rather than enforce widowhood.

66. W. LEE WARNER.—I have been told by Hindu gentlemen of high position that infanticide and the crime of abortion are a very common outcome of this most objectionable custom (enforced widowhood)...........The widows of India deserve the consideration of benevolent reformers. I go further, and dare state that their treatment is unworthy of the intelligence and of the progress of Hindu Society.

67. A. O. HUME.—It (enforced widowhood) is productive of great evils, much unhappiness, much demoralization. It is a custom against which common sense and all the best instincts of our nature write, as in the case of slavery, the verdict "*delenda est.*" But with all that, it does not, taking the country as a whole, produce so much evil as might be

theoretically inferred. It is bad enough doubtless, but it is not that gigantic cancer of the heart's core of society, that tremendous and cruel evil, the eradication of which is essential as the first step to national regeneration, that the casual reader unacquainted with the intricacies of social life in the East might well conceive it to be from your eloquent and earnest denunciations.

But besides this I have another difficulty. I must divide widows into titular or virgin-widows, and real widows. As to the former I have satisfied myself by a careful study of all the authentic and authoritative texts produced on both sides, that there is nothing in the Shastras to prevent *their* re-marriage; and there being positively no good that can be even alleged from enforcing their continued widowhood, while very grave evils unquestionably flow there-from, I have no hesitation in earnestly pressing and entreating every good Hindu, who loves his family, his fellows or his country, to combine to make re-marriages in such cases *customary* and thus, as it were, *legislate for themselves* on this matter.

68. CHOTALAL SEVAKRAM, PRIVATE SECRETARY TO H. H. THE RAO OF CUTCH.—The custom of enforced widowhood, which inflicts perpetual misery on Hindu widows of the upper classes, is a monstrous evil, far greater than that of early marriages, and, as such, ought to enlist the most lively sympathy of the educated and the reformer, of the statesman and the scholar, of the philanthropist and the philosopher, and of the Government, at least so far as to aid the efforts of those who would exert themselves to bring about the emancipation of the tens of thousands of the unfortunate victims...... Their forlorn condition, when viewed with a sympathetic consideration, cannot but melt the most adamantine heart.

69. RAI H C. SETH, (JHANSI).—Every one will admit that the state of our widows is deplorable. They lead a life of misery, and many of them become degraded and criminal.......

70. W. WORDSWORTH.—The condition of that unhappy class—the child-widows of India, though less pitiable

than that of infants married without their own choice or will to aged sensualists, is one which must command universal sympathy, and which no priestly casuistry can excuse or palliate. In a pamphlet by Mr. Raghonath Row, which I have been re-reading lately, there is a passage which portrays in sombre colours the hard lot of these innocent victims, and analyses the theological or metaphysical assumptious on which it is grounded. I have no more reason for questioning the substantial truth of Mr. Raghonath Row's representations than I have for questioning the truth of Manzoni's moving picture in the *Betrothed* of the fate of Italian noble maidens whom aristocratic pride condemned to a cloistered life before they were old enough to make a choice. But I must frankly say that, perverse and cruel as such practices are, I do not believe that their moral and social consequences have been, or are, so disastrous as eager reformers would wish us to believe. I do not believe that Italian Nuns, whose vocation was determined by their parents' choice, were necessarily either miserable or vicious, or that the same can be said of the great majority of Hindu widows. Human nature is marvellously plastic, and a state of life, which many women deliberately adopt, and which extrinsic circumstances impose on a multitude of others in all civilized lands, cannot be without compensating consolations. In those cases where it is sweetened by domestic affections, sustained by religious devotion, or fortified by intellectual passion, I have no doubt, that the lives of those who, from choice or necessity, adopt it, are neither unprofitable nor unhappy. I share, of course, your own judgment of that masculine egotism which has imposed on one-half of the human race in India a law of sacrifice from which the other half is relieved. But the feminine world of India is, I suppose, hardly conscious of this inequality and finds a consolation in self-sacrifice which we can hardly estimate.*

* In his minute recorded as Chairman of the Rukhmabai Defence Committee, Mr. Wordsworth wrote:—(vide the Indian Spectator of the

CHAPTER VI.

CAUSES OF ENFORCED WIDOWHOOD.

SECTION I. MADRAS PRESIDENCY.

1. C. SUBBARAYA AIYAR, B.A., B.L., THIRD JUDGE, APPELLATE COURT, ERNACOLLUM.—"Out of every 15 Brahman women of all ages, 3 are not yet married, 7 are married, and 5 are widows, and widows past remedy. There are proportionately 50 per cent more widows among Brahmans than among other castes, and this surplus may be wholly attributed to the greater extent to which infant marriages occur among Brahmans than is the case with other castes."

2. M. TILLAINAYAGAM PILLAI, DEPUTY COLLECTOR, MADURA.—One of the main causes of the existence of an unusually large number of these unfortunate creatures among the Hindus is early marriage.

5th June 1887) "Again, I need hardly say, that I consider the existence of the Hindu child-widow one of the darkest blots that ever defaced the civilisation of any people, and it is the direct and necessary consequence of the system of infant marriage. Some years ago, I should have expected that these sentiments would have found an echo in the bosom of every Hindu who had received an English education, and particularly among those persons who were attempting to appropriate the political method and ideas of Englishmen. I have no such delusion now. I find some of them employing all the resources of theological sophistry and cant, not simply to palliate but to vindicate what is plainly one of the most cruel, blighting and selfish forms of human superstition and tyranny. I find others manœuvring to arrest every sincere effort at reform, sophisticating between right and wrong, defaming the character and motives of reformers, and labouring to establish by arguments as ridiculous as they are insulting, that English domestic society offers a warning rather than an example to the Hindus. I find them vindicating early marriage as the only safeguard against universal sexual licence, a confession of moral incompetence which I should have thought that any people with a grain of self-respect would have shrunk from advancing."

SECTION II. BOMBAY PRESIDENCY.

3. NANDSHANKAR, ASSISTANT JOINT ADMINISTRATOR, RAJPIPLA.—The practice may lay claim to antiquity and has all the force of long established custom. It is associated with a high sense of honour and delicacy cherished by the people in respect of the status of females, and is commonly regarded as a sure criterion of the superiority of one caste over another. This mark of distinction.........is observed by some respectable Parsis of the old school, and Kasbatis, and other well-to-do Mahomedans living among Hindus.

4. JOTEERAO GOVINDRAO PHULAY.—It is (not) quite evident from the partial Arya religious institution that when it prohibits the widows from remarrying, why the widowers should be allowed to remarry...........There is no doubt that the selfish and wicked law-givers must have added such unjust and nonsensical clauses in their Shastras with malice towards the female sex.

5. KALIANRAI H. DESAI, OF BROACH.—The Hindu ideas about female chastity and integrity are so peculiarly delicate and refined that, it is almost impossible to convey an adequate notion of their influence on the social life of the people to any one who is out of the pale of the Community. The prevalance of the custom which Mr. Malabari so strongly condemns should be attributed to this religious and social aspect of the question.

6. RUNCHORLALL CHOTALALL (AHMEDABAD).—It is a point of religious belief and sense of honour that prevents a woman of a respectable family from remarrying. I learn that there are certain sects even of the Mussalman religion, such as the Sayads, who would not allow their young daughters to remarry. There are many castes of the Hindu Community such as Kunbis in which widow remarrage is freely allowed; but even among that caste there are some families who would

not remarry their widows on account of respectability of the family.

7. MR. JUGJIVANDASS (SURAT).—The Brahmins, Bannians, Jains, Tonis and a few other minor castes do not observe this custom (widow remarriage) generally under an impression that it is not allowed by the Shastras, presuming at the same time that by its adoption, distinction between higher and lower castes may cease to a great extent, and that the evil of poisoning or killing the husband of a wife who does not agree with him and who has a lover ready to take her, will easily find its way.

8. SAKHARAM ARJUN.—The introduction of this pernicious custom (Enforced widowhood) in the Non-Brahminical classes is due to that rage for imitating their superiors which constantly seizes an inferior class, whether in politics or religion, in literature or art. In our own days the eagerness for indiscriminate adoption of the foibles, nay even the follies of our English rulers, which many of our countrymen display, is an illustration in point of this passion for imitating our superiors.

9. NAGINDAS TULSIDAS.—I am inclined to believe that this custom (Enforced widowhood) must have been introduced when the number of females was greater than that of males.

SECTION III. BENGAL PRESIDENCY.

10. BRITISH INDIAN ASSOCIATION.—The Committee readily admit that the law of the remarriage of Hindu widows has not proved so fruitful of result as could be wished by its advocates.

But this is not a matter for wonder. Young girls under 13 or 14 years of age can be easily given away in marriage, without consulting their wishes, because they are not in a mental condition to judge for themselves; but the case is different when widows of 18 years and more have to be dealt with and who cannot but assert their will. In such cases courtship is the only means of influencing their minds, and courtship implies a change of dress, manners, habits and customs of Hindu Society: in short a complete boulversement of the Hindu social fabric, which cannot readily be accomplished. Hence it is futile to expect a rapid change.

SECTION IV. NORTH-WEST PROVINCES AND OUDH, THE PUNJAB, CENTRAL PROVINCES, BURMA, ASSAM, COORG, HYDRABAD (DECCAN.) &c.

11. Chief Secretary to Government, N. W. P. and Oudh.—It has been pointed out by Mr. Mayne .... that the prohibition against the second marriage of women ....has no foundation either in early law or custom. It is probable, he thinks, that the change of usage on this point arose from the influence of Brahminical opinion, marriage coming to be looked upn as a Sacrament, the effect of which was indelible. This view seems quite in accordance with the rnles actually followed by most Hindus in the North-Western Provinces...

It seems clear that, comparing the two countries, (North West Provinces and Oudh, and England) there are more widows in the North-West Provinces and Oudh, because (1) a larger proportion of the women get married, and (2) they get married very much younger. *Cæteris paribus*, a woman who marries at 15 stands a much greater chance of being left a-widow, than a woman who does not marry till 30; and as an Indian woman reaches a marriageable age earlier than a European, so she passes it sooner. *Mr. White's inquiries (at the time of the Census) went to show that at 30 years of age she is generally an old woman*, past the age for child-bearing and not likely to secure another husband. This most likely is the reason why.........the proportion of Hindu women living in widowhood only begins to get excessive in the fourth decade of life. Those left widows after 30 remain so for the rest of their lives, and this is a state of things which is likely to continue till some radical change in the national physique and constitution occurs, which may check the development and prolong the youth and vigour of the race. Males remarry freely even in old age, but they do not seem to marry their second wives from among the widows of 30 and upwards.

The excess of widows seems due in the main to physical and social causes which are not peculiar to Hindus, and are probably inseparable from the ethnological and climatic conditions of the country. The residuum of avoidable evil which can be safely set down to caste custom, is confined to the wealthier and more educated classes, who ought to be best able to help themselves without asking for Government interference.

12. MR. BAPUJEE HARI HEAD CLERK, OFFICE OF DEPUTY COMMISSIONER, BULDHANA.—Wedded to a child hardly capable of taking care of itself, a female child in a hundred cases out of 500, becomes a widow. She does not in many instances know whether she was ever married. She does not even realize the loss she has sustained in the death of her boy-husband. She does not comprehend the restrictions and privations, the usual lot of a Hindu widow, to which she is subjected. She does not comprehend the evil she has committed for which she is made to suffer all the rigors of widowhood. Her restrictions and privations grow more and more as she advances towards the dangerous state of widowed womanhood. Once at that age, and there is fear of fall, and what is the consequence of that fall but misery, imprisonment or untimely death. Shame is more formidable than death, it causes even the ill-gotten child to be thrown away or disposed

of in the way best known to a young Hindu widow. All these evils proceed from the evil and pernicious custom of early marriage. Prevention is better than cure. If infant marriage is stopped, the large number of India's widows will be diminished.

SECTION V. EXTRACTS FROM OPINIONS GIVEN TO MR. MALABARI.

13. P. C. MOZOOMDAR, BRAHMO MISSIONARY.—With the exception of a few men who marry widows out of principle, or of a small percentage who are indifferent whether they marry maids or widows, there is a clearly defined and quite extensive objection in marriageable men to take a widow for wife. In as well as outside the Brahma Samaj one meets with this objection so repeatedly that the inference suggests itself—there must be some natural cause for it. All notions on the subject of the holiness of the marriage tie are so absolutely and constitutionally puritanic amongst Hindus, that in spite of the revolutionary training of the young men, they theoretically uphold widow marriage as a reform, but they will not themselves marry widows when their turn comes. The remarriage of widows as a *separate* movement has not the same moral interest for every practical reformer. It may do very well as part of a larger and more sweeping measure. To the genuinely orthodox, it is quite as revolutionary as the most radical movement, despite all quotations from the Dharma Shastras. To the genuinely heterodox it is too fractional to deserve so much shot and powder! ....

It seems to me, my dear sir, a wise economy of Providence that quite an appeciable number of men and women in every civilized people, whether in the shape of the widowed or the unmarried, should remain disentangled from the anxieties and trials of matrimony for the ministry of sorrow, suffering, and other wants of general society.

14. Rai H. C. Seth, (Jhansi).—Hindu sons and daughters being generally married at an age when they even do not get over the ordinary diseases of childhood, the result is that many girls become widows before they know what conjugal bliss is, and are forced to pass the best portion of their life in widowhood.

15. W. Wordsworth.—In India, where for ages the thoughts and habits of men have been controlled and dominated by religious ideas, it is easy to understand how the sacramental or mystical conception of marriage as a binding tie for time and eternity,and the inferences which have been drawn from that conception, should have taken such deep root and possess such enduring vitality. In the primitive Christian society in which this temporal life was also darkened by the overpowering vision of the hereafter, the sacramental conception of marriage was among its earliest developments, and second marriages, as you know, were tolerated and barely tolerated, as concessions to human weakness. On this subject even St. Paul in whom practical judgment went hand in hand with mysticism, uses language which strikes harshly on modern ears. If European society had ever been as completely moulded by theological beliefs and priestly rules as Hindu society has been, I am persuaded that remarriage, or at least the remarriage of women would have also been prohibited in Europe. If this had been done, European society would certainly have suffered, but not perhaps so much in the direction which you would be inclined to suppose.

CHAPTER VII.

THE LAW ON THE SUBJECT OF ENFORCED WIDOWHCOD.

SECTION I. MADRAS PRESIDENCY.

1—Krishnaswami Rao Chief Justice Travancore.—The laws now in force contain adequate provisions for the protection of a widow. If against her will, she is compelled to go through the melancholy ceremony of tonsure, the offenders will be liable to prosecution on charges of assault, causing hurt, using criminal force, &c., under the Indian Penal Code. Ample provision is made in Act XV of 1856 for the marriage of widows and for the protectien of their civil rights. She is also protected from wanton insults, resulting from the offensive and unnecessary publication of bulls of excommunication, by the judgment of the Madras High Court in Empress *versus* Sri Sankarachary Swami. If widows have *unredressed* grievances, their existence is entirely due to their reluctance to bring them to public notice.

2. M. Tillainayagam Pillai.—I find the authorities on the subject to be contradictory; those against early marriage and in favour of remarriage of widows preponderating..

The following facts may, I think, be traced from the Sastras. In earlier days marriages appear to have been performed after women attained puberty or discretion, and remarriage of widows was an orthodox institution. Marriageable age for women was then reduced to 12 or 10 or 8, and an attempt at stopping the remarriage of widows was made by holding out to them hopes of heaven if they continued unmarried, and led a virtuous life after the death of their husbands. This was probably found to be not a sufficient inducement, to prevent remarriage of widows. It was then restricted first to childless widows and then to virgin widows and finally absolutely prohibited, and even death with her husband was prescribed. Even after all this widow marriage appears to have been practised. But the married couple occupied an inferior position in society.

The days of faith in the divine origin of these anthorities are fast vanishing. They are being believed to be human laws and marriage a human institution. If any Sastra, which is intended for the promoti on of human happiness, does not produce that end, but is on the other hand, found to be productive of evil, it may well be revised and a better law calc ulated to secure that end, may be substituted.

SECTION II. BOMBAY PRESIDENCY.

3. K. C. BEDARKAR LL. B. DEPUTY REGISTRAR, HIGH COURT.—I am content with expressing my conviction that those who say widow remarriage is not forbidden by the Shastras are correct ....
I would beg leave to draw attention to Sections 350, 352, 109, 89 and 90 of the Indian Penal Code. I think that the provisions of these sections are quite sufficient to put a stop to the forcible shaving of women, who have the misfortune to lose their husbands, provided the people themselves have the courage to invoke their aid.........It must, however, be admitted that there are great difficulties in the way of going to law. The task of ascertaining whether the consent to shave is given voluntarily or otherwise would be stupendous. Perjury would be unscrupulously resorted to in torturing the woman's inclination into her voluntary consent.

4. TIRMALRAO VENKATESH.—Supposing the *dates and numbers* of all Regulations and Acts passed up to now by the Government of India and all the Local Governments, together with the different *sections* in them, repealing former enactments, and stating the extent of country over which each enactment was intended to have force, were effaced, and the bare enactments, many of which are contrary to the others, placed in the hands of lawyers, who may in no way be personally acquainted with the order and arrangement of the Regulations and Acts, they would become quite confused, and would not know which Regulation or Act was rescinded and which was in force ; and yet the counsel of one party would take hold of one enactment, and that of the adverse party of a contrary one, and the Judge

would be at a loss as to which of the two enactments he was to follow. and there would be confusion every where. Such is exactly the state of the present Hindu law books. If the Legislature were to collect all Hindu law books, examine them, and declare which of them are to be acted upon, which modified and which rejected, it would be conferring a great benefit on the country.........Many native pleaders are of this opinion

5. RANCHODLAL K. DESAI.—It may now be taken as a point beyond dispute that the Hiudu Shastras allow of the marriage of widows.

6. KALIANRAI H. DESAI OF BROACH.—Notwithstanding the feeble endeavours of Pandit Ishwarchandra Vidyasagur and Vishnu Shastri Pandit, and their few followers, both here and elsewhere, Oriental Scholarship in India is unanimous in the condemnation of widow remarriage as an institution not recognized by the Shastras.

7. VARJEEVANDASS MADOWDASS.—I believe that the remarriage of widows is prohibited in the religious books of the Hindus and as long as this belief is entertained by the people interested, I think it will be unwise that Government should interfere in the matter.

8. VENKAT RANGO KATTI.—The reformers allege that many of the authorities adduced by their opponents are fabrications and that the single authority of Parashara whose Smriti is declared to be supreme in the Kali age, allowing widow remarriage in five cases of emergency is enough for their purpose. The oppositionists set forth this very authority to oppose remarriage by changing the last word "Vidhiyate" (is allowed) to "Navidyate" (is not allowed) and assert that it is their reading which is correct.........If we consult the Dharma Sindhu.........we find that the author dismisses the subject of widow remarriage by stating in a very few words that it is prohibited in the Kali age.

Widow marriage is objected to by some writers of the Dharma Shastra on the principle that a thing once bestowed on others cannot be given again. But these writers have at the same time given permission to girls themselves to choose their own husbands when they have none to give them away. (This gentleman gives an account of Rughunathrao's discussion with the Pandits one of whom adduced a verse from the Babhravya Smriti stating that the girl whose husband dies after Saptapaddi (the concluding ceremony of marriage) should not be given to another in the Kali age and refused to accept Raghunathrao's array of authorities in favour of widow remarriage on the ground that none of them specifically opposed the above text. Another explained away Parashara's text by stating that it was applicable to the portion of the Kali age which passed before the sacrifice of Janamejaya, as well as to cases in subsequent times wherein a husband died in the interval between marriage proper and Saptapaddi, and that at all other times Babhravya and other prohibitory authorities must be followed.)

9.—R. G. BHANDARKAR.—The Hindu Shastras do not make Suttee compulsory. Manu and Yajnavalkya, the principal law-givers, make no mention of it whatever. It is only some of the minor law-books that prescribe it, and they even make it optional, the other course open to women being perpetual widowhood. On the other hand there are distinct texts prohibiting the immolation of widows of the Brahmin caste and one law-book allows even remarriage. So that the general spirit of the Hindu Shastras is in favour of perpetual widowhood, self-immolation being allowed but not enjoined. And the practice was in keeping with this spirit.

10. CHATURBHOOJ MORARJI.—Remarriage (of widows) is expressly prohibited by our Aryan religion. There are only two duties enjoined for widows, the first is Sayyapalana (falling away from bed i.e. celibacy) and the other is Anugamana (dying after as of a widow) Of these two Sayyapalana is the chief one. Sayyapalana only has been enjoined in the Smritis of Manu and others.

11. GUNGADHAR SHASTRI DATAR OF POONA.—After the death of King Dasharatha his three wives led a life of

abstinence and protected their sons and subjects. Purshuram's mother Renuka burnt herself as a *Sati.* It is also evident that there did not exist, besides these two alternatives the third alternative of widows again marrying themselves. The above incidents are taken from the Purans. In recent times also, in the Kali yug itself, Ahilyabai's daughter burnt herself as a Sati. As to how Ahilyabai herself led a life of abstinence and managed the affairs of her state will be known from a perusal of Malcolm's History of Central India......... In the discussions held some years ago on this subject before the Jagadguru Shrimat Shankar-acharya and in the discussions lately held before Shriman Madhav-acharya, it was decided that the remarriage of widows was contrary to the Hindu Shastras, and that therefore a Brahmin who married a widow became an outcaste with whom as well as with the widow so married no intercourse should be held in matters of religion.

12. Pandit Gattulal.—As for the aphorism of Parashara "that (the husband being) lost, dead, banished, being impotent and outcaste," &c. the form पपौ is not possible, because the word पुति does not terminate in पि and therefore getting ऊपपे by dissolving the Sandhi, and the negative particle in अपपौ being construed as conveying the meaning of similarity, the aphorism applies to a girl betrothed.

13. Gokuldas Kahandass Parekh.—As things now stand, in several matters the legal and social position of an adulterous widow is superior to that of a remarrying one.......... Her Myjesty's Privy Council and the High Courts of Bombay and Calcutta have all laid down that adultery does not divest the widow of interest once vested in her (I. L. R. 5 Cal. 776 ; 13 B. L. R. 14 ; I Bom. H. C. R. A. C. 25); while the widow Remarriage Act effects that divesture (See Section 2 Act XV of 1856.) Then again an adulterous widow is entitled to retain the custody and guardianship of her children while the remarrying widow is deprived of them.

14. Babu Hori Mohun Chandra.—It has been proved that the custom of remarriage of widows was in force in our society...............It is highly probable that the rite of Sati began when the remarriage of widows was abolished.

It is a fact I believe, that the burning of widows on their husbands' funeral pile was unknown in the Vedic period and in the words of Dr. Hunter..........." the verses in the Veda which the Brahmins afterwards distorted into a sanction for the practice have the very opposite meaning."

SECTION IV. NORTH-WEST PROVINCES AND OUDH, THE PUNJAB, CENTRAL PROVINCES, BURMA, ASSAM, COORG, HYDRABAD (DECCAN.) &c.

15. Chief Secretary to Government N. W. P. and Oudh.—It has been pointed out by Mr. Mayne in his treatise on Hindu Law and Usage (pages 86 & 87) that the prohibition against the second marriage of women upon widowhood has no foundation either in early law or custom.

16. Honourable D. G. Barkley, Member of the Legislative Council, Punjab Government.—Expulsion from caste is not a civil injury,* though an attempt to give it

* In a recent case (I. L. R. 10 Mad. 133) the Madras High Court upset a decision of Mr. Muttusami Ayyar and ruled that a custom or usage of a caste to expel a member in his absence without notice given or opportunity of explanation offered is not a valid custom—that it is open to the Court to determine whether an expulsion from caste is valid, and that if the person excommunicated had not in fact violated the rules of the caste but had been expelled under the *bona fide* but mistaken belief that he had committed a caste offence, the expulsion was illegal and would not affect his rights. Mr. Justice Kernan said. " The maxim *audi alteram partem* contains a fixed principle of justice. It prevails in all countries subject to the British rule.........The caste institution is not above or outside the law. The usages and customs of caste exist only under and not against the law. Whenever a custom or usage is opposed to the law it cannot be a good custom. Colebrook. B. I. Chapter 2. Section 2 IX. on Usage. Practice which is founded on

undue publicity may be, see I. L, R. 6 Mad 38 ....A caste is really, from the point of view of the State, very much in the position of a voluntary association, and people who wish to continue to belong to it must submit to its rules, while it can only punish those who will not do so by expelling them, unless they submit to some minor penalty in order to avoid expulsion. It cannot take away any civil rights—see Act XXI. of 1850.

SECTION V. EXTRACTS FROM OPINIONS GIVEN TO Mr. MALABARI.

17. SERGEANT ATKINSON,—It is clear that unjustifiable expulsion from caste and the like are good causes of action in a Civil Court of Justice. And why the poor widow, amongst other sufferers from the tyranny and oppression of the Punchayet, who marries again, and who is *on that account* made an outcaste, does not appeal to the Laws of the land for redress of her grievances (an appeal, let her be assured, never made in vain) is to me inexplicable. Does it arise from ignorance of her legal rights, from fear of appearing in a Court of Justice, or because she is *inops consilu*.........I have not cited from my MSS. the legal authorities that justify me in saying that a suit for damages will lie for restoration to caste and the like; for no lawyer will dispute the proposition and laymen will not expect it of me.

18. A. O. HUME.—As to the former (virgin widows) I have satisfied myself by a careful study of all the authentic and authoritative texts produced on both sides, that there is

law prevails. Hence usage inconsistent therewith must be abrogated. A practice must be reasonable.........Immemorial custom cannot prevail against the principle contained in the maxim "*audi alteram partem.*" See Williams *vs.* Lord Bagot 3 B. and C. 786. It is thus clear that a widow cannot be expelled from caste, without being heard in the first instance in her defence.

nothing in the Shastras to prevent *their* remarriage......... For the remarriage of fully married or real widows, I cannot say as much. I entertain no doubt that according to the Shastras, the remarriage of such involved a loss of caste. I regret that this should be so, but I believe it to be the case.

CHAPTER VIII.

REMEDIES FOR ENFORCED WIDOWHOOD.

SECTION I. MADRAS PRDSIDENCY.

1. K. KRISHNASWAMY RAO, CHIEF JUSTICE, TRAVANCORE.—The best possible aid which the Government can give seems to me to be periodical donations to the Widow Marriage Fund upon such conditions as would not encourage idelness.

2. C. RAMCHANDRA AIYAR, SUB JUDGE, MADURA.—The decision law allows a Hindu widow to lead with impunity a life of open prostitution retaining possession of her husband's property while the hallowed tie of matrimony entails forfeiture of property according to Act XV. of 1856. This is cetainly an anomaly which ought to be remedied. It must be enacted that adultery on the part of the widow is a positive disqualification to hold property inherited from her husband.

The Criminal law of the country should also be amended so as to make open excommunication by priests and gurus and others, of those that contract a second marriage and their relations penal. They should also be protected from exclusion from public temples and public tanks and rivers.

3. C. SUBBARAYA AIYAR, B.A., B.L., THIRD JUDGE APPELLATE COURT, ERNACOLLUM.—(*a*)The law laid down in Kery-Kolitany *vs.* Moneeramkolita (I. L. R., V. Cal. 776) should be

amended in accordance with the views of Mr. Justice Dwarkanath Mitter, in other words an unchaste widow should be deprived of her inheritance.

(*b*) The criminal law of the land may be so amended as to make it a penal offence on the part of priests and gurus to excommunicate publicly those that contract second marriages and their relations.

(*c*) A statutory declaration that the rights of property as against husband and wife are inchoate till nuptials.

(*d*) Active sympathy on the part of Government with the objects of voluntary associations.

4. S. SUBBRAMANIA AIYAR, VAKIL, HIGH COURT.—Alienation by will by a Hindu coparcener of his undivided share to provide for his wife, daughter and sister is, I believe, not legal, and I think that the aid of the legislature can be sought for to legalize it. This rule will much tend to improve the position of women by making them far less dependent on their male relations than they are now. The modification which has been already introduced by decided cases in respect of alienations by coparceners is so great that the granting of the testamentary power recommended will not be looked upon as an undesirable innovation.

5. M. TILLAINAYAGAM PILLAI, DEPUTY COLLECTOR, MADURA,—There is...........one point in which Government interference will not, in my opinion, go much against the feelings of the people. They may pass an Act prohibiting the priests from excommunicating a widow who may choose to remarry, and her husband and others who may sympathise or associate with her. I do not see how the priests who have been permitting marriages between persons within the degree actually prohibited by the Smritis *i.e.* marriage between a man and his sister's or paternal aunt's or maternal uncle's daughter, can claim any right to interfere with widow marriages in favour of which authorities are not wanting.

6. Nandshankar, Assistant Joint Administrator, Rajpipla.—Let the isolated cases of widow remarriage which now and then occur prepare in some way the minds of the orthodox, let the leaders of society raise their voice against this inhuman custom, let poets sing the miseries and horrors of enforced widowhood and melt their audience into tears with the recital of the wrongs of the widows, let the school-masters, lecturers and authors of books and pamphlets inveigh as vehemently as they can against this evil—let associations be formed to ventilate their grievances and afford direct and indirect encouragement to the cause, let outside influence be exercised and gentle persuasion be tried, and in short let all legal measures be adopted to further the end in view, and in process of time the condition of Hindu widows will be ameliorated and the dreaded interdict will for ever be removed.

7. Joteerao Govindrao Phulay.—I propose that no barbers should be allowed to shave the unfortunate Brahmin widows.

8. Gurshidapa Virbasapa.—I say that these evils can be easily put down by Government with the assistance of the educated natives because no respectable individual would wish, if he could help it, to have an immoral woman in his house, and because the spiritual guides who have the power of excommunication will yield to the educated natives such as merchants, *Vakils* and Government servants who contribute largely towards the maintenance of these guides.

If however Government are not inclined to go this length then let the educated Natives come forward in a body, and have widow marriages performed in their own houses at first and I am sure the orthodox will soon follow suit. If the educated natives are afraid of losing their kith and kin and their dear and near (and they will have to lose some or all at the beginning by adopting the course indicated above, and no great reforms can be effected without some such sacrifice). then let Government and the educated natives strive hard to stimulate female education to the utmost extent possible, so that the females may have sufficient enlightenment to realize their present degraded position, and sufficient moral courage to assert their right to remarry if they choose to do so.

9. NARAYEN BHIKAJI, DEPUTY COLLECTOR, NASIK.—I am strongly of opinion that a law be passed that no widow below the age of 35 shall be shaved by a barber without the written permission of a Punch given by them after noting down the voluntary desire of the woman concerned.

The law...........should like the Gambling Act be made applicable to towns and villages on application of the inhabitants of the class whom the same affects.

10. GOPALRAO HURRY, DIWAN OF RUTLAM.—In my opinion it is necessary to amend the Widow Marriage Act so far as to declare (that) any public proceeding adopted by caste or others to excommunicate and molest any remarried couple or their friends is illegal and penal under Chap. XXI. and XXII. of the Indian Penal Code.

11. K. C. BEDARKAR, L.L.B., DEPUTY REGISTRAR, HIGH COURT.—The motto of reformers for some years to come must be agitation and discussion by means of organized bodies in every part of India. The subject must be brought home to the old and to the young, to the orthodox and to the heterodox. Constant familiarity with the question and the evils of prohibition of the marriage of widows must in course of a little more time lead to a healthier and better state of things........

I should not be disinclined if the Government made a fresh section 351 (I. P. C.) by declaring that "no Hindu widow under the age of 25 should be deemed to have given her consent to shave unless it be in writing signed or marked by her before a Magistrate and attested by the latter." I think the people are to a certain extent prepared to view such a measure with secret approbation, if not more, and Government might properly aid the cause by its introduction.

12. HURRICHUND SADASIV HATE A.M.I.C.E.—Enforced widowhood is, as a general rule, the result of early marriages, and as soon as the practice of early marriages is done away with, it will mitigate many of the serious evils of perpetual widowhood.

Several texts of the Shastras will be found in favour of widow remarriage. These texts should be collected and the opinions of learned Pandits both orthodox and of the new school versed in the Shastras obtained. These opinions should be extensively circulated and the scruples of the female sex on the point be thus overcome. Government may very humanely put a stop to the present barbarous custom of getting young widows at least under 30 years of age, shaved.

13. RANCHODLAL K. DESAI.—As the commission of adultery by the unfortunate widows leads them to commit suicides and infanticides either before or after birth, the Government may well be pleased to rule that the adultery by and with a widow shall be criminally punishable. This suggestion, if accepted by the Government, will lead many widows to perform marriages instead of committing adultery secretly without caring for caste-excommunication.

14. VEERCHAND DIPCHAND.—The best thing which I am inclined to recommend for the present is for Government and the public to come forward, and open as many foundling hospitals as the funds at their disposal permit, and this measure will apparently do away to a certain extent with the evil arising from the prohibition of widow remarriage.

15. DIVAN BAHADUR MANIBHAI JASBHAI, (DIWAN OF CUTCH.)—The idea of establishing a national association for social reforms suggested by Mr. Malabari is excellent and has my hearty approval.

16. M. G. RANADE, POONA.—A reform in the early marriage law would prove very helpful in preventing early widowhood. The interposition of independent non-official

gentlemen as intermediaries to ascertain whether the young widow understands the full misery of her situation, will go a great way to alleviate her lot.

17. Venkat Rango Katti.—An effectual suppression of the shaving of widows is paving the road for widow remarriage............Sections 320 and325 (of the Penal Code) contain ample provision for our present purpose. It is therefore only necessary that Government pass a general order not longer than 2 lines directing the attention of Magistrates to the serious crime of shaving a woman and ordering them to take complaints against it brought by any body whatever ....

No trace of a shaved widow can be found before Buddhism ....That faith required the shaving of its religious persons, men or women. Such widows in those days as had no attraction for this world turned Sanyasis of their own accord by getting their head shaved and wearing red cloth, and went to live in Viharas or monasteries. This custom was regarded at the time by the Indian nation as a great improvement on the former social condition inasmuch as it granted equal rights to women with men in religious matters. When the Vedic religion revived through the efforts of Kumarilabhatta and others who drove Buddhism to foreign lands, this custom was borrowed from it by the astute Brahmins along with other good customs, with the double purpose of making their own religion more attractive to the masses and exposing the dark side of the banished religion to the world. Shaving of widows, therefore, may be considered to date from the 4th or 5th century A.D., as part of the present Hindu religion.

18. R. G. Bhandarkar, Professor of Sanskrit, Deccan College.—Indirectly Government will greatly help the cause (of widow remarriage) if it pushes on vigorously the education of girls and especially their higher education. It grieves me, however, to find that the present generation of educated natives are not so enthusiastic about the elevation of women as they are about many other things ; while it is almost

disappointing to find that the lower strata of the body actually oppose any scheme that has for its object the amelioration of their condition.

19. NAGINDAS TULSIDAS.—It just strikes me that if bigamy, polygamy and remarriage be prohibited to males of the castes who obstinately refuse remarriage to widows, the object of Government will be attained sooner. But this, again, will necessitate legislation which Government may or many not be willing to undertake. It further occurs to me that Government may do much by requiring and diffusing information on the point.

20. LAKHMIDAS KHIMJI.—If the formidable, most pernicious and tyrannical power of excommunicating is taken away from the caste in the matter of widow remarriages by declaring it to be an offence in the caste or any of its members, to excommunicate or join in excommunicating any persons marrying a widow, or taking part in the widow remarriage ceremonies, or having intercourse with parties contracting such marriages, it would be a great boon conferred on the poor widows suffering under it.

21. LALSHANKAR UMIYASHANKAR.—(*a*) Vernacular translations of Act XV of 1856 should be published and largely distributed gratis.

(*b*) Government should strictly warn the officials to take all precautionary measures to assist and protect the remarriage party in all possible manners.

(*c*) As long as the persecution is very active, Government officers should give preference to remarried candidates (*i.e.*, candidates who have married widows apparently) in filling up places for which they may be qualified.

(*d*) The proposed associations should be recognized and registered by law, and some penalty should be prescribed for one, who, after joining the association in a specified manner, breaks the rules thereof. It may be said that many will not join the association owing to such a provision of law. But I think it is better to have a few members who would adhere to the rules than to have many who would do nothing, and leave the body at any time they please. The rules may vary according to circumstances, but if the associationists be legally bound to observe their rules, mutual confidence among the members will increase and much good will result.

22. ATMARAM PANDURANG.—Much can be effected by the exercise of personal influence by the officers of State, from His Excellency downwards, on heads of castes and leaders of native society, to facilitate the introduction of the required reforms in their several communities. As an illustration of what I mean, I beg to refer Government to the line of conduct followed in such matters by so high and judicious an authority as the late Sir J. Malcolm, as described in Vol. II. of his Memoir of Central India, 3rd Edition. As regards the present case, I may observe that the mere fact of Government asking for opinions on Mr. Malabari's 'Notes' has so far influenced some of those who were fiercely opposed, for instance, to widow marriage that they freely allow themselves to he talked to on the subject.........and admit that the matter is worth considering. I may also mention that some of these gentlemen who only a few years ago would not tolerate the presence of a respectable remarried Hindu lady at Government House, simply because she was a widow before, do not now feel any such objection to her presence, and the change of feeling is due to the sole fact that Government do not think the worse of a respectable Hindu lady for her remarriage, and in their invitations to Government House make no distinction on that account. I therefore believe that much unfounded prejudice and unreasoning opposition can be overcome in this manner.

23. PANDIT NARAYEN KESSOW VAIDYA.—The first step to be attempted is the appointment of a Commission....... The next step is to remodel our girls' schools on the model chalked out for us in 1867 by the late veteran lady of world-wide renown Miss Mary Carpenter....The police returns under

the heading of "Marriage, injuries to unborn children, concealment of births" should be collected and carefully analysed.

The people are quite prepared to receive any reform the Government would introduce on this subject. Already in Surat, a most conservative district, the widows have boldly appealed to the Nugger Sett for redress. But his fortitude (sic) is not equal to the occasion.

24. PANDIT GUTTULAL.—Manu says........

" On the death of her husband she should willingly waste away her body by (living upon) good flowers, roots and fruits, and should not even pronounce the name of a stranger..........

The father protects (a woman) in childhood, the husband in youth, the sons in old age. A woman does not deserve independence ....

From meretriciousness, inconstancy and hardness of heart, they howsoever well protected, act hostilely towards their husbands by nature.

Knowing that this their disposition has been implanted in them by the Creator, a man should strive hard to guard them.

Sleep, sitting, ornaments, (the possession) of love, anger, petulance, envy and evil conduct are predicated of women by Manu."

If all the widows in the world would practise their own duties night and day, such as avoiding music and singing of all kinds, associating with good men, devotion to God, not taking plenty of food and too many ornaments, then they would not at all be the objects of the accursed torments of love and such like. Where will then be there any occasion for them to cause miscarriage or commit countless other sins?

25. GOKULDAS KAHANDAS PAREKH.—I am of opinion that the legislature has a right to insist that so long as a caste considers adultery of its widows to be matter not falling within its cognizance and does not make it punishable by its rules, they (sic)cannot make punishable what according to their view

should be only another form of adultery, particularly when the law recognizes it and the religious ceremonies remove the taint of sin and immorality. I think a provision of the Legislature, rendering the excommunication of a remarrying widow, her husband and relations punishable when the caste rules do not visit adultery with punishment, to be a just and proper one. To my mind it is not very difficult to make legislative provisions in this matter which may not unduly increase the power of the caste in reference to the action of individuals, and at the same time leave its autonomy in other matters intact.

With a view to check miscarriages and sometimes the suicide or murder of the unfortunate widows themselves, I further propose that there should be a law compelling every widow of those castes in which remarriages are not permitted who is in the family way to get her condition registered ...... and on omission to get herself registered should be made criminally punishable. The establishment kept for this purpose should work independently of the Police.

26. His Highness the Rao of Cutch.—Preaching and persuasion should be employed by the reformers as their best agents for effecting a still greater and wider change in the opinions of the people on this important subject (enforced widowhood)

27. His Highness the Thakor Saheb of Bhavnagar—Relies upon the spread of education (Vide Remedies for Infant Marriage).

28. His Highness the Thakor Sahib of Morvi.—My opinion is that widow marriages should be made quite voluntary within certain ages and under certain prescribed circumstances.........I would propose therefore the adoption of some protective measures which may not savour of interference but which may serve the desired end, indirectly though, and that Government and its officers should use their private influence indirectly in encouraging these reforms.

29. JAYASING RAO REGENT OF KOLHAPUR.—When early marriages decrease, there will be a reduction in the number of young widows. And for widow marriage to be a general custom, it will require as much moral courage as to prevent early marriage.

30. SHANTARAM NARAYAN.—On the question of widow remarriage I do not see that much remains to be done by Government............Even if the State were to do its best, widows, for all that, would remain in widowhood, so long as society looked upon the practice as sinful.

There is one suggestion that I should deem it my duty to make on this point. The Act which has legalized the remarriage of a Hindu widow at the same time provides that, in the event of such remarriage, the widow shall not be entitled to the property of her deceased husband and that it will revert to his other heirs. The result is that the law, as it is now enforced, leads to ludicrous results. For instance, suppose a Hindu dies leaving a widow. The widow inherits his property and then leads an immoral life; yet she is not liable to be deprived of it and she continues its owner nevertheless. Suppose the same widow instead of leading an immoral life remarries; the result is, the property goes out of her hands at once. This is very unfair and is hardly calculated to encourage the remarriage of widows or even morality. The Government ought to remove this blot from the Statute book without any delay.*

---

* The Bombay Government in forwarding Mr. Shantaram's letter to the Government of India wrote as follows......" ....2.........Mr. Shantaram Narayan is the ablest pleader of the High Court........... and his views merit attention. 3.—The provisions of Section 2 of Act XV. of 1856 are certainly somewhat anomalous and might in the opinion of the Governor in Council, be amended. The law as regards Hindu widows in this Presidency is succinctly stated in Bechar vs. Bai Lakshmi (1 Bombay High Court Reports 56) in the following terms. ' The Hindu law existing on this side of India gives a widow absolute power over the moveable property of her deceased husband, which has

31. JASWANTSING, THAKOR SAHIB OF LIMBDI.—Government can *help* social reform as it did, I think, in 1856, by an Act passed in that year. It can aid progress by giving opportunity for progress. But it can do no more.

SECTION III. BENGAL PRESIDENCY.

32. LORD H. ULICK BROWNE, COMMISSIONER, RAJSHAHYE DIVISION.—I think Government might consult intelligent and reliable Hindus on the question of simply repealing Section 2 of Act XV. of 1856, and unless there is strong consensus of opinion against the proposal, I would repeal the section.

33. BABU HORI MOHUN CHANDRA.—It is said that the law in the Hindu State of Baroda punishes the enticing away of a widow for immoral purposes, and that even sexual intercourse with a widow is severly punished in those territories;

---

been inherited by her, but no power to alienate immoveable property except under special circumstances.' It would be reasonable to enact that a widow should not by remarriage forfeit any property over which she has absolute power. It is clear that she can avoid the forfeiture by conveying such property to her intended husband immediately before her marriage; and it seems undesirable that the Legislature should appear to give its sanction to a penalty of which it does not approve and which can be so easily evaded."

The Government of India wrote on this subject as follows :—

"5. Of the suggestions made in the course of the voluminous correspondence quoted in the preamble, the only two which do not seem to the Government of India to be open to serious objection on ground of principle are (1) the amendment of Section 2 of Chapter XV. of 1856 as to the forfeiture of property of a widow on remarriage, and 2 the supply of machinery by which a Hindu widow who fails to obtain the consent of her caste-fellows to her marriage, may nevertheless marry without renouncing her religion.

But although there is much to be said in favour of each of these suggestions, the Governor-General in Council, as at present advised, would prefer not to interfere, even to the limited extent proposed, by legislative action, until sufficient proof is forthcoming that legislation is required to meet a serious practical evil, and that such legislation has been asked for by a section important in influence or number, of the Hindu community itself."

but although our social customs prohibit the remarriage of widows, yet the law does not punish the enticing away of a widow for immoral purposes if she is over 16 years of age. It seems to me that here the law is inconsistent, and not in accord with the customs of the people ....

Licenses may be granted to priests for celebration and optional registration of widow remarriages, and remuneration of priest registrars by fees say from Rs. 20 to Rs. 100 to be paid by the parties.

It may be stated that the standard laid down by Malthus as to the number per square mile that can be supported in Europe does not apply to the conditions of life in India, and if it did, it could be proved that the large and fertile tracts of land yet uncultivated would be amply sufficient to support any probable increase of population (from widow marriages) for thousands of years to come. The statement that remarriage of widows would be the cause of more famines does not touch the real cause of these calamities, as although we have no widow marriage among us at present, yet we have had between 1769 and 1878, *i.e.* in 109 years, altogether 38 severe scarcities and famines in the continent of India

34. Tipperah People's Associbtion.—Recommend the repeal of Section 2 of Act XV. of 1856.

35. Kumar Pramotha Bhushana Deva, Raja of Naldanga.—Approves the suggestion regarding the formation of a national association.

SECTION IV. NORTH-WEST PROVINCES AND OUDH, THE PUNJAB, CENTRAL PROVINCES, BURMA, ASSAM, COORG, HYDRABAD (DECCAN) &c.

36. Diwan Ram Nath, District Judge, Hoshiarpur.—A section in the Penal Code providing punishment for those

who turn out of caste a remarried widow and her new husband would ultimately prove a great boon to society and to unhappy widows ; and though outward dissatisfaction might be shown by the majority of Hindus, the legislator of the law would have blessings of the young widows at large and of their parents generally.

If any enlightened Hindu Raja were to undertake to perform the duty first in his own territory by aid of Brahmins, I think it would be easier for our British Government to assure the ignorant classes of the public that legislation if made is purely made for public interests and no infringement of caste and religion is intended.

37. Denzil Ibbetson, Director of Public Instruction, Punjab.—I think I would allow a widow, as well ss a wife, to sue for and obtain separate maintenance on proof of social ill-usage and on condition of chastity. Social ill-usege is difficult to define but so are many other questions of fact upon which the courts have to decide.

38. Chief Commissioner, Central Provinces.—If the native gentlemen, who share Mr. Malabari's views regarding the nature of the evils he denounces, although they may differ from him as to the remedies to be adopted, would set to work in a business-like manner to promote female education, they would find themselves nearer to their object.

When a large number of Hindu women are educated, infant marriage and enforced widowhood will disappear.

SECTION V. EXTRACTS FROM OPINIONS GIVEN TO Mr. MALABARI.

39. Hon'ble J. Gibbs C.S.I., C.I.E.—As I told Lakhmidas Khimji, when he came to see me about it seven years ago, the course is for strong memorials to be got up by the reforming

party amongst the Hindus, urging the necessity of further legislation and pointing out the direction such should take..... Without pressure of this nature, it (the Government) could not take up a matter based on such deeply rooted social prejudice, (the religious point has long ceased to be urged).

40. Sir Alfred Lyall Lieut.-Governor N. W. Provinces.—In the case of young widows, Sir Alfred Lyall certainly thinks that the law should enable them to contract a valid and legal union by some simple system of civil registration, and this might be one of the earlist reforms proposed to Government.

You will not fail, however, to remember that in all countries the position of women is still more or less unsatisfactory, and that in no country does the Government interfere in this class of social questions without clear previous assurance that its interposition is called for by the ascertained wishes and feelings of a considerable section of the people.

41. Dinsha Ardeshir Taleyarkhan.—As in the matter of early marriages, so in this, I would take up the question of every caste separately and study the extent of widowhood prevailing therein, what facilities it offers for its removal, and the amount of good thereby calculated to be produced. While adopting the same measures for inciting each of the important castes to throw off the harsh usage, I would prepare a community or two to apply to Government to render widow marriages as innocuous (sic) as the ordinary marriages, the law not being so perfect in the former case as it is in the latter.

42. T. B. Dani, Editor Arya Vart.—There are numerous instances in which property is extorted by threats of excommunication from caste, and since the decision of the Bombay High Court in a recent case (Reg vs. Alja Dharma, decided on 17th August 1870) such an act does not amount to an offence under the Penal Code. Such sentences are passed by caste bodies under an implicit confidence that, however illegal or unjustifiable their actions might be, the aggrieved party shall be given no redress by the courts or any other

Government officer. It is, therefore, I apprehend, the duty of Government to legislate with a view to put some restraint upon the power of caste bodies to pass a sentence of excommunication; and that can be done by enacting that if any body is excommunicated without any reason whatsoever, or for having done an act which is not prohibited by the Hindu law or by any usage or custom such as is capable of being recognized in a court of justice, or for having omitted to do an act which he is not required to do by Hindu law or by such usage or custom, the person or persons passing the sentence of excommunication shall be liable to punishment.

43. K. VENCATRAO FIRST GRADE PLEADER BELLARY.—Numerous quotations may be made and authorities shown to prove that the mutts and other religious institutions do not possess legitimate authority to dictate or punish, but are merly to teach Vedas or their sectarian philosophies to their disciples. If the fear of excommunication be removed, the progress of social reform will be very rapid,

44. B. V. JOSHI (MOUNT ABU).—Let an institution be started...........where a Hindu widow will be afforded all the safeguards against immorality, and where she will be trained in some useful branch of human industry and given a home for all her life. I am sure if such an institution be once started, endowments will be pouring in.

45. RAI C. H. SETH, (JHANSI).—If our children were married at an advanced age...........my impression is that the number of our widows will be reduced to half, if not less. The mortuary returns show that there are always more deaths among children than adults.(VIDE CHAPTER IV. PAGE 138)

46. HON. SIR M. MELVILL C.S.I.—I see no reason why a widow, who wishes to remarry, should not be allowed to retain her life-interest in her late husband's property. Even as it is, a separated widow on this side of India can do what she likes with the *movable* property, and make a gift of it to her second

husband an hour before her marriage: so that it is somewhat absurd for the law to say that she shall lose this property on her remarriage............. ....

I see no objection to allowing remarriages, or indeed any marriages to take place before a Registrar, as in the case of Christians. Whether Hindus would take advantage of it, I do not know. Of course, the priests would set their faces against it, just as Christian priests do.

47. Hon'ble Mr. Justice West.

(Vide Chapter IV. Page 140.)

48. Right Hon'ble Leonard Courtney, Deputy Speaker House of Commons.—As regards enforced widowhood, I would go as far as possible in making punishable all attempts to over-awe or impede individual liberty; but we, who are apparently unable to put down boy-cotting at home, must feel some diffidence as to the possibility of liberating a widow, who presumes to marry again, from terrorism and persecution backed by religious sanctions. There was of course a similar struggle of authorities over Sati, but our fathers did not shrink from insisting upon having their own way, and the obligation of immolation has practically disappeared. I know not why in course of time the obligation of dedicating the *whole* of a life to the memory (say rather "to the dominion", of a husband with whom there may never have been married life, should not also vanish. Unhappy women now often suffer a fate worse than Sati.

CHAPTER IX.

REASONS FOR NON INTERFERENCE.

SECTION I. MADRAS PRESIDENCY.

1. A. Sankariah, B.A., President, Hindu Sabha. Madras.—The agitation against infant marriage and enforced

widowhood proceeds from persons, who, by reason of their Western education, or of their scepticism, or of their desire to check immorality and infanticide, cannot appreciate the religious sense of the Hindu, and particularly of the Brahmin community.

2. K. KRISHNASWAMY RAO, CHIEF JUSTICE, TRAVANCORE.—It is not in my opinion expedient to put the machinery of legislation to do what is now being done without it.

No legislature of the 19th century would attempt to make friends and unmake enemies by its laws.

3. C. SUBBARAYA AIYAR, B.A., B.L., THIRD JUDGE, APPELLATE COURT, ERNACOLUM.—Real reform in the marriage laws of the Hiudus must be initiated by the Hindus themselves …………If the Government were induced to give its executive authority a stretch in the direction suggested by Mr. Malabari, there would be no limit to interferences of the kind in question, and the Government might find itself confronted by questions of an embarrassing nature.

The intelligent and educated section of the Nair community have set on foot a movement to effect a change in the marriage laws of Malabar. But the opposition is so great that no reform is feasible giving to the Nair wife a distinct status in the family of her Nair husband. Should the Nair reformers seek the aid of Government in the manner suggested by Mr. Malabari, will the Government be prepared to countenance the reform by shewing preference to a particular section in the distribution of official patronage and honours?

Again there are certain customs among the Mahommadans which reduce their women to the condition of slaves. It is stated that according to the belief of the orthodox, women have no souls. The Government may be solicited to afford encouragement to reforms tending to ameliorate the social condition of the Mahommadan women on the lines suggested by Mr. Malabari. Will the Government be prepared to take action?

4. S. SUBRAMANIA AIYAR, VAKIL, HIGH COURT.—It is not desirable that the peculiar circumstances of this community should be lost sight of, and popular opinion, however unreasonable it may be considered to be by the go-ahead reformers, rejected in a consideration of these questions, and that changes entirely out of harmony with the feeling and even with the prejudices of the people should be suddenly introduced.

5. P. CHENTSAL RAO.—I do feel that infant marriage and enforced widowhood are evils and serious evils too, but I do not see my way to advising the Government to interfere in the matter directly or indirectly. While any such interference can be productive of no beneficial results, it is sure to shake the confidence of the people in the neutrality of Government in religious matters, and create a reaction in favour of the very evils which it is our wish to repress..................................

It would be contrary to all principle for Government to tell the priest that he ought not to advise his followers to do what he himself thinks to be right for his spiritual welfare.

6. M. TILLAINAYAGAM PILLAI, DEPUTY COLLECTOR, MADURA.—The best course for effecting the reform is to create a sufficiently strong public opinion in favour of it and all that Government can render is indirect aid.

What we want is, men to set examples, more Rajagopala Charlus and Seshayengars.

7. R. RUGHUNATH RAO.—The priest's excommunication is nothing more than the exercise of his private undoubted right, and to interfere with it would be illegal. The best remedy against excommunication of the priest is to show contempt of it openly and neglect it. If men of common sense and education would do this, there would be an end to the priest's tyranny.

8. T. PATTABHIRAM, HEAD SERASHTADAR TRICHINOPOLY CLLECTORATE.—I, for one do not much believe in young men or young women being always happy in their choice. Choice

after all is a blind guess, and is always more tempted or governed by symmetrical make and personal grace than by any insight into the quality of the mind and attachment of the heart.........If men of so much above the usual average run of mankind as Lord Byron &c, fail in their choice, and in a society which allows free scope for many a private talk and personal intercourse between the young lovers, can there be any meaning in the high-sounding phrase 'liberty of choice.'?

SECTION II. BOMBAY PRESIDENCY.

9. Lallubhai Nandlal, Native Assistant to the Commissioner, North Division.—The chief point, therefore, that is left for consideration is whether the general marriageable standard of the age of girls from 7 to 10 is objectionable.........The climate of India makes it desirable that girls should be married at this age, and though at the same time it would be very much desirable that the consummation should begin a little later, I think, to provide for this a remedy in checking marriage at the age abovementioned is rather fighting against nature itself.

10. Venayek Wassudev.—In my humble opinion education alone will bring about these changes in the social fabric so highly desirable, nay necessary, and any interference on the part of the State may provoke opposition to the reform which is at present slowly but surely in progress. Act XV of 1856 is quite sufficient to protect widows inclined to marry. When female education is better developed the progress of social reform will be rapid and remarkable.

11. Mahadeo Moreshwar Kunte.—My belief is that no legal enactment is necessary, and that reformers, as opposed to the orthodox, should work out the called-for reforms without any aid from the State, which cannot assist a small minority, however intelligent and well-informed.

12. Hari Parsad Santokram.—My own opinion is that the subjects of infant marriage and what Mr. Malabari calls "enforced widowhood" are important, and should be kept before the public by discussion, lectures &c., but strictly in a private and unofficial way.

13. Nanabhai Haridas.—Government cannot, consistently with its avowed policy, and ought not to, interfere in purely social and religious matters. However unreasonable certain usages and customs in India may appear to foreigners, it must not be forgotton that to the people at large, among whom they obtain, they appear in another light, and that the fact of their having existed for centuries is in itself some evidence of their being adapted to the circumstances of the people. Notwithstanding all that one hears now and then of "ill-assorted" marriages entailing "life-long misery," I am disposed to think that our conjugal relations are on the whole more satisfactory than those among other people. Our domestic differences are certainly fewer, and when they arise we arrange them without having recourse to matrimonial or other tribunals ....

Until the views of the people generally change, no action on the part of Government will have any appreciable effect in preventing infant marriage or promoting widow remarriage. Social reform associations exist, and have existed for years in almost all the large towns in the Presidency; but the reformers are a mere drop in the ocean, and up to this time they have not met with much success in their efforts. But they are gradually increasing both in numbers and influence, and as education advances they will be able to accomplish much which at present may seem almost impossible.

14. Sakharam Arjun.—The growing spread of primary education among the masses, the extension of higher education, the progress of railways, the closer contact with western thought and culture, the increasing facilities afforded and largely availed of of, a travel to Europe and England, all these

together and every one of them singly, is a nail in the coffin of blind prejudice and settled ignorance.

15. S. H. CHIPLONKAR.—Individually I desire to see complete equality between the two sexes, that is to say, if a widow of 40 chooses to remarry, I see no reason why she should be prevented from doing so, when a widower of over 50 can with impunity do so. But this consummation is a work of time, and no law can, as it were, create such a state of things to order ....

According to the English law, both civil and religious, a marriage with a deceased wife's sister is illegal, and though an advanced body of social and religious reformers in the United Kingdom have been making a strong effort for the last 30 years and more to legalize such marriages, and it is even stated that some members of the Royal family are strongly and actively in favour of the movement, the religious sentiment against legalizing such marriages is so strong that the effort of the minority has been hitherto altogether unavailing.

16. NARMADASHANKAR LALSHANKAR.—If we let these matters alone now, education would gradually but surely open the eyes of the people, and lead them to adopt a compromise between the venerable old and the dazzling new customs which will be both more consonant with the ideas, habits and traditions of the people because brought about by themselves, and more permanent because of its being based on popular convictions.

17. GANPATRAM G. SASTRI.—It is not unlikely that interference on the part of the State in this matter (widowhood) might create unforeseen difficulties in other directions which may tend as in the case of the abolition of the Sattee system, to aggrevate some evils undreamt of at present.

18. GAVARISHANKAR UDEYSHANKAR.—No observer of Hindu life can afford to ignore the fact that religion is the basis upon which the whole fabric of Hindu Society is built, and the reformer who chooses to pull out one brick from

here and another brick from there, with perhaps the best intentions in the world, to improve the shape of the structure, is bound to pause and consider whether his attempt, instead of mending matters, will not cause the whole structure to tumble down.

19. Pandurung Balibhadra.—I am of opinion that there is no necessity for appealing to Government on social matters............'Constitutions' it is said 'are not made but grow.' This is as true of social as it is of political development. True growth comes from within; not from without. Reform to be real, thorough, and productive of lasting good, must spring and emanate from the people themselves. It should never be forced upon them.

20. Ram Shastri Dikshit Apte of Poona.—Infanticide is not ordained by the Shastras but is considered a sin, and Government were therefore right in suppressing it, and it in no way interfered with the religion of the people. Killing one-self under the car of Jagannath was not also a religious practice. It is true that Government interfered with the religion of the people when they suppressed *Sati*...........but this was before the 1857 (or 1858) Proclamation which publicly declared the Government policy of non-interference. Moreover there was the alternative of widows leading a life of abstinence, and *Satis* were rare being one in a lakh or even a crore, in every year. This was again not a deliberate action of the widow, but an impulse of the moment and gave much pain to the relations.

21. Ambalal S. Desai.—To enforce any law that may be made, very wide powers must be given to the Police which will lead to certain corruption and oppression towards the weak, and inquisitorial proceedings will be often resorted to. No enquiry could be efficiently made without making a rude intrusion into the sacred domains of private life and disturbing the peace of families. Further there are mothers and fathers who

rather than their widowed daughters should remarry, would commit suicide. Practical reformers will put these resultant evils of the proposed measure in the balance, and see if they will not outweigh the anticipated good. I, for one, humbly conceive that they will.

22. MANMOHANDAS DAYALDAS.—It is useless to have a legislative measure in the matter (of infant marriage). The chastity of widows has disappeared with the putting down of the practice of becoming *Sati.* Girls should therefore be married between the ages of 8 and 12. If it be desired to preserve public health, then the best course is to drive away all prostitutes from cities. They are a source of immense mischief.

23. PANDIT PANCHANADI GUTTULAL GHANASHYAMJI OF BOMBAY.

Vijnyaneshwara says :—

" When a country is subjugated, the usages, laws, (and), family customs (prevailing therein) should be preserved intact" and adds " when a foreign country comes under subjection, the customs &c., (of one's) own country should not be mixed up with (those of the conquered country), but the usages, family customs or laws peculiar to that country should be preserved, provided they are not contrary to (their) Shastras"..............

" The king should by subjecting them to penalties, bring back families, tribes, sections, associations and even countries to their proper way when they swerve from their religion. "

With reference to his (Mr. Malabari's) statement that thousands of Arya wives bereft of their husbands, though of chaste lives and actions, yet pass their lives in misery only and support their existence in hopes of happiness in a future life, we ask, is it or is it not desirable to remove the miseries of dutiful, chaste and virtuous women also ....

Again the evils of infanticide that are pointed out are, for the most part, for obvious reasons, possible also in the case of women of some of those Aryas who having married here leave their wives and undertake long journeys occupying many years, to distant countries for the purpose of trade.

If it be still urged that the bearing of the torments of passion by a widow is not desirable then the legislature must also be asked to do away with celibacy and many other similar observances. Properly speaking, therefore, in order to avoid immorality, it is better to resort to independent means rather than to bring into existence immorality of a grosser type in the shape of marriage of widows. In this world there are many wicked persons such as adulterers, thieves, robbers &c., who if resistence is offered to them while they are engaged in perpetrating their evil deeds in lonely places, commit other evil deeds such as murder &c —But in order that such murders &c., may be prevented, the persons in question cannot be allowed to commit adultery, theft, robbery &c., as being only lesser evils.

The advantages of the non-violation of the bridal bed are evidently non-deviation from religion............preservation of modesty and family dignity and the observance of good moral conduct ....

It is not possible to admit equality between males and females in all respects;...........If there should be equality between males and females in every respect why.........do not the husbands live in the wives' houses for both their lives, and the wives in the husbands' houses for the remaining period......

Why does he (Mr. Malabari) not wish that in case a woman has no offspring by the first husband, she should marry again in his life-time another man; and that in case of daughters of kings&c., they should simultaneously have many men.

The thing called woman is the crowning piece of all the objects of enjoyment in this world, and being subject to the special power of the husband, is not like a house &c., capable of being enjoyed by the husband's relations. How much more incapable must she then be of being fit for remarriage and enjoyment by a stranger. Like a dining leaf* used previously by another person, she is unfit to be enjoyed by another person. The object of marriage is neither sensual intercourse alone, nor bringing forth children, these being attained without the restriction of marriage. But the end of marriage is chiefly the performance of religious rites enjoined to a householder by the Shastras, and secondarily the attainment of the indescribable pleasure to be derived through mutual affection.

Widow marriage is by steps likely to be the source of another danger namely that, in case a serious quarrel arises between the husband and wife it would be thought proper that both the parties should by mutual consent effect a dissolution of the marriage in their life time.

24. V. N. MANDLIK.—I may observe that the "age of consent" which is all that is required for marriages (when consent is necessary) is 12 for females and 14 for males even in such advanced countries as the United States of America. In New York an attempt was made to raise these periods to 14 and 17 respectively, but they were so disrelished by the people that a law was passed in 1830 restoring the old periods of 12 and 14 as before. In the old Hindu institutes the marriageable age for females is 12; but that for males has been contracted by the gradual curtailment of student-life and a change in the social usages of the people. As I have said before, the system has not apparently injured those who have lived properly under it ....

In my own opinion the drawback to these associations (for social reform) is that temptations to secede are often very strong, so that mental reservation and family necessities are sure to be pleaded, often with great force; and it will en-

---

* The Hindus use plantain and other leaves to eat their food upon.

courage hypocrisy and a departure from truth if such associations are formed ....

Mr. Malabari asks the Educational Department to prepare and disseminate tracts in the shape of a few Chapters in their text books on the subject.........Were the Department so to descend from its present height, such action would in my humble opinion tend to create most undesirable feelings of discontent, on the ground of improper State interference, whilst the alleged evils could in no way be diminished ....

It is hinted that official pressure was required to induce the establishment of girls' schools in the mofussil. Similarly it may be used now, is probably the conclusion suggested. If there was improper pressure used, as is here alleged, I regret the occurrence, because I feel sure it must have been injurious to all those who used it and to those on whom it was inflicted. There can be no waste of force in nature : it must produce good or evil...

Our greatest social and moral benefactors in Western India, Jnanadeva, Tukaram, Muktabai, Ekanatha, Ramadasa and others were not helped by the human agency of Armies, Councils and Governments. They depended on higher power. Their noble lives tell their own tale. We in Western India worship them. Their temples, their memory, their writings are now living powers. I say it with all submission that there is no royal road to these things any more than to others. People, must try to *be*, to *live* what they preach. It is a slow painful process but what is higher education, I should like to know, if it will not prepare men for such lives of self-sacrifice and noble self-abnegation ? All these saints, male and female, lived between the 14th and 17th centuries of the Christian era.

25. Jayasing Rao, Regent of Kolhapur.—Moral pressure of officials too, will not be so effectual as Mr. Malabari supposes. What did such pressure achieve in the early days of female education ? Not even pecuniary inducements could

tempt parents to send their girls to schools till the example of others brought home to them the advantages of doing so. The educated classes fully feel the evil (Infant Marriage). But it is want of moral courage that makes them simply talk and take no action in the matter. At this rate the state of things will never improve. Let the so-called leaders of society set an example themselves, and the rest are sure to follow.

SECTION III. BENGAL PRESIDENCY.

26. C. H. Tawney, Director of Public Instruction.—I have no wish to under-rate the value of the influence of "distinguished members of the ruling race," but I think that the days when such pressure could produce a magic effect are for ever gone by in this part of the country, and for my part I do not much regret them. Besides, official pressure is utterly incapable of dealing with a sentiment based on religion and long established custom, and allied with the best instincts of feminine delicacy. On the other hand, we have every reason to hope that, as the diffusion of enlightenment extends the dislike to early marriage that is gradually spreading with the spread of Western ideas, a feeling will spring up that it is unjust to debar child-widows from remarriage. This will perhaps bring with it as a natural corollary a shrinking from imposing restraints on human freedom even in the case of women who have lost their partners early in life and desire to re-enter the married state.

27. C. T. Metcalfe, Commissioner, Orissa Division.—There are many natives who would gladly see a change effected, but even those most opposed to the present practice depreciate Government interference for this reason that they feel that the purity of their families, the preservation of their caste and their social customs, are all wound up with the question of early marriage and enforced widowhood.

28. E. E. Lowis, Commissioner Burdwan Division.—It is urged that much has already been effected in mitigation of the evils complained of, that the feeling of the educated classes against infant marriage and enforced widowhood is becoming stronger, and that the movement should be allowed to devlope naturally without such official aid as Mr. Malabari suggests should be afforded.

29. F. M. Halliday, Commissioner, Patna Division.—I cannot do better than cite the following from Mr. Nolan's views: "If we exclude Hindus from the professions and the public services for marrying too soon, we may also exclude Europeans for not marrying at all, Mahommadans for marrying too often, Buddhists for marrying without exclusive possession, and men of all creeds for marrying rashly, and failing to keep their matrimonial engagements."

30. J. F. K. Hewitt, Commissioner Chota Nagpur Division.—Major Garbett..............after consulting with some of the leading and most intelligent native gentlemen of the District, states that the ideas embodied in Mr. Malabari's note are the ideas of all thinking men and of all well-wishers of India. But unfortunately the ideas are in advance of the times, and caste prejudices and superstitions are at present too strong..

I myself think that while it is most desirable that the opinions expressed by Mr. Malabari should become the current opinions of the community, yet the interference of the Government in the matter would tend to delay their final adoption. The present custom would be maintained out of a spirit of opposition.

31. Dr. R. Lyall Commissioner Chittagong Division.—The Magistrate of Tipperah sums up the question well in the following words with which I thoroughly agree.

"The tyranny of caste is the tyranny of religion as at present understood by the people, and it is immaterial whether the religious views now held are in accordance with the Shastras or not. If they are not, the best plan would be to correct public opinion. This is certainly not the business of Government Where Mr. Malabari's arguments are directed against caste, they are really assailing the Hindu religion as now understood. It is not possible for Government to maintain a policy of non-interference with religion, and yet assail caste prejudices based on religion or what is believed to be religion."

32. THE BRITISH INDIAN ASSOCIATION.—If native society is to be reconstructed on the lines of the views propounded by Mr. Malabari, not only would it be necessary to repress by indirect State influence infant marriage, but also marriage in violation of established mental and physiological laws as inculcated in our own ancient works and recognized by modern biologists.

The laws of the land already provide for acts of oppression implied by the terms 'rattening' and 'boy-cotting,' and nothing further can be done. The rule (proposed as to prohibition of excommunication of widows &c.,) contemplates the suppression of the civil right of the large majority for the comfort and convenience of a small minority.

33. UTTERPARAH PEOPLE'S ASSOCIATION.—He (Mr. Malabari) seems however not to recognize the law that all sound social growth must be a process of evolution, and not one of revolution. Even a revolution to be successful must have strong social forces to sustain it.

34. MYMENSING ASSOCIATION.—It is undesirable in matters like these to invoke Government interference, direct or indirect, legislative or excutive, unless it can be distinctly shown that society is powerless to check the *evils* or unless the *evil* be of the nature of a *crime* or a *wrong*. But no such case has been or can be made out of the present questions.

35. BALASORE NATIONAL SOCIETY.—A nation that has Savitri and Sita to boast of—characters which are the wonders of the civilised world—may well afford to put up with certain evils for the sake of charming things connected with female purity and chastity. "Frailty thy name is woman," so says Shakespeare. If there are failings here and there among our widows, there are also slips among our married women. Whatever shame and disgrace we come across in Hindu society are attributable to human nature.

SECTION IV. NORTH-WEST PROVINCES AND OUDH, THE PUNJAB, CENTRAL PROVINCES, BURMA, ASSAM, COORG, HYDRABAD (DECCAN) &c.

36. CHIEF SECRETARY TO GOVERNMENT N.-W.P. AND OUDE.—Statutory marriage by civil contract does not exist for persons of the Hindu religion. They are excluded from the benefits of Acts XV of 1865, III of 1872, and XV of 1872 except in the solitary case of marriage with a Christian. But it must be observed that this disability is not accidental or undesigned. The Legislature has deliberately refrained from authorizing civil marriage between persons professing the Hindu faith. The bill which in another shape became law as Act III of 1872, when introduced in September 1868, contained in its original form a provision legalising such contracts. It was met by such general opposition, and received with such wide-spread dissatisfaction by the Hindu community that it was withdrawn. The position assumed was that the Bill would by direct legislation change very deeply the native law upon marriage; while by recognising the existence of the Hindu religion as a personal law in the matter of marriage the British Government had contracted an obligation to enforce its provisions in their entirety upon those who choose to live under them. The discussion upon the bill exhausted all the

reasons and arguments which could be urged for or against grafting on the Hindu marriage law, liberty to individual members of the religion to contract marriage as they pleased without reference to the customs of the caste or the consent of the brotherhood or family. The Lieutenant-Governor and Chief Commissioner is not prepared to say whether since that date there has been any such considerable change in the social conditions of the community or any such material progress in the dissent from Brahminical orthodoxy, as to justify the Government in now re-opening the question. As the law now stands a renunciation of the Hindu law or custom which governs marriage involves renunciation of the Hindu religion. Persons who are willing to take such an extreme step in order to escape from the obstacles which now present themselves to the remarriage of Hindu widows, can effect their purpose by a recourse to the machinery provided under Act III of 1872. But should the movement ever assume large and popular dimensions, it will be necessary to improve and enlarge that machinery which is at present adapted only to meet the wants of the small Brahmo community, and Sir Alfred Lyall would meet any such movement half way.

On the subject of infant marriage.........it is very doubtful whether State interference in such a matter is desirable, and there is still more reason to doubt that it could be effectively attempted. To alter by legislation or executive action the social custom of an entire nation is a very difficult matter and can only be effected very slowly by taking advantage of, or occasionally anticipating gradual changes of, public opinion or of circumstances...........Any real reformation must await the impulse of a wide-spread desire for a social change, and State interference could at present do little good and would almost inevitably be misunderstood by the bulk of the people.

[In his letter dated 24th August 1884, Sir Alfred Lyall wrote to Mr. Malabari : " My present view is that the State should be ready to countenance any distinct movement of public opinion in the direction of these reforms" and in his Private Secretary's letter dated 27th March 1886 it was said "Sir Alfred Lyall quite agrees that the main point for your attack should be not so much early betrothal as premature cohabitation, and it may be added that legislation would probably deal more easily with the latter than with the former subject."]

37. HON'BLE D, G. BARKLEY, MEMBER OF THE LEGISLATIVE COUNCIL PUNJAB GOVERNMENT.—Even in the case of Christians. the age at which marriage may be entered into is not regulated by law, though when the parties are minors certain precautions are prescribed, and the consent of parents and guardians, if in India, is rendered necessary, and though the effect of S. 60 of Act XV of 1872 must be to render more difficult marriages between native Christians below the ages there specified. In the case of Parsis also no age is fixed, though the consent of the father or guardian is required, if any of the parties is below the age of 21 years, and Section 37 of Act XV of 1865 does not allow certain suits relating to marriages to be brought until the husband has completed the age of 16 years and the wife the age of 14 years. If legislation of a similar character were desired by Hindus, it might be useful to discourage too early consummation of infant marriages, though it would be no obstacle to the marriage relation being established in infancy. But it would probably be necessary to ascertain that at least a large number of Hindus desired such legislation before it could be proposed.

38. DENZIL IBBETSON DIRECTOR OF PUBLIC INSTRUCTION PUNJAB.—Would it be wise, even if it were possible, to tempt women to fly in the face of public opinion and the code of morality and decency in which they have been brought up? The large number of unmarried females in England leads to immorality. Suppose bigamy legalised, ought

the English Government to seek to induce girls to marry men who had wives living, public opinion being as at present. ?

39. CHIEF COMMISSIONER BRITISH BURMA.—(Sir C. Bernard). The analogy of the laws against Satti and infanticide is not quite applicable to the present questions. Those were hideous crimes, against the natural sense of mankind. Child marriages and child widowhood no doubt, sometimes lead to crime and cause loss of life. But drinking similarly leads to crime, and midwifery as practised by Easterns often causes death. Yet these things are not proscribed by law or put down by State interposition ....

The only safe way for the Government and the safest course in the interests of reform itself, is to leave the forces of education, of common sense, of enlightened public opinion, and of natural feeling, to work on as they are now working against the practices and customs which Mr. Malabari rightly characterises as harmful ....

Married undergraduates and scholarship-holders are not unknown at our English Universities. If such exclusion (i.e. of married students from honours and scholarship, &c.) were made the rule, questions would at once arise whether a betrothal or an unconsummated marriage operated as a bar to studentship.

40. J. G. CORDERY, M.A.. C.S., RESIDENT AT HYDRABAD.—The evil caused by the institution of the *pardah* is probably attended with far more general and more widely reaching evils than the social restriction against the remarriage of a widow, which is confined to a comparatively small section of women. But, beyond according a legal permission to the violation of such injurious customs by any women who may desire to break them, Government can hardly proceed, without engaging in an unequal conflict with social prejudice ....

Apart from this question of early widowhood, it may well be doubted whether the present system by which betrothals of children are arranged at an early age by their parents, is not well suited to the present status and character of the people taken as a whole, and especially to the masses of the agricultural villages. The obligation of the tie makes the honour of the child respected by others and by no means necessarily leads to premature consummation by the husband for whom she is safely reserved. It is of course true that, as in many other countries, the parties to the contract have little or nothing to say to their selection of each other. But could the principle of free choice be wisely advocated or safely introduced in a country where physical capacity for sexual intercourse exists at so early an age? The question is one beset with difficulties, for which he would be a bold man who would be confident that the people themselves had not found the best solution. At any rate it appears to me manifestly no subject for prohibitive legislation.

41. Vishnu Moreshwar Mahajani M.A., Head Master Akola.—Home is at present the centre of blind conservatism, and whatever efforts the educated natives might make to bring about social reforms, they are thwarted from day to day by women and elderly persons. So long as therefore, the wife has not become the real help-mate of her husband, so long as her mind is tied down by rules of immemorial custom, Hindu society cannot hope to move at a more rapid rate than we have hitherto done. Some of our English friends take the educated young men to task for not carrying out the first and greatest of reforms *i.e.*, those at home, and disappointed to see that they still observe practices which they profess to condemn, are led to think that their young friends are no better than a set of hypocrites, or, at the best, as persons that have no courage of their convictions. But outsiders know not what a life of daily trouble the educated natives lead at home, always arguing with their wife with their aunts with their father or uncles, always meeting with the stock objection "our ancestors were wiser than we." It should not therefore be supposed that the reformers have always been defeated. While they yielded much, the old

party had to yield a little and already we see in 25 years an advance in the marriageable ages of girls and boys from 8 to 10 and 13 to 16 respectively. This does not refer to Berar where the movement has scarcely begun. I am here referring to Poona and other similar districts of which I have personal knowledge.

We have no facts to warrant us in saying that if the reform be delayed, a permanent deterioration in physique will take place. Besides whatever danger there is, it does not proceed from infant marriage but from the early consummation of that marriage. But this the State cannot prevent, even if it rules that a girl under twelve cannot be married. For the girl reaches the age of puberty at the age of thirteen or fourteen and custom directs that the consummation should take place soon after. Her home-education, her surroundings, the talk among women, her sports, the proud celebration of the religious ceremonies attending the consummation, all work upon the imagination of the poor girl, and give an unnatural stimulus to her passion which is certainly mischievous. A girl as soon as the consummation takes place receives benedictions from old women and from priests: "Be you soon a mother of eight sons," and until she becomes a mother she has very little respect in the family. Her parents do not dine at her husband's until she gets a son. Under these circumstances, it is no wonder, that the consummation takes place at an age too early for her physiologically to become a mother. The evil consequences of this in the breaking down of constitution, giving up the studies of the boy, and the ushering-in of diseases and sickly children, we do not ignore, and we have been making constant efforts to mitigate them. These it is obvious no State legislation will prevent, unless public opinion is brought to bear on them. My view in short is this: if public opinion is strong, State legislation is unnecessary; if it is weak, State legislation is powerless. But in the latter case, it is worse than powerless...........The majority of the people *i.e.* outside the pale of educated classes have not yet begun to recognise the evils of the practice (infant marriage), and may resent Government interference in the most susceptible of their religious feelings, for the practice has to them a religious sanction. It is not desirable that the educated classes who already are alienated by their sympathies and education from the majority of their countrymen, should be still more alienated by their joining in league with Government apparently *to destroy their religion,* and thus ensure their permanent helplessness in carrying out reforms from within, and a perpetual dependence and looking up to Government for everything they wish to do.

I have hopes in my own people and am loth to call in the aid of Government. I have faith in education, I have faith in educated agency when it is well organised and sustained by united efforts, I have faith in the contagiousness of example, and more I do not want. Let Government Officers give us moral support, if they will, sympathise with us when we fight with ignorant masses on the one hand, and old people on the other, and we shall conquer. Perhaps the victory may not be won in our lifetime, but our children will take up the cause where we left it, and having made some advance themselves will leave it to their children to be taken up in the same manner. We want this continuity of progress—this silent though inevitable change *from within;* no revolution *from without,* and least of all by force.

42. Shrikrishna Narhar, Extra Assistant Commissioner, Ellichpur.—External interference has the unhappy effect of destroying the self-acting machinery by which a nation elevates itself, and by departing from its pronounced policy the Hindus will be put at least a few decades back.

43. Waman Narayen Bapat, Tahsildar of the Chandur Taluk.—Malabari says Modern India has made woman the inferior of man. But we say this is quite beside the mark. In classes which allow her to remarry, she is inferior still, but her inferiority is no bar to her re-marriage

over and over again. He thinks a Hindu widow is not able to appreciate and protect her rights. But we reply that Act XV of 1856 which was made specially for her, did not help her in the least in getting this appreciation and therefore other legislation can only follow in its wake. First make her fit and then legislate. He believes that it is not in her nature to publish her wrongs. We say, amen, but we ask why not alter that nature by education, when she will complain as many of her sisters have complained, and do complain ? Legislation can do nothing. Her appeals to the Mother-Queen will be equally helpless, so long as she is allowed to be ignorant ...... Malabari says that Government in rescuing the widow from self-immolation, is bound to see that she has full permission to substitute another husband in the room of the one lost, and that too without the least social inconvenience to her. No such thing. By a parity of reasoning, Government is bound to cure one of his disease, since it does not allow him to commit suicide which he seeks and constantly longs for, only because nothing else will put an end to his lifelong sufferings.

44. Raghunath B. Talvalkar, B. A., Head Master, High School, Amraoti.—Sir H. Maine says that moral opinion and social necessities are more cr less in advance of law. The only justification of a new law is that it is called for by the prevailing moral opinion, and by pressing social necessities.

SECTION V. EXTRACTS FROM OPINIONS GIVEN TO Mr. MALABARI.

45. The Marquis of Ripon, Viceroy and Governor General of India (in August 1884).—The two questions are practically branches of one and the same question, the position of women in India..............Indirectly these practices undoubtedly lead to great evils, but they do not in themselves involve crime, nor are they so necessarily and inevitably mischievous, as to call for suppression by law, if they are sanctioned by the general opinion of the society in

which they prevail* ....I shall rejoice if the result of your inquiries should show that there exists an opening for the Government to mark in some public manner the view which it entertains of the great importance of reform in these matters of Infant Marriage and Enforced Widowhood.

46. SIR CHARLES AITCHISON, LIEUT. GOVERNOR OF THE PUNJAB.—Very little good can result from Government action in such matters until the way is cleared by enlightened native opinion............I watch with the deepest interest the progress you are making with the great social reform with which your name will be for ever associated. You are going about it in the true way............I wish you very heartily God-speed.

47. HON'BLE W. W: HUNTER, C.S.I., MEMBER OF THE VICEREGAL COUNCIL—I have considered your points carefully, and the difference between us is not great. But the fundamental necessity of the initiative coming from the natives remains.

---

* Cf the Resolution of the Government of India, No. 35. 1616-26, dated 8th October 1886. "In dealing with such subjects as those raised by Mr. Malabari's notes, the British Government in India has usually been guided by certain general principles. For instance when caste or custom enjoins a practice which involves a breach of the ordinary criminal law, the State will enforce the law. When caste or custom lays down a rule which is of its nature enforceable in the civil courts, but is clearly opposed to morality or public policy, the State will decline to enforce it. When caste or custom lays down a rule which deals with such matters as are usually left to the option of citizens, and which does not need the aid of civil or criminal courts for its enforcement, State interference is not considered either desirable or expedient.

In the application of such general principles to particular cases, there is doubtless room for differences of opinion; but there is the common sense test which may often be applied with advantage in considering whether the State should or should not interfere in its legislative or executive capacity with social or religious questions of the kind now under notice. The test is, 'can the States give effect to its commands by the ordinary machinery at its disposal.' If not, it is desirable that the State should abstain from making a rule, which it cannot enforce without a departure from its usual practice or procedure.

The reforms advocated by Mr. Malabari, which affect the social customs of many races with probably as many points of difference as of agreement, must be left to the improving influences of time and to the gradual operation of the mental and moral developement of the people by the spread of education."

48. SIR LEPEL GRIFFIN, AGENT, GOVERNOR GENERAL.—I have the warmest sympathy in your views; but oriental as you are I do not believe that you realise the intensity of Hindu conservatism. You are sufficiently enthusiastic to be a Western reformer, and you are thrown away in a country which has had no enthusiast since Gautama.

49. M. G. RANADE, MEMBER OF THE LEGISLATIVE COUNCIL, BOMBAY.—It (widowhood) is a very delicate subject. When the victim of cruelty welcomes the disgrace and effacement, it is not to be expected that startling results will be achieved soon. We are slowly touching the consciences of the people, disarming the opposition of the terror of excommunication, and teaching the female sex to rebel or protest. These influences will be strengthened by our efforts to promote their higher education. Our people will not like any interference of the Police or Magistrate with such delicate matters, and Government can never be too cautious in its dealings in this connection.

50. A. MACKENZIE, C. S., SECRETARY TO THE GOVERNMENT OF INDIA.—Caste prejudice—their nursing mother—will not, we may be sure, die a violent death at the hand of the public executioner and by sentence of law, but will dwindle away as enlightenment advances and perish of inanition at the last, just as the belief in witchcraft did in Europe.

Social progress must everywhere depend upon intellectual progress. Turn up your Buckle for proof of that. The social reformer must trust to education and not to dictation, in his crusade against popular belief and prejudices. Compulsion can never be conviction, and without conviction both social and material reform is impossible now-a-days. Now conviction is a plant of slow growth, and the social reformer is apt, we know, to view with impatience the tardy progress of opinion, and to declare at times that no progress whatever is being made............The hours of night hang heaviest towards dawn; but just as your Indian sun leaps almost at a bound into the full blaze of day, so I expect to see (or if not I, those who next follow me may see) a "Reformation" in India of which that in Europe was but a faint and partial type.

[More than a year later Mr. Mackenzie wrote: Whether the Government would undertake to fix by legislation a minimum age for marriage, or to assimilate the legal position of the chaste to that of the unchaste widow (the difference in which at present certainly involves an anomaly) must depend entirely, I should say, upon the eventual strength of the demand for such action on the part of the Hindu community. *It may not be necessary to wait until Hindu opinion is unanimous on the point, but certainly there must be more unanimity than has yet been secured.**]

51. HON'BLE SIR AUCKLAND COLVIN, FINANCE MINISTER.—They are questions intimately connected with the religious practices of the Hindus, and while they are open to obvious objection in themselves, they cannot be suppressed, like Sattee or Infanticide, on the ground that they are in themselves grossly immoral or destructive of human life.

52. HON'BLE SIR STEUART BAYLEY, MEMBER VICEREGAL COUNCIL.—The sphere within which Government can usefully legislate in social matters is really very limited, and to legislate on marriage questions in the face of the whole bulk of conservative sentiment, custom and religious pride of the country, would be both useless and mischievous. Useless, because Government could not without most objectionable inquisition enforce such decrees, and mischievous because evil must always result from a Government roughly irritating the feelings of the people on such subjects ....

The agitation for reform is more likely to be well received, if dissociated from the idea of its being backed by Government action, and if left to the spontaneous energies of the people and their leaders, than if looked upon as forced on them by Government...........I feel thoroughly convinced that public

* (The Italics are ours.)

opinion, moulded and influenced by its natural leaders, is not merely the best, but the only instrument for giving effect to your reforms, and that the reforms themselves are so obviously beneficial that the question is only one of sooner or later.

53. Mr. Serjeant Atkinson of the Bombay Bar.—Reforms, as Lord Bacon says, should conform to the example of Old Father Time who indeed innovateth greatly but quietly and by slow degrees: and chiefly, for the reason that he gives, because the least change in any part of a social or political fabric necessarily brings with it more or less, some evil or inconvenience: not unfrequently much greater than human foresight could well provide against.

54. C. Suba Rao, Pleader, Bangalore.—It is quite impossible that any improvement can be effected in the practice of early marriage so long as our circles of selection remain so narrow as at present ....

In India where people look to Government or the king as their earthly God, and with Hindus the majority of whom are not filled with Western ideas, individual liberty is not much appreciated.

55. Hon'ble K. T. Telang, Member Legislative Council, Bombay.—The next recommendation is that an educated man should not marry a "girl too much under his age." This again, is not at all feasible under present conditions. Seeing that the practice of widowmarriage is very far from being at all wide-spread among the higher castes, and seeing that the practice of marrying girls before they are thirteen at the outside, is all but universal, it must needs be extremely difficult if not impossible, to arrange for a marriage which shall satisfy the condition now proposed. Are the proposers then ready to accept the alternative of enforced celibacy with all its attendant evils? I must confess that both these suggestions and the one last dealt with (taking of pledges by members of an association) strike me in some of their aspects as illustrations of the old recommendation to "bell the cat."

I maintain that it would be tyrannising over caste, to wrest out of its hands the power of excommunication. As Sir Joseph Arnould said in the famous Aga Khan case: "In fact, in every community, whether of a religious nature or not, whether church or chapel, caste or club—there must, as requisite for the preservation of a community and as inherent in the very conception of a community, necessarily exist a power, not indeed to be exerted except in extreme cases and on justifying grounds, of depriving of the privileges of membership those who persistently refuse, after due notice and warning, to comply with those ascertained conditions of membership to which by the very fact of being members of the community, they must be held to have given an implied, if not an expressed, consent." That is the doctrine which I hold, and paradoxical as it may seem, I hold it not merely as being what is demanded by considerations of justice, but also as being that which under our present conditions must accelerate the decline and fall of caste as a power hostile to progress.

56. W. Lee-Warner, C.S.—On the whole, I see no remedy against infant marriages except the growth of public opinion and a higher tone of morality. As society finds that girls can grow up without the least danger till they are physically and intellectually fit to be mothers, it will be ready to give up the unnecessary safe-guard of infant marriage. The education of girls will help more to bring about this result than anything else, and it is a reform which the upper classes of Hindu society must commence......................

I have often discussed your social question with others. The impression grows that the State might interfere in special localities, where the people are ready for it. To me, however, the question presents many difficulties. Lord Lawrence has a great name. He goes further than I do. I gave you therefore the reference, because my personal wishes are wholly on your side. It is only what the Greeks call Xnesis, my political instinct (which may be wholly wrong), which makes me lag behind.

57. G. H. R. HART, PRIVATE SECRETARY TO H. E. SIR JAMES FERGUSSON, GOVERNOR OF BOMBAY.—Sir James does not see that it would be more right for Government in India to take steps to deter young Hindus from early marriages or to encourage widows to remarry, than for Government in England to protect from social ostracism a young lady who married her father's footman, or for Government in France to insist on every husband being the man of his bride's choice.

58. A. O. HUME.—It is essential, I think, that we should all try to realise that, closely interwoven in humanity as are the physical, intellectual, and psychical factors, progress in any direction to be really permanent, postulates a corresponding progress in other directions—that though we may and must, most specially devote our energies to overcoming the particular adversary that circumstances have most immediately offered to us, we each form but one unit in a force contending against a common foe whose defeat will depend as much on the success of each of our fellow-soldiers as on our own. In the hour of battle, it signifies nothing whether a man is in the light or grenadier company, the whole regiment must advance—the individual can do little—it matters not whether he is in the cavalry, artillery, infantry, pioneers or what not, the success of each is the success of all, the defeat of any an additional obstacle to the triumph of the rest.........

Now, whether rightly or wrongly, it seems to me that sporadic crusades such as that you have now undertaken, not to capture the Holy Land, but merely destroy one little stronghold of the infidels therein, is an utter waste of power, in so much that even if crowned with momentary success, this would have no permanent result, while the Hills that command it and its water supply, are still in the hands of the enemy. It would be like our capture of the Redan before the Mammelon was in our allies' hands ....

The majority of the opposition with which your proposals have been met with in certain native circles, has had its origin in the conviction that our women and girls are not yet sufficiently educated to enable any great change in the social customs, which regulated their lives, to be safely made at present.

To me, personally, the promotion of female education (using the word in its broadest sense) as necessarily antecedent to the thorough eradication of the grievous evils you so forcibly depict, appears a more important and immediately pressing question than those selected by you ....

What I do desire to make plain is that without the proper education of our females, without their elevation to their natural and rightful position, no great and permanent political progress can be hoped for. It is by such education alone that the national intellect can be completed, and the East put in a position to compete fairly with the West.

As in the individual there are two brains whose harmonious co-operation is essential to the best mental work, so in the nation are those two intellects, the male and the female, whose equipoised interaction is indispensable to the evolution of a wise national conduct ....

Political reformers of all shades of opinion should never forget that unless the elevation of the female element in the nation proceeds *pari passu* with their work, all their labour for the political enfranchisement of the country will prove vain; and in so far as the two customs against which you righteously inveigh tend *inter alia* to depress that element, all are bound to sympathise and support you in your proposed reforms, not over-rating their importance, not pressing them too furiously before their time is ripe, but accepting them as two, amongst several reforms by which our women must be raised to their rightful status, before India, whether still affiliated to England or not, can become either truly prosperous or truly free.

59. W. Wordsworth.—I am certain, that no rhetoric, however pathetic or eloquent, will produce the smallest effect on the solid structure of Hindu habit, and that reason, whether starting from facts or first principles, can only slightly, and for the most part indirectly affect it. Hindu Belief and Usage are no more the products of conscious reflection than Christian Theology or our own English religious habits, and are as invulnerable as these are to criticism or irony. Religion and Habit were not created and cannot be destroyed by logic...............
......But let me say at once, before I pass on, that I have no thought of putting an absolute veto on efforts like those which you have recently been making. Rationalistic criticism, whether founded on a re-examination of ancient texts, or on moral presumptions, or on social statistics, is not wholly thrown away, because its direct efforts are, in most cases, impalpable. It is a part, at least, of the work of the Time Spirit, and no part of that work is lost. Everywhere it constitutes a specific element in that aggregate of causes, which shapes the character of nations and guides them, as some think, with the stringency of a fore-ordaining fate. Your own work, inspired by pity and passion, has drawn to itself the eyes of men. It must have quickened the sympathies and startled the intelligence of some of your readers, and it has certainly forced many opponents to reconsider their position, and take up new ground. I think, however, that the time has come, when you would act most wisely in suspending, at least *for the present*, that apostolate of criticism and rebuke which you have assumed...

A society divided as Hindu society is, and dominated as it is by religious tradition and priestly law, will never be reformed piece-meal and in detail. New energy must be generated, and new principles of association and sympathy formed and carried forward into resolute deeds. Religion, culture, war, have all at different periods of history, furnished nations with starting points for a new career. But the influence which England is fitted to exercise on others is stronger in the sphere of positive science and political life than in any of those mentioned above, and it is surely in these departments of human activity that India will display the results of England's impact on her thoughts and habits. It is from the reaction of scientific and political ideas on Hindu society, and above all, from the authority which the champions and exponents of these ideas will gradually acquire and wield, that I look for changes in the social and religious institutions of the Hindus. I have carefully watched if not the beginnings, at least the early growth of these new forces, and I must say the spectacle is one full of interest. The drama of history is a long one, and none of us who are sitting in the theatre will witness the catastrophe. *

60. HON'BLE MR. C. P. ILBERT, LAW MEMBER, GOVERNMENT OF INDIA.—I do not thinka sufficient case has yet been

* As Chairman of the Rukhmabai Defence Committee, Mr. Wordsworth wrote a minute from which the following extracts are taken: "We are all agreed in holding that the penalty of imprisonment ought not to be awarded for a refusal of conjugal society, and most of us, I hope, if not all, also hold that this penalty bears a peculiarly odious aspect when applied to marriages contracted at an age when the parties could have no rational knowledge of the obligations to which they were committing themselves, or have never lived together.

I have been led to believe, principally on Mr. Telang's own authority, that coercive provisions of this kind were unknown to the written laws of the Hindus, and also opposed to their moral feelings. I was not unaware that on this point, the customary law or practice obtaining in some Hindu States at the present day was very different, but I did not expect to find that there were men living under British authority who looked with envious eyes to that customary law, and would be glad to bring the law of our own courts into closer conformity with it. ....

I am by nature more inclined to trust to opinion than legislation as the instrument of social reform; and I quite accept Mr. Telang's view that it is no function of our Committee to agitate for any change in the law which would make infant marriage illegal. I should be personally prepared to support such a change in the law, if a sufficiently large and important section of Hindu society desired it. At present I do not see much prospect of this, and the new law would probably remain a dead letter. But there is a point in social development—witness Lord Shaftesbury's Factory Acts—when legislation gives a powerful support to the highest moral feelings of a community, and a great stimulus to practical improvement. It is one of the functions of the wisest minds in a community to discover and point out to others where this point is reached."

made out for legislative interference. I do not wish to suggest that, Indian legislation cannot influence or is not materially influencing Hindu usages, belief and opinions, or to dogmatize about the limits within which such influence can be usefully or effectually applied.

But after having considered very carefully the suggestions for legislation put forward at various times by yourself, by Mr. Ranade and others, I have come to the conclusion that most of them are beyond the proper sphere of legislation, and that no one of them has yet received that kind or amount of support from representative opinion which would justify a legislature in interfering with laws or customs relating to marriage, and to which the Indian legislature was able to appeal when it passed Act XV of 1856. In saying this I do not forget the short and easy method of dealing with infant marriage which has been suggested by my eminent predecessor, Mr. Whitley Stokes.

Nor do I think that much can be done by executive regulations, or by the action of Government officials as such...

The propaganda to which you have so nobly devoted yourself demand missionary effort and missionary enthusiasm. Any appearance or suspicion of undue official interference is more likely to retard than to advance your cause.

I have followed with the greatest interest the reports of your recent progress through the towns of Northern India, and I see in the reception which you have met with every ground for encouragement.

Experience shows that Indian customs and usages are not the unchangeable phenomenon which they were ever believed to be. What is remarkable about these is the rapidity and unexpectedness with which they occasionally give way under new influence. A belief or a custom which seems to be firm or immovable as a rock, suddenly topples over and disappears, without previous warning, like an iceberg which has drifted into a Southern sea. The prejudice which was once believed to be a fatal obstacle to the prospect of Indian railways has thus disappeared. The prejudices against crossing the sea seems destined to share its fate.

61. RIGHT HONORABLE LORD HOBHOUSE.—Such customs (as that of Infant marriage), are most difficult to alter even in communities where a large number of minds have, for generations, been accustomed freely to speculate on and to discuss the merits and grounds of human conduct, and of social arrangements. Much greater is the difficulty in India where the vast masses throughout the country are probably incapable of such discussion, and would certainly think it wicked, and where old traditions have acquired the force of a divine command. I am afraid that, the panic about ghee is an illustration of this. Such conservatism has its good side—but it presents heart-breaking difficulties to one who desires to abate an evil custom. The only way is for those who have convictions, to go on uttering them boldly and persistently, trusting that the seed they sow will fall into the more receptive soil of young minds and will produce its fruit in due season. As regards the action of Government, it is rarely wise to outrun general opinion, especially in matters such as marriage which are so mixed up with religion and with personal feeling. I suppose that you will never have any English Ministers who will not be glad to act in the direction you wish, the moment they see that their action will be consonant to the feelings and convictions of the bulk of intelligent and influential Indians.

HON'BLE SIR RIVERS THOMPSON, LIEUTENANT GOVERNOR OF BENGAL.—The people want more education in the matter; and any attempt to pass a compulsory law on the subject would, as you are quite aware, not only be far in advance of popular sentiment in Bengal, but would be resented by Hindus of influence and authority.

You may be sure, however, that you will succeed in the end.

APPENDIX I.

PUBERTY AND PUBESCENCE.

One of the most plausible arguments put forward to justify infant and early marriages is the following:—"That consummation which takes place just when the parties have arrived at the age of puberty is a direct call of Nature, and cannot be early or late. Nature is generally credited with being unerring and perfect. In cases especially where she writes in legible characters, and where it is impossible to misunderstand her, it is not always possible to disregard her. If she is opposed or slighted, she knows how to have her revenge. It may be less direct, longer in coming, but it is none the less certain. In these timely consummations if it is Nature that calls, we cannot be presumably wrong in responding to her. Hence, we should be disposed to argue that if Hindu children are comparatively more sickly and less robust, it should be the effect of causes other than these wrongly called untimely consummations."* It is assumed by this writer as well as by many others that a girl who has menstruated has attained her puberty. This fallacy appears in so many forms in the opinions published by Government, that it is quite time to expose it fully and set all doubts on the subject at rest.

The question is one in which physiologists and doctors ought to be taken as authorities, and we proceed to quote these authorities. We owe a debt of gratitude to Keshub Chunder Sen for obtaining the views of the eminent men whom we are about to cite on this point, and we would request all medical gentlemen who have bestowed any attention on this matter to favour us with their own experiences.

Dr. Chevers the author of "Indian Medical Jurisprudence" wrote:—"The Mahommedan law has frequent allusions to the principle that puberty sanctions marriage, and doubtless Bengal would make a great step in advance, if parents would admit and act upon

* *Vide* Government Selections on Infant Marriage, &c., p. 287.

the rule that marriage allowed before the establishment of puberty, even should that change be delayed until the 17th or 18th year, is contrary to the law of nature. *Still this is not enough. It stands to reason that a wife ought to be a parent whom the least observant would declare to be a 'woman' and not an immature 'child.' Therefore if safe child-bearing and healthy offspring are to be regarded as being among the first objects of marriage, this rite ought to be seldom allowed till the 18th year, the 16th year being the minimum age in exceptional cases."* This is a pretty strong opinion, coming as it does from a standard writer.

Dr. Fayrer, M. D., wrote to the same effect:—"The fact of a girl having attained the period of puberty does not by any means imply that, though *capable*, she is *fit* for marriage. *Physiological science, common sense, and observation, all teach that an immature mother is likely to produce weak and imperfect offspring.* Before the parent gives the birth to a child, she should herself have attained her full vigour. That cannot be looked for in female children of 10 to 14 years of age. I am told that in Bengal marriages do frequently take place at these very early periods of life. I am speaking of the subject now only in its physical aspect. Of the other disadvantages, moral, social and domestic, I need say nothing. They are so obvious that they must forcibly present themselves to the notice of all highly educated, thoughtful and intellectual natives of Bengal, among whom, it is to me a marvel, that such a pernicious practice could have so long been permitted to obtain."

The marvel has not yet ceased. The above was written in 1871. Sixteen years have now elapsed and the evil is almost as great as it was before. Turning to the Bengal Census Report of 1881, we find the following mournful passage. "Among that people (i. e. the Hindus) more than 10 boys in every 100, between 5 and 10 years old, are bridegrooms, while of the girls 28 in 100, or more than 1 in 4, are wives or widows at an age when, if they were in Europe, they would be in the nursery or in the infant school." And yet we hear so much cant about the evil being of a limited extent and of a harmless character.

Dr. J. Ewart wrote: "I am of opinion that the *minimum* age at which Hindu women should be encouraged to marry would be *after and not before the 16th year. But the race would be improved still more by postponing the marriage of women to the 18th or 19th year of age.*" What have the Maharatta lecturers to say to this? They pride themselves on deferring consummation to the period of menstruation. They forget that early marriage leads to early menstruation, a fact on which we will quote abundant medical testimony. They forget that the menstrual period is not coeval with maturity. They forget the very end of marriage—the begetting of a healthy progeny. And forgetting all these elementary facts, they flood us with tall talk about their glorious old customs, about the evolution of these customs, from primeval necessities, about their adaptation to the race, and about a thousand other things deduced from misinterpretations of Herbert Spencer and Drawin and Mill and Buckle. But let us proceed with our quotations.

Dr. S. G. Chuckerbutty, M. D., wrote:—"It is a vicious custom that as soon as a girl menstruates she must be married. This is not done in any civilized country, nor should it be done here. *The practice of abstinence which the deferment of marriage imposes on a girl is more beneficial to mankind than its reverse in early marriage.*

Dr. T. Edmonston Charles wrote:—"I would beg to be allowed strongly to insist on the fact that the beginning of menstruation should not be taken to represent the marriageable age. It is true that talking generally this may be said to be a sign that a girl has arrived at the age at which she may conceive. It is an undoubted fact, however, that out of many girls living in the married state at the time that menstruation begins, very few do conceive for many months or even years after the function has become established. *I believe that though this event may be taken to represent commencing puberty*, a girl ought not to be taken as having arrived at puberty, till various changes in her organization which take place gradually and occupy a considerable period, have been fully completed. It is also of great importance that the fact should be kept prominently in view, that there is a broad distinction between the age at which it is possible for a child to conceive, and that at which it is expedient, from a medical point of view, that she should be allowed to become a mother..........*I have seen so many mothers at fourteen, as to look on the occurrence of maternity at that age as the rule rather than the exception. I uniformly regard such instances of child-bearing as a misfortune*......................*..It would be improper to style a girl* *of* 14 *as a child, but we would be equally far wrong in regarding her as a woman. She is in a transition stage, and while she is only developing into womanhood, she is in a position as regards child-bearing which is very far from perfect.* The practical effect of this limit (i.e. the one proposed in the Brahmo Marriage Bill) will be to ensure that the young mothers will just be removed from the period of childhood, which I consider to be a very great desideratum, but it will not place them within the safe period of adult age. At present, I believe, the majority of women become mothers while they may be said to be children, and the proposed change will just bring them into that stage in which they may with propriety be regarded *adolescent. Child-bearing in the early stage of adolescence, I regard only as a little less injurious than during childhood.*"

Dr. D. B. Smith, M.D., wrote :—"Before the age specified (sixteen) a female cannot be said to be fully developed—either physically or mentally. Some parts of her osseous structure which are essential to the reproductive function are not yet consolidated. The first appearance of these sexual changes which mark 'puberty,' are by no means to be regarded as coincident with the most fitting time for marriage. They merely indicate the development of procreative power and a possible capacity for conception; although it is to be observed that a female may conceive before she has even menstruated, and also that infants have been known to menstruate. *The stomach digests, the brain elaborates thought, the voice gives utterance to such thought long anterior to the time at which these functions are performed with full force and in physiological perfection; and a similar law of Nature applies to the sexual system of the female.* She may present the initiative sign of womanhood, without its being at all desirable that she should at once become a mother. When a girl reaches the 'pubescent' or 'nubile' age she may be said to have acquired the 'Vis generandi,' but it is a few years after this that she arrives at what the Romans called her *pubertas plena,* which is physiologically, the most appropriate period for marriage."

"This is the best reply to the "direct call of Nature" argument. Yes—Nature is unerring—but we are not. We do not understand her—but like arrant fools are always cocksure that we do: hence we confound *pubescence* with *puberty.*

Dr. Nobin Krishna Bose wrote: "In determining the age in question, more regard is to be had to the period of life when, by its anatomical development, the female system is fitted to enter upon the functions and duties of maternity, without injury to itself, or the physical deterioration of the offspring begotton by it. I should say that *our girls should not be married before they have attained at least the* 18*th year of their age. Before this period their system would not bear with impunity the drain which maternity must establish in it.*" And these are the words of a Hindu doctor. Ponder over them all Hindu patriots—and decide whether it it not time to put your house in order.

Dr. Atmaram Pandurang, of Bombay, wrote: "puberty is not the best criterion of proper marriageable age, for it is not the period at which development of the parts concerned in gestation and delivery is completed, nor is then the mind well adapted for the requirements of the mother in taking proper care of her delicate and tender off-spring." Dr. Atmaram Pandurang was further of opinion that the proper age for girls to marry was *twenty*!

Dr. White, Professor of Midwifery at the Grant Medical College, Bombay, wrote: "Menstruation is no doubt the most important sign of puberty, but when it shows itself early, it is only the sign of commencing puberty, and in the absence of other indications, by no means implies that a girl is fitted for marriage and child-bearing. *It is not until puberty has been fully established that the minimum marriageable age has been reached, and this rarely occurs in my opinion among Native girls before the* 15*th or* 16*th year; but if marriages were delayed until the* 18*th year, the frame would be more throughly developed, the danger of child-bearing would be lessened and healthier off-spring would be secured.*" These are weighty words coming from a professor of midwifery. What have our Poona friends, who hiss Social Reform advocates, to say to them.

Dr. Mohendralal Sircar wrote:—"The commencement of the menstrual function is no doubt an index to the *commencement* of puberty. But it is a grave mistake to suppose that the female who has just begun to menstruate is capable of giving birth to healthy children. *The teeth no doubt are intended for the mastication of solid food, but it would be a grievous error to think that the child, the mo-*

ment he begins to cut his teeth, will be able to live upon solid food. Our anxiety, on the contrary, should be that the delicate masticatory organs are not injured or broken by giving the child too hard food. *So when we see a girl beginning to have the monthly flow, we should not only anxiously watch its course and regularity, but should also watch the other collateral developments of womanhood, to be able to determine the better the time when she can become a mother, safely to herself and to her offspring. For, it should be borne in mind that while early maternity results in giving birth to short-lived or unhealthy children, it at the same time seriously compromises the health of the mother also. I can speak positively on this subject from personal experience. A host of complaints from which our females suffer life-long, or to which they fall early victims, arise from the evils of early marriage—namely early pubescence and early maternity.*" This is the language of one of whom India may well be proud, for he has spent his life in the relief of human suffering and has spared no pains to spread scientific knowledge among his countrymen. The extent of misery and distress caused by this pernicious custom cannot be exaggerated. We appeal to all educated Hindus to say if it is right—if it is even utilitarian to subject so many women to the horrors of early maternity?—for the pain suffered by the young mother is simply heart-rending. In Heaven's name follow your utilitarian ethics and seize the greatest happiness—we would say *welfare* with Darwin—of the greatest number. Be true to this standard and you must—you ought at least to organize a Social Reform Mission and support it with your purse and your intellect. Have no legislation if you please—no executive interference. But is it too much to ask you to become missionaries of the doctrine you preach?—the doctrine of alleviating the misery of your fellow creatures.

II.

IS NOT EARLY MARRIAGE THE CAUSE OF EARLY PUBESCENCE?

It is often stated that so long as consummation is deferred there can be no harm in marrying children at an early age. The opinions published by Government repeat this supposed axiomatic truth almost *ad nauseam*. But the proposition is not true, far less axiomatic. Recently a Calcutta contemporary republished an article of Dr. Mohendralal Sircar, published in 1871, which clearly shows the fallacy of the view adopted by so many of the gentlemen consulted by Government. The opinion given by Dr. M. Sircar to Keshub Chunder Sen is to the same effect, as we shall presently show. It is extremely important to know what medical authorities have to say on this subject, and we proceed to quote them.

Dr. S. G. Chuckerbutty wrote in 1871. "The Hindu and Mahomedan girls, from the custom of early marriage, attain to *forced* puberty at an earlier age. This should, therefore, never influence our opinion as to what is the proper age for puberty under normal circumstances." Dr. D. B. Smith wrote on April 17, 1871. "The early betrothal system and bringing together of persons of immature age must be bad, as involving *a disturbance of imperceptibly gradual sexual development, and as lighting up what in medical phraseology might be called an unnatural Erythium !*"

Dr. T. E. Charles wrote :—" *The great cause which induce early menstruation is undoubtedly early marriage.* The girl is forced into menstruation prematurely by the abnormal conditions under which marriage places her.

" Horse-breeders are well aware of this physiological law ; and owners of racing steeds habitually take advantage of this natural law when it suits their purpose, by confining a pony under the same roof, though separated from the mare by partition, when they desire that her ovaries should be forced prematurely into that condition which is analogous to the state they are in, during menstruation in the human species.

" I believe, in the young widow, and in the girl kept separate from her husband, menstruation occurs uniformly later than in those living in a state of marriage. *I am also of opinion that the universality of early marriage has had a decided effect in determining the earlier appearance of menstruation, as it is well known that instances of early and late menstruation show themselves regularly in special families, and the age at which menstruation occurs may be regarded as in a great measure hereditary. A very large number of the instances of menstruation met with before the thirteenth year, is capable of very easy explanation on the supposition of early marriage having caused their premature appearance.* If marriage became generally delayed till menstruation has been fully established, I am quite sure that after a series of generations, menstruation would come on habitually at a later period, and much more closely approach to a Western standard."

Dr. Charles does not believe that climate has more than an insignificant influence on the development of the menstrual function. We shall in a separate contribution deal with the effect of climate—but in the meanwhile, is it not remarkable that some of our educated brethren in supreme contempt of physiology should argue that early marriage is a very beneficent institution which even Europeans would do well to adopt? Professor Bhandarkar, who differs from these gentlemen in regarding the custom as an evil, has nevertheless a great deal to say in its favour, and so has our friend Mr. Hume. "From childhood," says the learned Professor, "the girl and the boy are brought up in the belief that they are destined to be wife and husband, and that their mutual relation is as much the work of nature, and consequently inviolable, as the relation between brother and sister, or parents and children. This belief enters into the formation of their character, and they grow up as husband and wife and consequently become adapted to each other." Far be it from us to say that any evil in this world is an unmixed evil. We do not deny that some early married couple may be happy. But is the happiness of the married couple the sole object of marriage? Have our philosophic and scientific Poona Brahmins forgotton their Darwin in this instance? Darwin certainly does not believe that an institution which merely brings happiness to a given number of individuals is necessarily a good one. His test is: "Does it lead to the *welfare* of the race as a whole?", and this test is based on reasoning and in fact which the Poona Brahmins should be the last to disavow. Judged by this test, early marriage is certainly a most pernicious custom. Darwinism and Spencerism and all the *isms* in the world are certainly arrayed against it. Dr. Charles shows what a detrimental reflex action is exercised by early marriage on the young couple. It leads to early development and that early development perpetuates early marriage. This is exactly the way in which social evils propagate themselves. And yet, how often do we hear—"We come to maturity too early—and ought therefore to marry early"? This is rank nonsense—as rank as the talk about early marriage adapting the wife to the husband *as a rule*. Yes, the wife is adapted—but to the mother-in-law. Did Professor Bhandarkar ever read Mr. Mahipatram Rupram's *Sasu Wahu ni Ladai?*" Can he deny that even in Poona the adaptation is to the mother-in-law and not necessarily to the husband? The husband is the wife's god according to the Hindu religion—and the worshippers do not need much adaptation to the worshipped. But the mother-in-law rubs down her poor little daughter-in-law's angles in a very short time —in the domestic social mill. Her tyranny is a proverb. Does not Professor Bhandarkar know some of the pithy saws in which Hindus themselves have crystallized this sad truth? The mother-in-law has been curiously enough ignored by most of the educated gentlemen who favoured Government with their opinions. And yet the mother-in-law is one of the worst evils of early marriage. And as tyranny is always morally worse for the tyrant than the slave, the mother-in-law is more to be pitied than denounced. She is but a victim of an institution which, founded on a perversion of the laws of nature, seeks to create a second nature among those who come under its baneful influence—a second nature which blights the springs of human happiness—which dwarfs the race and impedes their progress in physical, moral, social and political vigour. Will the day ever dawn, when this upas tree of early marriage will crumble to dust, when a race once remarkably manly and upright will acknowledge its own imperfections and corruptions, and looking the evil full in the face uproot it from their midst? The very opposition to social reform is a sad token of the depth of moral deterioration which has pervaded Hindu society ever since its departure from purer laws and purer discipline led to its subjection to foreign rule. The outlook is certainly not very hopeful—but no patriot is worthy of this name, if on this account he has not the courage to give his *tan*, *man* and *dhan* to the cause.

Reverting to our quotations, we find Dr. D. B. Smith writing again in July as follows:—"I am inclined to believe that very early marriages in this country are mentally degrading as they are physiologically objectionable. It would be altogether unbecoming and out of place for me to enter into the subject of the moral objections to early marriage; the more so as it is almost self-evident that the *artificial forcing of physical instincts and the consequent unnatural stimulation of the sexual cannot be regarded as a mere error of judgment.* It certainly involves a degree of depravity the consideration of which may, however, safely be left to the 'intuitive moralist.'

"It may, I think, without any exaggeration or cynicism, be said that the present system of early marriage in Bengal panders to passion and sensuality, violates the requirements of nature, lowers the general standard of public health, lessens the average value of life, takes greatly from the general interest of existing society, and *allows the present race to deteriorate both to its own disadvantage and to the detriment of future generations.*" Mr. Malabari never used such strong language, and yet he was charged with exaggeration ! !

Dr. Nobin Krishna Bose wrote: "In this country the custom under notice has prevailed for centuries and generations, and it is not at all to be wondered at, therefore, that our boys and girls should attain to puberty at an earlier period of life than under a healthier system of matrimonial connections they would have done." Here is a Hindu Doctor of some eminence actually admitting the results of the horrid forcing-system practised for so many years !

Dr. Atmaram Pandurang wrote: "In some cases puberty is known to come on as early as 10 years and in others so late as 17 or 18 years. In some rare instances the *catamenia* occur regularly every month from infancy. This difference amongst girls is caused by some peculiarity in their individual constitution, *but in a large majority of cases chiefly or entirely by social influence—the influence on habits of thought and action which society has on each individual member.*" And yet how loth we are to improve our social influences !

Dr. A. V. White wrote:—"Early marriages, as they obtain in this country, have the effect of prematurely rousing the ovaries into a state of activity, and early menstruation is the result. *But this early menstruation is unaccompained with the other signs of development or advancing puberty, such as the special growth of the reproductive organs in conjunction with the general development of the frame and of the mental faculties. This pernicious custom has so long prevailed that it has now become the constitutional habit of Indian girls to menstruate early, and this habit, I believe, is transmitted from mother to daughter.* If Indian girls were not to marry until 16 or 18, I believe that in a few generations this habit would be broken and marked improvement in this respect would be observed." Here is hope indeed of regeneration—of the salvation of a whole race. But the doctors are crying in the wilderness, and no one hears them.

Dr. Mohendralal Sircar wrote: "If we take the age laid down in Susruta as the minimum, which is more likely from the language employed, then we must come to the conclusion that *the minimum age of menstruation has, since the day of Susruta, become much lower, a fact which demands serious consideration.* ....I have no doubt in my mind that high and luxurious living, and *early seeing and knowing of child-husbands and child-wives, favored by the anxiety of fond parents to see their little ones become fathers and mothers, are the chief causes of the forced puberty which we so much regret in our females rather than in our male children."* Little fathers—and little mothers! Little brides and little bridegrooms! Little widows and virgin widows! Are these to be proud of? Are these the only glory now left of the once glorious Aryan race? Are there no true son of Aryavarta to raise their voice against this iniquity, this abominable wrong to nature, to man, to woman, to children, to the present generation and to the future? Is India to have no Sitas, no Draupadis, no Savitris no Damayantis again? The little pigeons coo and woo and are happy. The whole of animal nature presents wonderful cases of sexual selection—of adult marriages—of happy couples and healthy offspring. When will India conform to nature in this respect? The little children of little fathers in Gujarat call the latter *Motabhai* (elder brothers). as the little progenitors are ashamed to be called fathers! When will all this unnaturalness end? Is there no light? Is it always to be "behind the veil, behind the veil"? This strife between foolish man and the laws of God—is it to last for ever? Is it irreligion only to discard certain beliefs? Is it not irreligion also to violate natural laws—as it is to violate primal moral laws? The laws proceed from the same lawgiver—their sanctions are the same—and they revenge themselves by the same self-acting machinery. And yet our countrymen consider early marriage hardly a sin!

III.

HAS THE CLIMATE ANYTHING TO DO WITH THE EARLY PUBERTY OF INDIAN GIRLS AND BOYS?

The answer to this question is: "a little only—so little as to be almost inappreciable." This may appear quite a novel answer to many, and yet those who have kept abreast of modern scientifi-research will feel little surprise at it. Carpenter in his 'Animal Physiology' proves that organization plays a more important part in reproduction than climate, and Darwin tells us in his 'Origin of Species' at page 113, that, "adaptation to any special climate may be looked at as a quality readily grafted in an innate wide flexibility of constitution common to most animals." It was at one time supposed that the colour of the skin depended solely on climate, "but Pallas first showed that this view is not tenable, and he has been followed by all anthropologists. The view has been rejected chiefly because the distribution of the variously coloured races, most of whom must have long inhabited their present homes, does not coincide with corresponding differences of climate" (Darwin's 'Descent of Man,' Vol. I. p. 242.) These we take to be the latest conclusions of science. Let us now see what the medical authorities consulted by Keshub in 1871 had to say on this subject.

Dr. Norman Chevers wrote. "*The general opinion among physiologists is that all collateral circumstances, except those of climate, being equal, all women would reach puberty at about the same age.*" In other words, judging from the context, given different climates but the same collateral circumstances, for instance what Dr. Mohendralal Sircar would call 'the late knowing and seeing of husbands,' and all women would reach their puberty at the same age. Dr. Chevers continued. "If, however, there does prevail in India an idea that a crime equal to that of child murder is incurred whenever menstruation occurs previous to marriage, it becomes difficult to obtain statistics showing the ranges of ages at which *naturally* Indian women would attain puberty. It would perhaps be well to obtain some statistics of the ages at which puberty was reached by some hundreds of *carefully brought up widows of child-husband*. This has never been attempted, I believe, and such a table would be valuable to science and of valid aid to the excellent purpose which you have in view." A false physiological doctrine made into a religious precept would appear, from this extract, to have been to some extent at the bottom of the practice of early marriage. Would some of our M. D.'s take the trouble to collect the statistics suggested by Dr. Chevers?

Dr. S. G. Chuckerbutty wrote:—"The usual sign of puberty (pubescence ?) in a girl is the commencement of menstruation which occurs as a general rule in all the countries between the ages of thirteen and fourteen,. though in some cases it may come on earlier or later. *The best standard for comparison would be the Native Christian girls on the one hand, and European girls on the other, for in respect of marriage they adopt the same rule. I am not aware that there is any practical difference between these two classes* of girls as to the age of puberty. The Hindu and Mahomedan girls, from the custom of early marriage, attained to forced puberty at an earlier age. This should, therefore, never influence our opinion as to what is the proper age for puberty under normal circumstances." We believe, there is some difference between Native Christian girls and European girls. Heredity plays a permanent part in sexual development, and it would take years before Native Christains whose ancestors were originally Hindus and practised early marriage, could minimise the effects of heredity.

Dr. Charles wrote: "Two points constituting grave and formidable impediments have come prominently before me while making enquiries to enable me to offer an opinion on the question. One lies in a wide-spread belief that the climate leads to early menstruation which points to early marriage, and the other a similarly extended opinion that the climate causes an early development of sexual passion. There is just sufficient truth in both these statements to render it impossible to give them a full and unreserved denial, and yet so little truth in them as to render the arguments based on them entirely valueless. Menstruation in Calcutta is undoubtedly earlier than it is in London, though the difference in this respect between the two places is not so great as is usually believed. The climate and other surroundings of young girls may have some influence in leading to this result, *but the great cause which induces early menstruation is undoubtedly early marriage*. The girl is forced into menstruation prematurely by the abnormal conditions under which marriage places her..........

" On the subject of early development of sexual passion, I write with great reluctance, and only write at all because I consider by not referring to the question, it will do more harm than by allowing it to enter into this discussion.

" I have long believed that the young Hindu female is usually totally devoid of all sexual feeling and special inquiries on the point made during the present investigation have completely confirmed me in this opinion. Believing the allegation to be without foundation, I consider the fear of seduction grounded on it to be needless and am convinced that such a misfortune befalling any Bengali girl of fourteen or fifteen years of age would depend on a train of events in which sexual passion would hold as unimportant a place as it would do under similar circumstances in Spitzbergen or the Northern shore of Baffin's Bay." It is a psychological truth that a desire satisfied as soon as it is felt has no need and no occasion to become intense. In India sexual passion is satisfied before even it is felt. What is the natural result? It has lost in intensity and, parodoxical as it may appear, Dr. Charles' conclusions appear to us to be no more than the truth.

Dr. Smith wrote as follows: " Montesquieu enunciated the dictum that 'women in hot climates are marriagable at eight, nine, or ten years of age'—adding (what under the assumed circumstances is certainly much more near the truth) that, 'they are old at twenty.' 'The age of marriage,' says Mr. Sale, 'or of maturity, is reckoned to be fifteen—a decision supported by a tradition of the Prophet, although Abu Hanifah thinks eighteen the proper age' (Prichard's Natural History of Man, Vol. ii. p. 655). Some physiologists believe that the catamenial function does not occur earlier in hot than in cold climates. Mr. Roberton, whose writings on this subject are well known, is a learned exponent of this view of the case. Allusion to his investigations may be found in Todd's 'Cyclopædia of Anatomy and physiology,' Article 'Generation,' vol. ii. p. 442.

"The experiences of Haller, Boerhaave, Denman Barnes, Dewees, and others were in support of a contrary opinion. There can, I think, be but little doubt that '*temperature, mode of life, moral and physical education* do produce decided variations in relation to puberty.' The late Professor Traill, Editor of the 8th Edition of the Encyclopædia Britannica, states that Fodere observed a difference in this respect between the inhabitants of the warm Maritime part of Provence and the elevated valleys of Entrannes and St. Etienne, and that he himself (Traill) had remarked a similiar difference in Spain between the children in the plains of Andalusia and among the mountains of Cataleena (Outlines of Medical Jurisprudence, p. 18).

"Dr. Tilt compiled from the works of various authors a table of the periods of first menstruation of 12,037 women, in hot, temperate and cold climates. The following are briefly the results arrived at.

	No. of observations	Mean Age.
Hot climates	666	13·19
Temperate	7,237	14·94
Cold	4,134	16·41
Grand mean of all countries		14·85

"The table referred to is to be found in Dr. Tilt's work on "Diseases of Women," 2nd edition, p. 35,

"Menstruation has been found to be accelerated amongst the Manchester cotton-spinners by continual exposure to a high artificial temperature. The effects of high temperature in hastening development of the organic functions generally were well demonstrated by Reaumer's experiments on Pupac and by Mr. Higginbottom's researches on the metamorphosis of the tadpole into the frog (Phil. Trans. 1850 p. 431, and Proceedings of the Royal Society vol. XI. p. 532.)

"Those who desire to study fully the subject of puberty, in all its bearings, should consult the writings of Raciborski, Costa, Pouchet, Bierre de Boismont, Whithead, Arthur Farre, Allen Thomson, Roberton, Mayer (Des Rapports Conjugaux) Meigs, &c., and different standard treatises on Medical jurisprudence as those of Beck, Orfila, Casper, Chevers, Taylor, &c."

This is sufficient to give a vertigo to the ordinary reader. Dr. Smith is too learned—but we hope his learning will not be lost on those who take a deep interest in Hindu Social Reform. Dr. Smith's own opinion as to the proper age of marriage has been already quoted, and it will be observed that his own conclusion is that temperature is one of several causes which determine early or late puberty. But the conclusion arrived at by Carpenter and Darwin after a careful study of its effects on the reproductive system of animals is that it has but little effect. Montesquien's opinion was probably based on the celebrated text of Angira which prescribed 8, 9 and 10 as the marriageable age for Hindu girls. He probably jumped to the conclusion that because a precept like this occurred in some of the Hindu Shastras, women actually reached puberty at these ages. Had the climate such a powerful effect we would expect English girls, born and bred in India, to attain puberty at an earlier age than their sisters in England. But this, we are informed, is not the case. Moreover, it is curious that in several parts of Africa, early marriages are unknown, while the Esquimaux who live in cold climate marry almost as early as the Hindus. All these facts show that the conclusion arrived at by Dr. Roberton is more likely to be correct than that arrived at by the various comparatively older writers mentioned by Dr. Smith. The case of the cotton spinners in England has been explained away by showing that the congregation of the two sexes is primarily the cause of the early puberty noticed in their case, and as regards Provence and Spain, it is clear that many more causes might be at work, as in India, than the apparent cause of climate.

Dr. Nobin Krishna Bose wrote:—" I do not think that climate exerts that degree of influence in modifying the age of puberty in different parts of the world which has been ascribed to it. Some difference it will produce, no doubt, but this, on examination, will be found to range within very narrow limits. On studying the age of marriage in different countries at different periods of time, it has appeared to me, on the other hand, that early wedlock has been the result of ignorance and of general degraded condition of the female sex, and hence at one time it was not unknown even in the latitudes of England and Russia. *And the mischief lies in this, viz, that when, the practice becomes a marked one, it tends to perpetuate itself by producing precocious prematurity (sic!) among the childern, in accordance with the organic laws which govern the hereditary transmission of physical and mental qualities.*" This consideration shows how cautious we should be in ascribing the prevalence of this custom in any country to climate, solely or principally.

Dr. Atmaram Pandurang wrote:—"You will find in all countries in the world that girls living in city, and especially in very crowded parts of it, and in the lowest strata of society, arrive at puberty at a much earlier age than those living in the agricultural or rural districts, and in the upper strata in whom high moral, feelings prevail. The custom of premature marriage thereby acting injuriously upon the morals of the people among whom it prevails, has an undoubted tendency to bring on early puberty, and this is strangely mistaken for 'climatic influence.' *Climate has no influence in the matter. The history of our own people in former years when this pernicious custom had no existence, will bear me out fully*, so that I need not point to other classes or tribes in this country or other countries, savage and civilized, where the custom of early marriage does not exist, to support the assertion that climate has no influence in the coming on of puberty."

Dr. A. White wrote: "From inquiries I have made on this subject, I have long since come to the conclusion that, there is a considerable difference with regard to the period at which menstruation first makes its appearance between English and Indian girls. Among English girls menstruation occurs more frequently at 15 years than at any other age, while among Indian girls, in the majority of cases, I believe it occurs at 13 or even less. *The cause of this difference of two years is not so much in my opinion the effect of climate as a difference in the condition of the two races.*

Dr. Mohendral Sircar, after showing how the age of menstruation and conception has become lower than in the days of Susruta, from valuable statistics collected by himself, writes about the effect of climate as follows: "As to whether climate, the degree of latitude, the position on the surface of the earth, the nature of the soil and other surroundings have or have not any influence—upon the menstrual function, its first appearance, its subsequent regularity, and its final decline, this is a question which may be still regarded as open to discussion. I do not think facts have been collected with sufficiently scrupulous accuracy, and other circumstances, social and domestic, have been allowed due weight in the balance of causation, to warrant any positive conclusion on the point. *A superficial view of available facts would seem to incline the mind to the belief that climate does influence the menstrual function delaying its first appearance in the cold and hastening the period in tropical climates. After weighing carefully all the circumstances which might have a possible influence on the function, I am led to believe that if climate has any influence, it is trifling, not to say infinitesimal.* There is no doubt as our table will show (the statistics collected by the Doctor) that, age of first menstruation here in Calcutta (I do not say, Bengal advisedly) is earlier than in London, but I am more inclined to attribute this difference to the difference as social and domestic economy that obtains in the respective places. I have not said Bengal, because *I have positive testimony that there is a striking difference between the ages of first menstruation in town and country. The earliest ages that I have quoted of early* menstruation were in some of the rich families in Calcutta. And I have no doubt in my mind that *high and luxurious living and early seeing and knowing of child-husbands, and child-wives, favoured by the anxiety of fond parents to see their little ones become fathers and mothers, are the chief causes of the forced puberty which we so much regret in our female rather than in our male children."* This passage cannot be repeated too often. Those who rely on the climate theory have to explain how rural girl attain puberty later than urban ones—how the old Aryas knew no such practice as early marriage—how even in England and Russia this practice prevailed, at one time, though neither country is tropical—how it prevails even now among the Esquimaux and how it does not prevail in several parts of Africa. We have seen how the old supposition that skincolour depended upon climate has been found to be untrue, and we think, we have sufficiently shown that the equally old supposition that early puberty is the natural result of a hot climate must share its fate.

APPENDIX II.

A SCHEME OF SOCIAL REFORM ON THE PRINCIPLE OF SELF-HELP AND "ON THE LINES OF LEAST RESISTANCE."

I.

There has been a great deal of talk on the subject of social reform. None can deny that the time for action has now arrived.

The result of the discussion establishes almost a perfect unanimity as to the necessity of well-organized Social Reform Associations. Indeed the strongest argument urged against Government interference is that, social reform must come from within, and the Hindus must help themselves.

There is only one gentleman, R. S. Vishwanath Narayen Mandlik, who is opposed to the formation of such associations. His reason is that the pledges usually taken by the members of such associations are seldom kept, and that, therefore, such associations generally discredit the cause which they ought to promote.

There is considerable truth in this objection—and it cannot be denied that most Social Reform Associations have failed. Let us see why they have failed.

Under the English law, a pledge by a member of an association to defer the marriage of his son and daughter until a certain age, is an agreement without consideration, and, therefore, void. The pledges taken cannot thus be enforced—nor of course any penalties provided for their breach. The gentlemen who take the pledges are aware of this fact—and the public is aware of it. There is of course a considerable difference between taking a pledge which can be legally executed, and which cannot be. In the former case, the outside public can understand that the pledge-taker is in earnest—that he has made a self-sacrifice—and that he means action. In the latter case, such presumptions are not possible. Moreover, as has been admitted almost on all hands, the pressure brought by the family—especially by the ladies of the household—brings about the violation of the pledges, and it is clear that this pressure has not much chance of succeeding when such violation carries with it an enforceable penalty.

The most important question, therefore, is—how to secure the fulfilment of pledges—for otherwise we would have no end of tall talk—but no examples. None denies the value of examples, and none denies their necessity.

I take it that in every community there are at least some earnest self-sacrificing men. Ten good men once saved a city from the wrath of the Most High—and at least seven good men must be found before the scheme I am going to sketch can be worked.

If the seven men however are found—the first question which each has to ask himself is—how much of his time and how much of his money he can devote to the cause of social reform. If the result of this questioning is a substantial self-sacrifice, let the association be started—but not otherwise.

In England corporate action succeeds—because it is well-understood that organization means self-sacrifice. Here associations fail, because no one wishes to pay the salary of a stipendiary Secretary, or the rent of an office, or printing expenses. The most successful associations in India are those which have not only "a local habitation and a name"—but a *paid full-time* Secretary able to devote all his energy to the promotion of their objects. The salary of such a Secretary is generally a first-rate investment—for the success of the association brings to it additional members and liberal donations, and in a short time it becomes self-supporting. One of the essential features of my scheme is, therefore, a paid full-time Secretary. If one of the seven workers can devote the whole of his time to the cause on a small pay—so much the better. But a full-time Secretary must be secured any-how.

The pay of the Secretary being provided for—the next thing to do is to select a house—humble and unpretentious—for an office. If one of the workers has a commodious dwelling, he can place one or two of his rooms at the disposal of the association—otherwise the workers must contribute the rent in addition to the salary of the Secretary. Besides these a small fund—say 10 Rs. a month—should be subscribed or collected, for the publication of pamphlets and tracts on the subject of social reform. Those who are not prepared to pay a Secretary, or keep an office, or publish such papers regularly, need not attempt this scheme at all.

These preliminaries being settled—let the workers determine, in consultation with the wisest in their community or caste, their programme of social reform. This is their look-out and they had better be careful to settle a programme likely to be carried out "on the lines of least resistance," as the Hon'ble Mr. Telang advises. Let them first definitely enunciate the objects for which they wish to form the association, and agree that none of them will make a profit by the association, or divide the assets, and that none of them in case of the dissolution of the association, will shirk his responsibility for the debts of the association to the extent of a fixed sum say 10 Rs. Usually when associations formed not for profit but for promoting useful objects, are dissolved—their property is conveyed by them to other associations having the like objects—and a clause to this effect must also be agreed to. Lastly provision should be made for the keeping and auditing of accounts. All these clauses should be inserted in the memorandum of association.

Besides this document—the articles of association should be drawn up. The memorandum is to contain the conditions on which the association is formed—the articles are to contain the regulations which are to govern its existence. In the articles it should be stated whether the number of the members is to be limited or unlimited—what their qualifications are to be—how they are to be admitted—how they can retire—what rights they will have—how the office-bearers will be appointed—how the association will be managed—what powers will be vested in the managing committee—what meetings will be convened and when—how the proceedings before such meetings will be conducted—and how branch-associations may be formed. The promoters should use the utmost care in drawing up the articles regarding the qualifications, admission and retirement of members. The most prominent feature of this scheme is that some pledges and the maximum penalties leviable on their infringment should be agreed to, that the agreement should qualify for membership, and that none can retire without paying the penalty adjudged by the association. The association is to be a self-governing body, and a domestic tribunal. It will judge in each case of default what amount within the maximum penalty should be levied from the defaulter—and so likewise it will determine, when a member applies for leave to retire, whether his real motive is or is not to violate his compact, and to escape the penalties, and it will mete out its punishment accordingly. What these penal clauses are to be is of course left to the collective discretion of those who covenant to abide by them.

But suppose that a member fails to abide by these clauses, and refuses to pay the sum adjudged by the association, how then is this sum to be recovered? I reply that it cannot be recovered unless the association is registered under Section 26 of Act VI. of 1882, (an Act for the incorporation, regulation, and winding up of Trading Companies *and other associations.*) The heading of Section 26, is "Associations not for profit"—and this Section read with the Sections it impliedly refers to lay down that any seven or more persons associated for a lawful purpose, and desirous of promoting any "useful object," can have all the privileges and obligations of a Company. But these persons must first satisfy the Local Government that they have a "useful object" in view, and obtain its license. Without such license, they cannot get their association registered, and it is only when the association is registered that the privileges and the obligations accrue. The procedure is not complex. Draw up first your memorandum and articles of association. The forms annexed have been approved by the Bombay Government. The form of the memorandum (excepting the clauses about the objects of the association, and the figure limiting the liability of the members in case of dissolution) is the form in use in England, and the clauses inserted in it (except as above) must be accepted—for without such acceptance the Government will not issue its license. The association however, are free to settle their articles—for only the headings of these last were supplied by Government. The memorandum and the articles should be printed, and then signed by at least 7 persons in the presence of one witness at least. They should then be sent to the Secretary to Government, General Department, with a letter praying for a license under Section 26 of Act VI. of 1882. In this letter all facts tending to prove the *bonâ-fides* of the association should be stated. When the license is obtained, the memorandum should be taken to the Registrar of Joint Stock Companies for registration. The Government of India have now reduced the fee for registration to 50 Rs. and of course this fee must be paid.

II.

For the benefit of those who wish to know the wording of the Sections alluded to, and also the privileges and obligations of the association, I give below the following *precis*. Section 26, runs as follows :—

"ASSOCIATIONS NOT FOR PROFIT."

"Sec. 26. Where any Association which might be formed under this Act as a limited Company proves to the Local Government that it is formed for the purpose of promoting

Commerce, Art, Science, Charity, or any other useful object, and that it is the intention of such Association to apply the profits if any, or other income of the Association in promoting its objects, and to prohibit the payment of any dividend to its members, the Local Government may, by license under the hand of one its Secretaries, direct such Association to be registered with limited liability without the addition of the word "Limited" to its name, and such Association may be registered accordingly, and *upon registration shall enjoy all the privileges and be subject to the obligations* by this Act imposed on limited Companies; with the exception that none of the provisions of this Act, that require a limited Company to use the word "Limited" as any part of its name, or to publish its name, or to send a list of its members, directors, or managers to the Registrar, shall apply to an Association so registered.

The license by the Local Government may be granted upon such conditions and subject to such regulations as the Local Government thinks fit to impose ; and such conditions and regulations shall be binding on the Association and may at the option of the Local Government be inserted in the memorandum and articles of association, or in both or one of such documents."*

The first question which requires elucidation in this Section is "what associations may be formed under this Act as limited Companies." The reply is contained in Sections 6 and 7, the former of which is as follows :—

"Any seven or more persons associated *for any lawful purpose* may, by subscribing their names to a memorandum of

---

* Mr. Justice West said in his Judgment in the celebrated Dakore case (P. J. of 1887, p. 169, Manohar Ganesh Tambekar and others *vs.* Lakhmiram Govindram &c.) "If its (a charitable association's) purposes are such as are contemplated by Section 26, of the Indian Joint Stock Companies' Act VI. of 1882, the Society may get itself constituted accordingly under the Act. Otherwise, though the individual members may have certain rights and privileges as members of a class, or answering to a certain designation, these advantages must be realized as against the world at large, through the proprietary or quasi-proprietary right of some other person or corporation."

association, and otherwise complying with the requisitions of this Act in respect of registration, form an incorporated company, with or without limited liability." Sec. 7 shows that if the members agree to pay a fixed sum, say one rupee, in the event of the association being wound up, towards the liquidation of the debts of the association, their liability will be limited.

The next question is "what are the privileges and obligations of Companies"—for these are also to be the privileges and obligations of Social Reform Associations registered under the Section.

The first great privilege is that the agreements of the members are to be "contracts"—that is enforceable covenants, for this is the meaning of the term 'contract' according to the Contract Act. So also the moneys due to the Association by the members are recoverable as debts. As in the case of societies registered under Act XXI. of 1860—the Association is bound to draw up a "memorandum of association" and its "articles of association" (SS. 6 and 37.) It is necessary as said before to print the articles, and each subscriber must sign them in the presence of one witness at least (S. 39.) The effect of this subscription is stated in the following words.

"When registered, they (*i. e.* the articles of association) shall bind the Company and the members thereof to the same extent as if each member had subscribed his name thereto, and *as if such articles contained a contract on the part of himself, his heirs, executors, and administrators to conform to all the regulations contained in such articles subject to the provisions of this Act*.

*All moneys payable by any member to the company in pursuance of the conditions and regulations of the company, or any of such conditions or regulations, shall be deemed to be a debt due from such member to the Company."**

---

* Cf S. 9 of Act XXI. of 1860, which is not so comprehensive. "Whenever, by any bye-law duly made in accordance with the rules and regulations of the society, or, if the rules do not provide for the making of bye-laws, by any bye-law made at a general meeting of the members

The second privilege is that in any suit brought by the Company against any member to recover any moneys "due from such member in his character of member, it shall be sufficient to allege that the defendant is a member of the Company and is indebted to the Company in respect of...... moneys due whereby a suit has accrued to the Company" (S. 94).

The third privilege is that conferred by Section 41, under which the association "shall.........be a body corporate by the name contained in the memorandum of association, capable forthwith of exercising all the functions of an incorporated Company, and having perpetual succession and a common seal." Its contracts with strangers are to be written or oral, unless any law requires any of them to be in writing, when of course they ought to be in writing (S. 67.) All its contracts "shall be effectual in law," and shall be binding upon the association" and their successors, and all other parties thereto, their heirs, executors or administrators, as the case may be." (S. 67.)

The fourth privilege is that "until the contrary is proved, every general meeting of the Company or meeting of directors or managers in respect of the proceedings of which minutes have been made, shall be deemed to have been duly held and convened, and all resolutions passed thereat or proceedings had, to have been duly passed and had, and all appointments of directors, managers or liquidators shall be deemed to be valid, and all acts done by such directors, managers, or liquidators shall be valid, notwithstanding any defect that may afterwards be discovered in their appointments or qualifications." (S. 92.)

---

of the society convened for the purpose (for the making of which the concurrent votes of three-fifths of the members present at such meeting shall be necessary,) any pecuniary penalty is imposed for the breach of any rule or bye-law of the society, such penalty, when accrued, may be recovered in any Court having jurisdiction where the defendant shall reside, or the society shall be situate, as the governing body thereof shall deem expedient."

The fifth privilege is that the certificate of the incorporation of the association given by the Registrar, "is conclusive evidence that all requisitions of this Act in respect of registration have been complied with." (S. 41.)

The sixth privilege is that the register of members kept by the association is "*prima facie* evidence of any matters by this Act directed or authorized to be inserted therein." (S. 60.)

The seventh is that the minutes of the resolutions and proceedings of its general meetings and of its managing committee, "if purporting to be signed by the Chairman of the meeting at which such resolutions were passed or proceedings had, or by the Chairman of the next succeeding meeting, shall be received as evidence in all legal proceedings." (S. 92.)

Lastly, the association has the privilege of modifying its articles. The regulations in the articles may be altered in general meeting (of which notice specifying the intention to propose a "special resolution" has been duly given) by passing such "special resolution, *i. e.* a resolution passed by a majority of not less than three-fourths of such members entitled to vote as may be present in person or by proxy (in cases where by the regulations proxies are allowed,) and confirmed by a majority of such members entitled to vote as may be present in person or by proxy, at a subsequent general meeting of which notice has been duly given, and held at an interval of not less than 14 days nor more than one month from the date of the meeting at which such resolution was first passed. A poll may be demanded, and in computing the majority when a poll is demanded, reference shall be had to the number of votes to which each member is entitled by the regulations of the Association. A printed copy of the special resolution would have to be forwarded to the Registrar within 15 days from the date of its confirmation (SS. 76,77,79.)

"Any regulations so made by special resolution shall be deemed to be regulations of the Company (or Association) of the same validity as if they had been originally contained in the articles of association, and shall be subject in like manner to be altered or modified by any subsequent special resolution." (S. 76.)

We now come to the obligations of the Association. These are :—

(1.) To forward a copy of the memorandum of association, having annexed thereto the articles of association to every member, *at his request*, on payment of such sum not exceeding one rupee as may be prescribed by the Association (S. 42.)

(2.) To keep a register of members in which the following particulars shall be entered :—

(*a.*) The names and addresses and the occupations, if any, of the members of the association.

(*b.*) The date at which the name of any person was entered in the register as a member.

(*c.*) The date at which any member ceased to be a member. (S. 47.)

(3.) At the registered office of the association, to keep the register of members "open to the inspection of any member gratis, and to the inspection of any other person on the payment of one rupee, or such less sum as the association may prescribe, for each inspection." The inspection to be allowed "during business hours," but subject to such reasonable restrictions as the association in general meeting may impose, "so that not less than 2 hours in each day be appointed for inspection." The association, however, may upon giving notice by advertisement in some newspaper circulating in the district in which its registered office is situate, and in the local official Gazette, close the register of members for any time or times not exceeding in the whole 30 days in each year. (SS. 55,56.)

(4.) To grant copies of the register or any part thereof, "on payment of two annas for every hundred words required to be copied." (S. 55.)

(5.) To be subject to the process of "the principal court of original civil jurisdiction in the district or place in which the registered office............is situate," in all matters affecting the rectification of the register of members. The Civil Court will only exercise its jurisdiction if an application is made to it by the aggrieved person, and such application may be made "if the name of any person is fraudulently or without sufficient cause entered in, or omitted from, the register of members............or if default is made, or unnecessary delay takes place, in entering on the register the fact of any person having ceased to be a member." (S. 58.)

(6.) To be liable to contribute to the assets under certain conditions. The liability of the members of the Association may be limited to such amount as the members may respectively undertake by the memorandum of association to contribute to the assets of the Association in the event of its being wound up (S. 7.) But no past member shall be liable to contribute to the assets if he has ceased to be a member for a period of one year or upwards prior to the commencement of the winding up, or unless it appears to the Court that the existing members are unable to satisfy the contributions required to be made by them in pursuance of the Act. No past member shall be liable to contribute in respect of any debt or liability of the Association contracted after the time at which he ceased to be a member (S. 61.)

(7.) To keep a registered office and to give notice of its situation to the Registrar (Sec. 63.)

(8.) To be bound by contracts entered into according to law by "any person acting under the express or implied authority" of the Association. (Sec. 67.)

(9.) To convene a general meeting of the Association within six months after the memorandum of association is registered (S. 75,) and "once at least every year" (S. 74.)

(10.) To make out and file with the Registrar within twelve months after registration, and once at least in every year afterwards, a balance-sheet containing a summary of the property and liabilities of the Association, after it is audited and laid before the general meeting. (S. 74.)

(11.) To have the accounts examined and the correctness of the balance-sheet certified by one or more auditor or auditors "once at least every year" (S. 74.)

(12.) To produce books and documents before, and to submit to an examination into its affairs by, a government inspector. Such an inspector can only be appointed upon the application of not less than one-fifth of the whole number of members, supported by such evidence as the Local Government may require for the purpose of showing that the applicants have good reason for requiring such investigation to be made, and that they are not actuated by malicious motives in instituting the same (SS. 83, 84.)

(13.) To cause minutes of all resolutions and proceedings of general meetings and of the managers of the Association to be duly entered in books to be provided for the purpose. (S. 92.)

It will thus be seen that an association formed under S. 26, of Act VI. of 1882, enjoys several important advantages—while the duties imposed on it are either such as are usually discharged or such as ensure the regular conduct of business.

III.

The Hindu Social Reform Association in Sind at first applied for the amendment of Act XXI. of 1860—and on their memorial the following resolution was passed.

"HINDU SOCIAL REFORM ASSOCIATION IN SIND."

No. 3765.

GENERAL DEPARTMENT.

Bombay Castle, *23rd October* 1886.

Letter from the Officiating Secretary to the Government of India, Home Department, Public, No. 1628. dated 8th October :—

"I am directed to acknowledge the receipt of your letter No. 372, dated the 29th January 1886, forwarding a memorandum from the Commissioner in Sind with a memorial to the address of His Excellency the Viceroy from the 'Hindu Social Reform Association, Sind,' in which the association prays for the amendment of Act XXI. of 1880 (an Act for the Registration of Literary, Scientific and Charitable Societies) so as to place that body on the same footing as charitable and other associations under the Act. For this purpose the memorialists are advised that it will be only necessary to amend the preamble and Section 20 of the Act by the addition of the words 'social reform.' The objects the memorialists have in view are stated to be 'to put an end in their community to the early marriage and early widowhood of girls, and at the same time to do away with the ruinous marriage expenses now incurred by fathers of female children.'

"2. In reply I am to say that, on a recent examination of the provisions of Act XXI. of 1860, it was found that they were defective in many respects, and that if the Act is to be amended it will probably require to be thoroughly examined and extensively altered. For such an extensive revision the present time is not opportune. I am, however, to point out that a more convenient mode of incorporating public bodies has since been provided by Section 26 of the Indian Companies Act VI. of 1882, and that numerous clubs and other societies formed for objects not unlike those contemplated by the Hindu Social Reform Association of Sind have been incorporated under the corresponding section of the English Companies Act. I am accordingly to suggest for the consideration of His Excellency the Governor of Bombay in Council whether the provisions of of the Indian Companies Act VI. of 1882 might not be made available in the present case, the necessity for the amendment of Act XXI. of 1860 being thus avoided."

Resolution.—Copy of the letter from the Government of India should be forwarded to the Commissioner in Sind, with reference to his memorandum No. 13, dated 7th January last, for communication to the Hindu Social Reform Association in Sind, and with a request that the views of the Association may be obtained on the suggestion made by the Government of India and reported to Government.

J. DE. C. ATKINS,

Under Secretary to Government."

On examining Act. VI. of 1882, the Association agreed with the Government of India that this enactment provided "a more convenient mode of incorporating public bodies," and acted accordingly.

The following memorandum and articles bore 230 signatures, mostly of heads of families, when sent to Government. Many more signatures will be given if the workers do their duty.

MEMORANDUM OF ASSOCIATION.

1. The name of the Association is "The Hindu Social Reform Association."

2. The Registered office of the Association will be situate in Hyderabad Sind.

3. The objects for which the Association is established are :—

(1.) The prevention of premature marriages.

(2.) The reduction of marriage expenses.

(3.) The promotion of female education, and the improvement of the status of woman.

(4.) The doing all such other lawful things as are incidental or conducive to the attainment of the above objects.

4. The income and property of the Association whencesoever derived shall be applied solely towards the promotion of the objects of the Association as set forth in this Memorandum of Association, and no portion thereof shall be paid or transferred directly or indirectly by way of dividend, bonus, or otherwise howsoever, by way of profit to the members of the Association.

Provided that nothing herein shall prevent the payment, in good faith, of remuneration to any officers or servants of the Association or to any member of the Association or other person, in return for any services actually rendered to the Association.

5. If any member of the Association pays or receives any dividend, bonus, or other profit in contravention of the terms of the 4th paragraph of this Memorandum, his liability shall be unlimited.

6. Every member of this Association undertakes to contribute to the assets of the Association, in the event of the same being wound up during the time that he is a member, or within one year afterwards, for payment of the debts and liabilities of the Association contracted before the term at which he ceases to be a member, and of the costs, charges and expenses of winding up the same, and for the adjustment of the rights of the contributories amongst themselves, such amount as may be required not exceeding Rs. 10 or, in case of his liability becoming unlimited, such other amount as may be required in pursuance of the last preceding paragraph of this Memorandum.

7. If, upon the winding up or dissolution of the Association there remains, after the satisfaction of all its debts and liabilities, any property whatsoever, the same shall not be paid to or distributed among the members of the Association, but shall be given or transferred to some other institution or institutions having objects similar to the objects of the Association, to be determined by the members of the Association at or before the time of dissolution, or in default thereof by such court as may have or acquire jurisdiction in the matter.

8. True accounts shall be kept of the sums of money received and expended by the Association, and the matters in respect of which such receipts and expenditure take place and of the property, credits and liabilities of the Association, and subject to any reasonable restrictions as to the time and manner of inspecting the same that may be imposed in accordance with the regulations of the Association for the time being, shall be open to the inspection of the members. Once at least every year the accounts of the Association shall be examined, and the correctness of the balance-sheet ascertained by one or more properly qualified Auditor or Auditors.

We, the several persons whose names and addresses are subscribed, are desirous of being formed into an Association in pursuance of this Memorandum of Association.

Names, addresses and descriptions of subscribers.

ARTICLES OF ASSOCIATION.

1. For the purposes of registration, the number of the members of the Association is declared to be unlimited.

2. These articles shall be construed with reference to the provisions of the Companies Act VI. of 1882, and terms used in these articles shall be taken as having the same respective meanings as they have when used in that Act.

3. The Association is established for the purposes expressed in the Memorandum of Association.

4. There shall be four divisions of members.*

Qualifications of Members.

The first division shall consist of those persons who agree :—

(1.) Not to marry their sons, or any other male relations under their control or guardianship, below the age of 16, and in each case of breach by them hereafter of such agreement, to pay to the Association a sum of Rs. 500 or any less sum adjudged by the division after giving such persons an opportunity of being heard in their defence.

(2.) Not to take from the family of any bride whom any of their sons or such other relation shall marry, any marriage or other presents in excess of any scale that may be laid down by the first division of members and, in each case of breach by them hereafter of such agreement, to pay to the Association a sum not exceeding double the excess which may be adjudged by the division after giving such opportunity as aforesaid.

(3.) To educate all their female children to the best of their ability and in case of their failure to teach them or to have them taught at least reading and writing and simple arithmetic, to pay to the Association a sum not exceeding Rs. 50 which may be adjudged after giving such opportunity as aforesaid.

(4.) To pay a subscription of not less than 2 annas monthly, or 1 rupee a year in advance.

The second division shall consist of those persons who agree to all the above clauses except the second.

---

* In small castes it will not do to have more than one or two divisions--viz. the division of pledge-takers and at the most honorary members. Even under these articles it is quite within the power of the first division to have no other members at all. (*Vide* articles 5 and 9.)

The third division shall consist of those persons who merely sympathize with the objects of the Association and agree to pay an annual subscription of not less than Rs. 6 or a monthly subscription of not less than 8 annas.

The fourth division shall consist of Honorary Members elected on account of their liberality towards the Association, or for eminent services to the cause of social reform or female education. No Honorary Member shall be bound by the Memorandum of Association or these articles.

None but Hindus of Sind are eligible for the first three divisions, but this limitation does not apply to the fourth division. Members of the first two divisions may become life-members on payment of Rs. 50, and members of the third division may become life-members on payment of Rs. 200, and such life-members will not thereafter be liable to pay any subscription.

Admission of Members.

5. All who subscribe these articles of association shall be deemed to have agreed to be members of the first division. All, who, after the registration of these articles, are allowed by the Managing Committee to sign their names in the Register of members of the first, second or third division shall be deemed to have agreed to become members of these divisions respectively. Honorary Members can only be elected at a General Meeting.

Retirement of Members.

6. Any member of the first or second division can retire at any time on payment to the Association of Rs. 500, or any lesser sum that may, after an opportunity has been given him of being heard, be adjudged by the division of which he is a member. Any member of the third division can retire at any time after payment of any arrears of subscriptions due.

An Honorary Member may retire at any time.

7. Every member shall have the right to use the Association's property in common with other members, and to receive, free of charge, such of the publications of the Association as the Association may determine to distribute gratis among the members.

Rights of Members.

8. The General body shall elect one of their members as Honorary Secretary, and it may appoint such Secretary as Treasurer or elect any other member as Treasurer. The General body shall also elect an Auditor or Auditors for the ensuing year.

Appointment of office-bearers.

The Managing Committee shall, subject to the approval of the General body, appoint a Stipendiary Secretary who shall work under the control of the Honorary Secretary, and it shall appoint, subject to the approval of the same body, such other persons as may be necessary to carry out the objects of the Association.

9. The subscribers to the Memorandum of Association shall determine who and how many shall be members of the first Managing Committee, provided that, until the Managing Committee is appointed, the said subscribers shall be deemed to be such Committee.

Management of the Association.

Every Managing Committee shall hold office for one year, but the members shall be re-eligible.

Every subsequent Managing Committee after the first, shall be elected at the Annual General Meeting of the Association out of the members of the first two divisions, and shall consist of as many members as the Association may think fit.

10. The business of the Association shall be managed by the Managing Committee for the time being under the control of the Association.

The Committee shall carry out all resolutions passed at any General Meeting of the Association or any meeting of a division.

Powers of the Managing Committee.

11. A General Meeting of the Members shall be held about every Christmas, in every year, for the purpose of receiving, discussing and approving the report of the Committee, electing a Committee, Honorary Secretary, Treasurer, and Auditor, for the ensuing year and also for electing Honorary Members, and transacting the general business of the Association. At General Meetings only those who are members of the Association and who have paid up all money due from them to the Association shall be allowed to vote or, except by permission of the Chairman, to address the Meeting.

Meetings, Proceedings &c.

Votes may be given by proxy at General, Divisional, or Committee Meetings, provided that the proxy is a member and has been appointed in writing. The Committee or any 7 members of the Association shall have power, through the Honorary Secretary, and in his absence through the Stipendiary Secretary, to convene a Special General Meeting or a meeting of a division.

The Managing Committee shall meet as often as it likes and may be specially convened by the Honorary Secretary and in his absence by the Stipendiary Secretary.

No business shall be transacted at any General or Divisional Meeting or at any Committee Meeting, unless a quorum of members is present.

In the case of General Meetings such quorum shall consist of not less than one-third of all the members of the Association, and in the case of Divisional or Committee Meetings of not less than one-half the members of the Division or the Committee, as the case may be; provided that no meeting can be held for the purpose of prescribing a scale of marriage and other presents unless three-fourths of the Registered members of the first division are present and no such scale can be laid down unless it is approved by a majority of three-fourths of the members present.

If there is no quorum, the meeting shall be adjourned and fresh notice of the adjourned meeting shall be given to all who were absent. At such adjourned meeting the business specified in the notice of the first meeting, but no other, shall be transacted even though there is no quorum.

The Managing Committee shall choose its own Chairman, and every General or Divisional Meeting shall choose its own Chairman.

Every Chairman shall have a second or casting vote in case of equality of votes.

Accounts, Audit &c.

12. The accounts of the Association's income and disbursements shall be kept by the Stipendiary Secretary, under the control and supervision of the Honorary Secretary and the Managing Committee, and shall be audited at least once a year.

13. The Committee shall have power of calling public meetings at such times and places as they may approve, for the promotion of the interests of the Association, and to invite the co-operation of any suitable persons, but such meetings shall have no power over the regulations or proceedings or funds of the Association.

Affiliation.

14. The Committee shall have also the power to connect with this Association any Association formed for the purpose of carrying the same objects into effect, and to give pecuniary or other aid to such Associations, although the funds raised by the latter may be devoted to local efforts, and be under separate control.

Suits.

15. The Association may sue and be sued in the name of its Honorary Secretary, and in the absence of such Secretary in the name of its Stipendiary Secretary.

Names, addresses and descriptions of subscribers.

An association on similar lines has been formed at Ahmedabad. Its distinctive features will appear from the following extracts—the first (A) from the Memorandum, and the second (B) from the Articles:—

A. 3 The objects for which the Association is established are:—

(1.) The prevention of premature marriages, specially by taking legally enforceable pledges from parents and guardians, and by persuading castes and sub-castes which can dine together to allow intermarriage.

(2.) The improvement of the status of woman, specially by discouraging Asura marriages, and male bigamy, in castes which practise either.

(3.) The doing all such other lawful things as are incidental or conducive to the attainment of the above objects.

Qualifications of members.

B. 4. There shall be three divisions of members, consisting respectively of persons who agree to adopt any of the following three limits of marriageable age, *viz.*, (1) 18 for boys and 14 for girls; (2) 16 for boys and 12 for girls; (3) 16 for boys and 10 for girls.

Every one of such persons must further agree not to marry his sons or daughters, or any other male or female relations under his control or guardianship, respectively, below the limit of age adopted by him, and in each case of breach by him, hereafter, of such agreement to pay to the Association a sum of Rs. 200, or any less sum adjudged by his division (or by any committee to which this power of adjudication may be, generally or specially, delegated by his division, or by the Association on behalf of all the divisions) after giving him an opportunity of being heard in his defence.

The minimum subscription payable by each member is eight annas a year.

Donors of Rs. 25 need pay no subscription.

Honorary Members may only be elected on account of their liberality towards the Association, or for eminent services to the cause of social reform or female education. No Honorary Member shall be bound by the Memorandum of Association or these Articles.

5. All who sign the following printed form in duplicate shall be deemed members respectively of the divisions chosen by them, and shall be registered as such by the Secretary under the control of the Managing Committee. The Secretary, under the control of the said Committee, may for recorded reasons forego the subscription in any case.

FORM.

I...... of ...... caste living at ...... after understanding the Memorandum and Articles of the Gujarat Hindu Social Reform Association hereby agree to become a member of the ...... Division.

Honorary Members can only be elected at a General Meeting.

APPENDIX III.

THE INDIAN LAW REGARDING THE SEDUCTION OF GIRLS—A CRYING INEQUALITY.

I have read the English Criminal Law Amendment Act, and I ask the Government most earnestly to contrast its provisions with those in our Penal Code on this subject. I put them here side by side.

How girls are protected by the Indian Penal Code.	*How they are protected by the English Criminal Law Amendment Act.*
1. A husband having intercourse with his wife who is *under ten* years of age, *with or without her consent*, is punishable with transportation for life. (Sec. 376.)	1. He is punishable with penal servitude for life.
2. A husband having intercourse with his wife who is *ten years old, with or without her consent*, is not punishable at all. The law in the most explicit language declares that this is not *rape*. (Sec. 375.)	*He is punishable with penal servitude for life.*
3. Any person other than a husband, having intercourse with a girl who is *ten years* old, *with her consent*, is not punishable.	*He is punishable with penal servitude for life.*

4. A girl under twelve years of age is not competent to consent to the commission of any offence upon her, or in respect of her, except that of rape or seduction. (Secs. 90 and 375.)	Any one having intercourse with a girl *under thirteen* years of age, *with or without her consent*, is punishable with penal servitude for life.
	Any one having intercourse with a girl *over thirteen* and *under sixteen* years of age, *with or without her consent*, is punishable with ten years' rigorous imprisonment.

Let the public, and the authorities, look upon this picture and upon that. Can there be any justification for such glaring divergencies and inequalities? In three out of these four cases, what is an offence in England—an offence punishable with penal servitude for life—is not an offence in India. The question affects not only us Natives, but Englishmen also. It is the Penal Code that governs them here, and not the Criminal Law Amendment Act. An English girl, ten years old, has not in India that protection which her sister under sixteen enjoys in England. Can there be a better reason for the reform of the law? And does not this show that it is the interest of every publicist, Anglo-Indian and Native, to protest against this shameful inequality?

II.

As the public may wish to have the *ipsissima verba* of our code, I quote those portions of it which relate to our subject.

We are first warned in Sec. 90, that "a consent is not such a consent as is intended by any Section of this code...... if the consent is given by a person who, from unsoundness of mind or intoxication, is unable to understand the nature and consequences of that to which he gives his consent; or, *unless the contrary appears from the context*, if the consent is given by a person who is under twelve years of age". Let us now turn to the context of Section 375:—"A man is said to commit 'rape' who, except in the case hereinafter excepted, has sexual intercourse with a woman under circumstances falling under any of the five following descriptions:—

Firstly.—Against her will.

Secondly.—Without her consent.

* * * * * *

Fifthly.—With or without her consent when she is under ten years of age.

Exception.—Sexual intercourse by a man with his own wife, the wife not being under ten years of age, is not rape."

This Section, therefore, lays down that if a girl is under ten her consent to her seduction is immaterial, while without this Section, Section 90 would make such consent immaterial in the case of a girl under twelve. Section 375, therefore, is contrary to Section 90, and so, it has been construed by that eminent commentator, Mr. Mayne.

Now, mark the absurdities:—"Whoever intentionally uses force to any person, without that person's *consent*, in order to the committing of an offence, or intending by the use of such force to cause, or knowing it to be likely that by the use of such force he will cause injury, fear, or annoyance to the person to whom the force is used, is said to 'use criminal force' to that other" and is punishable with three months' imprisonment. (Sec. 350 and 352.)

"Whoever assaults or uses *criminal force* to any woman, intending to outrage, or knowing it to be likely that he will thereby outrage her modesty, shall be punished with imprisonment of either description (rigorous or simple), which may extend to two years, or with fine, or with both." (Sec. 354.)

The maximum punishment for rape is ten years' imprisonment (Sec. 376) or ten years' transportation (Sec. 59). To such a serious offence, a girl ten years old is supposed capable of consenting, but not to petty criminal force or an indecent assault. If she consent to the latter, the law nevertheless rigorously enjoins that her consent is not a valid consent, and that the offence committed against her is in spite of it an offence. But if she consent to sexual intercourse—why, that consent is valid. The difference between her husband and any other person is simply this, that while the former is safe, whether she consents or not, the latter is not safe, unless she consents or is willing. But in the case of criminal force or an indecent assaualt, even a girl under twelve, and not merely a girl under ten, is supposed incompetent to give a valid consent. Is not this a most unjustifiable anomaly? Surely rape is a more heinous crime than criminal force or an attempt to outrage the modesty of a girl. Why, then, this pernicious distinction? Notice that the Penal Code holds out an indemnity, not only to the husband, but to others. The exception in favour of a husband is to a rule which is itself an exception to the general law laid down in Sec. 90. That general law prohibits us from taking a single ornament off a girl's person, even with her consent, if she is under twelve (Sec. 378). That general law prohibits us from conveying a girl of this age beyond the limits of British India, even if she consents. That general law punishes the least touch of her garments, the least contact with her person as criminal force, even if she consents (Secs. 349, 350 and 352). But the exception to this general law lays down that a girl, not under ten, is game to any one for sexual intercourse if she consents, and a further exception to this exception lays down that she is game to her husband, even if she does not consent. Is not this, then, fearful and shameful? I challenge any one to come forward to defend it. The truth is that at the time the Penal Code was framed, the English law was in a most unsatisfactory state. The English jurists held that mere physical consent was sufficient, that even though the woman was an idiot still if she consented from mere animal instinct, the offence of rape was not committed (Reg. *vs.* Fletcher). The Indian law was an advance upon this barbarous principle. It protected idiots, and even intoxicated women, from violation, but, curiously enough, while it placed girls and boys not twelve years old on the same footing as idiots and intoxicated persons in all other respects, so far as competency to consent was concerned, it allowed the former to be violated with impunity. The English law treated consent as a very simple fact, and held that "the consent even of a child under ten years of age to what otherwise would be an indecent assault, prevented the act being indictable" (Reg. *vs.* Johnson). Our Indian legislators were of a different opinion. They thought a child under ten was not competent to consent to such an act, and so they ruled it, but they were not prepared to make a greater advance upon the English law. Now that the English law itself has made a far more momentous advance than our Indian legislators ever dreamt of, it is time, I submit, for us to bring our code in harmony with the exigencies of society and the greater perfection of the English law. I am sure Lord Macaulay and his co-adjutors would be the first to move an amendment of Sec. 375, were they now living. I am sure they would now concede that they had stopped too short—that they had been content with making a very small improvement in the English law so far as children were concerned, though they had provided a thousand times better safeguards for unsound persons than any to be found in that law. Let the present Legal Member do the work left undone by them. Let him recognize the fact that a girl under 12 in India is really and truly as unable "to understand the nature and consquences" of seduction as a girl under 16 has been by law declared to be in England. Let him recognize the injustice of allowing her to give away her most precious possession—a possession dearer to her than riches or any earthly thing. The law punishes the thief of her jewels, even if she consent to the theft, but it lets go scot-free the thief of that priceless jewel of woman, her chastity, her honour, if she is just ten years old, and consents to the deprivation. Does she understand the nature and consequences of this larceny better than that of the former? Has she more education than an English girl of fifteen? If not, then why, in Heaven's name, should this absurd ungodly distinction disgrace our Penal Code any longer? We do not ask for special legislation. We simply confine ourselves to a most temperate, a most reasonable demand. We want the exception and the further exception to the exception in Sec. 375 to be done away with. We want no more for the present; and Heaven forbid that we should have occasion to ask for more at any future time!

III.

Our Legislature lays down:—"You shall not take or entice any boy under 14 years, or any girl under 16 years, out of the keeping of his or her lawful guardian, without such guardian's consent" no matter whether the boy or the girl consents or not (Sec. 361). Why this distinction? If so far as kidnapping is concerned, a girl is not supposed to be able to take care of herself before she is sixteen, while a boy is held to be so able when he is fourteen, why should the former be supposed capable of consenting at the age of 10 to an act which means her physical prostration and the ruin of her frame, while the latter is completely protected? May I ask if girls require less protection than boys? Who can doubt that they require one thousand times more protection? Nay, even the Legislature admits this in the case of kidnapping. I confess, I cannot for the life of me understand why a girl should be supposed thoroughly competent at the age of ten to dispose of her most valuable possesstion, while a boy under 12 is considered completely incapable of giving any valid consent to the transfer even of his jacket, or his boots, or his drawers. Will the Government redress this crying inequality? Why should there be an exception in the case of girls? Is it because they come to maturity earlier than boys? If so, then why raise the age of consent in their case to 16, and that of boy only to 14 so far as kidnapping is concerned? Besides, does any Indian girl reach maturity at ten? "With respect to offences upon girls," says Mr. Mayne, "the Legislature seems to assume that they come to maturity two years earlier here than in Europe." Let the age of consent, therefore, be fixed if you like at two years earlier than in England. According to Dr. Chevers, females in India begin to menstruate after the twelfth year, or at the beginning of the thirteenth......Menstruation at ten years is very uncommon, and probably does not occur in more than one or two instances out of a hundred females. It is equally rare that it should be delayed beyond the thirteenth year (p. 461 of Chevers' Medical Jurisprudence for India). "Perhaps in this country," says Taylor, talking of England "the most frequent age for the commencement of menstruation may be taken at 15 years. It is liable to be accelerated in its appearance by certain moral and physical conditions under which a female may be placed." The value of the revelations made by the *Pall Mall Gazette* consists in proving conclusively that girls even at the age of 15 do not understand the consequences of seduction. Here in India, it may be said with as great positiveness, that the child-wives under 12 hardly understand the consequences of sexual intercourse at such tender age. "Before the 14th August," it has been said "it is a crime to shoot grouse, lest an immature bird should not yet have a fair chance to fly. The sportsman, who wishes to follow the partridge through the stubbles, must wait till September 1, and the close time for pheasants is still later. Admitting that women are as fair game as grouse and partridges, why not let us have a close time for bipeds in petticoats as well as as for bipeds in feathers? ......Fish out of season are not fit to be eaten. ....The law ought at least to be as strict about a live child as about a dead salmon."

Our Penal Code in this matter was based more or less on the English law. The amendment proposed will be welcomed by the whole of India. No one dare come forward and say that girls should be allowed to be outraged when under twelve. Such a brutal act would undoubtedly be an outrage, a violation; and yet the law does not punish it. It may be said, no gross cases have been brought to our notice of such outrages. But how can they be? There is no *Pall Mall Gazette* among our vernacular papers. Instances, however, are not wanting.* But I say if one single instance can take place of such an outrage under the present law, the law ought to be amended. There may be only 12 murders committed in a province during the year—there may be only one case of rape—there may be no case of an unnatural offence—and yet the law provides punishments for all these. Does it not? Why, then, should it leave girls under 12 unprotected?

APPENDIX IV.

SOCIAL REFORM IN RAJPUTANA.

Early in March last was held at Ajmere a meeting of Sardars, Officials and Charans from all parts of Rajputana, for the purpose of adopting some rules for regulating the expenditure on marriage and funeral ceremonies among the Rajputs. It seems that Colonel C. K. M. Walter, Agent to the Governor-General for Rajputana, has been interesting himself very actively in the cause of social reform in Rajputana, and that the meeting at Ajmere in March last was a result of his long continued labours in that direction. We are enabled, through the kindness of a friend, to reproduce the rules and regulations

* I have had myself to try at least two cases which arose from the unwillingness of the child-wife to surrender her person to her husband. In the first the charge against the husband was of causing her grievous hurt. She had tried to run away from him to her parents, and he had pursued her and thrown her down and cut off the tip of her nose. In the other case the child-wife, to be rid of her nocturnal tortures, had plucked some Dhatura and put it in the rice cooked by her for her husband. The husband was anxious to have her back, and prayed for a nominal sentence.

agreed to by the Conference at Ajmere. These rules and regulations have been signed by about forty delegates from the different States of Rajputana. Among the signatories are to be found several Thakurs, Sardars and Charans. It was these rules and regulations which formed the subject of conversation in the House of Lords some time ago when Lord Northbrook, Lord Kimberley, the Bishop of Carlisle, and Lord Cross, the present Secretary of State for India, passed the highest eulogiums on the Rajput Princes and on Colonel Walter for the reform they have inaugurated throughout Rajputana. According to the London correspondent of the TIMES OF INDIA, Lord Cross is reported to have said that "it was the greatest advance made in the present century and might lead to changes which no man living could foresee." With these brief preliminary observations we give below the rules and regulations adopted at Ajmere in March last:—

All the Sirdars of the various States of Rajputana assembled at Ajmere, for the purpose of discussing arrangements for regulating the expenses incurred on the occasion of marriages, deaths, &c., having come to an unanimous decision. the following observances have been prescribed and will be binding on Rajputs of all ranks, except ruling chiefs :—

1. If the marriage is that of the Thakur himself, or an eldest son, or a daughter, the amount to be expended is fixed as under :—

When the value of the Estate is above Rs. 20,000, not more than ¼ of the annual income.

When rental is below Rs. 20,000, but not less than Rs. 10,000, not more than ⅓ of the annual income.

When the rental is below Rs. 10,000, but not less than Rs. 1,000, not more than ½ of the annual income.

When the income is below Rs. 1,000, not more than ⅔rds. of the annual income.

The above limits are in no case to be exceeded, but any body can spend less if he likes.

Note—In many Estates there is a rekh rating, while others are held on a fixed payment, according to which the rental is estimated. Sometimes the revenue does not correspond with the assessment, while in certain Estates no assessment has been made. When a rekh settlement obtains, or the rate has been fixed, and the collections accord with the rate of assessment, the income thus derived will be the basis for calculating the sum to be expended on marriage expenses. But if the collections fall short of the assessment, or there be no assessment at all, then the actual realizations will be taken into account.

2. Disputes arise regarding the gifts, which the girl's father sends to the father of her intended husband, the latter wishing to have the value increased, while the former is desirous of decreasing it. This controversy besides delaying the conclusion of the engagement, gives rise to other evils. It is therefore proper that the sending of 'teeka' (engagement presents) should be altogether stopped.

The customary presents of opium, betel leaves, &c., which are now sent on the occasion of the betrothal may continue, but the engagement itself should be arranged for by letter only.

3. Of the sum to be spent on 'tyag' under rule 1, Rs. 9, local currency per cent., on the annual income of the Estate, equivalent to Rs. 6-12-0, British currency, will be distributed as at present, by the father of the bridegroom, among the Charans, Raos, Dholis, &c., in the proportions fixed by the custom obtaining in each State. The share of this payment which the Dholis receive is inclusive of the amount given on account of 'Ghurcharhi.' Except the above percentage, the fathers of the young couple will not give any other item to Charans, Raos, and Dholis, on account of marriage.

4. Persons who hold property valued at less than Rs, 500 will pay nothing. When property is worth from Rs. 500 to 1,000, the amount to be given as 'tyag' or present to Charans, &c., will be half that specified in Rule 3, viz. Rs. 4½ local currency, or Rs. 3-6-0, Imperial rupees per cent.

5. A list will be made of the Charans, Raos, Dholis, &c., attending the celebrations; and the day after the completion of the

marriage rite, they will be paid their shares, and dismissed to their homes.

6. Only the Charans, Raos, Dholis &c., who are residents of the territory in which the marriage takes place, are entitled to the receipt of presents. Those of foreign territory are forbidden to come. Only the father of the bridegroom will make the payment; the father of the bride is liable for nothing.

7. In the case of the marriage of sons other than the eldest, and of brothers of the Thakur, who are dependent for support on the latter, the expenditure will be one-tenth of that specified in Rule 1, and the amount to be distributed as 'tyag,' one rupee local currency per cent. on the income of the Estate.

8. If sons and brothers are allowed separate maintenance, the expense will be calculated on what the Estate allows them, according to the usual proportions above fixed.

9. The scale of 'tyag' set forth in the preceding rules applies to a first marriage only. If a second or third marriage be contracted, the payment will be at the rate of Rs. 2 local currency per cent. when the income exceeds Rs. 5,000; when the income is less than Rs. 5,000 no 'tyag' will be distributed on the occasion of a second or third marriage, while in the case of a younger son or brother no 'tyag' will be disbursed if the marriage is other than the first, when as already settled, 1 per cent. will be distributed as 'tyag' on a second or third marriage, the eldest son only will be liable for 'tyag' according to the rate above stated.

10. The above rules settle what may be paid, but it must be understood that in the capital of the State itself no Sirdar is at liberty to distribute 'tyag.'

11. 'Tyag' will be distributed strictly in accordance with the scale laid down; no enhancement or reduction should be made. But, if some people, regardless of their reputation have never given 'tyag' they need not do so in future. Such people have not hitherto been taken to task by the State, nor will any claim lie agains- them hereafter,

12. The amount of presents fixed should be accepted with thanks and distributed before witnesses. The recipients should not

go to foreign territory, nor should they (if disappointed) use abusive language. Charans, Raos, Dholis, &c., should be guided by the intention of the rules, which have been drawn up, and each State should see that this is enforced.

13. Five years hence a Committee will assemble to reconsider the rules, which have been now fixed to regulate marriage expenses and the distribution of presents, and after another interval of five years, a similar Committee will be convened to report on the advantages or drawbacks of the arrangements.

14. In every State a Committee will be appointed, consisting of a Sirdar, an official, and a member of the Charan and Rao castes, or with such modifications in the constitution as the Durbar may be in favour of. It will be the duty of this committee to make arrangements for carrying out the regulations, regarding the expenditure to be incurred on marriages and deaths and on 'tyag,' as well as the other instructions embodied in these rules. When a marriage is to be celebrated one month's previous notice will be given by the head of the Estate concerned to this Committee, which will be required to see that the regulations prescribed are confirmed to. The Committee will be empowered to permit at their direction the attendance of those of their territory who are priviledged to be present or to make such other arrangements as they may deem expedient. The provisions of Rule 5 will remain in force for two years, after which it will be considered whether it is better to disburse the 'tyag' to the assembled Charans &c., or to have the money remitted to the Committee for distribution.

15. The father of some girls owing to their not possessing the means, obtain the necessary funds for their daughters' marriage from the bridegrooms' fathers. This is a most objectionable practice, and one that is opposed to the Dharam-Shasters. Many fathers, although without adequate means shun such impropriety and adjust the marriage expenses to their present circumstances. There are others again, who have neither land nor maintenance, are practically without any means, and only earn a daily livelihood as cultivators. If such

as these who elect to do so, take Rs. 100 and spend the lot on the marriage it matters little, but no greater sum should be taken, and they should as far as possible strive not to take anything. Should it be proved that the girl's father accepts, or the boy's father gives any sum contrary to this rule, the delinquents will be suitably punished.

16. As a rule boys and girls are married at an early age, notwithstanding that the evils of such a custom are well known to all and need no description. In inviting attention to the subject, it seems proper to lay down, that boys and girls should not be married before the age of 18 and 14 respectively.

Note.—As regards engagements concluded before this date, the marriage can take place, as soon as the girl complete 14 years, irrespective of the boy's age.

17. When a widower has attained the age of 45 years, and has a son living, he should not contract another marriage.

18. The expenses on the occasion of death will be on the following scale:—

When the value of the property owned is less than Rs. 1,000 $\frac{2}{3}$rds of income.

When the property is worth from Rs. 1,000 to 5,000 $\frac{1}{4}$ income.
Do. do. Rs. 5,000 to 10,000 ... ... $\frac{1}{4}$ „
Above Rs. 10,000 ... ... $\frac{1}{8}$

Less than the above proportions may be spent, but never more.

Note—The above rule fixes the expenses to be incurred on the occasions of deaths, but each State will make suitable arrangements for regulating other matters connected with the ceremonies.

19. The sums to be expended on marriages and deaths have been set forth above, but should the proportion which has been fixed, calculated on the value of the property, yield a very insignificant sum, or if there be no property, then notwithstanding what is contained in the preceding rules, the party concerned is at liberty to spend up to a limit of Rs. 100 on a marriage, and of Rs. 75 on a death.

20. Besides the Committee in each State, the premier Sirdar of each clan will superintend the arrangements for giving effect to these regulations.

21. It is very necessary that the rules should be given the widest publicity. To this end each State might have copies printed off, and distributed amongst all classes of Nobles, Jagirdars, and others. It would also be advisable to circulate copies among the officials.

22. As there are no Charans in Kerowlee, those from the adjoining State of Jeypore and Ulwar can go there as heretofore. The Kerowlee Motmid has agreed to this.

Dated the 10*th March* 1888.

SIGNATURES.

Fatteh Singh, Jagirdar of Dilwara, for Meywar.
Kavi Raj Shyamal Das for Meywar.
Bahadur Singh fer Bikanir.
Seth Nemi Chand do.
Rai Behari Pal of Kerauli.
Jewan Rao do.
Thakur Esri Singh do.
Gordhan Pandit of Kishengarh.
Rathor Bharut Singh do.
Barat Karni Dan do.
Kunwar Sher Singh of Kuchawan for Marwar.
Kavi Raj Murar Dan for Marwar.
Rajawat Jeet Singh for Jhalawar.
Sunder Lall do.
Kavi Raj Sheodan for Jeysulmere.
Barote Sheo Bux for Ulwar.
Thakur Biradh Singh do.
Hanwant Singh do.
Har Bux, Charan, for Jeypore.
Raja Ajit Singh of Khetree for Jeypore.
Thakur Gobind Singh, Chomoo, (Jeypore).
Kavi Raj Raghu Dan for Sirohi.

Singhi Poonam Chand Motamid for Sirohi,
Bohra Ratan Lal for Bundi.
Hara Mohkam Singh for Bundi.
Maharaja Hanwant Singh for Bundi.
Girwar Singh for Tonk.
Pertab Singh do.
Maharaja Chaggan Singh for Kotah.
Barote Isar Dan.
Chawand Dan Jawan Dan.
Kirni Dan for Jhallawar,
Mardan Singh for Partabgarh.
Kavi Raj Kesri Singh for Dungarpore.
Mohbat singh ditto.
Mehta Nehal Chand ditto.
Sahivale Urjan Singh for Meywar.
Raja Mangal Singh, C. I. E. of Bhinai (Ajmere).
Barote Biranh Singh for Bhinai.

APPENDIX V.

MEMORANDUM BY RAJA SIR T. MADAVA RAW.

1. According to the census of the year 1881, the num, ber of widows under ten years of age in all India is about 54,000.

2. According to the census of the Madras Presidency, for the year 1881, the number of widows under 10 years of age is about 5,600 in this Presidency.

3. The evil thus stated and the misery it implies are indeed terrible.

4. In this connection attention is earnestly invited to the following remarks from the Madras census report.

"This gives us roughly an estimate of the age at which Brahman girls are married. Some are married before 7 years of age, nearly all are married before 10. The figures suggest that between 6 and 7 is the average age of marriage for females among Brahmans. This has the natural result of a high percentage of widows, and we find that nearly one-third of the Brahman women are widows."

"There are proportionately 50 per cent more widows among Brahmans than among other castes, and this surplus may be wholly attributed to the greater extent to which infant marriages occur among Brahmans than is the case with other castes. Certainly one-third, probably a larger proportion of the number of Brahman widows are widows owing to this custom; that is to say, if Brahmans countenanced infant marriage only to the extent that other castes do, there would be nearly 60.000 fewer unhappy women in their caste. The total figures show that there are 80,000 widows under 20, and the foregoing remarks suggest that Brahman custom is responsible for threefourths of this."—Vol. I. pp. 71, 72.

5. It is evident that the earlier a girl is married, the greater are the chances of virgin widowhood.

6. It is also evident that if girls are married after they have attained 9 or 10 years of age, a vast number of virgin widowhoods will be altogether prevented.

7. It seems, therefore, desirable and necessary to establish some inducement to parents and guardians to delay the marriage of girls until they complete their 9th or 10th year of age.

8. *This much* of delay is quite permissible according to the Sastras and also according to the custom.

9. I do not propose to compel the delay, but, only to create an inducement in its favour, leaving everything else as it, at present, is.

10. The best form of such inducement seems to be a fine for performing the marriage before the fixed limit of age.

11. The fine will, of course, be according to the circumstances of the parties concerned and calculated to produce a deterrent effect.

12. The effect of this arrangement will be to make the parents or guardians delay the marriage up to the age limit if possible, and thereby escape the fine, but if not possible to so delay, then to perform the marriage before that limit and to pay the fine.

13. The effect of this will be to leave the existing order of things as little disturbed as possible and yet to diminish the number of marriages before the age limit, and thereby diminish the number of virgin widowhoods, which will be an important gain.

14. The inquiry into facts precedent to the imposition of fine may be safely left to a local punchayet.

15. The measure proposed will produce good only.

16. Any evil it may involve will be clearly outweighed by the good.

17. I prefer this moderate action to total inaction which I consider culpable in a high degree.

18. I decidly prefer fine to invalidity because the latter would involve the misery of the innocent children and cause deep and extensive popular discontent.

19. The fines should not be appropriated by the State, but applied to some purpose beneficial to virgin widows.

20. I would have two age limits; one for castes under obligation to marry the girl before puberty, and the other for castes at liberty to marry the girls after puberty.

21. More than this measure appears to me impossible at present, less than this measure would be culpable.

22. The friction attendant upon it will be at its minimum.

The List of the foregoing:

1. The longer the married life of a woman, the greater must be the chances of her widowhood.

2. The shorter the married life of a woman, the less the chances of her widowhood.

3. Therefore it is desirable in every possible way to shorten her married life.

4. The only way to shorten her married life is to delay her marriage.

5. Therefore delay the marriage as long as possible under existing rule and custom.

6. It may be delayed accordingly at least up to ten years of age.

7. This period is not inconsiderable in relation to the term of married life.

8. In many cases it may have the proportion of 25 per cent.

9. Therefore, in many cases it may prevent the chances of widowhood in that ratio.

10. Therefore I would create an inducement in favour of that much in delay.

11. The inducement being in the shape of a fine in preference to invalidity.

The best thing of all would be for parents and guardians to voluntarily delay the marriage of girls till the completion of the 10*th year in the case of Brahmans, and longer in the case of non-Brahmans.*

(Signed) RAJA SIR T. MADAVA ROW, K.C. S.I.

MYLAPORE, MADRAS,
10*th August*, 1888.

APPENDIX VI.

SHASTRIC TEXTS ON THE SUBJECT OF INFANT MARRIAGE.

One of the penalties of arrested civilization is that, while stopping further growth, it sows the seeds of decay and death in the paralyzed social organism. The 'stationary' East is one of those popular fallacies which died a very hard death, though killed and exploded a hundred times. It is not possible for a living being, be the unit an individual or a collection of individuals, to remain stationary at any stage of progress achieved, for any considerable time, without, in fact, undergoing the slow process of decay and degradation. The full importance of this fact is not realized, because the span of national life is not, like that of the individual man, easily encompassed within our ordinary vision, and even in ordinary human life, many people imagine that they stand still, when in fact they are sinking in health and vigour, and lapsing into decrepitude and dotage. Perhaps, no better illustration of this great truth can be cited than what is furnished by an historical survey of the changes which have taken place, during centuries of arrested growth, in the social usages regulating the institution of marriage in the Âryan population of this country. Without such a survey of the past, it is not possible to understand intelligently the present, or correctly to forecast or guide the future. The theory of evolution has in this country to be studied in its other aspect of what may conveniently be called devolution. When decay and corruption set in, it is not the fittest and the strongest that survives in the conflict of dead with living matter, but the healthy parts give way, and their place is taken by all that is indicative of the fact that corruption has set in, and the vital force is extinguished.

The study of the morbid symptoms of a nation's decay is no doubt very irksome, but the pain must be endured, and the scruples set aside. The Gordian knot of centuries of involution cannot be cut asunder by any spasmodic violence. The successive stages of slow decay must be closely watched and diagnosed, if we would work out the solution of the difficulty. Fortunately, unlike the individual, the doom of death is not irrevocable as fate in the case of a nation so large as the Âryan population of India, numbering one-sixth of the human race. The process of recovery may be slow, but if we stimulate the stifled seeds of health and growth, and lop off dead excrescences, decay may be arrested, and death averted, successfully. It is this hope which must cheer all those who desire to see the dead bones in the valley heave again with the breath of resurrection, and the sleep of centuries disturbed by the penetrating rays of living light.

It is proposed here to take such a survey of the growth and decay of the Âryan social usages regarding the institution of marriage in this country during historic times, *i.e.*, the times of which we can trace the history in records or institutions or customs. Such a survey presents many stages of growth as also of decay, but it is not proposed to dwell on them all here. It will be enough for the purpose of this introduction to note only two stages: the one stage associated with all that is truly old and venerable, associated, moreover, with all that is best and noblest in our traditions; and the other stage when the civilization which promised so well was arrested in its growth, internal decay set in, and foreign invasions paralyzed all activity, and brought in with them political subjection and social slavery. This distinction of two stages fits in with the orthodox view of looking at these matters. The most orthodox interpreters of our Shâstras admit that the present is separated from the past by a distinctly laid-down land-mark. The Vedic age is separated from the Purânic age, in which Âryan society now lives and moves and has its being. The Shâstris profess veneration for the past, but their allegiance is given not to the venerated Vedic past, but to the more modern transformation represented by the developments of the Purânic period; and owing to a false rule of exegesis, they try to distort the old texts so as to make them fit in with what is hopelessly irreconcileable with them. This desperate attempt must be abandoned, if it is desired to look at the subject in its true historical aspect. Two propositions may safely be laid down in this connection:—(1) that Âryan society of the Vedic, or, more properly speaking, the Grihya Sûtra, period presents the institution of marriage in a form which recognized female liberty and the dignity of womanhood in full,—very slight traces of which are seen in the existing order of things, except, fortunately, in the old Sanskrit ritual which is still recited, and the ceremonies which are still ignorantly performed; (2) that, owing to causes which it is not possible to trace, there was a revulsion of feeling, and the Vedic institutions were practically abandoned or ignored, and in their place usages grew up which circumscribed female liberty in various directions, and seriously lowered the dignity of woman in the social and family arrangements. By clearly separating the texts relating to each period, the confusion of thought and ideas, which marks all orthodox discussion of these subjects, will be avoided, and the whole history presented in a way at once intelligible and suggestive.

It may be noted here that the stage of civilization represented by the texts of the Sûtra period, has itself a back-ground of pre-historic times when the arrangements of family life and marriage were admittedly archaic and barbarous. In the Mahâbhârata, there are traces of this time when married life had no sanctity, and the tie of wife and husband was felt to be very loose. The well-known story of दीर्घतमा (Dírghatamâ) may be referred to as an incident of these pre-historic times. The Yajur Veda texts which described a woman as necessarily अनंश, (Anaṇṣa), disentitled to inherit, like those male heirs who were deformed or afflicted with an incurable malady, point to the same time, and their influence was recognized by some of the old Sûtra writers, Baudhâyana and Âpastambha. The possession of a wife by a family of brothers, as common property, is a relic of the same period. The lower forms of Âsur and Paishâchha marriages are survivals of the same period. Slowly, Âryan society out-grew this savagery, and one by one female heirs, first the wife, then the daughter, afterwards the mother and sister, began to be recognized as heirs to a separated Âryan householder. Monogamy became the rule of life, and rose in national estimation, as the story of Sitâ and Râma so nobly illustrates. Woman's freedom and dignity were preserved, in the Khshatriya caste especially, by liberty to choose her husband in the form of Svayamvara, so well illustrated in the stories of Sitâ, Damayanti, Rukmiṇi, and Draupadi. Among the Brahmins, women given up to study and contemplation refrained from marriage altogether, and lost none of their importance by this act of self-sacrifice. Marriage took place in all castes at comparatively mature age, and remarriage was not looked down upon as disreputable, seeing that Damayanti was permitted by her father to make a feint of it to find out her longlost husband, and Krishnâ's son married a widow of his enemy Shamber, and Arjuna married Uloopi. This was the classical age of Indian history when the nation throve along all lines of activity. Later on, some reason or another caused a change. Svayamvara fell into disuse, single life became unfashionable, late marriages and remarriages became disreputable, women's rights as heirs were also circumscribed in favour of distant male heirs, monogamy lost its strictness so far as males were concerned, the *Dân* form of marriage was recognized as the best form, and women were denounced as being on a level with the Shûdrâs in respect of claims for Vedic learning and performance of Vedic rites, and they were condemned to lifelong pupilage, first to the father, afterwards to the husband, and lastly to the son. The Shâstris explain this revulsion of feeling by accounting it to be the result of the change of Yuga, *i.e.*, the setting in of the Kali Yuga. The explanation is not satisfactory or complete, since the same texts which ushered in these restrictions on female rights were equally explicit in regard to many other customs, such as *sanyása,* or renouncing the world, and the keeping up of Agnihotra fire in Brahmin houses. In these matters the restrictions did not form a bar to the continuance of the old institutions, and their continuance as honoured institutions. The causes of this change, as I have attempted to show elsewhere, were really the reflex action of the rise of Buddhism with its horror of female charms, the invasion of barbarous hordes from outside, and the rise of non-Âryan tribes to power, which deluged the land with bloodshed, and extinguished the spirit of chivalry, and learning, and independence, and reduced the nation to the subjection of peoples with a low type of civilization. This destructive work was completed by the invasion of the Mahomedans, with a distinctly lower ideal of family life and respect for the female sex. The revulsion in feeling was not confined to the marriage institutions only. It equally affected the law of inheritance, by discouraging partition, and encouraging living in union under the authority and protection of the eldest living male. It similarly affected the notion of individual property in land, and substituted in its place communal or tribal ownership of the soil. The intermixture of castes was discouraged, and the subdivisions became more numerous and rigorous than before. Foreign intercourse by sea and land was similarly eschewed and discredited. The domination of the priesthood became more pronounced than ever, and led to the foundations of numerous dissenting sects and heresies. Whatever may have been the cause of this change of front all along the line, the fact is indisputable, and cannot be denied.

Having thus presented the pre-historic, the classical or Vedic, and the Purânic stages in one view, it will be now convenient to refer more in detail to the institution of marriage, and to trace its downward course step by step. The following conclusions may safely be laid down on this point:—

(1) In the Grihya Sûtrâs no definite age-limit for the marriage of females is laid down. The age limit for males is laid down by inference, seeing that the studentship commences at 8 for Brahmins, and at a later age for other castes, and the study of the three Vedâs, or of two, or of one Veda is prescribed for 36, 24, or 12 years in the preceptor's house, as a preliminary to the Brahmin student entering upon the life of a गृही (grihi), married householder, with his preceptor's permission.

(2) While no definite age-limit has been laid down for females, the texts indicate clearly enough what they mean, by prescribing certain qualifications as necessary in the case of females. The Hiranya Keshi Grihya Sûtra lays down that the female should be नग्निका (nagnikâ), defined in Sanskâr Ratna Mâlâ as मैथुनार्हा, (maithúnârhâ) fit for bodily association with her husband, and ब्रह्मचारिणी (brahmachârini), similarly defined to be one who has not associated with a male person. This requisition of ब्रह्मचारिणी is a qualification prescribed in all the Sûtrâs of the different Vedâs and Shakhas.

(3) It might be said that the interpretation put upon नग्निका and ब्रह्मचारिणी is too far-fetched, and cannot be accepted as representing the general sense of the Sûtrâs. Such a contention will not be urged by any one who reads the texts in full for himself. The texts in all the Sûtrâs require that for three days at least—some texts prescribe twelve days, others a year—the husband and wife should be व्रतस्थ (vratastha), *i. e.*, should observe certain forms of self-restraint, and among these restrictions are (1) that they should abstain from the use of salted food, (2) should sleep on the ground, (3) and it is in this connection that they are required to observe the ब्रह्मचारि व्रत (brahmachâri vrata) also. There could thus be no mistake about the sense of the words, even if the texts which permit a girl to look out for a husband only when she desires to be joined in marriage, be left out of account.

(4) No doubt, however, is left on this point by the ceremony of the fourth night, which used to be common in former times after the व्रत (vrata) of the three nights. This ceremony is still kept

up in name in the rituals of all the Sûtrâs, except the Âshwalâyana where only the three nights' व्रत (vrata) is mentioned. In other Sûtrâs, the fourth night's ceremony is intended to sanctify the ground, that is the female body, so as to make it fit for association, for purposes of cohabitation, and the ritual prescribes the union of the bodies and of the members thereof, of both husband and wife. Even the texts which refer to a later period, recognized the completion of the three nights' व्रत (vrata) and the union of bodies on the fourth night, as the final step which made marriage complete so as to make them both एक ऋषी (eka rishi) *i.e.*, incorporated the woman with the man's Gotra, and entitled her to receive and offer the Pinda after death. Even the Âshwalâyana as interpreted by the Prayoga Farijâtaka has stated the efficacy of the त्रिरात्रव्रत, (trirâtravrata) or the 12 days' or one year's ब्रह्मचर्य (Brahmacharya), to be that it took the girl out of her father's Gotra, and gave her her husband's Gotra. The rite is now performed not at the marriage time, but part of it is performed after the girl arrives at age at the time of the गर्भाधान (gharbhâdhâna) and the omission to perform the rite at the proper time is atoned for by a प्रायश्चित (prâyaşchita), or penance. The fourth night's ceremony was understood to join the husband and wife in actual bodily cohabitation, and the ब्रह्मचर्य व्रत (brahmacharya vrata) then ceased. This fact can leave no doubt as to the correctness of the interpretation put upon नग्निका (nagnikâ) and ब्रह्मचारिणी (Brahmachârini) by the commentator, and it shows that the marriageable age was fixed at a mature period of both husband and wife.

(5) This circumstance also accounts for the fact that a great many of the Smriti texts favour the remarriage of अक्षतयोनी (akshatayônî) girls widowed in their childhood, even when these texts did not permit, in the way Pârâshara, Manu and Nârada authorised, such remarriage in the case of all women suffering from five forms of distress. There is thus a recognized distinction between the status of a wife married with the fourth night's ceremony, which was most in vogue in those days, and a girl given in marriage who had not known her husband. There was no occasion for any such distinction in old times. With the restrictions of age limit, this distinction had to be made as a concession to popular feeling.

(6) The marriage ritual, it may also be noted, has no place in it for the girl's father after the कन्यादान (kanyâdâna)

ceremony. The subsequent rite is entirely an affair of the husband and wife. The mutual promises and assurances of love and protection and obedience, pre-suppose a much greater capacity in both than can be attributed to them in their childhood. The marriage rite is no doubt a sacrament, but a sacrament which pre-supposes the age of discretion on both sides. As now performed, it loses all its significance, because neither party understands what is said or done.

(7) The circumstance that स्वयंवर (svayamvara) was much in vogue in royal families, and among Khshatriyas generally, is evidence of the same fact, namely, that marriage was contracted after a girl had arrived at age and years of discretion, and that it was not a matter in which she was allowed no choice. Even after the Smriti texts greatly restricted female liberty, they have expressly reserved to her the power of marrying herself after waiting for some time for the father's choice.

(8) To the same effect is the evidence of the Purânic legends which expressly state that many girls refused to abide by the choice of their fathers. The well-known story of Sâvitri is proof of this, and stories of Rukhmiṇi and Subhadra are similarly instructive. The choice of the daughters of Kâshi Râjâ, and of Mandodari in the Devi Bhâgawata legend, tends to confirm this. In some of these cases, the girls chose to remain unmarried, and their fathers did not think they were bound to constrain their choice.

The several points noticed above can leave little doubt upon the question at issue, and they show beyond doubt that marriages took place after years of discretion, and were matters of choice, and not of parental constraint.

To come next to the Smriti texts, there is no doubt that when these texts were written, there was a revulsion of feeling, and it was generally regarded as a matter of necessity that no girl should remain unmarried, if the parents could help it, after twelve or before puberty. In their inability to fix the relative locality or order of date of the Smritis, and under stress of a false theory of exegesis, the Shâstris lump the Smritis together, and attempt the hopeless task of reconciling opposite texts by inventing fictions. No fair view of the subject can be secured by this violence of interpretation. The better plan appears to be to take the texts as they are, and arrange them in an intelligent order, and ascertain on which side the balance of authority rests. The following observations have been recorded with this view, and may prove useful:—

In regard to the marriageable age of males, there is not the same diversity of view as in regard to the age of females. Marriage is not compulsory on males. If a man desires to marry, the lowest permissible age according to the Smritis is eighteen, and the highest is thirty, as the following texts will show clearly:—

(1) बृहस्पति (Brihaspati) :——A man 30 years old should marry a girl of 10 years. In another place the text reads that a man of 30 should marry a girl of 16.

(2) मनु (Manu)
(3) यम (Yama) } :——A man at the age of 30 should marry a कन्या (kanyá.)

(4) देवळ (Devala) :——A man at the age of 18 should marry in due form a girl of seven who is then called गौरी (gauri).

(5) आश्वलायन (Ásvalâyana) :—A द्विज (Dwija) of 25 should marry a कन्या of 8 years. A man of less than 30 should marry a रोहिणी (Rohinì) of 9 years. She becomes गांधारी (Gândhârì) after 10, and he who wishes long life should marry such a girl before she attains her menses.

(6) व्यास (Vyâsa) :——A द्विज (Dwija) of 26 years, who has fulfilled all observances, and finished his studies, should, with his preceptor's permission, if he desires to be a householder, marry a faultless and grown-up girl.

(7) गौतम (Gautama) :——A householder should marry an unmarried grown-up girl of less age than himself. Wise men have said that after 50 a man should not marry in Kali Yuga.

(8) वृद्धगौतम (Vriddha Gautama) :—A man should study in his बाल्य (bâlya) age, and marry in the यौवन (yauvana) period after finishing his ब्रह्मचर्य (brahmacharya).

(9) चतुर्विंशति स्मृति (Chaturvi Śati Smriti) : After studying and understanding the Vedâs, a man should bathe in oil at 16, and marry a well-born girl.

(10) बुध (Budha) :——After finishing the study of the Vedâs and the service of his preceptor, and

after having completely observed all व्रत (vrata) a man should marry a girl of his own caste.

(11) आश्वलायन (Âśvalâyana):—After finishing four Vedâs, or three, or two, or one, and satisfied his preceptor, a man should, after completing one-fourth of his life's period (25 years) become गृही (grihi) for the second portion of 25 years of his life, and then retire into the forest.

(12) मनु: (Manu)—**A**. A man 30 years old should, after finishing the study of the Vedâs, or two Vedâs, or one, or after a fair mastery thereof, and having remained a ब्रह्मचारी (brahmachârì) all the while, should become गृहस्थ (grihastha).

B. A man should, in the first quarter of his life, stay with his preceptor. In the second quarter of his life, by marrying a wife, he should stay in his house as a householder.

(13) याज्ञवल्क्य (Yâgnyavalkya):—A male should be chosen who is श्रोत्रिय (shrotriya) and well-endowed, one who is युवा (yuvâ) intelligent and beloved by men.

(14) शातातप (Sâtâtapa):—A man should be युवा (yuvâ) who desires marriage.

(15) दक्ष (Daksha) :—A man who has finished his study of the Vedâs should marry a well-endowed girl. Before 16 a man is not qualified for marriage. After he has finished his study of the Vedâs and completed his ब्रह्मचारी व्रत (brahmacharí vrata), he should bathe and become गृही (grihi).

(16) मनु (Manu):—The Keshânta ceremony may be performed in the case of a Brahmin at 16, in the case of a Khshatriya at 22, and in the case of a Vaishya at 25. After bathing he becomes Snâtaka, and fit for marriage.

These texts leave no doubt on the point that the majority of the Smritis favour the age after 25 in the case of males. One text fixes the age at 18, and two at 16. The maximum limit is also fixed at 50. The text of देवल (Devala) about 18 is counter-balanced by his own text which fixed the age at 25. The चतुर्वि शति स्मृति (Chaturvi Shati Smriti) text is only a modern collection of what the compiler thought to be authorities, and has no independent value. दक्ष (Daksha) specifically lays down a minimum limit of 16 below which no man may legally marry. Manu's text about 16 relates to केशांत (keshânta) ceremony, and is balanced by his own other text which fixes 30 as the limit of age. The medical works also favour the higher ages. सुश्रुत (Sushruta), वृद्ध वाग्भट (Vriddha Vâgbhata), fixed 21 and 12 for the marriageable ages of boys and girls, and 25 and 16 for the consummation of marriage by cohabitaton. "Children born of parents who are respectively less than 25 and 16 years old are either still-born, or if born alive, are weaklings." All these authorities are thus clearly in favour of late, as against early, marriages. Nobody now proposes to wait till 25, though that would not be unreasonable, but surely a proposal to raise the minimum age to 18 or 20 for males is not an unreasonable concession to the weakness of the Kali Yuga.

To proceed next to the consideration of the age for females. It will be noted that the Sûtrâs laid down no minimum or maximum age-limit, but left marriages optional. Those who desired to marry might do so at a time of life signified by the use of words कन्या (Kanyâ), कुमारी (Kumâri), युवा (Yuvâ), कांता (Kântâ), नग्निका (Nagnikâ), and ब्रह्मचारिणी (Brahmachârinî), which in those days were sufficiently indicative of their being grown-up girls. The way in which the स्मृति (Smriti) writers proceeded to restrict the freedom was, (1) by prohibiting the choice of single or unmarried life to females, (2) by making it compulsory on fathers or guardians to see their daughters married before puberty at the risk of damnation, (3) by laying down new texts limiting the age significance of the words नग्निका (Nagnikâ), कन्या (Kanyâ), कुमारी (Kumâri), &c., used by the Sûtra writers. It is a very interesting study to mark the successive stages of the gradual process of restriction and degradation. Notwithstanding this manipulation, it will be seen that the majority of the texts favour the age of twelve or the age of puberty as the marriageable age of girls. As might be expected, the स्मृति (Smriti) texts, which bear the same names as some of the older Sûtrâs, are naturally the most in accord with the ideas of the Sûtra period. बौधायन (Baudhâyana), for instance, prescribes that a girl must be both a नग्निका (Nagnikâ) and a ब्रह्मचारिणी (brahmachârini), words obviously used in the sense of the Sûtrâs, *i.e.*, as a girl fit for sexual connection, but who has had no such intercourse before. आश्वलायन (Áśvalâyana), शंखलिखित (Shankha Likhita), and पैठीनसि (Paithinasi) also use the same words नग्निका (Nagnikâ) and कन्या (Kanyâ), but obviously use the words in a sense different from the Sûtrâs. कात्यायन (Kâtyâyana) similarly uses the word कुमारी (Kumâri) in the same way. शौनक (Saunaka) in his कारिका (Kârikâ) keeps up the memory of the traditions of the three nights' observance of व्रत (Vrata) to be followed on the fourth night by actual consummation. Owing to the change of habits, the three nights' व्रत (Vrata) was enlarged to 12 days' or a year's period for the final consummation of cohabitation. सत्यव्रत (Satyavrata), another writer of the same early period, also refers to the three nights' observances, and the fourth night's union as completing the marriage. Even when less liberal notions were clearly in the ascendant, बौधायन (Baudhâyana) clearly permits the girl to wait for three years after she attains her menses, and if till then her father did not give her in marriage she was at liberty to contract a lawful marriage herself. वशिष्ठ (Vaśistha) belongs to the same early period. According to him, the girl eligible for marriage is one who is अस्पृष्टमैथुना (Asmrishtamaithúnâ) *i. e.*, who has not had sexual intercourse, in other words who is ब्रह्मचारिणी (brahmachârini) in the old Sûtra sense.

The first decisive step in the downward course of restriction and constraint was taken when the maximum age for marriage was brought down to the period before a girl attained her menses, and the words नग्निका (nagnikâ), कन्या (kanyâ), कुमारी, and others were defined accordingly, and a new word of opprobrium, वृषली (vrishali), was invented for the girl who remained unmarried after menstruation. The authorities on this point are numerous, and belong decidedly to a later period, contemporary with the compilation of the अमरकोश (Amarakosha) lexicon, which defines नग्निका (nagnikâ) by its equivalent of नागतार्तव (nâgatârtava), one who has not attained her menses. The omission of the word ब्रह्मचारिणी (brahmachârinì) is easily explained, for there was no occasion for the use of that test when the age was brought down. The descent from नग्निका

(nagnikâ) who was fit for sexual intercourse (मैथुनार्हा) (maithunârhâ) to one who had not attained her menses is a clearly marked one, and constitutes the first step in the retrograde descent. यम (Yama), आश्वलायन (Âśvalâyana), बौधायन (Baudhâyana), देवल (Devala), पैठीनसी (Paithinasi), गौतम (Gautama), शंखलिखित (Sankha Likhita), बृहस्पति (Brihaspati), वशिष्ठ (Vaśistha), मरीचि (Marichi), all prescribed the gift of a नग्निका (Nagnikâ) girl as the most eligible form of marriage called ब्राह्मविवाह (brâhmavivâha); and the following स्मृति (Smritis), बृहस्पति (Brihaspati), पराशर (Parâshara), शातातप (Śâtâtapa), व्यास (Vyasa), अत्रि (Atri), मरीचि (Marichi), कश्यप (kasyapa), शाटयायन (Sâtyâyana), देवल (Devala), याज्ञवल्क्य (Yâgnyavalkya), हारीत (Hârîta), नारद (Nârada), गौतम (Gautama), संवर्त (Sanvrata), अंगिरा (Angirâ), आपस्तम्ब (Âpastamba), पैठीनसि (Paithinasi), यम (Yama), विष्णु (Vishnu), expressly contain texts, laying down that a girl who attains her menses while living in her father's house unmarried, becomes a वृषली, (Vrishali) and her father, brother, &c., incur the guilt of fœticide भ्रूणहत्या (bhrinahatyâ), or, more vaguely, "go to hell," and her husband is a वृषलीपति (Vrishalipati), unfit to be associated with, or invited for, श्राद्ध (Shrâddha). Paithinasi (पैठीनसी) prescribes another reason why a girl should be given in marriage before she attains her menses. The reason is—"A girl should be married before her breasts are developed." अंगिरा (Angirâ) and कश्यप (Kaśyapa) also require that a girl whose breasts are not developed, or who has not attained her menses, should be given in marriage.

These texts, it will be seen, say nothing about the girl incurring any guilt. On the contrary बौधायन (Baudhâyana) permits her to give herself in marriage after waiting for her father doing so for three years, and according to the Smriti writers, namely व्यास (Vyâsa), अत्रि (Atri), देवल (Devala), वृद्धात्रि (Vriddhâtri), मरीचि (Marichi), लौगाक्षी (Laugăkshí), शौनक Saunaka), आश्वालायन, (Âśvalâyana), आपस्तंम्ब (Âpastamba), वृद्धपाराशर (Vriddhapârâśara), even when a girl becomes impure in the course of the performance of marriage rites, these rites are only delayed by three days of impurity, at the end of which she is to bathe, and after a small penance she is eligible for marriage, as if she had not attained her menses. But in the further development of this same retrograde tendency it was afterwards laid down that she herself incurred guilt, and that she should be abandoned by her father, and her face should not be seen according to गौतम (Gautama) and

मार्कंडेय. (Mârkandeya). According to बृहस्पाति (Brihaspati) and अत्रि (Atri) the marriage of a girl after she had attained her menses destroyed the welfare of the giver's ancestors. The word वृषलि (Vrishali) was apparently at first applied to a barren woman, or a woman who gave birth to still-born children. It was obviously about this time, as shown above, made to embrace the unmarried girl who had attained menses, and as such the denunciation against connection with a वृषली (Vrishali) of the old sort contained in यम (Yama), हारीत (Hârita), उशानस् (Uśânasa), मनु (Manu), वशिष्ठ (Vaśistha), शौनक (Śãunaka), and गौतम (Gautama), were made applicable to marriages with girls after they had attained menses.

The next step in order of further restriction was taken by fixing the time of the first appearance of the menses at the age of 12. यम (Yama), पाराशर Pârâshara, and बृहस्पति (Brihaspati) laid it down that girls attain their menses when they have reached the twelfth year, and they condemn the father who neglects his duty in getting his girl married before that age to the fearful penalty of the sin represented by his drinking the impure flow from month to month. मनु (Manu) and यम (Yama) accepted the limit of 12 years for a full grown-up man of 30, and संवर्त fixed upon 12 years as the age when a girl became a वृषालि (Vrishali). This was thus the third step, and must have been later in time than the age of अमरकोश (Amarakosha) noted above.

In keeping with this view, or in exaggeration of it, a नग्निका (Nagnikâ) was defined in the Purâna to be a girl who did not feel the desire of concealing her limbs in a male's presence, or was still playing like a child in the dust, and did not know what was proper and improper. But a time came soon after when the limit of 12 was thought to be too liberal by the text writers, and the words नग्निका (Nagnikâ), कन्या (Kanyâ), and कुमारी were subjected to further manipulation. The Sûtrâs prescribed the marriage of a कुमारी (Kumâri) and a कन्या (Kanyâ), (daughter), among whose qualifications they had stated that she should be नग्निका (Nagnikâ) and ब्रह्मचारिणी (Brahmachârini). In the Sûtrâs the words कन्या (Kanyâ) and कुमारी (Kumâri) were never intended to signify any particular age or state of bodily development, any more than भार्या (Bhâryâ) or स्त्री (Stri) used in बृहस्पाति (Brihaspati) and आपस्तंम्ब (Âpastamba). They are general words, and used as such in मनु (Manu), यम (Yama),

आश्वलायन (Âsvalâyana), शौनक (Sáunaka), and बौधायन (Baudhâyana) intheir texts in various places, where girls of 12 and after maturity are still called कन्या (Kanyâ), as also in बृहस्पति (Brihaspati), यम (Yama), पाराशर (Pârâshara), and विष्णू (Vishnu), where a father is condemned to the sin of child-murder who leaves his कन्या (Kanyâ) unmarried after she attains menses. When, however, a desire began to be felt to bring down the age below 12, the device of defining कन्या (Kanyâ), नग्निका (Nagnikâ), कुमारी (Kumâri) as a girl who had reached a particular age was adopted, and turned to account. Thus (Kashyapa) कश्यप styled a girl of 7 गौरी (Gauri), and a girl of 10 was called कन्या (Kanyâ), and a girl after 10 was called रजस्वला (Rajasvalâ). Another reading of this same text states that a girl after 10 becomes कुमारी (Kumâri). A third states that at the age of 12 she becomes रजस्वला (Rajasvalá). संवर्त (Sanvarta) styled a girl of 8 years गौरी (Gauri), of 9 years नग्निका, (Nagnikâ), and of 10 कन्या (Kanyâ), and of 12 वृषली (Vrishali), which last thus became synonymous with रजस्वला (Rajasvalâ). यम (Yama), गौतम (Gautama), गर्ग (Garga), and पाराशर (Pârâsara) called the girl of 8 गौरी (Gauri), of 9 रोहिणी Rohini), of 10 कन्या (Kanyâ), and after 10 she became रजस्वला (Rajasvalâ). By this device of merely calling a girl रजस्वला after 10, these writers attempted to cancel the definition adopted by previous texts noted above of fixing the age of 12 as the age of menstruation. आश्वलायन (Âsvalâyana) and देवल (Devala) also adopted the nomenclature गौरी (Gauri), रोहिणी (Rohini), and कन्या (Kanyâ) as the names of girls in their 8th, 9th, and 10th years, and they called the girl after 10 a गांधारी (Gândhâri). अंगिरा (Angira) called the girl before she attained menses नारि (nâri); a girl who had attained menses was called रोहिणी (Rohini); and one who had developed breasts was called कन्यका (Kanyakâ). The great confusion seen in these texts, and their open contradiction of each other and of the large number of the texts quoted before fixing the age of marriage by the limit of monthly courses or 12 years, condemns them as being later tamperings with old texts, or later additions. By this ignoble device, the marriageable age of girls was cut down by 2 years and reduced from 12 to 10, for, after 10 a girl was supposed to be रजस्वला (Rajasvalâ) against all the facts of experience, and the authority of texts which fixed the वृषली age at 12.

As if the limit of 10 was not low enough, and to complete the degradation, it was later on suggested that as girls had not, like boys, any उपनयन (Upanayana) ceremony, the marriage sacrament should be taken in the place of the उपनयन (Upanayana) ceremony of boys, and therefore the texts laying down the age for उपनयन (Upanayana) of boys were by analogy made applicable to girls for their marriage. अंगिरा (Angirâ) and संवर्त (Sanvarta) laid it down that wise men have commended the age of 8 as fit for a girl's marriage. But as Manu's authority was required to support the fraud, a text of Manu (मनु) was made to order, laying it down that 5 years from birth or conception was the best time for a boy's उपनयन (Upanayana) or a girl's वरण (Varana). The word वरण (Varana) in the text is not exactly equivalent to विवाह (Vivâha), as in Angirâ's text, but it supports the confusion of ideas on which the fraud was based. आश्वलायन (Âśvalâyana) and देवल (Devala), as also मरीचि (Marichi) and बृहस्हति (Brihaspati), were laid under contribution as assigning particular blessings or particular portions of heaven to the man who married or who gave his daughter in marriage when she was a गौरी (Gauri), रोहिणी (Rohiní) or a कन्या (Kanyâ).

In this indirect way, a few solitary and apparently fraudulent additions have been made to do duty, and the eligible marriage age reduced to what it now obtains in a large number of castes. That some texts have been manipulated can hardly admit of doubt; for instance, the text of मनु (Manu), नारद (Nârada), and यम (Yama),* which allows a girl to remain unmarried even till death rather than be wedded to a man who is of a bad character, has been made in some books to read that such a girl should on all accounts be given to a man, howsoever bad he might be, and her forcible abduction is not at all a sin. In the काश्यप (Kâśyapa) text a similar manipulation of 10 for 12 years in the third line is proved by the reading in different still extant books. There is a similar instance of manipulation in respect of the text त्रिशत्वर्षोदशाब्दातु—a man of 30—should marry a girl of ten, The same text in Mahâbhârata is त्रिशत्वर्षोषोडशाब्दा—a man of 30—should marry a girl of sixteen. These instances will suffice for the present.

Taking a review of the whole subject, it will be seen that the authorities for marriages of girls before 8 are

---

*काममामरणात्तिष्ठेदगृहे कन्या ऋतुमत्यापि॥नचैवैनां प्रयच्छेत गुणहीनाय कर्हिचित्
The last two lines are turned into तथैवैनां प्रयच्छेत गुणहीनाय कर्हिचित्

obviously later additions, and are limited to two obscure Smritis, of which full texts have not been preserved, and the मनु (Manu) text quoted is evidently not to the point. The authorities which support marriage at 10 are similarly of no great weight, being based on a device by which the words कन्या (Kanyâ), &c., have been distorted from their correct sense to mean a girl of 10 years. These authorities are eight in number. The largest preponderance of authorities is for 12 years as the safe but not compulsory limit. Properly speaking, these authorities lay down the limit at the period when a girl attains the first sign of puberty —menstruation. But taking these texts as they have been since interpreted, the limit of 12 is supported by nearly thirty text-writers of repute, and as such it may be taken as representing the correct sense of the Smriti writers generally. It is also supported by the orthodox works on medicine. Marriage at 12 and consummation at 16 appear thus to be the normal and authoritative ages for girls just as 18 and 25 are for boys.

Here these observations must be brought to a close. Leaving the old Sûtra period as too remote to influence the present condition of our population, no such objection can be urged to the minimum limits laid down above, 12 and 18, and 16 and 25 as supported by the vast majority of the really authoritative texts. Those who seek reform in this matter do not desire to turn marriage into an affair of mutual romantic love. They do not want to thrust aside the parental authority, or to diminish the sense of responsibility now felt. They advocate a return from modern corruptions to the real sense of the old Smriti texts, and their request is therefore fairly entitled to consideration.

On the subject of enforced widowhood, the writer of this essay has already published a small pamphlet, setting forth all the texts bearing upon the subject. That pamphlet is republished as an appendix to this work. The reader will thus have the whole of the Shâstra literature on the subject available on this side of India at the present day on both these subjects. It is hoped that after the present reaction subsides men will come to see that, in clinging to the existing order of things, they are really setting at naught the traditions of their own best days and the injunctions of their own Shâstras, leaving aside all considerations of duty and expediency; and that, in calling for a change on the old lines, the reformers seek not to revolutionize, but only to lop off the diseased over-growth and excrescence, and to restore vitality and energy to the social organism.

APPENDIX VII.

VEDIC AUTHORITIES FOR WIDOW MARRIAGE.

Dr. Fraser, in his learned judgment in the great Poona Defamation Case, has very clearly stated one of the grounds on which the advocates of remarriage found their argument, that remarriage is permitted to the high-caste Hindu widow in this present age. As the learned Judge has so forcibly put it, in seeking this reform, the advocates are only endeavouring to restore the purer institutions of old times. People who are, however, not conversant with the merits of the question, may be misled by the special prominence given to one minor argument in the judgment, *viz.*, that the central period of Kali age, which is the Yuga proper, and to which alone the prohibitions against remarriage and other institutions can apply, has not yet commenced, and in fact, will commence only after some 31,000 years from this date. This special mention of it in the judgment may mislead people into thinking that the advocates have after all a very narrow basis to build their great argument upon, and it is deemed necessary that this false impression should be removed. So far from this argument being the only one the advocates ground their movement upon, the truth is that it occupied only a very secondary place in the late discussions at Poona. Dr. Fraser's attention was specially directed to it by reason of the fact that one of the accused, Vyankat Shástri, was the first to discover this line of argument, and he communicated it to Vishnu Shástrí Pandit, the great apostle of this movement on our side of India who made use of it in the late discussion at Poona and there it stood its ground, for the orthodox disputants gave no answer to it. In itself, it is, however, a very lame argument, for it has no force if the antagonist denies the validity of remarriage even in the previous ages. This was the position taken up in the late discussions, although as it is a very unsafe one, the Panch on the orthodox side in their joint decision wisely confined themselves to a statement, "that by reason of the prohibitions (which apply only to this Kali-yuga) the practice of remarriage derives no countenance from the Shástras in this Kali age," thereby impliedly admitting that in the previous ages, when the prohibitions did not exist, it was valid by the Shástras. And this is a position about which there is a general consensus of opinion of all the authorities most opposed to the concession of this liberty to widows in this age. Once however it is admitted that remarriage is authorized by the Shástras for the previous ages, Vyankat Shástri's argument comes to the assistance of the advocates of remarriage much in the way of a plea in abatement. It simply asks both parties to put up their quarrels for the present, and for 31,000 years more at which distance of time alone the prohibitions will come into force, even allowing them to have any binding character.

The advocates of remarriage are, however, in a position to make out a much stronger case. They are able to show in the first instance that the remarriage of widows has the positive authority of the Shástras, which Shástra authorities hold good for all the four *Yugas, i.e.*, for all time. They are also able to establish, that, allowing the prohibitory texts for the Kali-yuga to be in force now, they only restrict, and do not totally abrogate, the privilege enjoyed before, and that the widow's case falls under the class of the permitted circumstances of distress, in which it is lawful for a woman once married in due form, if she is unable to live a life of single devotion to her deceased husband's memory, to marry another man. Before we proceed to arrange the texts in due order, it is necessary to bear in mind that the Vedas, the Smritis, and the Puránas and Itihásas are the three-fold authorities which constitute our Law, and that the Veda texts override all Smriti texts, and these latter override all Puránas, in cases of direct conflict. When the former class of authorities are silent, then the latter are held binding and authoritative. The fiction is that all these Smriti texts proceeded from one and the same source, and they must all be reconciled together, a place being found for every text by force of the rules mentioned before, and also by a rule which allows to one institute a sort of presidential authority for its age controlling all others, if in direct conflict with it. The ordinary rules of interpretation are the same in Hindu law as in English law, that words are to be understood in their plain and grammatical meaning, that technical words are to be understood in their technical sense, that a general law is restricted in its operation by a special and particular one, and so on.

With these prefatory remarks, we enter upon the argument by which we hope to establish in this number, that the Shástras common to the four ages permit or authorize the remarriage of widows in all castes. The only difficulty in the way of the right of the widow to marry again is the fact of her completed first marriage. All texts, therefore, which permit or authorize or prohibit an *údhá* (or a woman whose first marriage is perfected) to marry again under certain enumerated cases of distress, authorize or prohibit, *a fortiori*, the remarriage of widows. We shall now enumerate the texts in their order; the Vedic texts first, the Smritis next, and after them the references in the Puránas and the Itihásas.

The Vedic texts :—

I. "Get up, oh woman, you who lie down by the side of this your lifeless husband. Come to this crowd of living people about you here, and may you become the wife of some person desirous of taking the hand of a widow in remarriage."

This text occurs in Yajurveda, Taittiríya Aranyaka, sixth Prapáthaka, 14th S'loka. It occurs in all the other Vedas also, and is quoted in A'svaláyana 4,2,58, and also in Baudháyana. It was discovered by the industry of Dr. Bühler. It is addressed for the wife of an Agnihotrí Brahmin, deceased, who it seems had in old times by way of expressing her grief to lie down by the side of the corpse of her dead husband. Some near relation, says the Sútra, is to go to her after having recited this text, and with the right hand raise her up, and bring her back to the crowd of her relations. This is an express text, and the translation as given is taken word for word from Sáyana's Commentary. If the wife of an Agnihotrí, who has even borne children to him, may marry, all objection to the remarriage of helpless girl-widows is, *a fortiori*, removed.

2. "Therefore many wives to one husband there may be, but not many husbands *together* to one wife."

This text occurs in Aitareya Bráhmana, 3 Panchika, 22 Khanda. The word *saha (together)* is very significant, no such word occurs in reference to the husband. It indicates that one woman cannot have many husbands together at the same time, impliedly sanctioning a second marriage when the first husband is dead and gone, &c.

3. "Your first husband was the moon, after him Gandharva became your husband. Agni was your third husband, and those born of men will be your fourth husband."

This text occurs in Rigveda, 8th Ashtaka, and is recited on the occasion of marriage. Every girl is thus the wife successively of three superhuman beings, and what is the most significant part of the text, it says, those born of men (the word is in the plural number) will, altogether, as belonging to the order of human beings, be your fourth husband, impliedly giving sanction to successive marriages with human husbands.

4. "Oh Ashviní Kumára, where do you stay during the night? Where do you remain during the day? Where do you get your desires satisfied? Where do you dwell? What priest offering sacrifices invites you to the sacrifice as a widow attracts her second husband, or a wife attracts the man who is her husband, to be present with her in her bed."

This text occurs in Rigveda, VII. 8. 18. It is useful to show that in those archaic times, it was a common illustration to speak of widows blessed in the company of their second husbands. It was no more strange, no more disreputable, than for a wife to be happy in the embrace of her husband.

5. "The mention of a *didhishu* husband, *i.e.*, a man who marries a widow, or a woman who has been married once before, occurs in several places in the Vedas, as, for instance, in Taittiríya Bráhmana, 3, 4, 4, this passage occurs:—

"To the Goddess Arádhi, the sacrifice of a *didhishu* husband is enjoined," which passage contains an enumeration of human sacrifices to the different gods, and to some god, it seems the sacrifice of a man who was married to a widow was specially acceptable, just as others liked children or women or old men, or even Brahmins learned in the Vedas.

6. Lastly, in a passage in Atharva Veda IX., 5, 27 which was discovered by Dr. F. Kielhorn, it is expressly said, that—

5. "She who having had a first husband subsequently marries another second husband, provided they two give an Aja Panchodan, they should not separate."

The following verses are still more emphatic :—

6. "This second husband goes to the same place in heaven with the twice married woman, if he gives an Aja Panchodan and additional offerings to the sun. IX. 5, 28.

Such married couples after giving a cow with her calf, a bullock, a bed, clothes and gold go to the best of heavens IX. 5, 29.

We fail to see what more man or woman can desire after this assurance.

Against all this mass of express permissive texts and incidental references, (and incidental references have in the case of the Vedas the same force as express permission,) against all this mass of evidence, there is nothing to be advanced on the other side except one solitary text.

"As about the same sacrificial post, two cords can be tied round, so one man may marry two wives. As one cord cannot be tied round two sacrificial posts, so one wife cannot marry two husbands."

This text occurs in Black Yajurveda, Ashtaka 6, Adhyaya 6, Prapáthaka 4, Anuváka 3. After all, it comes to no more than this, that one woman cannot marry two husbands at the same time. For there is nothing to prevent one cord, when loosened from the first post to which it was tied, from being wound round another post. And that this is the correct rendering will be seen by comparison of this text with the second text translated before, where the significant word 'together' occurs.

Besides this solitary text, no text expressly prohibiting the marriage of widows, or the re-marriage of a girl once married in due form, has been discovered. The Benares Pandits have sought to derive some prohibition from the use of the word *Kanyá* (daughter) in the *mantras* which are recited at the time of the first marriage:

The father says to the bridegroom 'I give this my *Kanyá* (daughter) by pouring this water on your hand.' Now it is contended that the word Kanyá, daughter, should be restricted to the artificial sense of an 'unmarried daughter,' as if the relation of the father and mother to the girl, expressed by the word Kanyá or daughter, ceases at the time of the marriage, and ever after. This position however cannot be sustained, for the daughter remains Kanyá to her father, inherits as such, sits in mourning as such, offers oblations to him as such as long as she lives, and long after through her sons. Moreover, there are innumerable texts in which the word Kanyá is applied to a married daughter. The Vedic texts recited at the time of the first marriage, as they contain no word of limitation, apply with equal effect to any second marriage when the father gives away his widowed daughter. The father in giving away his daughter does not part with all his rights over her. He only creates other rights and other relations, good for the time they stand. Just as when a prince gives land in service Inam, the grantee is the proprietor so long as he lives, or has issue capable of carrying into effect the objects for which the gift is made, and the prince, on failure of issue, may make a second gift of the land, the gift of a daughter in marriage is a conditional one, and not an out-and-out gift. The fivefold objects for which the gift of a girl is made are defeated by the husband's death, leaving the girl widowed behind him, desolate and hopeless, and the father has every right by the analogy to make a second gift of his daughter or *Kanyá*. We have thus shown that the Vedas, the highest authority on matters of law, recognise re-marriage as a permitted thing even to the wife of an Agnihotrí, that the Vedas enjoin that the widow married should not be abandoned, but that she should be allowed to remain as wife, and that it was an ordinary thing in those days to speak of the felicity of widows and their second husbands."

II.

SMRITI AUTHORITIES FOR WIDOW MARRIAGE.

Vyása in his Smriti 1, 4 says:—"When a conflict is seen bet, ween the Vedas, the Smritis and the Puránas, then the Vedas are the authority. In case of conflict between the latter two-the Smritis are to be preferred." As among the Smriti texts themselves, there are two rules of construction. 'If one set of institutes contradicts the other, then there is option.' (Mitákshara, Commentary on Yájnavalkya v. 5.) And, again, each age has its presiding institute. "In the *Kritayuga* the institutes of Manu, in Tretá the institutes of Gautama, in Dvápára the institutes of S'ankha and Likhita, and in the Kali age, the institutes of Parásara, are held to be binding" in cases of conflict. With the help of these rules of interpretation, we shall now enumerate the Smriti texts in their order, continuing the enumeration of the authoritative texts which permit the remarriage of a woman whose marriage has once been completed.

Manu :—

7. "In the case of five afflictions, viz., when the husband has gone abroad and no tidings of him have been obtained,

when the husband is dead, when the husband becomes a Sanyási (recluse), when the husband is a eunuch, and lastly when the husband being guilty of the five great sins, becomes a *patita*, *i.e.*, one who accepts no atonement or for whom no atonement is prescribed; in these five afflictions another husband is permitted by the institutes to women."

This is explicit enough. This text does not occur in the institutes as they are extant, but Madhavácharya cites and copies it as from Manu, and it is found in the Nárada Smriti which professes to be an epitome of Manu Smriti and it is acknowledged by all that it is a text of Manu. The fact is, it is the law of the dissolution of the marriage tie which this text expounds. It will be at once obvious that outlawry, or civil death in modern law, constitutes the fifth justification here enumerated. As the modern law allows seven years' unheard-of absence as a justification for re-marriage, these institute-writers did the same. Unheard-of absence, death, imbecility, renunciation of the world or becoming a monk, and lastly, outlawry, these are all valid justifications for the dissolution of the marriage tie by natural law, for in all these cases the great objects of marriage are defeated.

8. Nárada.—This same text occurs in Nárada Smriti IX. 12, 97.

The verses which come immediately after the text in this Smriti explain the first word of the text, *Nashte*,—explain the length of the period during which a wife should wait for her absent husband of whom no tidings are received. "A Brahmin wife should wait for eight years for her absent husband; if she has never borne children, she should wait for four, and then accept another husband." In a similar manner, periods of six and three years, and four and two years, are prescribed for women of the Kshatriya and Vaishya castes. No period is prescribed for a Shudra's wife. "In all cases when tidings of his being alive are received, the period of absence should be double. This is the view of Prajápati about absent husbands. If after the period prescribed, the woman associates with another husband, there is no sin in the act." About the other afflictions similar uncertainty does not exist, for the period is certain when the disability commences and the Smriti is silent.

9. Nárada.—" In the case of the husband belonging to four of the different sorts of eunuchs, their wives should abandon them *though they have cohabited with them*, IX. 12, 15. In the case of two others of the imbecile class, *A'kshipta* and *Moghabíja*, another husband is permitted to their wives after six months' trial, though they have cohabited with them. 16. In the case of a seventh kind of imbecile, who feels passion only in the company of women other than his wife, the wife should marry another husband."18. These texts are important,for they afford a sure index of the meaning attached by the writers of the institutes to the main text quoted before. In both the texts the word used is *Pati*, and one of the arguments in the recent discussion at Poona, and in fact the chief argument on the other side was, that the second word Pati, occurring in the main texts (7 and 8) should be rendered into a protector, which meaning is plainly out of place here. The texts translated in this and the preceding para. remove all doubt on this head. The latter come immediately after the main text, and in them the same word Pati is used all through in a manner where it can be understood as husband and husband alone. The limitation of the period of absence is different in the case of a woman who has borne children from that in the case of her who has borne none from her first husband. Then in the texts about eunuchs, though the first husband has lived and cohabited as Pati *(Kritepi Patikarmáni)*, yet as he is incapable of Patikarma, (the functions of a Pati), another Pati, or husband, is prescribed. This settles all doubts as to the sense in which the word is to be understood that it is a perfect Pati, and not a candidate proposed to be a husband that is spoken of in these and other texts.

Moreover, in the text from Manu and Nárada about the five afflictions, translated above, the first word Pati being understood in its proper sense as husband, it is not possible to give any other meaning to the second word Pati. The same woman, who has lost her first Pati, husband, is, according to the text, to take another Pati. If by this were meant that she was to seek a *protector* he cannot be *another* (*anya*) Pati. He can be *anya*, (another,) only with reference to the first. Besides, a mere *protector* can be of no help in remedying the affliction which the loss or incapacity of the first husband brings with it. A husband who is a eunuch does not become unfit to be a protector of his wife, for he can protect and maintain her most comfortably.

This same word *Pati* is, moreover, not an ordinary undefined word. Nearly all the institute writers have defined it. Manu, Nárada, Yama, Vasishtha, Brihaspati, and others have said :—

"Not by the pouring of water on the bridegroom's hand, nor by the offer by word of mouth, is the bridegroom called Pati or husband of the *kanyá* or daughter. It is after the ceremony of taking hold of the hand that, at the seventh step (which the bride and bridegroom take together), the bridegroom becomes Pati of a certainty."

This definition of the word ought to silence all doubts as to the interpretation to be put upon the word Pati in the texts from Manu and Nárada quoted before. Together they establish that a second marriage is lawful to a woman under the enumerated five afflictions, which, in the jurisprudence of all other nations, have been held to justify dissolution of the marriage tie with consequent liberty to marry again.

To proceed with the argument :—

10. Manu—

"She (who is abandoned by her husband or is a girl widow,) if she has never cohabited with a man, she is fit to be married to a second husband. If she leaves her first husband, and returns back without having cohabited with another man, the first husband may go through a second ceremony of marriage with her." IX. 176.

Besides the five cases of distress before mentioned Manu in this text adds two more, only with the qualification that she should be free from impure cohabitation.

11. Vasishtha—

"On the death of the husband of a girl-wife, who has been merely married with the recital of the Mantras, but has never cohabited with her husband, she is fit to be given in marriage again." XVII.

12. Prajápati—

"If she is a girl widow or has been abandoned by her husband by force or violence, then she is fit to be taken as a wife by any man upon a second ceremony of marriage."

13. Nárada—

"Even if the marriage rites have all been completed, if the daughter has not cohabited with the husband, she is fit to be married again. She is like an unmarried daughter, or as though no marriage was celebrated."

14. Shátátapa—

"A husband from a low family or of bad disposition is not fit to be united in marriage to a daughter. Though the Mantras, (marriage texts,) have been repeated, *i.e.*, though the marriage rites have been performed, they are not binding. If she has not cohabited with him, she should be wrested back from him by force, and given in marriage to another who is qualified."

This and another text to the same effect of this Institute are of importance. They show what importance is attached to the complete performance of marriage rites. They are not allowed to work injustice even when the first husband is living, and *a fortiori*, it cannot have been intended that they should stand in the way of the widow after his death.

15. Kátyáyana—

"If after having married the girl, the husband dies or disappears, the girl may marry again after an interval of six months."

16. Kátyáyana—

"If the husband is of another caste or a *patita*, or a eunuch, or of bad disposition, or belongs to the same Gotra or clan, or is a slave, or is afflicted with chronic malady, in all such cases, the daughter, though the marriage rites have all been performed, is fit to be given in marriage to another person with clothing and ornaments."

This text is important as it shows that a husband who is afflicted with chronic sickness does not stand in the way of a second marriage. *A fortiori*, a husband dead cannot put in a claim to keep the girl a widow all her life.

17. Vasishtha—

"If he comes of a low family or is evil-disposed, or is a eunuch, or is *patita*, or is afflicted with epilepsy, or is diseased, or is an actor, or belongs to the same Gotra or clan, in all these cases, the daughter, though given in marriage, may be wrested back and given again."

Many other texts may be cited, but these will suffice. There are thus no less than eight different Institutes which permit the remarriage, under peculiar circumstances of distress, of a girl once married in due form. Of course, they do not all enumerate the same particular justifications, but five of them expressly allow remarriage in the case of the husband's death, and the others, by implication or by analogy. By way of summing up, it may be stated, that there are no less than seventeen afflictions upon the happening of which different Institutes permit a second marriage to a girl once married in due form.

III.

All the texts cited hitherto are texts which have efficacy for all the *yugas*. They will be held satisfactorily to establish that as in the Vedas, so in the Institutes, so far from there being no recognition of the validity of remarriage, there is an express provision for no less than seventeen cases in which remarriage is justifiable. Against this mass of authorities, what have the other side to show?—not a single express text which negatives this permission. Manu, in his chapter on the duties of a widowed woman who wishes to live in single devotion to the memory of her deceased husband, says very naturally, in the exaggerated way so common with him, that—

"The widow should emaciate her body by subsisting on fruits, roots, and flowers, let her not, when her lord is deceased, even pronounce the name of another man."

Moreover—

"The widow who from a desire of children proves unchaste to her husband, and has unlawful intercourse with another, brings disgrace on herself, and will not attain the place in heaven where her husband goes.

"The children begotten on her by any other than her husband is not her progeny, nor the progeny of such begetter. In respect of chaste women, this other is nowhere spoken of as her second husband."

These are the only texts which have been urged on the other side, and, strange to say, relied on by a few European scholars of some authority on points of law. They all lay down the line of conduct which a widow who wishes to live a life devoted to the memory of her deceased husband should observe. They only prohibit unlawful connections. The advocates of remarriage have never maintained that a woman after her husband's death should not live a life of single devotion to her deceased husband. They freely allow that such heroic self-sacrifice to a sentiment is peculiarly meritorious. But a woman who cannot live this species of life, a woman who is widowed when a girl, before she knew who was her husband, before she knew what her duties as wife were,—surely such a woman cannot practise this devotion. It is on behalf of such women that this reform is a peremptory and crying want, and to require them to live a life of devotion in the manner Manu prescribes is a simple mockery of all religion and justice And, after all, the woman is directed not to prove unchaste, not to have unlawful intercourse with another. To the same effect is another passage from Manu often quoted :—

"To whomsoever the father or the brother with the consent of the father gives her in marriage, she should serve him while living, and not prove unchaste to him even after his death."

The word used is *Langhayet*, which Kulluka Bhatta, the commentator, interprets to mean having unlawful intercourse, *Vyabhicharet.*

Manu, again, "A girl can only be given away once in marriage. Three things occur once only. Inheritance from the same ancestor can only take place once, a daughter can only be given away once, and the same thing can be given away to another once only." By the analogy of the illustrations, it is apparent, that this text only determines the finality of the first marriage as a general rule, except where other texts intervene by way of exceptions. Except in places where these texts, intervening, allow a second marriage, the girl, it is admitted, can only be given away once. The exceptions where remarriage is allowable are as much law as the rule. Otherwise the host of texts which sanction forcible separation, which justify the reversal of a gift, which allow a second gift, would become simply meaningless. This is all that has been adduced on the other side against the positive permission of the Institutes. The general rule no doubt is that a first marriage is final, but the very Institutes, which prescribe this finality, enumerate seventeen different exceptions to this general rule in which second marriage is allowed to women as a permitted resource, not of equal merit with the life of a devoted widow, but still of legal force and efficacy. Much indeed has been made by the Benares Pandits of a text of Yájnavalkya which enumerates the qualifications of a girl who should be selected for a wife :—

"He who has never had sexual intercourse, should, after having completed his studies, marry a well-qualified girl, one who has not been given away in marriage to another before, who is handsome, who does not belong to his *sapindas*, and who is younger in years, who has no disease, who has brothers, who is not of the same Gotra, who is not within the prohibited degrees both on the father's and mother's side, whose ancestors for ten generations have been well known, who comes of a distinguished family learned in the Vedas, prosperous, and without any defect or hereditary disease. The bridegroom should also possess these same qualifications, be of the same caste, proficient in the Vedas, of potency proved with care, young, intelligent, and liked by all."

The qualifications of both the girl and the boy are enumerated at greater length in Manu and the other Institutes. But it is plain from the quotation that all these circumstances are mentioned as recommendations only. They are not essentials. For if it were not so, no man could marry a second wife on the death of the first, for the text requires that he should be one who has had no intercourse with woman before, a consequence which will not at all be welcomed by those who so strenuously assert that a virgin girl alone can contract legal marriage. So much in the way of answer to these objections.

From these quotations it will appear that both in the Vedas and in the Smritis which are common to all the four ages, there are no less than seventeen circumstances of distress under which a woman married once may lawfully contract a second marriage, and there is not a single express text negativing the permission given in these excepted cases. For this express negation is essential to establish the opponent's case. The advocates and the opponents both allow that a first marriage is, as a rule, final and binding; the advocates, however, further assert that the law allows exceptions to the rule in the enumerated cases of affliction which form so many justifications for divorce or second marriage. It is for the other side to show that there are other texts which negative the force of these express permissions. Mere general recommendations or assertions of the finality of first marriages will not be good answer against definite exceptions allowing remarriage.

The proposition then is established that in these seventeen enumerated instances, remarriage is permitted by the Smriti texts. It should be borne in mind that these are the only Smritis which speak anything either way. The others are simply silent.

To come now to our own *yuga*, we meet at the threshold for the first time with general negations of this permission accorded by the unanimous consensus of all the Smritis in the three first ages. Remarriage along with several other practices are prohibited in the Kaliyuga by the following texts. Most of them, it is to be observed, are Puránas, of inferior validity to Smritis, and a few, which profess to be Smritis, are the works of inferior authors, whose names are not enumerated among the leading Institute writers.

These negative texts are :—

Kratu :—

"The practice of begetting a son from the husband's brother after the husband's death, the remarriage of a daughter who has been once given away in marriage, killing of cows in sacrifices, and becoming a Sanyási, these four things are prohibited in Kaliyuga."

Now, it is to be observed upon this, that the last practice, so far from being abolished in Kali, is at present in force, and Shankarácharya himself comes within this exception. If the text is to hold good against one forbidden practice notwithstanding the generality of its words, it must hold good for the same reason against the other.

A′di Purána:—

"The remarriage of a girl once married in due form, the excess portion due to the eldest brother, the killing of cows, begetting a son on brother's wife, and becoming a Sanyási are prohibited in Kaliyuga."

Brahan-Náradiya Purána:—

"The gift in remarriage to another of a girl once given away in marriage is prohibited in the Kaliyuga."

A′ditya Purána, Brahma Purána, Gálava and Devala,—the latter two inferior Institute writers, whose Institutes have perished as entire works, and are only extant in rare quotations by modern authors,—contain the same or similar prohibitions.

Now, it is to be observed with regard to them all, that they are all texts of a very general sort. None of them contemplate the particular case of the remarriage of a widow. Nobody ever maintained that, *as a rule*, a girl once married in due form might be given away in marriage to another. Even in the previous three *yugas*, it is only under special circumstances, which the authors of the Institutes have been careful to enumerate, it is only on the occurrence of those particular contingencies, that remarriage is allowed. Such particular permissions are not interfered with by general texts prohibiting the remarriage of a girl once married in due form, a position which nobody ever disputes. None of them, moreover, contemplating the case of a widow, negatives the permission accorded by the texts common to all the *yugas* quoted before. The fact, however, that so many writers of the Puránas, who lived comparatively in very modern times, thought it necessary expressly to prohibit the practice, shows convincingly that, as they understood it, the practice was very common in the previous *yugas*, and they wished to restrain the liberty of archaic times. This is the strongest argument in favour of those who maintain that the remarriage of widows had the express countenance of the Shástras in the previous *yugas*, and in extensive use and favour in those days. However, to proceed with the argument, these texts above quoted being merely general prohibitions against the remarriage of a girl once married in due form,—a position which nobody ever contended against,—do not come into conflict with the general law as we have ascertained it before, which allowed liberty to women to remarry under certain enumerated circumstances, and among others, on the death of the husband. Besides most of them being only found in the Puránas they have no force against express Smriti texts by a well-known rule of construction.

Allowing, however, to these texts an operation in excess of the force of the words used, it is to be borne in mind that the leading Smriti for the Kaliyuga, the production too of one who is ranked among the most authoritative Institute writers,—expressly sanctions the practice of remarriage in five enumerated cases. As if to anticipate all objections, Paráshara, in his celebrated texts, simply reproduces the texts of Manu and Nárada (7, 8) quoted before, and, by thus expressly re-establishing these old Institutes as the law for this age, removes all manner of objections out of the way.

Paráshara's Institute, it will be seen, is intended expressly for the Kaliyuga, and this presidency of his Institute, his authority to control all other conflicting Smritis and *a fortiori* all Puránas as a matter of course, has been acknowledged by all the commentators, among others, by the author of Nirnaya Sindhu, by Nilkantha, the author of the Mayukhas, (see Sanskára Mayukha and Samaya Mayukha,) and by Shankar Bhat, the author of the Dvaita Nirnaya. This right of controlling all other conflicting texts has been allowed by all orthodox writers, and it is their acknowledgment of this supreme right of Paráshara to dictate the law for the Kali age, that has forced them to distort the meaning of this text in some way or other which will not conflict with their favourite prejudices.

It is to be remarked then, that this text of Paráshara reviving or re-enacting for this age the old law is very pregnant with sense. In the first instance, it is expressly intended for the Kaliyuga in which, moreover, it has precedence over all others. Secondly, it enumerates the particular cases of affliction when remarriage is allowed. Thirdly, it refers to the first three castes, for the word *pravrajita* means a *sanyási*, and only members of the higher castes can aspire to the dignity. Fourthly, it permits remarriage, though the first marriage has been in every sense completed. "On the death, &c., of the first *Pati*, husband, his widow may marry a second husband or *Pati*." Now nobody can become a *Pati* or husband, by any ceremony short of the walking the seven steps together which is the binding and concluding rite. In these four respects, this text is special in its permission and authorization. None of the prohibitory texts has this character. They simply contain a general prohibition which in no way conflicts with the spirit of Paráshara's text. Mr. Vithobá Anná of Karáda has collected two new texts from inferior Smriti writers, which seem to be more particular than those mentioned before. They are as follow:

Bábhravya:—

"After the completion of the marriage ceremony, if the separation takes place of the husband, wise men should not give away their daughters in marriage again in the Kali age."

Váyusamhitá:—

"The husband living or dead, his wife should not beget children from her husband's brother. In this Kaliyuga, a girl who has been married once in due form should not be accepted in second marriage."

Now in the first place, these texts are fragmentary ones, the books where they are to be found do not exist; secondly, they are the works of very inferior Smriti writers and not to be pitted against Manu, Nárada, Paráshara, Vasishtha, &c.; thirdly, they are not so special in their particulars as the text of Paráshara which, therefore, controls them; fourthly, that even if they were so special in their particular circumstances, the superior efficacy of Paráshara as the law-giver of the Kali age must prevail; and fifthly, that even if it did not prevail, this conflict of two Smritis can only create an optional duty. It will be thus seen that those who advocate the Shastraical validity of remarriage are able to give a very satisfactory account of the prohibitory texts which apply to this Kaliyuga. At the most, giving them the most extensive operation, they only restrict the liberty given in the previous yugas in seventeen different cases, they restrict this liberty to five occasions out of the seventeen, and by this method of reconciliation, all the authorities are reconciled. This great argument of the reconciliation of the texts was first laboured out by Pandit Ishvarachandra Vidyaságar, and has stood its ground against all attacks notwithstanding the great ventilation of the subject since. By his research and originality, and the noble devotion of his life's best days and all that is prized in human possessions to the promotion of this great emancipation of the women of his race, Pandit Ishvarachandra has become a household name for all that is great and good in human nature throughout India, and a potent influence for good in the ages to come.

The proposition then stands true beyond all power of dispute that there is express authority in the Shástras permitting the remarriage of a girl once married in due form, on the happening of certain defined contingencies, and that none of the prohibitory texts do more than restrict the greater liberty allowed to women in the previous yugas.

There is one solitary and suspicious text in A'shvaláyana Smriti, which requires a brief answer.

"If a twice-born marries a widow from ignorance, as soon as he knows her character, he should abandon her and do penance."

Now about this text, it is to be remarked that A'shvaláyana Smriti is not intended specially for the Kaliyuga, and even if it has force, it cannot have more force now than it had in the previous yugas, against the whole current of express permissive texts, especially against Paráshara whose Institute is the supreme authority for the age; and lastly, that the passage quoted from Atharva Veda which prohibits a husband from abandoning a widow so married upsets all the little force this text might otherwise claim.

There is thus express permission in the Vedas, express permission in the Smriti law common to all the yugas, and express permission in the special law for the Kaliyuga; and it has been shown that all the prohibitory texts are mostly very vague and general, and so, far from abrogating, only restrict the number of contingencies when remarriage is permitted by the law. And such of them as are more particular are controlled by the Paráshara text, first because it is so special, and secondly, because it is the binding authority for the age.

In furtherance of this great conclusion, the argument from the texts discovered by Vyankat Shástri comes opportunely to aid. The demarcation line which separates one age from another is only an imaginary one. The theory is that the race is gradually retrograding and degenerating in virtue, in capacity for austere endurance, and longevity of life, and as the old law would press too hard upon these decaying generations, and old permissions would be abused into wild license, it was deemed necessary to provide a graduated scale of duties and observances, some common to all ages, and others specially intended for each age. The world's duration is in all 12,000 years of the gods, which is divided into four yugas, and one yuga is made to slide into another, the intervals being called Sandhyá and Sandhyánsha or Junction periods of the yugas.

To provide for this gradual retrogression, a graduated central period of 4, 3, 2, and 1 thousand celestial years is, in the Bhágvata Purána and the Mahábhárata, assigned to the four *yugas* in succession, supplemented in each case by a morning and an evening twilight lasting for as many hundred years each, constituting in all 12,000 years of the gods as the duration of the world. The prohibitions and the observances prescribed for each particular age have effect only in the central periods, and in the junction or twilight periods, the law of the previous yugas may be followed (Bhágvata Purána.) The human year consisting of 360 days is a celestial day, whence a celestial year is equal to 360 mundane years. The duration of the Kaliyuga being 1,000 celestial years, its morning twilight or transition period is, as will be seen from the above, 100 divine years, that is, 36,000 human years, and as, according to the received mode of calculation, it is only 5,000 human years since Kali commenced, there are yet 31,000 human years to run before the Kali *sandhyá* or morning twilight will end. By that time, it is thought, caste distinctions will be obliterated, the Vedas will not be studied, the Ganges will lose its sanctity, and the gods become silent. So long as these evil prognostics are not realised, so long the practices prohibited in the Kaliyuga may be observed. And the orthodox commentators base their justification for the continuance of ascetic retirement, the domestic worship of sacred fire, and many other rites on this ground alone. Re-marriage being like them admittedly a valid practice in the previous ages, it continues to be a lawful rite now and for 31,000 years more, when it is hoped there will be little occasion to dispute its validity.

IV.

TRACES OF WIDOW MARRIAGE IN THE PURÁNAS AND ITIHÁS AND IN MORE MODERN TIMES.

To proceed with our main argument, we think it has been satisfactorily established that the remarriage of widows among the twice-born classes is a thing known and recognized in Hindu law, and that whether we look to the Vedas or the Smriti or Institute writers, the widow remarrying has the legal status of a wife. Except in very archaic times as illustrated by the references from the Vedas quoted before, the practice of remarriage, however, may never happen to have been very popular, as is but natural with a people who habitually married very late in life, and prided themselves upon a life of the severest austerity. This observation holds good of the Brahmin caste only. The warrior-caste, being more free to enjoy the sweets of life, seem not to have been equally averse from such indulgence; and this brings us to the Purának and the Itihás, the latest addition to our Shástra lore. A few studious scholars have investigated this subject from a desire to remove one great stumbling-block out of the way of the favourable reception by the orthodox population of this innovation, by showing that the practice of remarriage was common in past times, in the time of their wise ancestors, and accordingly that it may be revived in our present age. The industry of those who have searched for such illustrations in the Purána myths has succeeded in discovering three well-attested instances.

The first on the list is the remarriage of *Ulúpi*, the widowed daughter of a patriarch of the Nága tribe, who, on the death of her first husband, was given in marriage by her father to the famous Arjun, the hero of the Mahábhárata story. Ulúpi, in so many distinct words, is described to have become one of Arjun's many wives, the son she bore to him is emphatically described to be his legitimate-born son, and not one of the inferior sorts of sons. The entire narrative in the Mahábhárata, and still more emphatically in Jaimini's continuation, corroborates this assertion.

The second illustration is from the story of Nala and Damayantí. The latter Princess, after having been abandoned by her husband in the forest, found her way after much suffering to her father's house. While there, she bided in hope for some time, but could get no news of her absent lord. Thereupon, with the consent of her mother, she contrived a plan for finding out her long-lost Nala. She secured the services of a learned Brahmin to advertise to all the neighbouring princes that she was going to have a second Svayamvar, and make a second choice of a husband for herself, in consequence of the disappearance and probable death of Nala, her first husband. This Brahmin carried his message to the court of the king of Ayodhyá, with whom Nala had sought shelter in the disguise of an obscure charioteer. The king of Ayodhyá, on hearing this news, prepared to go to the Svayamvar, and Nala drove the chariot for him with extraordinary speed, the secret of which was known to him only. This display of skill and certain other circumstances led to his subsequent recognition, whereupon all idea of the second marriage was given up. This story has its importance, for it shows the received opinion among the people of the day, to whom such an invitation did not appear in any heinous light, did not appear more extraordinary than the invitation to the first marriage. That a woman like Damayanti, so renowned for her devotion to her husband, should, with the consent of her parents, try to discover the whereabouts of her lost husband by this stratagem, at once shows that remarriage did not strike people in those times as an abomination, but as an ordinary commonplace thing.

The third illustration is from Padma Purána, the story of the unfortunate daughter of the king of Benares, who was married no less than twenty times, it being her peculiar misfortune that as soon as the marriage rites were all performed, the husband so married died, but though this happened over and over again, the father, with the consent of the sage Brahmins of his court, solemnly gave her in marriage as often as she became a widow. The emphatic words used in the text preclude the supposition contended for by some disputants, that the several husbands were removed by death before, and not after, the binding marriage rites had been celebrated.

These are the only instances as yet discovered in the mythic Puránas and Itihás. In a book of the last century called Smrityarthasár, or an epitome of the Smritis, the compiler mentions without comment or disapproval that 'a girl given by word of promise may be given away in second marriage, that some maintain that before the Saptapadi rite is performed, a girl may be given away to another in second marriage; that others maintain that she may be given away after the rite is performed till the days of puberty, that some texts maintain she may be given away though she has had sexual intercourse with her first husband, and even after she conceives a child from her first husband. This statement comes from entirely orthodox quarters, and has an interest which the student of history alone can understand. This shows satisfactorily what orthodox writers thought of the Shástra texts in the last century. It is a matter of history also that in several Brahmin communities in Cutch, Sind, and Guzerat, the practice of *Pát* marriages still obtains.

We know there are those who are not satisfied with such few traces, and would fain have many more. To them we have a word or two to say. The position taken up by the advocates is, that the innovation sought for is peremptorily required in the present circumstances of our society. Being, however, a matter not for individual conscience, but a central part of all our social arrangements, a strong base of legitimacy must be established before the mass of Hindu society can be asked to help their unfortunate daughters and sisters out of their unmerited and irremediable misery. To ask them to change national institutions upon grounds of expediency is a thing they cannot understand, and will not tolerate. When this legitimate basis is once established beyond all danger of being shaken, to crave for more examples of the practice is very unreasonable, in respect of an institution which is professedly an innovation in every practical sense of that word, though it may be true, for the matter of that, that it is a renovation or a return to the manners of old and purer times.

Popular conscience have never been dead to the claims of this subject on its attention. In two recorded instances, the claims of the womankind for kinder consideration under this misfortune moved the souls of the great Jayasing, the Rajah of Jeypoor, and of the famous Pandit Appayá Dixit to rebel against custom. On both these occasions, however, the dead inertia of ages at last prevailed against the promptings of nature. In more modern times, the question was raised in our own part of the country, by the famous Parshuráma Pant Bháu Patvardhan, the co-adjutor of Lord Cornwallis in the wars of Tippoo Sultán, and the last of the terrible leaders of the Maratha conquering hosts. He had a young daughter, and Durgábái, we believe, was her name. She was given in marriage at a very tender age, varying in different accounts from five to nine years old, to a scion of the Joshî family. The young bridegoom died of small-pox fever, while yet the marriage festivities were not over. The brave old father was so moved by this calamitous termination of his fond hopes to see his daughter blessed, that he wrote to the Peishwa at Poona, tendering his resignation of his command of the army, and expressing a determination to retire from the world. The Peishwa's durbar, who knew the value of the man, and felt with him in his sufferings, assured him that he need not despair, for they would try to find a remedy for his irremediable sorrow. The Shankaráchárya of the time was then referred to, and his kind offices were prayed for by the men in power. The old man had some grudge against the Bhàu, and he answered that he would have nothing to advise in the way of giving comfort to a man who was worse than a *yavan*. The Peishwa's durbar, therefore, wrote to the Benares Pandits, the Pandits of the Poona court having shown a perverse disposition. These Benares Pandits sent a letter of assent signed by many hundred persons, in which, moved by the extreme infancy of the bride, and also by the consideration that the cause of Brahmin supremacy would be greatly checked by the withdrawal of Bháu from public affairs, they found out that the Shástras favour the remarriage of girls like Durgábái, widowed in infancy. On receipt of this letter of the Benares Pandits, the Shankarácharya of the day thought it wise to yield, and the Poona Pandits were about to follow suit, for none dared to hint a threat against the lion of the Deccan, as he was called. The astute Pandits, however, waited on Parshuráma Pant Bháu's wife, and through her they gained their object. The mother expressed her readiness to bear with her daughter's bereavement, rather than see a new innovation introduced. Parshuráma Pant Bháu was much surprised at this resolution and yielded the point to the Pandits, declaring that he insisted upon it solely with a view to console his wife, and if she wished for no consolation, he had nothing more to say. Thus the matter ended. The above account of the affair represents accurately what happened on the occasion. It is taken *verbatim* from one who has himself seen the original papers in the possession of the family, in his capacity as one of its old servants in charge of the records. The account is, moreover, corroborated by the received understanding of all the old people in the Patvardhan service, who have often said to us that they felt much surprised to find that the opponents of remarriage still had anything left to say after the solemn settlement of the question in Parshuráma Pant Bháu's time.

We have said all that is necessary to be said in illustration of the main theme of these observations. The agitation of the last three or four years has placed the legitimacy of the movement beyond all danger, and the Poona discussions brought this fact out in a most prominent manner. No question was raised there as to the Vedic texts, though special attention was drawn to the point; the argument of Vyankat Shástrí was not even noticed. The Smriti texts were jumbled up together, the main text, common to Manu, Náràda, and Paráshara, was twisted and tortured in all manner of ways, some of them most ridiculously absurd, and absolutely no attempt was made to show that the only true and natural meaning of the text was not the one contended for by the advocates. In fact this point was allowed, but it was urged that if the text were so understood, it would come in conflict with others, as if this was not the most common thing in the world with these Smriti writers. The orthodox disputants made a mess of their case, and though their Panch gave utterance to a foregone conclusion, the truth cannot be so hidden in these days. If these observations help the student to form his independent judgment upon the merits of this great argument, the writer will deem himself amply compensated for his pains.

INDEX

A

B

Pages.

M

N

P

R

S

T

V

W

Z